Christ Our Life

8

The Church Then and Now

Authors

Sisters of Notre Dame
Chardon, Ohio

Reviewers

Sister Mary Judith Bucco, S.N.D.

Sister Mary Grace Corbett, S.N.D.

Sister Margaret Mary Friel, S.N.D.

Sister Mary Jean Hoelke, S.N.D.

Sister Mary Cordell Kopec, S.N.D.

Sister Mary Carol Marek, S.N.D.

Sister Mary Donnalee Resar, S.N.D.

Sister Eileen Marie Skutt, S.N.D.

Sister Mary Jane Vovk, S.N.D.

LOYOLA PRESS.
A JESUIT MINISTRY
Chicago

Imprimatur

In accordance with c. 827, permission to publish is granted on April 16, 2014, by Most Reverend Francis J. Kane, Vicar General of the Archdiocese of Chicago. Permission to publish is an official declaration of ecclesiastical authority that the material is free from doctrinal and moral error. No legal responsibility is assumed by the grant of this permission.

Christ Our Life **found to be in conformity**

The Subcommittee on the Catechism, United States Conference of Catholic Bishops, has found this catechetical series, copyright 2016, to be in conformity with the *Catechism of the Catholic Church.*

Acknowledgments

Excerpts from the *New American Bible with Revised New Testament and Psalms* Copyright © 1991, 1986, 1970 Confraternity of Christian Doctrine, Inc., Washington, DC. All rights reserved. No portion of the *New American Bible* may be reprinted without permission in writing from the copyright holder.

Excerpts from the English translation of *The Roman Missal* © 2010, International Commission on English in the Liturgy Corporation (ICEL); excerpts from the English translation of *Rite of Penance* © 1974. All rights reserved.

Excerpts from the *Compendium of the Catechism of the Catholic Church* © 2005, Libreria Editrice Vaticana. Used with permission. All rights reserved.

Excerpts from the *United States Catholic Catechism for Adults* © 2006 United States Conference of Catholic Bishops (USCCB). Used with permission. All rights reserved.

The *Suscipe* and the Prayer for Generosity © 2004, Institute of Jesuit Sources. All rights reserved.

Loyola Press has made every effort to locate the copyright holders for the cited works used in this publication and to make full acknowledgment for their use. In the case of any omissions, the publisher will be pleased to make suitable acknowledgments in future editions.

Cover art: Lori Lohstoeter
Cover design: Loyola Press and Think Design Group
Interior design: Think Design Group

ISBN-13: 978-0-8294-3966-3, ISBN-10: 0-8294-3966-8

© 2016 Loyola Press and
Sisters of Notre Dame, Chardon, Ohio

For more information related to the English translation of the *Roman Missal, Third Edition,* see www.loyolapress.com/romanmissal.

Dedicated to St. Julie Billiart, foundress of the Sisters of Notre Dame, in gratitude for her inspiration and example

LOYOLA PRESS.
A JESUIT MINISTRY

3441 N. Ashland Avenue
Chicago, Illinois 60657
(800) 621-1008
www.loyolapress.com

20 21 22 23 Web 10 9 8 7 6

Contents

(continued next page)

(continued from previous page)

The New Evangelization

Gather and Go Forth pages at the end
of each chapter support faith, knowledge,
and the goals of discipleship.

Note to Students

Dear Students,

Every two years the world rivets its attention on the Olympic Games. Weeks before the games begin, an athlete ignites a torch in Olympia, Greece, the original site of the games in the eighth century B.C. He or she runs several miles with the burning torch and then passes it to another athlete, who carries it the next lap. This goes on until the flame arrives at the site of the current Olympic Games. There the last runner lights the Olympic flame in the stadium. It burns brightly throughout the games, as each contestant tries to live the Olympic motto: faster, higher, stronger.

How does this relate to you and your faith? The light of faith handed down through the past 2,000 years has been passed to you. Jesus, the light of the world, enkindled the flame of eternal life by his death and Resurrection. He promised his followers that he would be with them until the end of time. At Pentecost, his Spirit came to them in fire and wind, and they set out to inflame the world with faith and love. Countless Christians have been entrusted with this light.

In this book, you will see how the Church shone like a light in the Dark Ages. You will see how the Church has survived social systems, political systems, and persecutions. You will be encouraged to think in newer, more profound ways about Catholic truths. The Holy Spirit, the four gifts that mark the Church, and Mary's role will become more apparent to you. You will learn how the commandments are a sign of loyalty to Christ, who said, "If you love me, you will keep my commandments." (John 14:15) God's law will become clearer to you as a guide for doing today what Jesus did 2,000 years ago. You will meet Church members who bring joy and hope to the world.

The flame of Catholic Christianity is being passed to a new generation—yours! Will you accept the challenge of carrying it bravely? You alone can hold the torch of your faith higher and let your love for Christ and his Church grow stronger. Union with Jesus in prayer will help you meet the challenge. Let your motto be "Christ and I, an amazing team!"

> Do you not know that the runners in the stadium all run in the race, but only one wins the prize? Run so as to win. Every athlete exercises discipline in every way. They do it to win a perishable crown, but we an imperishable one.
>
> 1 Corinthians 9:24–25

Note to Students

Keeping a Reflection Notebook

In seventh grade, you saw how keeping a reflection notebook can help deepen your commitment to Jesus and strengthen your relationship with the Church. A reflection notebook is more than a diary. It is not just a collection of events, but what we think and how we feel about those events. Writing about your thoughts and feelings

can make you more aware of who you are and how you are living your life. In a reflection notebook, we take the time to reflect and to pray about our life.

Tips for Writing Reflections

1. Plan to set aside time regularly to write in your reflection notebook.

2. Write what you are honestly thinking and feeling. This notebook is for you and your relationship with Jesus.

3. Pray to the Holy Spirit to give you guidance and inspiration.

4. As you write your reflections, listen to how Jesus is speaking to you through the people, events, and thoughts in your entries.

5. Keep your reflection notebook private. Remember, these reflections are for you to question, explore, and discover how God is working in your life.

6. Make your reflection notebook special and neat, but do not worry too much about spelling and punctuation.

7. Reread your reflection notebook every now and then. This will help you see how God has spoken to you and how he has been acting in your life.

Louis Comfort Tiffany, stained glass.

The Mystery of the Church

"[Y]ou are Peter, and upon this rock I will build my church, and the gates of the netherworld shall not prevail against it."

Matthew 16:18

Family Feature
Our Universal Church

For most of us, our primary connection with the Church is through our parish. The first unit of the *Christ Our Life* program invites your eighth-grader to take a broader view. The word *catholic* means "universal." Being a universal Church means that

- we are a worldwide Church with a world-wide vision.
- we are a multi-cultural Church that welcomes people of every race and culture.
- We believe that the message of Jesus is true in every time and in every place.

The universal nature of the Church prepares us to be citizens of the world. We are called to love our neighbor, both near and far.

Catholic Insights
One of our eucharistic prayers highlights the universal nature of the Church in an especially beautiful way:

> "Through the gospel proclaimed by your Son, you have brought together in a single Church people of every nation, culture, and tongue. Into it you breathe the power of your Spirit, that in every age your children may be gathered as one."
>
> (The Church on the Way to Unity)

Faith Connections
Saints — Universal Faces: A good book on the lives of the saints can show how people have lived out their faith in various cultures and times. As a family, read about the saints and share stories about your favorite saints.

Some excellent resources on the saints include *My Life with the Saints*, James Martin, S.J.; *My Best Teachers Were Saints*, Susan Swetnam; *By Way of Grace*, Paula Huston; *Loyola Kids Book of Saints* and *Loyola Kids Book of Heroes*, Amy Welborn; *The Loyola Treasury of Saints*, David Self; *The Seeker's Guide to the Saints*, Mitch Finley; *Mystics and Miracles*, Bert Ghezzi.

Make a universal Gospel connection: Take time to read the Sunday Gospel with your family and then discuss these questions together:

- What line or image of the Gospel reading stands out for me?
- Name issues that are in the news around the world. What message does this reading hold for these worldwide concerns?

Address a universal concern: As a family, study a global issue that concerns you and make a decision about how to respond. For example, if you are interested in protecting the environment, you might join your family in neighborhood recycling efforts. If you are concerned about world hunger, you might contribute to an international relief organization.

Pray for the universal work of the Church: Choose an article from the diocesan or local newspaper that highlights the universal work of the Church (for example, missionary efforts in a developing country or a special event such as World Youth Day). Share the story with your family at dinner. After the meal, pray for the success of this ministry or event.

Visit **www.christourlife.com** for more family resources.

A Community of Disciples

What is your earliest memory of **Church**? Who was involved? How did you feel?

Church experiences have probably been a part of your life since you were born. You are now at the age when you look at familiar things in a new light. You form attitudes and make decisions that will affect your whole life and the lives of many other people. This book will encourage you to think about and deepen your relationship with the Church. You can be a Catholic in name only, you can be a Sunday-only member, or you can be an active and involved member of the Church. The choice is yours.

The first step in studying the Church is to grasp what the Church is. This is not so easy because the Church is a **mystery.** A mystery of faith is something that can be known but never fully understood because it relates to God. Even when God reveals himself through his great works, he remains a mystery beyond words.

What the Church Is and Is Not

Check the photo that best matches your present idea of Church, or describe a photo that would fit your idea.

☐ a large stone building

☐ all the people in the parish

☐ people who do not have much fun

☐ people who help those who are poor and in need

☐ saints who always do everything right

☐ everyone who believes in God

☐ the pope, bishops, and priests

☐ other:
_____

The People of God

No matter what your notion of the Church, you can be sure it is not complete. Some things cannot be neatly captured in words. The mystery we call the Church is perhaps most simply defined as the People of God. It is the people from all times and all countries who, like you, believe in God and have responded to Jesus' call to be holy and to serve the common good of all people.

We know that God exists because of creation and our own human reason. God has revealed himself to us as Father, Son, and Holy Spirit through his great deeds and words. Believing is a free human act—a gift made possible by the Holy Spirit. We are made by God to live with God. Therefore, we are religious by nature and by God's call. The Church is the means and goal of God's plan for us.

The word *church* means "convocation," or people called together. Jesus made possible our response to God's call. When sin separated us from God, Jesus—God the Son—became fully human and redeemed us. He died and rose, enabling us to be God's people. Jesus— the visible image of the invisible God—is the founder and head of the Church. He gathers his disciples—all those who believe in him—into a community, the Church. The Church, then, is a community of disciples and a **Communion of Saints.** Through the Church, we come to know God's plan of salvation.

Community comes from the Latin word for oneness. Church members are one in their faith in Jesus. Your belief in Jesus and your love for him bind you together with all the other members of his Church.

Jesus promised his followers, "I am with you always, until the end of the age." (Matthew 28:20) Jesus is alive and acting in the world today through the Church—through you!

Through you, he continues to proclaim the Good News and reach out to others with love. Like Jesus the God-Man, the Church is both human and divine. It is a human society in which God is present and acting. As a member of the Church through Baptism, you have the responsibility to let Jesus act through you as you work to bring justice to the world and peace to all people.

Who Is Jesus to You?

Your relationship with Jesus will determine your relationship with the Church. Do you believe in him? Do you believe that he saved you by his Death and Resurrection? Do you believe that he loves you and wants you to be his friend? Are you his disciple? Do you want to follow him? If your answer is yes to any of these questions, then you will be interested in the Church.

In and through the Church, Jesus has been present to his people since he returned to his Father over two thousand years ago. He is present with us today. Once you are convinced of this, the Church means a lot to you. You love it and desire to grow in your understanding of it. You are faithful to it because it was given to us by Jesus. And while it may be easy to give up a set of rules and customs, it is not so easy to give up a person.

Images of the Church

Scripture uses images that help us understand the mystery of the Church. It compares the Church to things we know. As you learn about the following images, answer the questions on a sheet of paper.

Saint Paul called the Church the *Body of Christ.* He referred to Christ as the head and to us as members of that Mystical (spiritual) Body.

- Think about the relationship of your body and its parts, or members. Why does your body need its members? Why do its members need one another? What happens to the rest of your body when one member hurts or is injured?
- The image of the Body of Christ shows we are a close-knit community. What does this image say about Christ and us? about our relationship with one another?

Read 1 Corinthians 12:12–31.

The Church is also called a *temple of the Holy Spirit* because God dwells with his family in the Church. Jesus is the cornerstone, and we are the living stones that build it.

- Think about the purpose of a temple. Why was the Temple so special to the Jewish people?
- The cornerstone of a building is the most important stone. What made Jesus the cornerstone of the Church?
- Why is each stone in a building important?

Another scriptural image of the Church is the *bride of Christ.* Christ loved her so much that he died for her. He constantly cares for her and gives her gifts. He joins her to himself in a covenant of love. Some day she will be united with Christ in glory.

- What kind of love do a bride and groom have for each other? What does this love tell you about Jesus and the Church?
- You are the Church. Reread the above paragraph about the bride of Christ, substituting *me* for *her* and *I* for *she.*
- How is the Church a mother? Why does Jesus call heaven a wedding feast?

How Jesus Saw It

Jesus spoke of the Church as a sign of his kingdom on earth. He used images in parables to tell us about it. Read each Scripture passage and then use the checklist to note ways you will become a more active member of the Church.

The Sheepfold John 10:1–16

Jesus tells us that he is the Good Shepherd and that his kingdom is like a sheepfold. The Good Shepherd's love is so great that he lays down his life for his sheep. Jesus also calls himself the gate for the sheep because only through him can we enter the kingdom. All those who have faith in Jesus and his Church belong to the sheepfold.

Listening to the Good Shepherd

What does Jesus say will happen when all people listen to his voice? (John 10:16)

_____

Check one way you will respond because you belong to the Good Shepherd.

I will

☐ be loving and generous like him.

☐ pray for the growth of the Church.

☐ share my faith with others.

☐ show Jesus that I rely on him by regularly celebrating Reconciliation and the Eucharist.

The Leaven Luke 13:20–21

The power of Jesus spreads through the whole world like yeast spreading through dough. It is a hidden power that moves slowly but surely. You are the leaven of Jesus when you become like him and proclaim the kingdom with your life. You are also his leaven when you work to change the world into a better place.

Rise to the Occasion

Check one way you will be leaven.

I will

☐ bring a spirit of forgiveness and unselfishness to all my dealings with others.

☐ do what I can to bring love and peace to my family.

☐ find secret ways to be generous.

The Vine and the Branches John 15:1–8

Jesus is the vine. Members of the Church are the branches. Through Jesus, you and other Church members live and grow. When you are united to Jesus and share his life, you are a healthy branch and bear much fruit. In other words, you recognize God's goodness in your life and you share it with others.

A Committee for Jesus

Imagine you are part of a committee whose job is to explain the meaning of Jesus' parables. Write a brief letter based on John 15:1–8 to people who are not familiar with the stories of the New Testament. Explain what it means to bear fruit and mention some of the fruits we bear when we are close to Jesus. Also note what the reading tells us about how we can glorify God.

To Whom It May Concern:

_____

_____

_____

_____

_____

_____

Sincerely,

_____

A Moment with Jesus

Each of these images—sheepfold, vine and branches, leaven—gives you a glimpse into who and what the Church is.

Take a moment now to reflect on one of these images. Silently read the Scripture passage that describes this image. Pause for a few moments and ask Jesus to help you deepen your relationship with him and with his Church. Thank Jesus for making you a member of his Church.

Mary: The Best Image

At the Annunciation, Mary became the mother of Jesus. She was united with him in the work of salvation—bringing about the birth of all believers in the Church. At the foot of the Cross, Mary became mother of Jesus' Mystical Body, the Church.

While Jesus hung on the Cross, he saw Mary and his faithful disciple John standing there. He said to his mother, "Woman, behold, your son." (John 19:26) Then he said to John, "Behold, your mother." (John 19:27) John represented all beloved disciples of Jesus. By referring to Mary as John's mother, Jesus was saying she was the mother of all who believe.

Mary believed and responded to God all her life. She was close to Jesus and always open to what God wanted. Because of this, she is an example for all of us. Mary, the first disciple of Jesus, showed us what it is like to be a perfect follower of him. That is why Mary is the best image of the Church. The qualities of Mary should be found in the Church: humility, obedience, love, and compassion. During the **Second Vatican Council,** Mary was given the new title *Mother of the Church.* If we resemble Mary, our Mother, and turn to her for help, we will be strong members of the Church.

Full of Grace

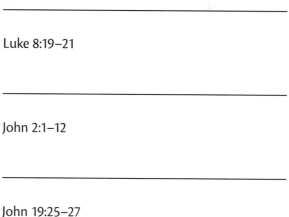

Look up the following Scripture passages. For each passage write one or more words that describe a characteristic or quality of Mary portrayed in the passage.

Luke 1:38

_____

Luke 8:19–21

_____

John 2:1–12

_____

John 19:25–27

_____

The Sanctifier

As Jesus is the Word of God, the Holy Spirit is the breath of God, the life-giver. Being one with the Father and the Son, the Spirit brought about creation. This Spirit is the Spirit of Jesus. They have a joint mission to save us and bring about a new creation. At the end of his life, Jesus promised to send the Holy Spirit from the Father. The Spirit did come and remains present and active in the Church, much as he was present and active in the life of Jesus.

When the Holy Spirit overshadowed Mary, Jesus came into being in his humanity. The Church came into being through the power of this same Spirit. The Spirit formed the disciples of Jesus into a community of love, worship, and service. Just as the Spirit directed Jesus throughout his life on earth, the Spirit shapes and guides the Church today. He guides not only the community as a whole but also individual Christians, who are filled with the Spirit at Baptism.

The Holy Spirit builds, animates, and sanctifies the Church. For this reason, the Holy Spirit is called the *sanctifier. **Sanctify*** means "to make holy." The Spirit helps you be holy, that is, devoted to God. Through grace, which is a sharing in God's own life, the Spirit dwells in you and forms you to be like Jesus. You are given the strength to act as Jesus would act and to love as he loves. You become a sign of Jesus' presence in the world by upholding the life and dignity of all people.

The Ever-Present Spirit

The early Church was very aware of the presence and action of the Holy Spirit. Read chapters 1, 2, and 4 of the Acts of the Apostles. Then create a slogan and design about the Holy Spirit to go on the T-shirt pattern below. Your T-shirt should focus on the Spirit's presence among us. For example, you might have flames around the words "The Spirit: This fire is always burning."

Saint Joseph

The patron saint of the Church is Saint Joseph. Why is he a good choice for patron saint?

_____

_____

_____

_____

Remember

What is the Church?

The Church is the People of God, a community of disciples. It is the Body of Christ alive and acting in the world today.

What are some images of the Church?

Images of the Church are the Body of Christ, the temple, the bride of Christ, the sheepfold, the vine and branches, leaven, and Mary.

Why is Mary the Mother of the Church?

Mary is the Mother of the Church because she is the mother of Jesus. He gave her to us as our Mother while he was dying on the Cross.

What does the Holy Spirit do for the Church?

The Holy Spirit builds, animates, and sanctifies the Church and helps its members become holy.

Words to Know

Church
Communion of Saints
mystery
sanctify
Second Vatican Council

Respond

In your reflection notebook, write your feelings about being a Catholic Christian. What does it mean to you to go to Mass, to participate in religion classes, or to belong to a parish community? In what ways would you like to see yourself change as a member of the Church?

Reach Out

1. Write and illustrate a modern-day parable of the Kingdom of God based on one of the following Scripture passages. You might write the parables as skits and present them.

Matthew 13:3–9	Matthew 13:47–50
Matthew 13:44	Matthew 25:1–13
Matthew 13:45–46	Luke 19:11–27

2. Show you are a member of the Church by
   - participating in the presentation of gifts at your parish church.
   - encouraging prayer in your family, especially before meals.
   - welcoming a new classmate.
   - giving one of your personal belongings or part of your allowance to those who are poor and in need.

3. Pray to the Holy Spirit, the sanctifier, for your bishop, parish priests, and all who minister in your parish that they may be spiritual leaders whose words and actions lead others to holiness.

4. Ask your teacher or catechist to help you find a copy of the Litany of Loreto, a popular prayer to Mary. Look through it and find titles that could also apply to the Church. Choose one title and explain how members of the Church can live it.

5. Tell someone what you learned about the Church. Invite a friend who is not Catholic or who does not practice the faith to go to church with you.

6. Research the history of your parish. Find out when it was founded and how it has grown and changed over the years.

7. Check to see if your parish (or a neighboring parish) has a Web site. Visit the site to see how the parish describes its mission and to see what kinds of services it offers.

Nothing but the Truth Check (✓) the statements that are true. Change the false statements to make them true.

_____ **1.** We will some day fully understand the Church.

_____ **2.** Jesus is the founder of the Church.

_____ **3.** The Church is both human and divine.

_____ **4.** We are like living stones in the Church.

_____ **5.** Jesus called the Holy Spirit the Good Shepherd.

_____ **6.** The best image for the Church is heaven.

_____ **7.** Through grace the Holy Spirit makes us like Jesus.

_____ **8.** To sanctify means to join the Church.

The Church in a Word Fill in the blanks. Use the clues to help you. If you fill in the blanks correctly, the boxed letters will spell *mystery*.

1. The Church is called this because God dwells in it. ___ ___ ☐ ___ ___ ___

2. Members of the Church ___ ___ ___ ☐ ___ ___ ___ ___ ___ ___ ___

3. Jesus' kingdom is like one of these. ☐ ___ ___ ___ ___ ___ ___ ___ ___

4. Christ died for her. ___ ___ ___ ___ ___ ___ ___ ___ ___ ___ ___ ☐

5. Jesus' power spreads like this. ___ ☐ ___ ___ ___ ___

6. Show how we are united with Jesus ___ ___ ___ ___ ___ ___ ___

___ ☐ ___ ___ ___ ___ ___ ___

7. Mother of the Church ___ ___ ___ ☐

Glimpses of the Mystery For each question, underline the truth about the Church.

1. What do we call the people from all times and countries who believe in God and have responded to Jesus' call?
   community   **People of God**   **apostles**

2. Jesus loves the members of the Church so much that he did what for them?
   preached   **prayed**   **died**

3. How far does the Church spread?
   throughout North America, South America, and Europe   **throughout the world**
              throughout your archdiocese

4. Members of the Church have life as long as they are united to whom?
   Jesus   **Saint Peter**   **Mary**

5. The Church is called a temple of what or whom?
   the Eucharist   **mystery**   **the Holy Spirit**

6. Jesus spoke of the Church as a sign of what?
   the end times   **his kingdom on earth**   **the coming of the Good Shepherd**

Gather and Go Forth

Know and Proclaim

We are the community of disciples. We learn about our faith so that we can proclaim it to others.

We Know Our Faith	We Proclaim Our Faith
The Church is the People of God. Jesus gathers all those who believe in him into a community, the Church.	Catholics show they are members of the Church by performing Works of Mercy, such as feeding those who are hungry or consoling those who mourn.
Mary was the first disciple, and she shows us what it is like to be a perfect follower of Jesus. Mary is the best image of what the Church should be.	Catholics honor Mary by observing holy days like the Feast of the Immaculate Conception and by praying prayers like the Hail Mary.
The Holy Spirit makes the Church holy. The Spirit's presence builds and animates the Church.	Catholics pray to the Holy Spirit for guidance when confused or troubled, using such prayers as Come, Holy Spirit or the Litany of the Holy Spirit.

As Catholics, we gather to hear the Word of God and celebrate the sacraments. The Holy Spirit sets our hearts on fire and sends us forth as disciples to live our faith.

"Go into the whole world and proclaim the gospel to every creature."

Mark 16:15

Test Your Catholic Knowledge

Fill in the circle that best answers the question.

What event do Catholics celebrate with the Feast of the Annunciation?

◯ the Last Supper

◯ the wedding feast at Cana

◯ the birth of Jesus in Bethlehem

◯ the message that Mary will be the mother of Jesus

A Catholic to Know

In the 1200s, Saint Hedwig, the daughter of a count, was considered a living saint. She married King Henry I of Silesia, and as queen, she was admired for her kindness and love for those who were poor. Among her many works of mercy, Saint Hedwig founded a hospital for people with leprosy, and she invited the religious to build monasteries in her kingdom. She welcomed travelers and those who were homeless and sick into her castle. Saint Hedwig also sought out those who needed her help, visiting them in their cottages. The example of Saint Hedwig's love and service inspired Catholics to serve one another with love throughout the centuries.

Saint Hedwig

Witness and Share

These sentences describe what Catholics believe. Listen carefully as they are read. Ask wyourself, "How strong are my Catholic beliefs?"

My Way to Faith

- I believe that the Holy Spirit is present and active in the Church today.

- I see myself as a member of the worldwide community of the Church.

- I look to Mary as an example for how to follow Jesus.

- I live as a sign of Jesus' presence in the world.

- I participate in parish activities that serve the needs of others.

Share Your Faith

Consider ways in which you can be more active in your parish community through participation at Mass, serving others, or joining a group. Write your ideas on the lines and invite a family member or friend to join you in at least one action during the coming week.

_____

_____

_____

_____

Tracing Our Roots

Tracing your ancestors is a fascinating hobby. This kind of research is called *genealogy*. Have you ever discussed the history of your family with your relatives? Try to answer these questions.

1. What is your father's family name?

_____

2. What is your mother's family name?

_____

3. What is your ethnic background?

_____

4. List some characteristics of your family.

_____

_____

_____

_____

5. Is there an occupation or profession that has been in your family for a long time? What is it?

_____

6. Which family member from the past is most interesting to you? Why?

_____

_____

7. Who would you say is an outstanding member of your present family? Why?

_____

_____

Your Spiritual Roots

Did you know that you have a spiritual history too? You inherited this history at your Baptism, when you joined the Church, the community of believers. Your spiritual history is part of **salvation history**—the story of God's loving relationship with his people. It is the story of God's redeeming love and the response of others to that love throughout history. It is also the story of your response to God's love.

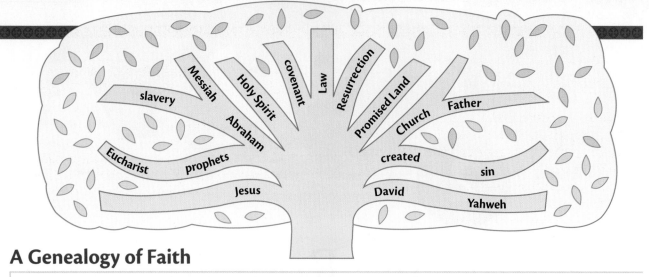

A Genealogy of Faith

Check your knowledge of your "spiritual roots" by filling in the blanks.
Use the words on the Family Tree of Faith if you need help.

From the beginning of time, God was a good, loving (1) _____ . God (2) _____ the whole universe and human beings. When God's friendship with Adam was broken by sin, God offered people hope by promising to send a (3) _____ who would save them from death and (4) _____ . God revealed who he was to our father in faith, (5) _____ . God made a special promise called a (6) _____ with him and called a special people to be his own. God showed deep care by revealing to them the divine name, (7) _____ .

When God's people were in Egypt, God led them out of (8) _____ to the (9) _____ through Moses. On Mount Sinai, God gave them the (10) _____ : love God and love others. God made a covenant with them.

When the Israelites arrived in the Promised Land, their leaders, the judges, led them in warfare. Finally, under King (11) _____ , they found short-lived unity and peace.

God made a personal covenant with David, promising that the Messiah would be from his family.

Whenever the Chosen People became discouraged and strayed from God's will, God would send (12) _____ to lead them back. Soon God's representatives realized that the Kingdom of God would come through one person. That person was (13) _____ , God's Son, true God and true man. He showed God's love and care in his life, especially in his passion, Death, and (14) _____ . Before Jesus died, he promised to send us the (15) _____ to help us.

Jesus commissioned his followers to carry on his teachings through the guidance of the Spirit in the (16) _____ . The Holy Spirit guides the leaders of the Church and helps its members proclaim the kingdom.

The Holy Spirit is active in your life. By participating in the sacraments of the Church, especially the (17) _____ , you can know God better and live the teachings of Jesus. You will be writing your spiritual history for the rest of your life.

The Master Plan

In salvation history, God has revealed deep love and mercy for us. When we were in the state of sin, God moved us to a state of grace so that we can be holy and righteous like God. We call this act of God **justification**. God's plan of salvation was fully revealed in the life of Jesus. Through the **Paschal Mystery** (the suffering, Death, Resurrection, and ascension of Jesus), God freed us from sin and death. Jesus made it possible for us to share in his eternal life and to glorify God in all that we do. His redeeming love comes to us through the Church. At Pentecost, the Holy Spirit helped the apostles to understand the divine plan. They saw that the Holy Spirit lives in each Church member through Baptism and faith in the risen Jesus. (Acts of the Apostles 2:1–41) The Holy Spirit leads Church members to holiness and helps them proclaim the Kingdom of God.

The Book

The story of your spiritual heritage is found in the Bible, our sacred writings. **Scripture** is the written record of God's love for us. It has two main parts. The first part is the **Old Testament.** Christians revere the Old Testament as God's inspired word to us, as do the Jewish people. The 46 books of the Old Testament tell about God's relationship with the Jewish people before Jesus came.

The second part of the Bible is the **New Testament.** The 27 books of the New Testament reveal to us the life and message of Jesus Christ. They tell of the beginning and growth of his Church. Both Catholics and Protestants believe that God speaks to us in the New Testament books: the Gospels, the letters, the Acts of the Apostles, and the Book of Revelation.

In the first few centuries after Jesus' Death and Resurrection, the Church decided which books were inspired by God. The Spirit guided the Church in making this decision. With the Spirit's guidance, the Church also helps us understand the meaning of these writings. As Catholics, we believe that God is the author of the Bible because he inspired its human writers.

Besides giving us knowledge of our faith, the Bible contains God's personal messages for us. To read it is to hold a conversation with God.

Favorite Scripture Stories

Write down your three favorite Scripture stories. Write down the title of the story if one already exists. Create a title if you are not aware of one.

	Chapter and Verse	Title
1.		
2.		
3.		

A Living Faith

Sacred Tradition is the lived faith of the Church. It is the beliefs taught by the Church that have been passed down by word, by customs, and by example. This Tradition is usually written with a capital *T* to distinguish it from ordinary tradition. God's Revelation comes to us through Scripture and Tradition. *Revelation* is all that God makes known to save us. Together, Scripture and Tradition form a single deposit—something entrusted to us for safe keeping—of faith. They help us to know God's Revelation in Jesus Christ.

Your Spiritual Family

Who belongs to your family of faith? The Catholics in your own parish are the members of the Church who are closest to you. However, your family in faith also includes more than one billion baptized Catholics around the globe. In addition, all those who are preparing to be baptized, known as catechumens, are members of your family of faith. You also have countless ancestors no longer living on this earth who are bound to you through the Church. You will be learning about some extraordinary ancestors, the saints, as you study the history of the Church. Saints are men and women in heaven who, while on earth, responded to God's call and now share eternal life with Christ. They are able to intercede for you in prayer, which means they can pray to God on your behalf.

People who have died and are in **purgatory** also belong to the Church. Purgatory is the state of those who are not yet ready to see God face-to-face. Those in purgatory are being purified from the effects of sin so that they can be wholly united with God. Through the Mass, your prayers, sacrifices, and acts of charity, you can help these people become prepared for heaven. As for children who die without Baptism, we trust God's mercy. Jesus' words, "Let the children come to me" (Luke 18:16), give us hope that there is a way of salvation for them as well.

Together all the members of the Church—those on earth, in heaven, and in purgatory—are called the Communion of Saints. We are all related in a special way in Christ. We can have a powerful influence on one another.

Christians who are not Catholic share our faith in many ways. Protestants believe in Jesus and his teachings. They believe that the Bible is God's holy Word. They celebrate Baptism and the Lord's Supper. Clearly they are closely linked with us in the Holy Spirit. Jewish people, too, are related to the Church in a special way because of their faith in God. They are God's Chosen People and Jesus' ancestors. All other believers are related to us as well, such as those who practice **Islam (Muslims).** All those who seek God are also related to us. To a lesser degree, people who do not know God but who live according to their conscience are also joined to us.

On the Move

We are a pilgrim people, because, like pilgrims, we are on a journey. The Spirit is leading us to eternal life with the Father. Our life on earth is just part of our journey of faith—a faith that comes to us from the Church and a faith that is necessary for our salvation. As a pilgrim, you need the support of others along the way. You see people of faith around you who help you understand what it means to belong to the Church today. By their words and example, they help you recognize Christ's presence in the world and in others. With the help of the Holy Spirit, you then are able to stand in solidarity with and support people in need, especially those who are poor, homeless, sick, or hungry.

Summary

Remember

What is salvation history?
Salvation history is the story of how God revealed deep love for us.

Where is God's Revelation found?
God's Revelation is found in Scripture and in Tradition.

What is the Communion of Saints?
The Communion of Saints is all the members of the Church on Earth, in heaven, and in purgatory.

Words to Know

Islam (Muslims)
justification
New Testament
Old Testament
Paschal Mystery
purgatory
salvation history
Scripture

Respond

Imagine that your favorite saint came to visit you to give you advice on how to follow Christ as a member of the Church. What would he or she tell you so that you too could come to follow God more closely? Write your conversation in your reflection notebook.

Reach Out

1. Work with a group to make a calendar on which the feast day of each student's patron saint is marked. Celebrate each feast by reading about the life of that saint.

2. Choose a patron saint for your class this year. Research the lives of various saints and then narrow your options to a few candidates. Decide on one and give reasons why this saint would be appropriate as your class patron.

3. Draw a mural of salvation history with your classmates.

4. Prayerfully read Matthew 13:31–32. Think of a practical way you could reach out to someone and spread the news of God's kingdom.

5. List ways in which we are all saints.

6. Talk with your family about the presence of a Bible in your home. If your family already has a Bible, ask about any historical significance it may have. (For example, it may have belonged to your great-grandparents.) If you do not yet have a family Bible, talk with your parents or guardians about acquiring one and placing it prominently in your home.

7. Find out the names of family members and relatives who have died and offer prayers for them, especially when you are at Mass. Pray that these family members and relatives will intercede for you.

CHAPTER 2 Review Activities

Putting History in Order Number these events in salvation history in the order in which they occurred.

_______ Exodus from Egypt led by Moses

_______ Jesus' Death

_______ Coming of the Spirit on Pentecost

_______ The call of Abraham

_______ Creation of the first persons

_______ God becoming Mary's Son to save us

_______ Giving of the Law on Mount Sinai

_______ Jesus' Resurrection

_______ Your Baptism

_______ Reign of King David in the Promised Land

A Church Directory Complete this directory of people who belong to the Church or who are related to the People of God in various ways.

People of God

Founder, J_______________

Sanctifier, H_______________

Mother, M_______________

Saints in H_______________

People in P_______________

Those Preparing for Baptism,
C_______________

All C_______________ on earth

C_______________ who are not Catholic

J_______________, God's Chosen People

M_______________ and others who believe in God

All who seek God

All who do not know God but live according to their conscience

Sentence Sense Use these terms in sentences to show that you know their meaning.

salvation history ____

____

Paschal Mystery ____

____

Communion of Saints ____

____

Tradition ____

____

Gather and Go Forth

Know and Proclaim

The Church, which began with God's Chosen People, includes all the living and dead who have responded to God's love.

We Know Our Faith	We Proclaim Our Faith
The Bible tells the story of God's love for his people and their response throughout history.	Catholics recognize God's love for all people, and they respect people of all religions.
Revelation is all that God makes known through Sacred Scripture and Sacred Tradition to save us.	Devotion to the Sacred Heart of Jesus is a tradition that acknowledges people's desire for Jesus' redeeming love.
Our spiritual family includes the saints—men and women who responded to God's call while they lived on earth.	Catholics commemorate the lives of the saints by celebrating their memorials and remembering the departed in prayers at Mass.

Test Your Catholic Knowledge

Fill in the circle that best completes the sentence.

The Communion of Saints includes:

○ people who do not believe in God but live according to their conscience.

○ all members of the Church on earth, in heaven, and in purgatory.

○ the Jewish people, who are God's Chosen People.

○ people of other religions, such as Islam.

As Catholics, we believe in the power of the Holy Spirit to guide what we say and do, just as the Spirit guided the apostles at Pentecost. The Holy Spirit speaks through Sacred Scripture and Tradition.

And they were all filled with the holy Spirit and began to speak in different tongues, as the Spirit enabled them to proclaim.

Acts of the Apostles 2:4

A Catholic to Know

Teresa of Ávila was an energetic and willful child. She entered the convent at the age of 20, but her experience of conversion did not occur until many years later. An image of the crucified Christ made her aware that she was not living in true relationship with God. Her resolve to devote herself to intense prayer, strict poverty, and tireless labor for God's people brought about a life-changing realization of the depths of God's love. Teresa's conversion led her to become a religious reformer, an author, the founder of many convents, and a master of Christian prayer. In 1622, the Church canonized her. She and Saint Catherine of Siena were the first women to be declared Doctors of the Church.

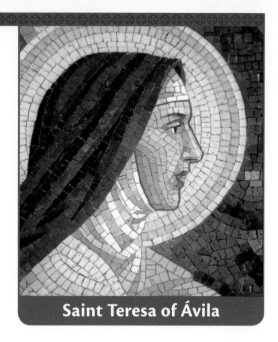

Saint Teresa of Ávila

Witness and Share

These sentences describe what Catholics believe. Listen carefully as they are read. Ask yourself, "How strong are my Catholic beliefs?"

My Way to Faith

- I spend time thinking about how God acts in my life.

- I use Scripture to pray.

- I respect people of other faiths and traditions.

- I think it is important to listen to our priest, our bishop, and the pope.

- I look to the saints as models for how to be holy.

Share Your Faith

Identify a quality of a saint that inspires you to take action in the form of prayer, service, study, or reaching out to others. How can you imitate this saint's example? Write your ideas on the lines. Invite a family member or friend to talk about a saint who inspires him or her.

_____

_____

_____

_____

A Closer Look

You have grown in many ways over the years: physically, mentally, and spiritually. You have grown in your relationships. When you were very young, you knew only your family members and a few neighbors. Then you made more friends when you went to school. Now you look forward to high school, where you will reach out even further in your relationships.

Who Helped You Grow?

Name people who have helped you become a better person. Tell how each one helped you grow.

_____

_____

_____

How the Church Got Started

Like many other organizations, the Church started out small. A group of disciples followed Jesus, listening to his words about God's love for us and about the kingdom. When Jesus was arrested and crucified by the Roman officials, that could have been the end of his movement. Instead Jesus' disciples became more excited about Jesus and more determined than ever to spread his message. Why? Because something tremendous convinced them that Jesus was the Messiah. That something was the Resurrection.

When the apostles encountered the risen Christ, their lives were changed forever. Jesus' Resurrection was the ultimate proof of his divinity. The Church was born when Jesus, its founder, died on the Cross and then rose from the dead on the third day. Before Jesus ascended into heaven, he promised his disciples that he would send the Holy Spirit to strengthen them to witness to others their faith in Jesus.

A Spirit-Filled Church

As Jesus had directed, the disciples gathered in a room in Jerusalem to await the Spirit. Together with Mary they prayed and waited for nine days. Then, on the Jewish feast of **Pentecost**, the Spirit came to them in the form of wind and tongues of fire. The disciples burst out of the room and began to preach. People had come from all parts of the world for the feast. Although these people spoke different languages, they could all understand the disciples' amazing words. About three thousand people were baptized that day.

Read Acts of the Apostles 2:38. In your own words, summarize what Peter told the people they must do to be saved.

_____

_____

_____

The Church Is Made Known

The Church was made known to the world on Pentecost. The Holy Spirit united the first Christians in Jerusalem and formed them into a community of faith. They were one in their belief in Jesus and his teachings, in the Eucharist, in prayer, and in their love for one another. The Holy Spirit poured out on them grace to witness, heal, and work wonders in Jesus' name.

Past and Present

If you had lived in Jerusalem at the time of Pentecost, why might you have wanted to join the Christian community?

_____

_____

What are some of the reasons for wanting to belong to the Church today?

_____

_____

Guided by the Spirit

The Spirit enlightened the disciples about the life and teachings of Jesus. Even today the Spirit is with the Church, giving us new insights into truth. We are still growing. We are still getting to know ourselves as a Church.

Models of the Church

A theologian is someone who studies the truths of our faith and tries to understand and explain them better. Cardinal Avery Dulles, a theologian, proposed six ways to look at the Church. These six images, or models, will help you go deeper into the mystery of the Church. They are

- institution
- mystical communion
- sacrament
- herald
- servant
- community of disciples

A person who plays various roles in life is said to wear many caps. You might think of the models of the Church as caps that the Body of Christ wears. Each one represents a different aspect or role of the Church. The models are explained in the following sections. Each section begins with a quotation from the Acts of the Apostles, a book about the early Christian community. These quotations show the model present in the infant Church.

INSTITUTION

Then they prayed, "You, Lord, who know the hearts of all, show which one of these two you have chosen to take the place in this apostolic ministry from which Judas turned away to go to his own place." Then they gave lots to them, and the lot fell upon Matthias, and he was counted with the eleven apostles.

Acts of the Apostles 1:24–26

The Church is organized in a hierarchy under the guidance of the Holy Spirit. All the baptized share in the one priesthood of Christ.

The Church also has ordained ministers to serve and lead the baptized. They do so by teaching, calling us to holiness through the sacraments, and governing. The highest authority in the Church is the pope, Christ's visible representative. The pope, who is the Bishop of Rome, is joined by other bishops. The bishops are the successors of the apostles.

Together with the pope, they lead the Church and serve the baptized. They also guard and transmit Church Tradition.

Priests and deacons support the bishop in their diocese in serving the community. The priests are responsible with the bishops for the people in their particular parish. These three degrees of ordained ministries—bishops, priests, and deacons—are essential for the Church.

Like any institution, the Church has laws and traditions. The *Code of Canon Law* contains rules that guide all aspects of Church life.

MYSTICAL COMMUNION

> The community of believers was of one heart and mind, and no one claimed that any of his possessions was his own, but they had everything in common.
>
> Acts of the Apostles 4:32

Human beings are social by nature. We like to be with other people. Recall how good it is to work together on a family project or to have fun together. Maybe you belong to a club or team whose members have a common goal.

As a Church, we are a group of people who share our lives. We are bound together by our belief in Jesus and our desire to do God's will. We talk, pray, and work together. We support one another and depend on one another. We are united, especially in the Eucharist. Nourished by the Body of Christ, we become the Body of Christ, the People of God, a mystical communion. In this mystical communion, there is diversity of members and functions. Our shared lives are a sign of the kingdom in the next world, where we will all be united in love forever.

SACRAMENT

> Every day they devoted themselves to meeting together in the temple area and to breaking bread in their homes. They ate their meals with exultation and sincerity of heart, praising God and enjoying favor with all the people.
>
> Acts of the Apostles 2:46–47

A sacrament is an outward sign that indicates an inward grace. It is an encounter with Christ. This definition describes the seven sacraments of the Church. At the same time, it also describes the Church itself. The Church is composed of individual persons who can be heard and seen. Within the Church we discover the presence of God. The Church is the sacrament of the Trinity's communion with people. In fact, Jesus himself is a sacrament. He is a visible sign of God— God made flesh. We continue to meet Christ through the Church in the Eucharist and in the members. As members of the Church, we are called to be a living sacrament. The more we follow Jesus' way, the better we represent the Kingdom of God.

HERALD

> All day long, both at the temple and in their homes, they did not stop teaching and proclaiming the Messiah, Jesus.
>
> Acts of the Apostles 5:42

A herald is a messenger sent to announce something. Sent by Christ, the Church continues to announce the Good News of Christ's teaching. Every day the *Gospel*, which means "good news," is proclaimed at Mass when the community gathers to celebrate.

We are called to take the Gospel to others. Christians do this because Jesus sent his disciples to "Go, therefore, and make disciples of all nations." (Matthew 28:19) The Good News is just too good to keep to ourselves. We want everyone to know. So Church members go to the ends of the earth to proclaim that God loves us, saves us, and calls us to join the community of believers.

Advertising the Good News

Imagine that you write advertisements to be aired on the radio. Write a creative radio ad to promote the Good News of Christ.

_____

_____

SERVANT

> And one of them named Agabus stood up and predicted by the Spirit that there would be a severe famine all over the world . . . the disciples determined that, according to ability, each should send relief to the brothers who lived in Judea.
>
> Acts of the Apostles 11:28–29

Over and over, Jesus told his followers that they must serve one another with love. He taught his most dramatic lesson the night before he died. At the Last Supper, he washed and dried the feet of the apostles. Then he told them to serve one another the same way.

The Church serves others by caring for their needs. Love for Jesus and others leads us to serve others as Jesus did—by healing, comforting, feeding, welcoming, and forgiving. Together we strive to promote the well-being of all, especially those who are poor and vulnerable. We serve people in our own families and neighborhoods, and we also stand in solidarity with our brothers and sisters around the world.

COMMUNITY OF DISCIPLES

> So the Twelve called together the community of the disciples and said, "It is not right for us to neglect the word of God to serve at table. Brothers, select from among you seven reputable men, filled with the spirit and wisdom, whom we shall appoint to this task."
>
> Acts of the Apostles 6:2–3

Young children enjoy playing follow the leader. Like many kids' games, it helps children become aware of a basic reality in life: there are leaders and there are followers. In the Gospels, we learn that Jesus was a leader who called others to be his followers. These followers were called *disciples*.

To be a disciple of Jesus is to follow him in all situations. As a Church, we are a community of disciples. Jesus is our one true leader, and we are united in our following of him. In order to follow Jesus, we need to be looking and listening for all the ways he is calling us to be his disciples. To be a member of the Church means to follow Jesus at every moment of our lives.

A Moment with Jesus

As a baptized member of Jesus' Church, you are being called to share in Jesus' mission. Jesus does not expect you, at your age, to personally go to the ends of the earth to proclaim the Gospel. He is, however, calling you to do so in your own community—at home, at school, and in your neighborhood.

Pause for a moment to thank Jesus for calling you to share in his mission. Ask him for the grace you need to share his Good News with others through your words and actions. Ask him to help you be a good member of his Church.

The Domestic Church

The family has been called the *domestic church*—a Church in miniature. The Christian home is a community of grace and prayer and a school of human virtues and Christian charity. If you think about it, the domestic church reflects each of the six models. On a separate sheet of paper, describe how a Catholic family lives each model. Share your answers with the class.

Summary

Remember

How did the Church get started?

Jesus founded the Church through his Death and Resurrection. The Resurrection convinced the disciples that Jesus was the Messiah, so they continued to spread his message. Lives were changed when they encountered the risen Christ.

How was the early Christian community united?

The Holy Spirit united the first Christians in Jerusalem and formed them into a community of faith. They were one in their belief in Jesus and his teachings, in the Eucharist, and in their love for one another.

What are six models used to describe the Church?

Institution, mystical communion, sacrament, herald, servant, and community of disciples are the six models used to describe the Church.

Words to Know

canon law
Pentecost

Respond

The Holy Spirit is present within you, moving you to action. It is important to listen in prayer so that you can follow the Spirit's lead. Read the following prayer from the Votive Mass of the Holy Spirit, and then write to the Spirit in your reflection notebook. Write about a time when you had to make a decision or about something difficult that happened to you.

> Father,
> as your Spirit guides us and your
>   loving care keeps us safe,
> be close to us in your mercy and
>   listen to those who call on you.
> Strengthen and protect by your
>   kindness
> the faith of all who believe in you.

Reach Out

1. Read Matthew 5:13–16 and find the two images it gives for a witness to Christ and his Church. Then write in your reflection notebook one way you have already witnessed to Christ today.

2. Make a poster depicting the six models of the Church. Include the Scripture passages from the Acts of the Apostles identified in this chapter. Draw or cut out pictures from magazines to illustrate the models.

3. On Pentecost, the Church was made known to the world. Today one of the ways that the Church makes itself known to the world is through the use of Web sites. Find out the URL of your parish and/or diocesan Web site and explore how the Church is making itself known to those who visit the site.

4. When you visit your parish and/or diocesan Web site, look up information about how the ministries of the parish and/or diocese are organized. Make an organizational chart to illustrate the institutional aspect of the Church in your parish and/or diocese.

5. Think of someone in your life who is a "living sacrament"—a visible sign of God's love and presence. Write about this person in your reflection notebook. Send this person a note or card, thanking him or her for being a living sacrament for you.

6. Together with a few friends, think of a way that you can be of service in your community. As you perform your service, remind yourself that to serve others is to be a good member of the Church and to act in the image of Jesus.

CHAPTER 3 Review Activities

News Flash **Complete this news brief about the first day of the organized Church.**

Yesterday, in the city of ______________________, a group of disciples of Jesus converted about ______________________ people. The disciples claimed that Jesus, who had been crucified, was ______________________. They preached with such enthusiasm that they were thought to be drunk. They claimed to be filled not with wine but with the ______________________. Although people from many lands were gathered for the feast of ______________________, somehow they all understood the language the men spoke.

Beginnings **List four characteristics of the early Christian community.**

1. ____
2. ____
3. ____
4. ____

Models of the Church **Match each model of the Church with the description that best describes it.**

_____ **1.** institution	**a.** Jesus washed the feet of his apostles.
_____ **2.** mystical Communion	**b.** The Church is a visible sign of Jesus' presence.
_____ **3.** sacrament	**c.** Groups of people need official organization.
_____ **4.** herald	**d.** Nourished by the Body of Christ, we become the Body of Christ.
_____ **5.** servant	**e.** Jesus is our leader and we are his followers.
_____ **6.** community of disciples	**f.** The Church continues to announce the Good News.

Gather and Go Forth

Know and Proclaim

We learn more about our Catholic faith as we grow in relationship with God. What we know, we can proclaim.

We Know Our Faith	We Proclaim Our Faith
The Church began as a small group of disciples who followed Jesus and listened to his words. The Holy Spirit united them into a community of faith.	On Pentecost, some Catholics wear red to recall the tongues of fire that appeared over the heads of the apostles.
The Church is an institution, a mystical communion, a sacrament, a herald, a servant, and a community of disciples.	Catholics support agencies like Catholic Charities, which serves as a voice for people living in poverty and promotes their well-being.
The Christian home—the domestic church—is a community of grace and prayer; it is the Church in miniature.	Catholics decorate their homes with signs of their faith, such as crucifixes, pictures of saints on their walls, and statues of saints in their yards.

God calls us, as he called the people of Israel, to be a light for all nations by working for peace and justice.

I, the LORD, have called you for justice,
* I have grasped you by the hand;*
I formed you, and set you
* as a covenant for the people,*
* a light for the nations.*

Isaiah 42:6

Test Your Catholic Knowledge

Fill in the circle that best answers the question.

Which best describes the Church as a mystical communion?

◯ the Acts of the Apostles

◯ the Bishop of Rome

◯ the Magisterium

◯ the Body of Christ

A Catholic to Know

Saint Robert Bellarmine (1524–1621) is the patron saint of catechists and students because he guided children in the Church's catechism. As a Jesuit priest and one of the outstanding scholars of his day, he was called upon to serve as personal theologian to Pope Clement VIII during the years of the Protestant Reformation (1517–1648). He became known as a great defender of the Catholic Church and its teachings through his writing and preaching. His sermons were so powerful that people were attracted from all over to hear them and many were converted. In 1931, Robert was declared a Doctor of the Church. We celebrate the life and works of Saint Robert Bellarmine on September 17.

Saint Robert Bellarmine

Witness and Share

These sentences describe what Catholics believe. Listen carefully as they are read. Ask yourself, "How strong are my Catholic beliefs?"

My Way to Faith

- I thank God for people in my life who have helped me become a better person.

- I share in God's love by proclaiming my Catholic faith.

- I support people in my family, parish, and community as they grow in their faith.

- I look to members of my family as examples of discipleship.

- I represent the Kingdom of God in the way I treat people who are less fortunate than I am.

Share Your Faith

Help make your home a community of grace and prayer. How do you and your family pray together? Write your ideas for praying with your family. Invite family members to choose favorite prayers or write original prayers to say together as a family every day or on special occasions.

_____

_____

_____

_____

A People of Prayer

During the last days of March 2005, it became apparent that the health of Pope John Paul II was severely declining. The Holy Father, who had been known for his vitality, had been slowed in recent years by Parkinson's disease and arthritis. Throughout the month of March, his health deteriorated. By April 1, he was slipping in and out of consciousness.

In St. Peter's Square, thousands and thousands of people, young and old, gathered to pray. Some sat together on the pavement, singing hymns. Others stood alone or in small groups, praying the prayers of the Rosary. Many sat quietly with their eyes closed, contemplating the mystery of the moment. Some gathered in groups and prayed the **Liturgy of the Hours.** Others meditated on passages from the Bible and prayed quietly to God in their own words.

Around the world, billions of people prayed for the Holy Father. Many Catholics attended Mass or other prayer services to keep vigil during the Pope's final hours. Christians and people of many religious backgrounds offered prayers at home and in churches, temples, and synagogues.

Finally, on Saturday evening, April 2, 2005, the Holy Father passed away. In the midst of their grief, people continued to turn to prayer as a way of seeking strength, guidance, and consolation over the death of one of the greatest figures of the 20th century. This man of prayer was surrounded by the prayers of millions of people as he passed.

Prayer Is . . .

Most likely, when you were very young, your parents or guardians taught you to say your prayers. The family is usually the first place where people learn to pray. Now that you are older, you understand that there are many ways to pray. You can pray aloud, or vocally. You can also pray silently, such as when you meditate, or think about God. Another way to pray is to contemplate, or rest silently in God's presence. Prayer takes many forms. Check those forms that best express your experience of prayer.

- ☐ talking to God in my own words
- ☐ loving God with all my heart and knowing I am loved by God
- ☐ participating in prayer services with others
- ☐ asking for strength when things are difficult
- ☐ listening to and reading the Word of God
- ☐ asking God for things I need or that my family and friends need
- ☐ participating in the Mass
- ☐ thanking God for his blessings
- ☐ saying traditional prayers I have learned
- ☐ enjoying the company of a friend
- ☐ praying with the Bible

A good definition of **prayer** is the lifting up of the mind and heart to God.

Prayer: A Must

Prayer is an expression of faith and love. It is as necessary to the life of the Church as breathing is to our natural life. We have to stay in contact with God to live as the People of God. Personal prayer nourishes our relationship with God. Communal prayer—praying with others—strengthens our unity in Christ. The Church was made known to the world after Jesus' followers prayed for nine days. Their shared prayer bound together the Church's members. In being a people of prayer, the Christians were imitating Jesus.

Jesus prayed the traditional Jewish prayers: meal prayers, the psalms, and the Shema, the central Jewish prayer of faith in the one God. Taken from Deuteronomy 6:4–5, it is prayed at least twice each day. Jesus prayed in the synagogues and in the Temple. He prayed at his baptism, before choosing his apostles, and at the multiplication of loaves. He prayed when he was transfigured, when he raised Lazarus from the dead, and during his agony in the garden. Jesus practiced deep personal prayer.

> Rising very early before dawn, he left and went off to a deserted place, where he prayed.
>
> Mark 1:35

Jesus' active life flowed from his prayer. The Church continues the prayer of Christ.

Jesus' Words on Prayer

Jesus told his followers how to pray. He told them a parable about the necessity for them to pray always without becoming weary. (Luke 18:1) He also gave them the following advice:

> Pray for those who persecute you.
>
> Matthew 5:44

> Ask and you will receive; seek and you will find; knock and the door will be opened to you.
>
> Luke 11:9

Christ Praying, The Palma Collection.

Above all, Jesus taught his followers to pray the Lord's Prayer, the most important prayer of the Church:

> This is how you are to pray: Our Father . . .
>
> Matthew 6:9

Great Pray-ers

Mary, the Mother of the Church, was a woman of prayer. Scripture tells us very little about her. It does say that, as the profound experiences of Jesus' life unfolded, she pondered the events in her heart. A pondering heart is a *listening* heart.

At the Annunciation, the angel announced to Mary that she would be the mother of the Savior. Mary's prayerful response expressed her openness to God, her willingness to listen. "May it be done to me according to your word." (Luke 1:38)

Mary listened to God's word in her life. When her relative Elizabeth was pregnant, Mary listened to God's call and went to help her. At the wedding feast of Cana, Mary listened to the needs of the people. She listened and believed in Jesus as she told the servants, "Do whatever he tells you." (John 2:5)

In the upper room on the feast of Pentecost, Mary listened to the Holy Spirit and supported the early Church by praying for its needs. Mary's willingness to listen in prayer and in her relationships with others made her one with God and God's will.

All the saints prayed. No matter how busy they were, they always took time for God. Saint Francis of Assisi praised God as he hiked along the country roads. Saint Elizabeth Ann Seton, the mother of five children, prayed as she rocked her babies to sleep. Saint Thérèse of Lisieux, a simple French sister, said, "I just tell our Lord all that I want, and he understands."

The Prayer of the Church

Since the time of the early Church, Christians have been taught by the Holy Spirit to come together to pray. In doing so, we find spiritual strength. We also make the Church a sign of that kingdom, where we will be one in praising God forever.

The **liturgy** is the public worship of the Church. In its broad sense, it includes the celebration of the seven sacraments and the prayer called the Liturgy of the Hours. Of course, the eucharistic celebration, the Mass, is the Church's great community prayer. The Mass includes adoration, contrition, thanksgiving, and supplication (petition). From the Mass, we are sent forth to live lives of charity and justice.

From the start, Christians were united every day in the Word and the Eucharist. Early Christians, most of whom were Jews, were familiar with the prayers of the Temple that honored God at various times of the day. As Christians, they wanted to extend their worship of Jesus throughout the day. This led to the practice of the Liturgy of the Hours, a prayer based on readings and prayers from the Mass of the day. This prayer is part of the living Tradition of the Church.

At first, the Liturgy of the Hours was prayed by a large number of people with their bishop in the cathedral. Later it was prayed only by priests and religious. It was called the Divine Office. Today the Church calls it the prayer of Christians and invites all Christians to pray it.

The Liturgy of the Hours includes hymns, psalms, Scripture readings, petitions, the Lord's Prayer, and times of reflective silence. It includes the three major expressions of the life of prayer: vocal prayer, meditation, and contemplative prayer. This prayer of the Church can be prayed at seven "hours" or times during the day. It makes the whole day holy. The morning and evening times are called hinge hours. Like a hinge that opens and closes a door, morning and evening prayer open and close the day. At morning prayer, or Lauds, Christians remember Christ and give praise to the Father at the beginning of the day. They also ask him to be with them throughout the day. At evening prayer, or Vespers, Christians pray at the setting of the sun that Christ, the light that never ends, will always be their hope.

Most Christians choose from among these hours (traditional names in parentheses).

- Readings (Matins)
- Morning Prayer (Lauds)
- Daytime Prayer (Terce, Sext, and None)
- Evening Prayer (Vespers)
- Night Prayer (Compline)

All through the day, Christians pray for the needs of the Church. They praise God and ask that God's will be done. They listen for God's will in their lives and ask for help. On pages 26 and 27 is a sample of the Liturgy of the Hours Wednesday Morning Prayer for Week III of a four-week cycle.

Night Prayer

This antiphon is prayed every night in Night Prayer. You might memorize it and pray it before going to bed.

Protect us Lord, as we stay awake; watch over us as we sleep, that awake, we may keep watch with Christ, and asleep, rest in his peace.

Praying the Liturgy of the Hours

Leader: O, Lord, open my lips.

All: And my mouth will proclaim your praise.

Song

Psalm 98

Leader: Let us celebrate with joy in the presence of our Lord and King.

Side 1: Sing a new song to the Lord for he has worked wonders. His right hand and his holy arm have brought salvation.

Side 2: The Lord has made known his salvation; has shown his justice to the nations. He has remembered his truth and love for the house of Israel.

Side 1: All the ends of the earth have seen the salvation of our God. Shout to the Lord all the earth, ring out your joy.

Side 2: Sing psalms to the Lord with the harp with the sound of music. With trumpets and the sound of the horn acclaim the King, the Lord.

Side 1: Let the sea and all within it thunder; the world, and all its peoples. Let the rivers clap their hands and the hills ring out their joy.

Side 2: Rejoice at the presence of the Lord, for he comes to rule the earth. He will rule the world with justice and the peoples with fairness.

All: Glory to the Father . . .

All: Lord Jesus, you have revealed your justice to all nations. We stood condemned, and you came to be judged in our place. Send your saving power on us and, when you come in glory, bring your mercy to those for whom you were condemned.

Reading   Job 1:21; 2:10

Reader: A reading from Job.

"Naked I came forth from my
mother's womb,

and naked shall I go back again.
The LORD gave and the LORD has
taken away;

blessed be the name of the LORD! . . .

We accept good things from God;
and should we not accept evil?"

Responsory

Leader: Incline my heart according to your
will, O God.

All: Incline my heart according to your will,
O God.

Leader: Speed my steps along your path,

All: According to your will, O God.

Leader: Glory to the Father . . .

All: Incline my heart according to your will,
O God.

Canticle of Zechariah

Leader: Show us your mercy, Lord; remember
your holy covenant.

*(Recite canticle [Luke 1:68–79],
alternating sides with each verse.)*

All: Show us your mercy, Lord; remember your
holy covenant.

Intercessions

Leader: Christ nourishes and supports the
Church for which he gave himself up to
death. Let us ask him:

All: Remember your Church, Lord.

Leader: You are the Good Shepherd who has
given life and light today,

All: make us grateful for these gifts.

Leader: Look with mercy on the flock you have
gathered together in your name,

All: let no one whom the Father has given
you perish.

Leader: Lead your Church in the way of your
commandments,

All: may your Holy Spirit keep her faithful.

Leader: Nourish the Church at the banquet of
your Word and Bread,

All: strengthened by this food may she follow
you in joy.

All: Our Father . . .

Leader: Lord, as daylight fills the sky, fill
us with your holy light. May our lives
mirror our love for you, whose wisdom
has brought us into being and whose care
guides us on our way. We ask this through
our Lord Jesus Christ, your Son, who lives
and reigns with you and the Holy Spirit,
one God, for ever and ever.

Leader: May the Lord bless us, protect us from
all evil, and bring us to everlasting life.

All: Amen.

Prayer Times

You know that God is with you always. He never forgets to pay attention to you. Jesus wants your friendship with him to be strong at all times. He taught us to "pray always." (Luke 18:1) It is important to schedule a time each day to pray. Friends agree to get together at certain times to talk. Let it be the same with you and God.

When do you pray? Color the box green if you *always* pray at this time, yellow if you *sometimes* pray at this time, or red if you *never* pray at this time.

☐ in the morning when you get up

☐ before and after meals (at home or school)

☐ in the evening (before going to bed)

☐ waiting for the bus or riding the bus

☐ during a test

☐ when you hear an ambulance or police siren

☐ when you see anyone hurt

☐ when you see beauty in nature

☐ when you see kindness in people

☐ in times of temptation

☐ when reading Scripture

☐ when preparing for the Sacrament of Reconciliation

Prayer Places

The Holy Spirit helps us pray anywhere and at any time. Churches are sacred places where people gather to pray with others. But most people have places where they talk to God by themselves. It could be outdoors or in their own room. It could be a quiet place in their home. What is your favorite place for prayer?

Never Give Up!

Praying is not always easy. We face many distractions. Even saints had difficulty. The important thing is to have faith, be open to conversion, and be vigilant. In other words, keep trying!

Read the following stories. What answers would you give these people who are having difficulty with prayer? Write them on a sheet of paper.

1. Jung-Hee was on his way to Mass Saturday evening. Then Josh called, inviting him over to his house. "It won't matter if I skip Mass this once," Jung-Hee thought.

2. At Sunday Mass during the opening song, Rachel and Kaitlyn were catching up on what they had done on Saturday. During the first reading, they were reading the bulletin announcement about the youth group ski trip.

3. Mrs. Okotie announced that the class would spend some time in private prayer. Flora hated the idea. "Prayer is boring. I never know what to do and just fall asleep," she said.

4. Anthony listened as his parents discussed their plans for Sunday. It would be useless to ask them to drive him to Mass. They often did not go themselves, and they were on vacation. "I cannot go," he decided.

5. When Liam's parents were getting a divorce, Liam prayed that God would stop it. He felt his prayers went unanswered. "God doesn't care about me," he thought. Liam stopped praying.

Ora et Labora

These Latin words mean "pray and work." Ultimately prayer should lead us to action so that, guided by the Holy Spirit, we can serve the needs of others. We should especially serve the needs of those who are poor and vulnerable.

Summary

Remember

What is prayer?
Prayer is the lifting up of the mind and heart to God.

What are the two basic forms of prayer?
Personal prayer and communal prayer are the two basic forms of prayer.

What is the Liturgy of the Hours?
The Liturgy of the Hours is a prayer based on readings and prayers from the Mass of the day. It extends the worship of Jesus throughout the day.

What prayer of Jesus' is the most important prayer of the Church?
The Lord's Prayer is the most important prayer of the Church.

Words to Know

liturgy
Liturgy of the Hours
prayer

Respond

Evaluate your prayer life. How could you improve your personal prayer? your prayer with others? In your reflection notebook, write a conversation with Jesus about your prayer habits. Begin with "Jesus, teach me to pray . . ." Assemble the Scripture Prayer Booklet at the back of this book and begin to use it.

Reach Out

1. Teach a prayer to a younger child. Talk about the meaning of the words.

2. Memorize a new prayer by saying it often. Tell the class why you like it.

3. Make a list of prayers that you know. Include private prayers, devotions, and communal prayers.

4. In your reflection notebook, write three or more intentions you wish to pray for. Set aside at least a minute every day this week to pray for these intentions.

5. Copy one of the quotations on page 30 onto a card and decorate it. Display it at home as a reminder to pray.

Reasons to Pray Match the lines from familiar prayers to the following forms of prayer.

    a. blessing and adoration   **b.** contrition   **c.** thanksgiving   **d.** petition

_____ **1.** Give us this day our daily bread.

_____ **2.** Glory be to the Father, and to the Son, and to the Holy Spirit.

_____ **3.** Grant us by the same Holy Spirit a love and relish of what is right and just.

_____ **4.** I am heartily sorry for having offended you.

_____ **5.** We give you thanks, O almighty God, for all your benefits.

_____ **6.** Lord, make me an instrument of your peace.

_____ **7.** We praise you for your glory.

_____ **8.** Lord, hear our prayer.

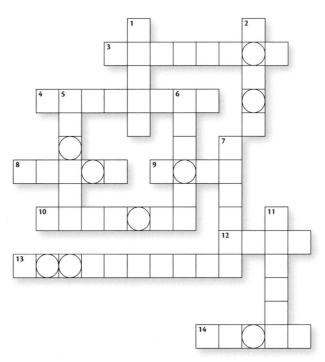

Prayer Facts Work this puzzle.

Across

3. Prayers of supplication are prayers of _____ .
4. Describes prayer said with others
8. Prayer is an expression of _____ and love.
9. The central prayer of the Church
10. Another word for evening prayer
12. Someone known for listening in prayer
13. The Liturgy of the Hours is a good prayer for all _____ .
14. The Liturgy of the Hours has prayer at seven _____ each day.

Down

1. Our chief model for prayer
2. The Liturgy of the _____ is the official Christian prayer.
5. Another name for the Liturgy of the Hours: Divine _____
6. Jesus taught us to pray _____ .
7. Song-prayers in the Old Testament
11. Lifting up of the mind and heart to God

Unscramble the circled letters to spell the name of a traditional prayer.

_____

Gather and Go Forth

Know and Proclaim

As Catholics, we are people of prayer. We offer our joys and sorrows to the God who loves us.

We Know Our Faith	We Proclaim Our Faith
Prayer is the lifting up of one's mind and heart to God. Jesus told his disciples to "pray always."	As Catholics, we bring our whole lives to the celebration of the Mass where we are nourished and sent forth to love and serve others.
Liturgy is the public worship of the Church. The Mass is the Church's greatest community prayer.	Catholics pray the Lord's Prayer during every Mass and in the morning and evening prayer of the Liturgy of the Hours.
The Liturgy of the Hours is the prayer of Christians. It is a traditional form of prayer that has been prayed by Catholics for centuries.	Catholics pray psalms during the Liturgy of the Hours, which are traditional prayers said by Jesus himself.

We pray to God to give praise and thanks as well as to ask for guidance and help. Through prayer, we grow in our relationship with God and receive God's grace and strength.

Give ear to my words, O LORD;
understand my sighing.
Attend to the sound of my cry,
my king and my God!
For to you I will pray, LORD.

Psalm 5:2–3

Test Your Catholic Knowledge

Fill in the circle that best answers the question.

What is the most important prayer of the Church?

○ the Hail Mary

○ the Lord's Prayer

○ the Liturgy of the Hours

○ the lifting up of the mind and heart to God

A Catholic to Know

Saint John Vianney grew up during the French Revolution, when attending Mass was illegal. His family traveled long distances to pray in secret. Although John wanted to be a priest, his struggles as a student made him an unlikely candidate. John's sincerity of heart triumphed, however. He was ordained and named pastor in the tiny French village of Ars. He was known for his devotion to prayer and his ability to "read people's souls" during confession, bringing them closer to God. People traveled from all over France and other countries to pray with him, celebrate the sacraments, listen to his homilies, and confess their sins.

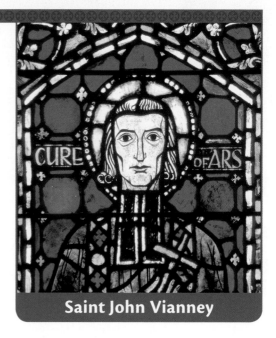

Saint John Vianney

Witness and Share

These sentences describe what Catholics believe. Listen carefully as they are read. Ask yourself, "How strong are my Catholic beliefs?"

My Way to Faith

- I talk to God using my own words.

- I attend Sunday Mass regularly and participate fully.

- I believe that prayer brings me closer to God and other believers.

- I pray for the needs of others.

- I thank God for the beautiful things in the natural world.

- I use the Bible to help me pray.

- I express my openness to God by listening to his Word.

Share Your Faith

Think about what you want to say to God today. What are you thankful for? Where do you need God's guidance in your life? Who is in need of prayer? Write your prayer using your own words on the lines below. Invite a family member or a friend to pray your prayer with you.

_____

_____

_____

_____

A People of Service

Have you ever thought about what it would take to build a structure or be a construction worker? In a way, we are all construction workers for God, since we are called to help build Christ's Church.

Describe a time when you acted in one or more of the following ways.

- Gave away something you really wanted because you saw that someone else needed it

  _____

- Volunteered for a job no one else wanted

  _____

- Freely chose to finish a project when you really wanted to do something else

  _____

- Chose to act like a Christian when those around you were doing the opposite

  _____

- Paid attention at Mass because you believed that Jesus was present

  _____

- Helped break up a fight that others were cheering on

  _____

- Went out of your way to show concern for someone in need

  _____

As a Catholic, whenever you do any of the above, you are a type of construction worker: you are building Christ's Church by serving God's people and by practicing virtue.

Building of Stone

After two hours in the hot sun, François gladly follows his father and other workers into the shade of the building. As he leans against the cold stone wall, François thinks back to the early days.

He still remembers the day: June 1, 1194. He was eight when the call came to the village of Chartres to build a cathedral. Everyone was enthusiastic, and each day François would run out to see how far the structure had progressed. Gradually the outer walls rose above the wheat fields—a grand sign of God's ever-present love.

François longed to join the builders. His father was teaching him to carve statues from stone. He hoped he and his father would be allowed to work on the cathedral. After years of waiting, the day came! He and his father were among the stonecutters chosen to work on the statues. At last, along with the glass cutters, carpenters, and stonemasons, he could share *his* special gifts and training. He had never been so excited.

"Back to work," his father says, returning him to the present. On the way back to the tools, François stops to watch as a cart piled high with stone and wood is pushed by some of the wealthiest women and men in town. Already the cathedral is becoming a sign of the faith and generosity of the people, from those who are very rich to those who are very poor. Often François hears the townspeople talking about the pilgrims who will one day visit the cathedral and be inspired to live more fully for God.

Happily, François picks up his chisel and says to himself, "It is great to be a builder, to be a part of such an important project."

LIVING STONES

[Y]ou are fellow citizens with the holy ones and members of the household of God, built upon the foundation of the apostles and prophets, with Christ Jesus himself as the capstone. Through him the whole structure is held together and grows into a temple sacred in the Lord; in him you also are being built together into a dwelling place of God in the Spirit.

Ephesians 2:19–22

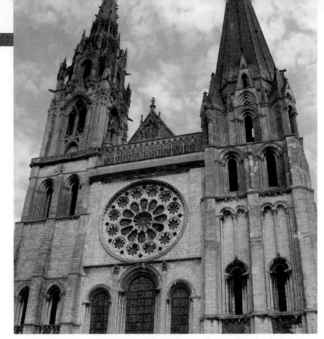

Chartres Cathedral, France.

Through your Baptism, you became a part of the Catholic Church. Every baptized person is called to share in the mission of Christ and his Church: to love and serve God's people, to spread the Kingdom of God, and to build up the Body of Christ, his Church. Unlike the cathedral at Chartres, this Church is not made of stone and glass. It is composed of people chosen by the Father, gathered together in Christ through the Spirit, and called to live lives of holiness.

Building a Cathedral

We can learn many things from François' experience of building a cathedral.

1. What common goal unites the villagers?

   _____

2. What does the cathedral represent?

   _____

   _____

3. How do the villagers work as a group?

   _____

   _____

   _____

4. How do the villagers work individually?

   _____

   _____

Be a Builder

François wanted to be chosen for the cathedral building project. You have been chosen as a member of the Church to help build up the Church. You can do this by sharing in the mission Christ has given to all his disciples: to spread the Kingdom of God through witness, worship, and service.

God asks you to serve every person in your life. When you serve, you **witness** to your family, your friends, your school, your neighborhood, your parish, and the whole world.

BUILDING IN LOVE

There are different kinds of spiritual gifts but the same Spirit; there are different forms of service but the same Lord; there are different workings but the same God who produces all of them in everyone.

1 Corinthians 12:4–6

As you grow in your life of service, you will discover how much you need the Holy Spirit and the special gifts that the Spirit has given to you. Jesus once said, "Without me you can do nothing." (John 15:5) He has united you with himself at Baptism and strengthened you with supernatural gifts. Through the sacraments, he continues to bless, nourish, forgive, strengthen, and heal you.

No one person has every gift or talent. Nor can any one person work for the kingdom single-handedly. The only way that the Church and each member can be faithful to the mission of Christ is for each member to share his or her special gifts. When one member is not willing to share, the whole Church suffers. On the other hand, when all share their gifts in various forms of service, every person benefits. The Kingdom of God becomes more visible.

Recognizing Your Gifts

Unique! Special! Amazing! These words describe you and the special blend of gifts and talents that God has given only to you, for you

to share. Only you can decide to share these gifts with others.

In the story, François had to wait many years to be chosen as a builder. While he waited, he learned stonecutting. He discovered his own strengths and weaknesses. Finding that he could cut stone into magnificent statues and ornate designs, he decided to use his talents for others. How can you prepare for your special way of serving? First, you can recognize the natural and supernatural gifts you have received, not earned. These gifts are designed to help you serve. Second, you can remember that you are called, above all else, to follow Jesus and to participate in his mission of service to others.

Answer these questions in your reflection notebook.

1. What gifts or talents do people recognize in me?

2. For what do I receive the most compliments?

3. How do I spend my free time?

4. What activities do I enjoy?

In Matthew 10:8, Jesus says, "Without cost you have received; without cost you are to give." Think of one practical way that you can use your gifts for God, for others, and for yourself. Among the many **vocations** available to you, consider whether you are being called to serve the Church as a priest, deacon, brother, or sister.

Two Job Descriptions

A Christian's responsibility is to build up Christ's Church and the world. The Gospel of Matthew contains two job descriptions for a follower of Christ: the **Beatitudes** (Matthew 5:3–10) and the **Corporal Works of Mercy** (Matthew 25:31–46). The Beatitudes teach us that we are all called to work for the kingdom, the only true way to have our desire for happiness fulfilled.

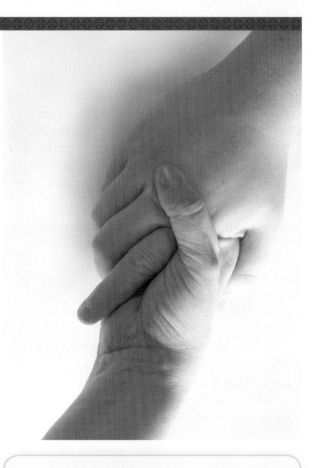

Read the Beatitudes, Matthew 5:3–10. Then, with your Bible closed, try to complete the following statements.

"Blessed are the poor in _____ , for theirs is the kingdom of heaven."

"Blessed are they who _____ , for they will be comforted."

"Blessed are the _____ , for they will inherit the land."

"Blessed are they who hunger and thirst for _____ , for they will be satisfied."

"Blessed are the _____ , for they will be shown mercy."

"Blessed are the _____ of heart, for they will see God."

"Blessed are the _____ , for they will be called children of God."

"Blessed are they who are _____ for the sake of righteousness, for theirs is the kingdom of heaven."

Describe a time when you put one of the Beatitudes into practice.

_____

_____

A Moment with Jesus

One of the ways that disciples of Jesus build up the Church is through the Corporal Works of Mercy. These works are described by Jesus in Matthew 25:31–46. Take a moment to slowly and prayerfully read this passage silently to yourself. Ask Jesus to open your eyes so that you may recognize his presence in those who are hungry, thirsty, lonely, without basic necessities, sick, or in prison. Ask Jesus for the grace to treat them as you would like to be treated.

You Make a Difference

Christ calls you to share in his mission to bring all people to the Father. You can do so by being united with him and by depending on his power. The Church needs you and the gifts of all its members. Others, especially those who are poor and vulnerable, need you to bring them the hope, peace, and justice that Jesus offers. Who knows the number of people you have already influenced? How many more wait for you to brighten their lives?

Remember

To what mission is every Christian called?

Every Christian is called to share in the mission of Christ and his Church: to love and serve God's people, to spread the Kingdom of God, and to build up the Body of Christ.

The Gospel of Matthew contains two "job descriptions" for a Christian. What are they?

The two "job descriptions" are the Beatitudes and the Corporal Works of Mercy.

How does Jesus view our actions toward others?

Jesus said, "[W]hatever you did for one of these least brothers of mine, you did for me." (Matthew 25:40)

Words to Know

Beatitudes
Corporal Works of Mercy
vocation
witness

Respond

Read and reflect on My Call to Service. Choose a part of the prayer and write it in your reflection notebook. Then write an explanation of what the prayer means to you.

My Call to Service

God has created me to do him some definite service;

He has committed some work to me which he has not committed to another.

I have my mission . . . I have a part in a great work;

I am a link in a chain, a bond of connection between persons.

He has not created me for naught.

I shall do good, I shall do His work;

I shall be an angel of peace, a preacher of truth in my own place, while not intending it,

if I do but keep His commandments and serve Him in my calling.

John Henry Cardinal Newman

Reach Out

1. **Read the following Scripture passages. Then write a paragraph on the attitudes needed for Christian service.**

   Galatians 6:1–10

   Philippians 2:3–4

   Colossians 3:16–17

   1 Thessalonians 5:12–18

2. **List 10 services performed by professional people. Then list 10 services Christians offer to others. Explain the differences between Christian service and other kinds of service.**

3. **Write a description of how members of your family have lived the Beatitudes. Illustrate your examples.**

4. **As a class, make an awards chart for people who show willing service as Jesus did. List the name of each person, the job or area of service, and the reason for the award.**

5. **Copy My Call to Service onto a sheet of paper and decorate the edges. Put it in a place where you will see it every day.**

Service with a Smile Draw a ✓ on the blank before each sentence that describes Christian service.

☐ **1.** Only certain members of the Church are called to serve the others.

☐ **2.** By serving others, we serve Jesus.

☐ **3.** We have supernatural gifts that help us serve.

☐ **4.** When we serve, we witness to our faith.

☐ **5.** Jesus expects his followers to enjoy life, not to serve.

☐ **6.** Everyone has the same gifts for service.

☐ **7.** When we fail to serve, the whole Church suffers.

☐ **8.** Service might call for sacrifice and risks on our part.

Beatitude Scramble Unscramble the letters in key words of the Beatitudes.

Blessed are the

1. _____
    NECLA FO TREHA

2. _____
    FELMUICR

3. _____
    OROP NI RTIPIS

4. _____
    EKEM

5. _____
    KAREESPCMEA

Blessed are they who

6. are _____ for righteousness
    TPRCDEEUSE

7. _____
    UNROM

8. hunger and thirst for _____
    SSSUHIOEETRGN

Mercy Today Match each Corporal Work of Mercy from page 291 with an example of how you can carry it out today.

_____ **1.** Feed the hungry.

_____ **2.** Give alms to the poor.

_____ **3.** Clothe the naked.

_____ **4.** Visit the sick.

_____ **5.** Shelter the homeless.

_____ **6.** Visit the imprisoned.

_____ **7.** Bury the dead.

a. Donate clothes you have outgrown to the St. Vincent de Paul Society.

b. See a friend who is at home with a broken leg.

c. Give money to Catholic Relief Services or some other agency that combats global poverty.

d. Attend the funeral of a classmate's relative.

e. Volunteer to support a shelter for homeless women and children.

f. Help a prison ministry prepare Christmas cards.

g. Contribute to a food drive at your school.

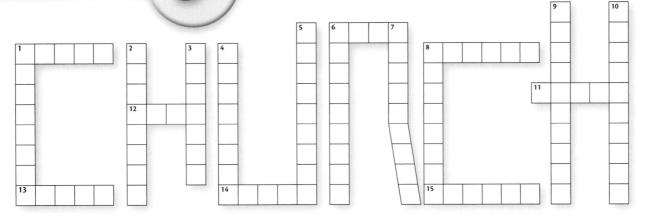

Belonging to the Church   Fill in the Church puzzle.

Across

1. The bishops look to the pope as their leader just as the apostles looked to Saint ____ .

6. The ____ and the bishops are infallible in solemn, official declarations on matters of faith and morals.

8. When a priest celebrates the sacraments, he exercises his role as ____ .

11. The Church is a mystery of ____ .

12. The Church is ____ because she was founded by Christ and is guided by the Holy Spirit.

13. Christ has conquered ____ .

14. A member of the Church who has loved like Jesus and who has died is a ____ .

15. The Holy ____ leads the Church to be faithful to the teachings of Christ.

Down

1. In purgatory we are ____ from sin's effects.

2. Since the Church is for all and preaches the Gospel to all, the Church is ____ .

3. Members of the Communion of Saints help one another by their ____ .

4. Bishops continue the ministry of the ____ .

5. The Old ____ tells about God's relationship with the Jewish people.

6. The Spirit formed the Church as a community on ____ .

7. We show that we rely on Jesus when we celebrate the ____ .

8. The pope and bishops are the official teachers in the Church; they have the role of ____ .

9. We grow in holiness when we celebrate the ____ .

10. Living our baptismal commitment, we are believing, serving, and ____ Church members.

Catholic Promises   Living up to your baptismal promises is important. Here are ways to live as a Church member. Mark each sentence, using the correct letter or letters: *W* = worship; *B* = believe; *S* = serve.

_____ 1. Pray for deceased members of your family.

_____ 2. Read about the lives of saints to learn more about living your faith.

_____ 3. Help a classmate who missed several weeks of school because of illness.

_____ 4. Take time to be friendly to everyone in your class.

_____ 5. Volunteer to participate in the offertory procession.

_____ 6. Refuse to shoplift because it is against God's law.

_____ 7. Participate in Sunday Mass.

_____ 8. Speak up in front of your friends for what is right.

_____ 9. Volunteer to do a job no one else will do.

_____ 10. Read Scripture on your own.

_____ 11. Ask or answer questions in religion class to know more about your faith.

_____ 12. Clean the garage when no one else has time to do it.

Called to Be Church

Opening Song

Leader: We begin our prayer:
In the name of the Father
and of the Son
and of the Holy Spirit.
Amen.

The Church was made known to the world on Pentecost. The Spirit enlightened the disciples about the life and teachings of Jesus. Even today the Spirit is with the Church, giving us new insights into truth. We are still growing. We are still getting to know ourselves as a Church. Let us pray today that the Holy Spirit will guide us and help us to grow as a Church.

Reader 1: Then they prayed, "You, Lord, who know the hearts of all, show which one of these two you have chosen to take the place in this apostolic ministry from which Judas turned away to go to his own place." Then they gave lots to them, and the lot fell upon Matthias, and he was counted with the eleven apostles.
Acts of the Apostles 1:24–26

Leader: We pray for the leaders of the Church, who serve the baptized. May the Holy Spirit inspire them to teach God's word, to call people to holiness through the sacraments, and to govern the Church with wisdom.

Holy Mother of the Church,

All: Pray for us.

Reader 2: "The community of believers was of one heart and mind, and no one claimed that any of his possessions was his own, but they had everything in common."
Acts of the Apostles 4:32

Leader: As a Church, we are a group of people who share our lives. We are bound together by our belief in Jesus and our desire to do God's will. May the Holy Spirit help us support one another and depend on one another. May we be united, especially in the Eucharist. Nourished by the Body of Christ, may we become the Body of Christ, the People of God, a mystical communion.

Holy Mother of the Church,

All: Pray for us.

Reader 3: Every day they devoted themselves to meeting together in the temple area and to breaking bread in their homes. They ate their meals with exultation and sincerity of heart, praising God and enjoying favor with all the people.
Acts of the Apostles 2:46–47

Leader: Jesus is a visible sign of God: God made flesh. We continue to meet Jesus through the Church in the Eucharist and in the members. As members of the Church, we are called to be a living sacrament. May we continue to follow Jesus' way and better represent the Kingdom of God.

Holy Mother of the Church,

All: Pray for us.

Reader 4: [A]ll day long, both at the temple and in their homes, they did not stop teaching and proclaiming the Messiah, Jesus.

Acts of the Apostles 5:42

Leader: A herald is a messenger sent to announce something. Sent by Christ, the Church continues to announce the Good News of Christ's teaching. May we enthusiastically take the Gospel to others. May we go to the ends of the earth to proclaim that God loves us, saves us, and calls us to join the community of believers.

Holy Mother of the Church,

All: Pray for us.

Reader 5: [A]nd one of them named Agabus stood up and predicted by the Spirit that there would be a severe famine all over the world . . . [T]he disciples determined that, according to ability, each should send relief to the brothers who lived in Judea.

Acts of the Apostles 11:28–29

Leader: Over and over, Jesus told his followers that they must serve one another with love. May we serve others by caring for their needs. May we serve others as Jesus did— by healing, comforting, feeding, welcoming, and forgiving.

Holy Mother of the Church,

All: Pray for us.

Reader 6: So the Twelve called together the community of the disciples and said, "It is not right for us to neglect the word of God to serve at table. Brothers, select from among you seven reputable men, filled with the spirit and wisdom, whom we shall appoint to this task."

Acts of the Apostles 6:2–3

Leader: We are called to be disciples of Jesus, following him in all situations. As a Church, we are a community of disciples. Jesus is our one true leader, and we are united in our following of him. May we look and listen for all the ways he is calling us to be his disciples.

Holy Mother of the Church,

All: Pray for us.

Leader: As baptized members of Jesus' Church, we are being called to share in Jesus' mission. Jesus does not expect each of us to personally go to the ends of the earth to proclaim the Gospel. He is, however, calling us to do so in our own communities— at home, at school, and in our neighborhoods.

All: Thank you, Jesus, for calling us to share in your mission. We ask for the grace we need to share your Good News with others through our words and actions. Help us be good members of your Church. Amen.

Closing Song

Images and Insights Match each image with the insight it gives us into the mystery of the Church.

_____ 1. vine and branches

_____ 2. temple

_____ 3. sheepfold

_____ 4. Body of Christ

_____ 5. Mary, Mother of the Church

_____ 6. leaven

_____ 7. bride of Christ

a. Jesus loves us very much.

b. All those who have faith in Christ and his Church are under his care.

c. The power of Christ spreads slowly through Christians who do God's will and evangelize.

d. We can bear the fruit of love for God and others only through our union with Christ.

e. To be a follower of Christ demands openness to all God wants us to do.

f. God dwells in us.

g. We are united with one another.

Believe It or Not? Write *T* or *F* for each statement. Change the false statements to make them true.

_____ 1. God has revealed himself to us as Father, Son, and Holy Spirit through his great deeds and words.

_____ 2. During the Council of Trent, Mary was given the title *Mother of the Church.*

_____ 3. Some of the people who believe in God are related to the Church.

_____ 4. The 27 books of the New Testament reveal to us the message of Jesus.

_____ 5. The three degrees of ordained ministry are bishops, priests, and deacons.

_____ 6. The *Code of Canon Law* contains rules that guide Church life.

_____ 7. Prayer is not particularly important to the life of the Church.

_____ 8. The liturgy is the public worship of the Church.

_____ 9. It is a Christian's responsibility to serve mainly his or her own needs.

_____ 10. One of the Beatitudes states, "Blessed are they who hunger and thirst for glory, for they will be satisfied."

Essential Information Imagine that one of your classmates was ill and unable to study Unit 1. Write five sentences highlighting what you believe are the most important ideas for your classmate to understand. Provide one sentence per chapter.

1. _____

_____

2. _____

_____

3. _____

_____

4. _____

_____

5. _____

_____

Self-Evaluation As you complete this unit, ask yourself three questions:

1. What has this unit taught me about how the Holy Spirit helps me to be a faithful member of the Church?

2. How have I grown as a friend and follower of Jesus?

3. What practical steps can I take to show others that I love my faith and am proud to be a member of the Church?

Gather and Go Forth

CHAPTER 5

Know and Proclaim

We are the hands and feet of Christ in the world. We use our gifts to share the love of Christ through service to others.

We Know Our Faith	We Proclaim Our Faith
Every baptized person is called to share in the mission of Christ and his Church.	As Catholics, we bless ourselves with holy water to remind ourselves of our baptismal call to share in the mission of the Church.
The Holy Spirit gives people natural and spiritual gifts to help them follow Jesus and share in his mission of service.	Catholics are inspired by the Holy Spirit to recognize and share their gifts at home, in their neighborhoods, and at their parish by donating their time, talent, and treasure.
The Beatitudes teach Christians that they are all called to work for the kingdom.	As Catholics, we act as peacemakers in our daily lives. We often pray the Peace Prayer of Saint Francis, "Lord, make me an instrument of your peace . . ."

The Holy Spirit gives gifts to all of us so that we may serve the People of God in Jesus' name.

There are different kinds of spiritual gifts, but the same Spirit; there are different forms of service but the same Lord; there are different workings but the same God who produces all of them in everyone.

1 Corinthians 12:4–6

Test Your Catholic Knowledge

Fill in the circle that best completes the sentence.

We participate in the Church's mission of evangelization by:

◯ serving others.

◯ choosing a vocation.

◯ profiting from our gifts.

◯ helping only other Catholics.

A Catholic to Know

Saint Lawrence lived at a time when the Roman emperor ordered all citizens to worship the gods of Rome. Those who refused were tortured and executed. As a deacon of the Christian church, Lawrence handled the church's money. When ordered to deliver the treasures of the Church, Lawrence gathered many people who were blind, sick, and poor to present as the church's true treasures. Government officials, believing that Lawrence was making fun of them, sentenced him to death by fire. Lawrence is said to have laughed and joked with his executioners even as he burned. We remember Saint Lawrence as a witness for Christ on August 10.

Saint Lawrence

Witness and Share

These sentences describe what Catholics believe. Listen carefully as they are read. Ask yourself, "How strong are my Catholic beliefs?"

My Way to Faith

- I follow Jesus even when other people don't.

- I affirm people for their gifts and talents.

- I show gratitude to the people who help me develop my gifts and talents.

- I strive to be generous with my time, talent, and treasure.

- I pray to Jesus that he will open my eyes to see the needs of others.

Share Your Faith

Think of ways to use your gifts to serve the People of God this week at home or in the community. What are some of your gifts? How can those gifts be used to serve others? Write your ideas on the lines. Invite your family to join you in serving or praying with you in support of your service.

_____

_____

_____

_____

The Marks of the Church

I believe in one, holy, catholic and apostolic Church.

Nicene Creed

Family Feature

One, Holy, Catholic, and Apostolic Church

Our beliefs and way of living are rooted in the beliefs and actions of the first apostles. This connects our lives today to the time of Jesus. Being apostolic means that the mission of the Church today is to continue the work entrusted to the apostles—to bring Christ's love and healing presence to the world.

Serving the world's needs can be overwhelming. The good news is that when we join with Catholics around the world, we are part of an organization capable of great things. With your family, try to become more aware of the Church's apostolic work and how you can contribute.

> "Our times call for a new readiness to assist our neighbors in need."
>
> (*Deus Caritas Est*), Pope Emeritus Benedict XVI

The Apostolic Work of Catholic Relief Services

Catholic Relief Services feeds families, shelters refugees, rebuilds shattered lives, protects health, develops sustainable communities, and restores hope in 99 countries around the world. Take time with your family to learn more about the work of CRS and how you can be part of it. The inspiring stories on their Web site showcase modern-day disciples reaching out with compassion and dignity to those who are the poorest of the poor.

The Apostolic Work of Catholic Charities

Catholic Charities is one of our nation's largest social-service networks. Catholic Charities' agencies and institutions provide vital social services to people in need, regardless of their religious, social, or economic backgrounds. Investigate ways your family can become involved in the apostolic work of Catholic Charities in your community.

Apostolic Relationships

The apostles modeled their ministry on the way Jesus lived his life. Jesus spent time with the people he served. He walked with those who were poor, ate with those who were hungry, comforted those who were sick, and listened to those who were lonely. Look for ways to build relationships with people you serve. Take time to learn their names and listen to their stories. Be open to ways you can receive as well as give.

Apostolic Action

Make a decision with your family to contribute to an outreach ministry of the Church that serves people in need and promotes justice and peace (for example, Catholic Charities or Pax Christi USA). Contribute money to support the organization's efforts. Pray for the organization and for those being served.

Apostolic Homework

Look to the Corporal Works of Mercy for ways your family can carry on the work of the apostles close to home: feed those who are hungry, clothe those who are naked, shelter those who are homeless, and visit those who are sick or imprisoned.

Visit **www.christourlife.com** for more family resources.

One in the Spirit

Think of times when you had experiences such as these:

- You meet someone your age and discover that like you, he or she is very interested in music. You instantly become friends.
- You are in another state or country and find someone from your hometown. Excitedly you plan to do something together.
- You walk into an auditorium filled with people. You spot someone you recognize and go over to sit with him or her.

Having things in common creates unity, a sense of oneness among people. Unity is one of the four visible signs, or **Marks of the Church,** that make the Church what it is. Just as you can tell a brand of clothing by its characteristics, you can identify the Church by its marks. Besides being **one,** the Church is **holy, catholic,** and **apostolic.** In this chapter and the next three, you will learn about each of these marks.

All for One and One for All

Ana's mother watched her daughter walk across the living room and sink into a chair. Ana looked tired and unhappy.

"How was the car wash?" Ana's mother asked.

"It went well. But that's not the problem. Theresa and I were the only ones who showed up to work!"

"Where were all the others?" asked her mother gently.

"Denise said she had to stay home. Juanita couldn't get a ride. Clare had piano lessons. What upset me is that last Thursday when we talked about it, all of them acted as if they would be there."

Ana's mother walked over and put her arm around Ana's shoulder. "You and Theresa must be tired. You've been working since eight o'clock this morning."

"It's not that, Mom. What bothers me is that all of us are on the basketball team. We all want new uniforms, not the boring gym suits we have now. We all said we would come and work on the car wash to earn money for the team. Where's the spirit of the team? Where's their loyalty?"

How do you know that Ana's basketball team lacks unity?

_____

_____

How could the members of the team have built up unity?

_____

_____

_____

Unity—The Catholic Church Is One

When we say that the Catholic Church is one, we are describing the unity of the Church. A group might work together and eat together but still not have unity. Unity is possible only when people have the same convictions, values, visions, and goals. Time, distance, suffering, and even death cannot break this unity. It is real and solid.

Unity comes from God who, as Father, Son, and Holy Spirit, is one. Human beings, made in the divine image of God, are called to establish unity among themselves and to live in solidarity with one another. The unity of the Church serves as a sign of the unity intended by God for all people.

Unity has been a strong and visible sign of the Catholic Church since its beginning. "The community of believers was of one heart and mind." (Acts of the Apostles 4:32) They were one because Jesus sent the Spirit to unite them in his love. Our unity flows from and reflects the unity of the Trinity. The gift of unity that comes from the Spirit helps us live the way Jesus showed us.

The Catholic Church is one in faith, worship, governance, and charity. The Spirit leads us to ever greater unity in each of these ways.

One in Faith

We are one in what we believe. We believe that Jesus is Lord and that all he taught is true. A *creed* is a statement of the truths we believe. At Sunday Mass, we pray the Nicene Creed to profess our faith in God and in the Church. At the beginning of the Rosary, we pray the Apostles' Creed.

An Invitation to Faith

One way to build unity is to include others in your plans. What you would say in an e-mail to invite someone to attend Mass with you?

To: _____

Subject: _____

_____

_____

_____

_____

_____

One in Worship

All members of the Church are united in our celebration of the sacraments. We are especially united in the celebration of the Eucharist. When we gather for Mass, we are united with Jesus and with one another. We offer praise to our heavenly Father. With, through, and in Jesus, our head, we thank the Father and ask for what we need. As we share his Body, the one bread, and his precious Blood from the one cup, we symbolize and strengthen our oneness. Nourished by the Word and the Body and Blood of Christ, we are empowered to work for unity.

What parts of the Mass are signs of our unity?

_____

_____

A Moment with Jesus

Celebrating the Eucharist is one of the most powerful ways we are unified as Catholics. Take a moment to thank Jesus for the gift of the Eucharist. Ask him to deepen your desire to be one with him and with others.

One in Governance

We are joined together under the leadership of the pope and bishops, who are successors of the apostles. They teach us the truths of our faith through Church councils, papal encyclicals (letters from the pope to the whole Church), pastoral letters, and talks. We follow the teaching of the pope and the bishops who, inspired by the Spirit, govern the Church. The bishop of your diocese is a visible sign of the unity of the Catholic Church. We are one with the whole Church through our diocese and parish. As of 2013, two hundred and sixty-six popes have led the Church through the ages.

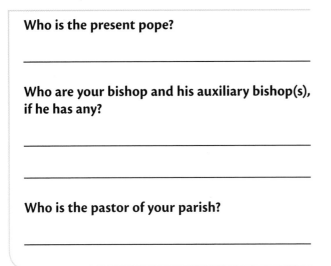

Who is the present pope?

_____

Who are your bishop and his auxiliary bishop(s), if he has any?

_____

_____

Who is the pastor of your parish?

_____

One in Charity

By practicing the virtues of faith, hope, and love, we come to live in a relationship with the Trinity. We are one with Christ and with one another in love. By putting our faith in God, we deepen our friendship with God and grow in love. By observing Christ's command to love one another, we create a community actively concerned about its members. By sharing in the Eucharist together, we are strengthened in Christ's love to serve with greater generosity.

The Letter to the Ephesians teaches that charity is the greatest gift in building unity. Read Ephesians 4:1–3 and then answer these questions.

How should we show love for one another?

_____

What binds the unity that the Spirit brings?

_____

How can your love help others in each of these examples?

- Acting friendly and cheerful at school
- Voluntarily doing more than your share of the work at home
- Asking a friend who often skips Mass to attend with you
- Asking forgiveness after an argument
- Expressing an interest in the things that concern your parents or guardians

Gifts for Everyone

Unity in the Church is not only the responsibility of the bishops and priests. It is the responsibility of all the members of the Church. We are to work together, using our individual gifts so all may be one. Within the unity of the Church, there is a diversity of gifts. Paul lists the charismatic gifts in 1 Corinthians 12:4–11. A charismatic gift is a special, spiritual gift used for the good of the entire Church.

> **Read 1 Corinthians 12:12–20 and then answer these questions.**
>
> **Who unites us all in the one body?**
>
> _____
>
> _____
>
> **How does Paul apply the many parts of the body to the Body of Christ?**
>
> _____
>
> _____
>
> **Why do you think there are so many different parts?**
>
> _____

Mending the Breaks

Chances are, not everyone in your neighborhood is Catholic. Christians are divided into hundreds of faith traditions.

The Spirit guides you and all members of the Church to work for unity with other Christian churches. This effort to unite all Christians is called **ecumenism.** *Ecumenical* refers to the whole world. Christ knew the importance of unity in his Church. At the Last Supper, he prayed "that they may all be one." (John 17:21) Christians would attract more people to Jesus if they were united. Because of misunderstandings in the history of the Church, however, the Body of Christ has divisions.

The Holy Spirit is calling you to use your gifts and be ecumenical too. You are needed! What can you do? You can pray every day that everyone may be united in Christ.

A good motto for ecumenical work is "Be respectful, but be faithful." Give all Christians the respect and dignity they deserve. We can often learn from other Christians. At the same time, you show how much you love the Catholic Church by faithfully following its teachings. Be proud of your Catholic faith.

> **If a friend of yours criticized the way other people worship, how would you respond?**
>
> _____
>
> _____

Summary

Remember

What are the Marks of the Church?

The Marks of the Church are one, holy, catholic, and apostolic.

What are the visible signs of unity in the Catholic Church?

The Catholic Church is one in faith, in worship, in governance, and in charity.

What was Jesus' prayer for the Church at the Last Supper?

Jesus prayed, "[T]hat they may all be one, as you, Father, are in me and I in you, that they also may be in us, that the world may believe that you sent me." (John 17:21)

Words to Know

apostolic
catholic
ecumenism
holy
Marks of the Church
one

Respond

Read Mark 10:35–45. Even the apostles did not get along perfectly. Jesus had to teach them to think more about others than themselves. How do you and your friends spend time serving others instead of thinking of yourselves? When have you helped others work together recently? Answer these questions in your reflection notebook.

Reach Out

1. Cliques and peer pressure can interfere with unity. Read 1 Corinthians 1:10–11. What does Saint Paul say about this? Discuss with some classmates the problems of cliques. How can your class avoid such problems?

2. The family is a miniature Church, so unity is important. Suggest something your family can do together this weekend, or try to cooperate in some other family project.

3. Read Precepts of the Church on page 292. Select one duty and make a poster based on it. Write down an example of how you have seen these duties lived out.

4. Search the Internet or a library for information about the Week of Prayer for Christian Unity, and prepare to celebrate it.

5. Think about a conflict you are experiencing with someone in your life. Strive to approach it with an attitude in which you and the other person both win and peace is maintained. Remember that the other person is sacred, a son or daughter of God who deserves respect.

6. Talk with your parents or guardians about relatives who are not Catholic. Learn what you can about their religious beliefs and practices. Learn more about your Catholic beliefs and practices so that you can join with them in respectful discussion.

Witness to Oneness The following statements express our unity. Mark the type of unity each one expresses most clearly. Use this code:

F = unity in faith   **W** = unity in worship   **G** = unity in governance   **C** = unity in charity

_____ **1.** At Sunday Mass, we all stand and recite the Nicene Creed.

_____ **2.** When the Nguyens' house burned down, people in the parish gave them food, clothing, and a place to stay.

_____ **3.** If you travel to a foreign country, a Catholic Mass will be basically the same there as it is in your parish.

_____ **4.** Sometimes a letter from the bishop is read at all Masses in a diocese.

_____ **5.** When Mr. Willis had a heart attack, parishioners sent him cards and flowers, visited him, and had a Mass offered for him.

_____ **6.** The Martínez children participate in religious education to learn Catholic beliefs.

_____ **7.** The U.S. bishops decided for the people of the United States which days were holy days of obligation.

_____ **8.** The parish supports the organization Birthright International because the people believe that abortion is seriously wrong.

_____ **9.** Many parishioners participate in the Easter Vigil and celebrate the Sacraments of Initiation with the catechumens.

_____ **10.** A Bible study group meets weekly to read and discuss the Bible.

The Power of One Match the descriptions with the correct terms.

a. mark

b. charismatic gift

c. one

d. Eucharist

e. encyclical

f. ecumenism

g. creed

h. Holy Spirit

_____ **1.** A statement of belief

_____ **2.** A spiritual gift given to certain members of the Church to be used for the good of all

_____ **3.** The mark of the Church that is shown in its faith, worship, governance, and charity

_____ **4.** A letter from the pope to the whole Church

_____ **5.** Efforts to unite all Christians

_____ **6.** A visible characteristic of the Church that makes it what it is

_____ **7.** The Person of the Trinity who brings unity to the Church

_____ **8.** The sacrament that expresses and strengthens our unity

On the Marks List the Marks of the Church.

1. _____   **3.** _____

2. _____   **4.** _____

Gather and Go Forth

Know and Proclaim

We seek unity by knowing and proclaiming our faith as one Church.

We Know Our Faith	We Proclaim Our Faith
The four visible characteristics of the Church—one, holy, catholic, and apostolic—are called the Marks of the Church.	Catholics express unity during Mass when they receive Holy Communion. By participating in the Eucharist, Catholics are united with Christ, and through him, with one another.
The Catholic Church is one in faith, worship, governance, and charity.	At Mass, during the Eucharistic prayer, Catholics pray for the bishop of their diocese and for the pope, people who are visible signs of the unity of the Catholic Church.
The Holy Spirit guides Catholics to work for unity with other Christian churches.	Catholics believe that Christ founded one universal Church. Every year Catholics celebrate the Week of Prayer for Christian Unity to restore unity among all Christians.

United to Christ in Baptism and brought together in one body through the Eucharist, Catholics are one in the Spirit and one in Christ the Lord. The unity of the Church serves as a sign of unity for all people.

"And I have given them the glory you gave me, so that they may be one, as we are one."

John 17:22

Test Your Catholic Knowledge

Fill in the circle that best answers the question.

Which of the following best describes the unity of the Catholic Church?

○ The Catholic Church has one pope.

○ The Catholic Church is based in Vatican City.

○ The Catholic Church is made up of many dioceses.

○ The Catholic Church is concerned only about Christians.

A Catholic to Know

In a letter to the people of Philippi, in northeastern Greece, Saint Paul wrote about a coworker named Clement. About 30 years later, Clement became Bishop of Rome and the third successor of Saint Peter. It is known that Clement wrote an epistle to the Christians in Corinth who were arguing among themselves. A group of believers refused to follow the legitimate authority there and split off from the main Church. Clement encouraged peace and harmony and urged the Christian community to remain united. Clement's letter is one of the earliest Christian documents we have, and it is valued as one of the earliest expressions of Christian unity. His feast day is celebrated on November 23.

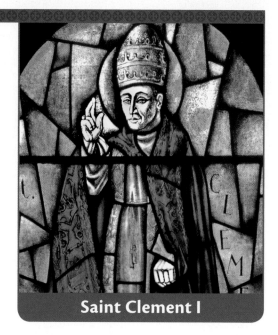

Saint Clement I

Witness and Share

These sentences describe what Catholics believe. Listen carefully as they are read. Ask yourself, "How strong are my Catholic beliefs?"

My Way to Faith

- I am united with Jesus and all Catholics when I receive Holy Communion.

- I reach out to others so that they do not feel left out.

- I serve others instead of thinking of myself.

- I show unity with the Church by paying attention to what the pope teaches.

- I am willing to make peace after an argument with a friend.

- I recognize non-Catholic Christians as fellow followers of Christ.

Share Your Faith

Consider ways in which you can promote greater unity in your parish community through prayer or dialogue. Write your ideas on the lines. Invite an adult relative or friend to discuss how he or she promotes unity in the family, at work, and in the world.

_____

_____

_____

_____

Made Holy in the Spirit

Mike bounded out of the school at the ring of the dismissal bell. Zach trailed glumly behind.

"Come on!" shouted Mike. "Let's bike over to the park."

Mike started to whistle as he unchained his bike from the post.

"Not today," Zach mumbled. "I got a D on the science test and my parents have to sign it."

"I got a D, too," Mike answered casually." But my parents will never know. I'll study harder for the next test." "How are you going to get away without having your test signed?"

"That's easy. I'll sign their names to the paper myself."

"That's forgery. You know, Mr. Thomas checks every test."

"He doesn't check that carefully. I've done it lots of times before. Try it. Other kids do it too. Why get your parents upset over nothing?"

Zach agonized over the thought all the way to the park. Forging his parents' names sounded simple. He could study harder for the next test. His parents would never find out. After all, others did it. He knew how upset his parents could get over one test. Zach argued with himself all evening. Finally he picked up the science test and headed for the living room. "Dad, could I show you something?"

Why do you think Zach made this decision?

_____

_____

The Source of Holiness

Zach chose to do what is right and pleasing to God. The power to choose what is right, to be holy, comes from the Holy Spirit. At Baptism, you were given a share in the life of the Trinity. You received God's grace not because you earned it, but as a gift that God freely chose to give you. The Spirit helps you to do good, to turn away from sin, and to be holy.

The Church is holy because

- it was founded and redeemed by Jesus.
- it is guided and given life by the Holy Spirit.
- its members are led to be holy like God.
- its members participate in Christ's holy mission of saving all people.

The Church is holy and yet always in need of purification, following the path of penance and renewal. All of us in the Church are sinners, already saved in Jesus Christ but still on the way to holiness. Because the Church is holy, it can make room for sinners.

Celebrating Life's Mysteries

The sacraments are one way you participate in the Church's holiness. Through the seven sacraments, you are bound closely to Christ, the head of the Church. You are strengthened in faith. You are empowered to share in the mission of the Church and to work to promote the well-being of all people, especially those who are poor and vulnerable.

The Seven Sacraments

The seven sacraments are often arranged into three categories: **Sacraments of Initiation**, **Sacraments of Healing**, and **Sacraments at the Service of Communion**. Baptism, the Eucharist, and Confirmation are Sacraments of Initiation. Reconciliation and Anointing of the Sick are Sacraments of Healing. Matrimony and Holy Orders are Sacraments at the Service of Communion.

Read the descriptions of experiences in people's lives and then write the name of the sacrament that matches them.

1. For three months, Beth has not spoken to Cecilia for what she did to her. Beth wants to grow in God's grace and live in holiness. Now she is going to ask forgiveness in the Sacrament of

   _____ .

2. Kneeling before the bishop on ordination day, Carlos thanks God for his vocation to serve God's people in word, sacrament, and service. He rejoices as he celebrates the Sacrament of

   _____ .

3. Mrs. García smiles at her husband, Jim, and turns toward the door of the hospital room as she hears a guest approaching. Jim's heart surgery is set for 8 A.M. tomorrow. Tonight Father Tan is coming to administer the Sacrament of the

   _____ .

4. Bridget's older brother is to be married in May. She notices that he and his fiancée are attending pre-Cana classes to prepare for the Sacrament of

   _____ .

5. Deng and Mei Chen have brought their baby to be initiated into the Church. They are glad the whole parish can rejoice with them, as during Mass their child will celebrate the Sacrament of

   _____ .

6. Juana writes in her reflection notebook as she prepares to be strengthened in the Spirit. She records how the acts of service and what she is learning about her faith will help her long after she celebrates the Sacrament of

   _____ .

7. Tom arrives at his parish church five or ten minutes early each Sunday. He did not eat or drink anything but water for the past hour or so. Now he wants to have a little time before Mass to prepare for the Sacrament of the

   _____ .

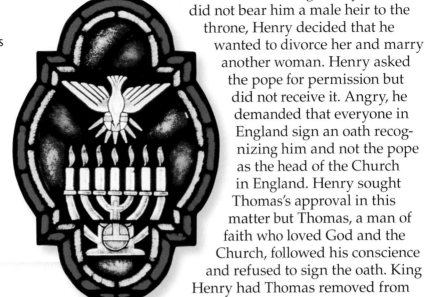

We've Got What It Takes

Discuss how the following lead us to holiness:

- Scripture
- the lives of the saints
- the teachings of Jesus
- acts of penance
- sacramentals
- prayer
- devotions such as the Rosary and the Way of the Cross
- service

The Gifts of the Spirit

Everyone is called to be holy. The Gifts of the Holy Spirit (based on Isaiah 11:1–3) help us grow in holiness and live lives of virtue. These are seven permanent, spiritual gifts as named in the *Catechism of the Catholic Church*. (The terms used in the Rite of Confirmation are in parentheses).

- **wisdom**
- **understanding**
- **counsel** (right judgment)
- **knowledge**
- **fortitude** (courage)
- **piety** (reverence)
- **fear of the Lord** (wonder and awe)

We receive these gifts at Baptism, and they are strengthened at Confirmation. Through these gifts, the Holy Spirit increases our ability to believe in Christ, to love and serve God and others, and to avoid sin. Saints and good Christians in every age have witnessed to Christ by living lives of outstanding faith and charity. They have shown us how the Gifts of the Spirit can lead us to become holy.

Holy Through Wisdom

Saint Thomas More was the chancellor of England under King Henry VIII. He was known as a wise and holy man, a famous scholar, writer, and lawyer. Thomas was a loving husband and father. So why was he executed by King Henry VIII?

When the wife of King Henry VIII did not bear him a male heir to the throne, Henry decided that he wanted to divorce her and marry another woman. Henry asked the pope for permission but did not receive it. Angry, he demanded that everyone in England sign an oath recognizing him and not the pope as the head of the Church in England. Henry sought Thomas's approval in this matter but Thomas, a man of faith who loved God and the Church, followed his conscience and refused to sign the oath. King Henry had Thomas removed from office, jailed, and condemned to death.

Once, when Thomas's daughter Margaret visited him in prison, she begged him to sign the oath in order to save his life. She asked him to say the words of the oath but to think otherwise in his heart. Thomas's answer to his daughter showed the kind of wisdom that guided his choice. He explained that when a man takes an oath, it is as if he is holding himself in his hands. He cupped his hands and told Margaret that it is like holding water in your hands. He said that if he opened his fingers (meaning, if he took the oath), he would lose himself just like he would lose the water. Thomas used the gift of wisdom to put God first and to make decisions based on how God sees things, not on how people see things.

Life is filled with choices. The gift of wisdom is the ability to put God first and to love the things of God. It enables you to see things from God's point of view and to recognize the sacredness of all people and the real value of things. Are you facing decisions? Pray to hear the voice of wisdom within you, helping you choose wisely.

Whom do you know who has the wisdom of Saint Thomas More?

_____

Holy Through Understanding

Barney Casey was the oldest of 16 children of an Irish-American family from Superior, Wisconsin. Barney had academic difficulties, and he took manual-labor jobs such as lumber worker, prison guard, and streetcar operator. Then, hearing the call to priesthood, Barney left for Detroit to enter the Capuchin order. There he took the name Solanus.

At the monastery, however, Solanus's academic struggles continued. He was ordained a priest, but his teachers recommended that his priestly duties be severely restricted. He was not allowed to hear confessions unless it was an emergency. Instead Father Solanus offered to help people in distress by listening to their problems. His superiors were shocked by the insights that Father Solanus had to offer to the people. It seemed that Father Solanus, though not academically gifted, had the gift of understanding. Word spread quickly and people came from all over to speak to Father Solanus. Even in his old age, he received hundreds of letters each day.

Father Solanus, who died in 1957 at age 86, had insights into the truths of faith. He grasped what they meant and lived by them. You have the gift of understanding too. By learning more about your Catholic faith, you can gain insights and understanding into the meaning of life. You can recognize that we are all brothers and sisters with the responsibility to care for one another. In 2017 the Church recognized Father Solanus's heroic virtue and sanctity and declared him a saint.

> **Whom do you know who has the gift of understanding? How does this person help you?**
>
> _____
>
> _____

Holy Through Counsel (Right Judgment)

Since the time of Saint Peter, the pope of the Catholic Church has been the bishop of Rome. However, from 1305 to 1378, seven popes chose to live in Avignon, France. Saint Catherine of Siena felt strongly that the pope should lead the Church from Rome, where Saint Peter had been. In a letter to Pope Gregory XI, she wrote with daring and force: "Be a man, Father! Arise! . . . Begin the reform of the Church by appointing worthy priests. Make peace in Italy, not by arms, but by pardon and mercy. Return to Rome." It was Saint Catherine who finally convinced the pope to make the move back to Rome.

It was highly unusual that a woman should tell the pope what to do. In the Middle Ages, holy women were expected to stay in convents and pray. Catherine did pray very much, but she was not afraid to take action in following God's will. Though she had little education, in 1970 she was named a **Doctor of the Church.**

Catherine had the gift of counsel, also known as right judgment. This gift helps us know what to do in life, to make good decisions, and to accept our responsibility to care for others. It makes us seek good advice from others and follow it. It enables us to advise others. You use the gift of counsel when you seek advice about living your Catholic faith. You use it when you participate in the Sacrament of Penance or when you ask others for help or offer help to others.

> **Whom might you ask about the following?**
>
> A high school to attend
>
> _____
>
> A solution to a family problem
>
> _____
>
> A way to help a friend in trouble
>
> _____
>
> Learning more about the Mass and why it is important
>
> _____

Holy Through Knowledge

Angela Merici was born in northern Italy around 1470. Her mother died while she was young, so she went to live with her uncle. Angela was concerned about the lives of girls, who were largely uneducated at the time. She was driven by a deep relationship with Jesus and the belief that we all are meant to know, love, and serve God. Angela knew that if families could help their young girls deepen their relationship with Jesus and their knowledge of God, their lives could be improved immensely.

In 1535 she and some of her friends founded a religious order called the Order of Ursulines. It was named after Saint Ursula, virgin and martyr.

The Ursulines lived as religious sisters, but they did not go off to live in monasteries or convents. Instead they continued to live in their homes and went to others' homes to teach them. The Ursulines helped young girls develop a knowledge of God as well as skills in reading and writing.

Saint Angela Merici had the gift of knowledge: she knew God and knew who she was. She used her experiences and faith to act according to Jesus' message.

> **How can we grow in knowledge of God and our faith?**
>
> _____
>
> _____
>
> _____
>
> _____

Holy Through Fortitude (Courage)

Blessed Miguel Pro, a lively, fun-loving young Jesuit priest, faced the firing squad without flinching. He had refused the blindfold and asked only for time to pray. In 1927 the Mexican government was against the Church. Father Pro secretly had done the work of Christ among the Mexicans. His quick thinking helped him in many narrow escapes. Finally he was arrested and falsely accused of an assassination attempt on a general. With no witnesses and no trial, he was condemned to death. A moment before Father Pro was about to be shot, he spread his arms out as if on a cross and shouted, "Long live Christ the king!" Then the bullets silenced him.

Followers of Christ have shown heroic fortitude, even giving up their lives for him. The risks you take to follow Christ may be small, but they are challenging. The gift of fortitude, also known as courage, gives you inner strength to do what is right in the face of difficulties.

> **Name one way you can endure a difficulty for Christ today.**
>
> _____

A Moment with Jesus

Living as a Catholic in today's society is not always easy. Although you most likely do not face the dangers that Father Miguel Pro encountered, you still face challenges in living as a follower of Jesus. Take a moment to ask Jesus for the courage you need to be his follower. Thank him for the times he has helped you do what was right in the face of difficulties.

Holy Through Piety (Reverence)

Saint John Chrysostom was born in 347 to a wealthy family of nobility. As he matured and began his studies in preparation for the priest-hood, he began to live a very simple life, giving up the wealth he was born into. He became an inspirational preacher and spoke powerfully about the importance of being generous to those in need. He spoke out strongly against the abuse of wealth and personal property.

In 398 John Chrysostom was made the bishop of Constantinople. He was not happy with the fact that this position entitled him to great privileges. He refused to host lavish events, something that angered the wealthy. John also made great efforts to reform the clergy, who were growing accustomed to being part of the wealthy class.

Saint John Chrysostom recognized the importance of showing reverence and worshiping God through the liturgy. He expressed his reverence for prayer, telling people that "It is simply impossible to lead, without the aid of prayer, a virtuous life." His piety was not limited to the time he spent in church. Rather, he believed that we cannot separate our reverence for God from our reverence for all of God's people. He expressed this in his writings: "Do you wish to honor the body of Christ? Do not ignore him when he is naked. Do not pay him homage in the temple clad in silk only then to neglect him outside where he suffers cold and nakedness."

Piety, also called reverence, is a gift of the Spirit that helps us love and worship God. Praying is one way to show reverence. Other ways are showing respect for the dignity of others, because they are sons and daughters of God, and being concerned for all that God created.

Holy Through Fear of the Lord (Wonder and Awe)

Saint Clare of Assisi sat down next to her Aunt. "Aunt Bona, guess who I saw today."

Bona looked at Clare suspiciously. "Who?"

"Francis, all dressed in a brown robe. I know that Francis has decided to live for God, but he dresses so poorly and owns nothing. Why?" asked Clare.

"Francis wants to trust God, his Father, completely," her aunt explained. "That is why he has given up his property and riches. He depends on God rather than on things."

"Papa says Francis is a madman," said Clare. "What do you think?"

Aunt Bona laughed. "I think Francis is just crazy about God. He adores God. He obeys God as a child joyfully obeys his father and is afraid to make God angry. The next time he preaches, Clare, I'll take you to hear him."

Saint Francis possessed the gift of fear of the Lord, also called wonder and awe. He marveled at God's greatness and love. This gift kept him from offending God.

The following actions show reverence. Check the ones you practice.

☐ Paying attention at Mass

☐ Praying regularly

☐ Staying for the entire Mass

☐ Refusing to use God's name in vain

☐ Making visits to the Blessed Sacrament

☐ Giving to those who are poor

Psalms praise the almighty God, who loves us. Write a line of praise from Psalm 146.

_____

_____

Remember

Why is the Church holy?

The Church is holy because she was founded by Christ, she is guided by the Holy Spirit, and she leads all people to holiness.

How do the sacraments help us grow in holiness?

In the sacraments, we are bound closely to Christ. We are empowered to share in the mission of the Church and to promote the well-being of all people.

What are the Gifts of the Holy Spirit?

The Gifts of the Holy Spirit are seven permanent, spiritual gifts received at Baptism and strengthened at Confirmation.

Words to Know

counsel	Sacraments at the
Doctor of the Church	Service of Communion
fear of the Lord	Sacraments of Healing
fortitude	Sacraments of Initiation
knowledge	understanding
piety	wisdom

Respond

Copy into your reflection notebook the Prayer to the Holy Spirit on the inside front cover of this book. Substitute *me* for *them* and *us*, and *I* for *they* or *we*. Then read the prayer again. The Holy Spirit really comes to you with these wonderful gifts. Draw on the strength of the Spirit and think about whom you could help. What could you do to help the person(s)? Write your thoughts in your reflection notebook. Then pray the following prayer for the person(s) you have noted.

Send your Holy Spirit upon them to be their helper and guide. Give them the spirit of wisdom and understanding, the spirit of counsel and fortitude, the spirit of knowledge and piety. Fill them with the spirit of fear of the Lord in your presence.

Reach Out

1. If you have not yet been confirmed, start to prepare for your Confirmation and for the strength you will receive from the Holy Spirit by doing one of the following:
   - Read and reflect on one of these Scripture passages: Matthew 16:24–28; Mark 1:9–11; Luke 4:16–22; John 14:15–17,23–26; Acts of the Apostles 2:1–6.
   - Talk to your parents or guardians about choosing a sponsor for the time when you will begin preparing for Confirmation. Look for someone who lives a good Catholic life and could help you in your faith.
   - Try harder to be a follower of Christ.
   - Pray more. For help on how to do this, see pages 281–288.

2. Read the following Scripture passages about the Spirit in the life of Jesus and his followers. For each one, think about how the Spirit can help you in a similar way and write it in your reflection notebook: Luke 1:26–38; Luke 4:1–2; Acts of the Apostles 4:13–31; Acts of the Apostles 9:1–9.

3. Ask your parents or guardians to help you think of a modern-day example for each Gift of the Holy Spirit. Think about the people you know, search the Internet or newspapers, and talk to others for ideas.

4. Think of a way you can take a stand for what is right and then act on it. You might ask your parents or guardians to help you write a letter, make a phone call, or help an organization that works for justice.

5. Participate as a family in the celebration of one of the sacraments in your parish other than the Eucharist. As members of the Church, pray for those people who are receiving the sacrament.

Wholly Holy Fill in the blanks.

The Church is holy because

it was f _____ by Jesus, it is guided by the S _____, its members

are made holy in the s _____, its members participate in Jesus'

m _____, and its m _____ strive for holiness.

Sanctifying Our Lives Unscramble the names of the sacraments.

Sacraments of Initiation

tabpsim _____   ihaucrest _____   oancftnoimri _____

Sacraments of Healing

accoirleinoitn _____   onantigni fo eth cisk _____

Sacraments at the Service of Communion

rmtiyonam _____   yhlo sdroer _____

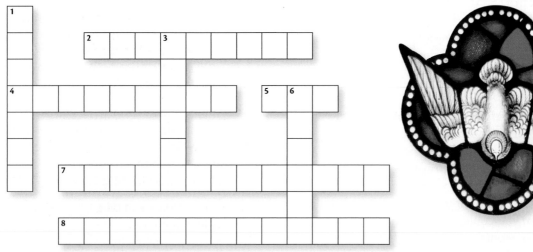

Gifts from the Spirit Fill in the crossword puzzle.

Across

2. The gift of knowing the truths of the universe and learning about them from experience

4. The gift that helps you love and worship God and show respect for others and for all God created

5. The gift of marveling at God's goodness and love that makes us avoid displeasing God

7. The gift of having insight into the truths of faith, grasping what they mean, and living by them

8. The gift of giving or seeking advice about the Christian life

Down

1. The gift of doing difficult things for Christ

3. Same as 5 Across

6. The gift of putting God first in your life and seeing things as God sees them

Gather and Go Forth

CHAPTER

7

Know and Proclaim

We seek holiness in the truths of our Catholic faith. We proclaim our beliefs to bring others to holiness.

We Know Our Faith	We Proclaim Our Faith
The Church is holy because it was founded by Jesus, it is guided by the Holy Spirit, and it leads all people to holiness.	Catholics perform acts of penance such as fasting, prayer, and almsgiving to foster conversion and to grow in holiness. Performing acts of penance helps us acquire freedom of heart.
Catholics participate in the Church's holiness through the seven sacraments. Through the sacraments, Catholics are bound closely to Christ.	The Sacrament of Reconciliation is one of the Sacraments of Healing. Through this sacrament, Catholics are reconciled with God and with the Church.
The seven Gifts of the Holy Spirit help Christians grow in holiness and live lives of virtue.	Catholics nourish their love of God and the Church by learning about their faith through parish missions and Catholic literature, radio programs, and online resources.

God calls us to holiness through the worship and sacraments of our Church. By living the life of the Church, Catholics become holy through the grace of the Holy Spirit.

The LORD said to Moses: Speak to the whole Israelite community and tell them: Be holy, for I, the LORD your God, am holy.

Leviticus 19:1–2

Test Your Catholic Knowledge

Fill in the circle that best answers the question.

Which Gift of the Holy Spirit gives you inner strength to do what is right in the face of difficulties?

○ piety

○ chastity

○ wisdom

○ fortitude

A Catholic to Know

Ambrose became a Christian and quickly rose to prominence in the Church. When the bishop of Milan, Italy, died unexpectedly in 374, an angry dispute erupted in the basilica over electing his successor. As the governor of Milan, Ambrose intervened and pleaded with the crowd for peace. Without warning, the people cheered for Ambrose as bishop. Ambrose begged them not to elect him, but he eventually accepted what appeared to be God's will. Within one week, Ambrose was baptized, confirmed, ordained a priest, and consecrated bishop. In his role as bishop of Milan, he is credited with providing capable and stable Church leadership at a critical time.

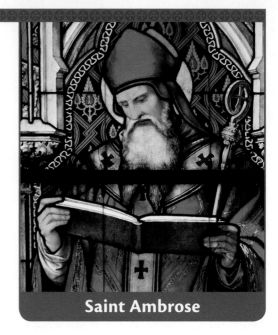

Saint Ambrose

Witness and Share

These sentences describe what Catholics believe. Listen carefully as they are read. Ask yourself, "How strong are my Catholic beliefs?"

My Way to Faith

- I follow the way to holiness.
- I acknowledge and atone for my sins.
- I use the Gifts of the Holy Spirit to grow in holiness.
- I seek out people who can give me good advice.
- I participate in my religious education lessons.
- I pay attention to the priest's homily during Mass.

Share Your Faith

Consider ways in which the Holy Spirit is at work in your home, class, or parish community. Write your ideas on the lines. Invite family members or friends to share ideas about how they experience the Holy Spirit at work in their lives.

_____

_____

_____

_____

A Church That Is Catholic

Jarius got a little nervous as he watched Miguel moving toward him on the crowded school bus. Today was Thursday, and Jarius had waited all week for someone to invite him to the party on Friday night. Only three other boys and two girls in the class had not been invited yet. How could Jarius face the class on Monday if he should be one of those who was left out? Maybe he should just turn to Miguel and ask if he could come to the party.

What will happen? Finish the story.

_____

_____

_____

Like Jarius, we might sometimes worry, "Will I be included? Will I be ignored?" Everyone wants to be included and accepted.

As Wide as the Universe

In God's plan, everyone is included! No one is left out. God the Father's love is universal. It is for everyone. Jesus, sent by his Father, showed that God loves all people and wants to save everyone from sin and death. In the parable of the great feast, we see the scope of God's love. Recall the story or read it in Luke 14:15–24.

The Great Feast: Take 1

Imagine you are the director of a television series that strives to teach viewers about the Kingdom of God. For the next episode, you are depicting a scene from the parable of the great feast. Keeping in mind your goal, answer the following questions:

TITLE
DIRECTOR
CAMERA

DATE   SCENE   TAKE

What is the title of your series?

_____

What will you emphasize about the parable of the great feast?

_____

_____

_____

To Jesus, it does not matter where people live, how much money they have, what they look like, or how successful they are. The Church recognizes the dignity of all people and strives to work for the common good. If people accept Jesus' invitation and follow him in faith, he will welcome them into the kingdom. They will be left out only if they choose to stay away. Jesus sent his apostles and their successors to share in his mission of inviting all people to salvation.

The Church Is Universal

Through the power of the Holy Spirit, the Church is Jesus present in the world. The Church carries to the whole world the Gospel and God's love for all people. We say that the Church is catholic, meaning that it is "universal, worldwide, total, for all." When we say that the Church is *catholic,* we mean that it

- strives to preach the good news of salvation to all people, effectively communicating to every **culture** and nation in the world.
- teaches the total message of Jesus Christ.
- offers all that is necessary for salvation.
- proclaims the Good News of Christ's teaching in every age until the end of the world.

The Church conveys all that it believes through its doctrine, life, and worship. From a small core of believers in Palestine, the Church has grown to include about one billion living members all over the world!

Blessed Mother Teresa.

To All Nations

The catholic, or universal, quality of the Church is visible in the lives of dedicated Catholics. Read the following summaries of what various missionaries have done. Underline the groups of people they reached out to.

- In 1873 a Belgian priest, Father Damien, began serving persons stricken with leprosy on the island of Molokai, Hawaii. He showed Christ's love by preaching the faith, building houses, and caring for those who were sick. Eventually he died of leprosy himself. He was canonized a saint in 2009.

- In 1891 Katharine Drexel founded the Blessed Sacrament Sisters to bring Catholic education to African Americans and Native Americans. She used $20 million of her money to establish almost 60 schools to serve these people. Katharine Drexel was canonized a saint in 2000.

- In 1902 Charles de Foucauld began his witness to the Gospel among the Tuareg of northern Africa. He prayed often and welcomed all who passed by his shabby hut. He said, "I want everyone here, Christian, Muslim, Jew, pagan, to look on me as a brother, a universal brother." Charles was named blessed in 2005.

- In 1948 Albanian-born Mother Teresa began the Missionaries of Charity in Calcutta, India. Until her death in 1997, she taught others how to see Jesus in the poorest of the poor. Her sisters minister to those who are dying, to abandoned babies, and to people who have AIDS. Mother Teresa was named blessed in 2003.

> ### A Moment with Jesus
>
> Take a moment to prayerfully read Matthew 28:18–20. Thank Jesus for inviting you to hear his message of Good News. Ask Jesus for the grace you need to participate in his mission of inviting all people to salvation.

Because the Church is catholic, those who are not Christian are related to us in various ways. Jewish people have already responded to God's revelation in the Old Covenant that God made with Abraham. That call cannot be taken away. Followers of Islam profess to hold the faith of Abraham as do Christians and Jews and with us adore the one, merciful God. The Church believes that all the goodness and truth found in religions around the world are a preparation for salvation, because God wishes all humanity to be saved. We approach all these religions with respect and dignity. When we strive to increase understanding between different religions, we call that **interreligious dialogue**.

In Your Parish

Because it is part of the universal church, your parish shares in the quality, or sign, of being catholic. When members gather for the Sunday eucharistic liturgy and then go forth to promote the well-being of all people, this sign of the Church becomes visible. The whole message of Christ is proclaimed to all people.

UNITY AND DIVERSITY

To the weak I became weak, to win over the weak. I have become all things to all, to save at least some. All this I do for the sake of the gospel, so that I too may have a share in it.

1 Corinthians 9:22–23

To be truly catholic, the Church has learned to take into consideration the unique differences between various nations and cultures around the world. In the face of such diversity, the Church has worked to guard the message of the Gospel and maintain unity.

In the early Church, the apostles learned to effectively communicate the Gospel to people in different parts of the Roman Empire. The Church is universal because of its mission to the whole world. When it puts down its roots in a variety of cultural and social settings, however, it takes on different expressions and appearances.

Greek Christians in the East and Roman Christians in the West used their own languages and customs and formed their own liturgical rites, or ways of worshiping. They also formed their own church laws and traditions for living the Christian life. People who celebrate their own liturgical rites and follow their own church laws and customs have always been considered distinct churches. This variety within the Church does not harm its unity but makes it more visible. The various Eastern Churches are encouraged to hold on to their traditions. The Eastern Churches traditionally celebrated Mass in their local languages, while the Western or Roman Church celebrated in Latin.

Unfortunately some of the cultural and political differences led to a split in 1054 between the Eastern and Western Churches. Those Eastern Churches are referred to as Orthodox. Today the Roman Catholic Church is committed to healing the rift that continues to exist with the Orthodox Churches.

Over time, some members of the Orthodox Churches have rejoined with the Roman Church. Today 21 Eastern Catholic Churches are in communion, or united, with Rome. There are about one million Catholics of the Eastern Church in the United States. The six major Eastern Catholic Churches are the Chaldean, Syrian, Maronite, Coptic, Armenian, and Byzantine. Even with all our diversity, we are held together in unity because of our faithfulness to the Tradition we have received from the apostles.

Visiting a Byzantine Church

If you attended a eucharistic liturgy in a Byzantine Church, you would notice that it is very different from the Roman Mass. Here are some of the differences:

- people bowing from the waist when entering the church.
- the Sign of the Cross made with the thumb and first two fingers together to represent the Trinity and the other two fingers outstretched to represent the two natures of Christ.
- religious images, called icons, in places of honor.
- an ornate icon screen between the altar and pews.
- prayers, music, vestments, and architecture that stress God's greatness and majesty.
- singing and praying in constant dialogue.
- the Eucharist under the forms of tiny bread cubes mixed with wine that people receive on a spoon.

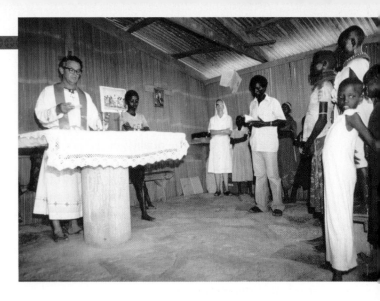

Enriching and Enriched

In all Catholic Churches, Eastern and Western, the essentials are the same: communion with the pope, the bishop of Rome; the fullness of the Gospel; the Mass, and sacraments. Unity is assured by fidelity to apostolic Tradition.

The Eastern Catholic Churches are a sign to the whole Church of our catholic nature. The Church respects all values and customs that reflect God's truth. The Church identifies what is good and meaningful in a culture and shows how it is compatible with the Catholic faith. At the same time, the Church also identifies the aspects of a culture that are contrary to the Gospel and seeks to transform them. Because of this process within the catholic Church, people of all cultures are united in Jesus and with one another.

Getting the Job Done Today

Jesus commissioned the Church to carry on his work. The Greek word for "good news" is *evangelion.* To proclaim the Good News of Jesus to others is called evangelization. When members of the Church teach, heal, serve, work for justice, and live as Christ did, they are evangelizing as he did. The purpose of evangelizing is to have all people become one in Christ. Evangelization is the essential mission of the Church.

In the 1990s Pope John Paul II (now Saint John Paul II) called for a "new evangelization." He explained that today there are many parts of the world where baptized Christians are losing their faith and are in need of evangelization. This type of evangelization is new because it is directed toward people who have heard the Good News but are indifferent to it. They have yet to experience a real conversion of heart. The new evangelization is a mission you can join without traveling to a distant country.

Missions: Near and Far

The Catholic Church continues to send generous priests, religious, and lay people to spread the Gospel in many countries. Others evangelize in cities or rural areas near their homes. All missionaries teach, heal, serve, work for justice, and love others as Jesus did.

Circle the word that you think best describes the kind of person needed for missionary work.

hopeful   hardworking   joyful

patient   courageous   trustworthy

How can the Eucharist be the greatest source of strength for a missionary?

_____

_____

_____

_____

The Holy Childhood Association

The Holy Childhood Association, founded in 1843, is an international organization of students in Catholic elementary schools and religious education programs dedicated to fostering awareness of the missionary nature of the Church. The Holy Childhood Association is unique in that the help it provides to less fortunate children comes almost entirely from those their own age. Money raised goes toward shelters, schools, hospitals, refugee camps, and centers for disabled people. It provides food, medicine, clean water, shelter, and education. Through efforts such as the Holy Childhood Association, you can become more conscious of the catholic nature of the Church and learn to show respect for the dignity of all people and to work for the common good.

Remember

What do we mean when we say the Church is catholic?

The Church is catholic because it teaches the whole message of Jesus to all people, effectively communicating to every culture and to every age.

What is evangelization?

Evangelization is the proclaiming of the Good News of Jesus to others. This means proclaiming it to those who have not yet heard it and to baptized Catholics who have yet to experience a conversion of heart.

Words to Know

culture
interreligious dialogue

Respond

As a member of the Church, your life can reflect its catholic quality. By your attitudes and actions, you can show the love and respect that God has for everyone.

Think of the people you meet who are different from you. In your reflection notebook, list people to whom you could give more love and respect. Write one way you could show that you care about and respect these people.

Then think about your call to spread the Good News. Each day for a week, write in your reflection notebook how you have spread the Good News to others.

Reach Out

1. Explain the idea that the Church will always have missionaries because it is catholic. Write your response and be ready to discuss it in class.

2. Write about someone you have seen

   ☐ trying to include others in a conversation

   ☐ being friendly to a visitor at school

   ☐ sitting with a variety of people at lunch or on the bus

   ☐ showing interest in younger students.

   Put a check (✓) next to the actions above that you will do in the future.

3. Go with your parents or guardians to the library to search for information about the Eastern Catholic Church.

4. Make a list of the Catholic television and radio programs and Catholic publications with which your family is familiar. Discuss with your family ways to support Catholic programming and the Catholic press.

5. Write to the diocesan or national office of evangelization. Request information about their programs.

6. Find out about other mission organizations and missionary communities. Work with your family to raise money to donate to one of them.

7. As a family, go to a Mass that is celebrated in a language other than your own. Talk about what it means to be a member of a Church that is catholic, or universal.

8. With your parents or guardians, search the Internet or a phone book for Eastern Catholic and Eastern Orthodox Churches in your area. If possible, make arrangements to visit one.

9. As a family, make a commitment to learn more about the Holy Childhood Association. Visit their Web site for more information.

All in All

Circle the people Jesus died to save.   **most people   all people   a select few**

Circle the centuries Jesus' message is for.   **only the first   only the 21st   all**

Circle the people the Church is for.   **all   only those who are poor   only those who are rich**

Circle the people included in God's kingdom: **only Protestants   only Chinese   all people**

Check (✓) the teachings of Jesus that the Church proclaims.

_____   Love your enemies and pray for those who persecute you.

_____   Pray only for your friends and family.

_____   Pray always.

_____   Jesus sacrificed so that we do not have to.

_____   Whoever wishes to come after me must deny himself, take up his cross, and follow me.

To Be Catholic   Check (✓) the correct endings to the statements.

1. To be catholic means to be

☐ Roman   ☐ saved   ☐ universal.

2. People who will not be in the kingdom will be outside it because

☐ God did not choose for them to be in it.   ☐ they chose not to belong.

3. The Church   ☐ makes everyone worship as they do in Rome.

☐ incorporates elements of various cultures into its worship when appropriate.

4. Evangelization is directed   ☐ only to the nonbaptized.   ☐ to all people.

5. In the Catholic Church, there is/are   ☐ is only the Roman Church.

☐ are Western Churches and Eastern Churches.   ☐ are only Eastern Churches.

A Worldwide Church   Fill in the following statements.

1. A religious image honored by Eastern Catholics is an _____.

2. Byzantine Catholics belong to the _____ Catholic Church.

3. Proclaiming the Good News of Jesus to others is _____.

4. People who evangelize to those who are not baptized in their own countries are called

_____.

Gather and Go Forth

Know and Proclaim

The work of Jesus is the work of the Church. We learn about our Catholic faith to do the work of Jesus in the world.

We Know Our Faith	We Proclaim Our Faith
The Church is universal, or catholic, because she preaches the Good News of Jesus to every culture and nation in the world.	Catholics are encouraged to learn about the various rites in the Catholic Church—Coptic, Byzantine, and Armenian—which accommodate different cultures and traditions.
God wants all humanity to be saved. The Church believes that all the goodness and truth found in other religions are a preparation for salvation.	Catholics come together with people of other faith traditions in events such as the National Catholic-Muslim Plenary. At these events, people come together to share stories, pray, and enjoy meals in an effort to build trust and dialogue.
The essential mission of the Church is to proclaim the Good News of Jesus Christ.	Lay Catholics participate in the Church's mission of evangelization through the example of their lives and good works.

Test Your Catholic Knowledge

Fill in the circle that best answers the question.

What is the essential mission of the Church?

○ interreligious dialogue

○ to commission catechists

○ worldwide recognition

○ evangelization

The Catholic Church is universal, calling people of every race, nation, time, and place to believe in the Gospel. The Church preserves, perfects, and raises up all that is good for the glory of God.

"Go, therefore, and make disciples of all nations, baptizing them in the name of the Father, and of the Son, and of the holy Spirit."

Matthew 28:19

A Catholic to Know

Francis Xavier was born into an aristocratic family in Spain in the 1500s. Along with Ignatius of Loyola, Francis was one of the six priests who founded the Society of Jesus. At that time, the Church needed missionaries in the East Indies. Ignatius assigned two of his men to go, but one of them became sick, and Francis was sent as a replacement. Francis worked in India and Japan, where he learned the language and culture of the people to share with them Jesus' message. Following his work in India and Japan, Francis set out for China, only to become seriously ill and die before reaching his destination. We celebrate his life of service on December 3.

Saint Francis Xavier

Witness and Share

These sentences describe what Catholics believe. Listen carefully as they are read. Ask yourself, "How strong are my Catholic beliefs?"

My Way to Faith

- I invite other people to know Jesus.

- I respect people who have different religious beliefs and cultural backgrounds.

- I help my parish act as a sign of the Church's universal nature by participating in events sponsored by the diocese.

- I am nourished by the Eucharist, which gives me the strength I need to be a disciple.

- I represent the mission of the Church by the way I show God's love for everybody.

Share Your Faith

All people are created in the image of God, regardless of culture, language, and faith traditions. How do you show respect for other people? How can you share the Gospel with them in a way that respects them? Invite someone of a different faith to discuss his or her understanding of God.

_____

_____

_____

_____

An Apostolic Church

As you get older, your responsibilities increase. Answer these questions with an *X*.

Are you responsible for	Yes	No
1. getting your homework done on time?	____	____
2. making sure you get sufficient rest and the right food?	____	____
3. paying the bills at home?	____	____
4. telling the truth?	____	____
5. giving back what you have borrowed?	____	____
6. getting a job to support yourself?	____	____
7. accepting advice from adults?	____	____
8. doing your fair share of work at home?	____	____
9. making decisions for your friends?	____	____
10. thinking about your future?	____	____

Christian Responsibility

At your Baptism, you became responsible for being a worshiping, believing, and serving member of the Church. To be a worshiping member means to participate in the sacraments, especially the Eucharist at Sunday Mass. To be a believing member means to put your faith in Jesus. Through the Spirit, you can live up to what he teaches. You can share your faith and give witness to it. Your friendship with Christ leads you to choose good and refuse evil. To be a serving member means to give loving service to all of God's people. It means you strive to be generous, respectful, and courageous and to promote the well-being of all people.

The Apostolic Church

When we say that the Church is apostolic, we mean that it is rooted in the teachings of the apostles and that it continues their mission. Church leadership goes back to Saint Peter and the other apostles. Scripture and Tradition show that Peter was the head of the apostles. In Matthew 16:18, Jesus told Peter "upon this rock I will build my church." Jesus entrusted the leadership of the Church to Peter, the first pope, and Peter's successors. Through them, Christ leads the Church. With their help and with the guidance of the Spirit, the Church is faithful in living the teaching of Jesus. The Church has a teaching authority called the *Magisterium.* Through the Church's teachings, life, and worship, the Church passes on a living faith to every generation.

The First Leaders

Jesus gave the apostles a share in his own mission. He sent them forth, with Peter as their leader, to proclaim the Kingdom of God. The word *apostle* actually comes from a word that means "sent."

Peter and the other apostles wanted the whole world to know about Jesus. Beginning on Pentecost, they set out to preach the Gospel, which Jesus had taught them. They followed his example. Their enthusiasm and courage inspired others to become Christians. Soon more leaders were needed. Through the Holy Spirit, others were called and sent forth to lead the Church. A Church leader is a servant and a shepherd who is willing to give his life for his flock, as Christ was willing.

Who Leads Us Today?

You belong to the same community Christ founded and built on the apostles. The pope and bishops continue the ministry of Peter and the apostles. They strive to effectively communicate the message of Jesus to today's world. The **pope,** the bishop of Rome, is the spiritual leader of the Church. He lives in Vatican City, an independent, 108-acre state in Rome. *Pope* comes from *papa,* the Greek word for "father." The pope is also called the Vicar of Christ. He represents Christ on earth and is the leader of all Catholics. Around the world, countless people of many faiths respect the pope as a spiritual leader.

The other **bishops** join the pope in leading Catholics. All the bishops together form the college of bishops. When the bishops work together with the pope to lead the Church,

we say that they are practicing **collegiality.** The special responsibilities of bishops are to teach, govern, and sanctify God's people within their own **diocese,** or territory. A bishop's church in his diocese is called a cathedral. *Cathedral* comes from the Latin word for "chair." The bishop's chair is a sign of leadership. Together with his priests and deacons, a bishop teaches the faith, celebrates the Mass, and guides the Church in his diocese.

The bishops of the United States form an organization called the United States Conference of Catholic Bishops. They meet twice a year to discuss issues and better lead the Catholic Church in their country.

Just as the Holy Spirit guided the apostles to teach the Gospel and continue the mission of Jesus, so the Spirit guides the pope and bishops today. Just as in the early Church, the apostles looked to Peter as the visible head of the Church, so the bishops look to the pope today.

Service in Three Roles

In the Acts of the Apostles 1:15–26, the apostles selected a successor to Judas. Peter said, "It is necessary that one of the men who accompanied us the whole time the Lord Jesus came and went among us . . . become with us a witness to his resurrection." (Acts of the Apostles 1:21–22) Peter knew that the Church needed leaders. Leaders are important in any group. Together the pope and bishops, inspired by the Spirit, guide us to be faithful to Christ and the Gospel. Popes speak Jesus' message to meet the needs of their times. All bishops, the successors of the apostles, receive the fullness of the Sacrament of Holy Orders. They are the source of unity in their own churches. They have the responsibility in the Church to share in Christ's ministry as priest, prophet, and king.

Sharing in Christ's ministry as priest, the pope and bishops celebrate the Eucharist and the other the sacraments. They direct the way the sacraments are celebrated. Their role is to lead the people to holiness through the sacraments.

Sharing in Christ's ministry as prophet, the pope and bishops are the official teachers in the Church. Inspired by the Holy Spirit, they hand on the teachings of Christ. The Church has the gift of **infallibility.** This gift means that when the pope proclaims a teaching solemnly and officially on faith or morals, we can be assured that the teaching is without error. It does not mean that the pope is perfect and can never make a mistake. It means that God preserves the pope from error when he definitively teaches a doctrine of faith or morals. The bishops also have this gift when, together with the pope, they teach on matters of faith or morals.

Sharing in Christ's ministry as king, the pope and bishops speak with authority and serve as Jesus did. They make decisions to guide us in living as Christians. They serve us by caring for our spiritual needs. They challenge us to live as Jesus did. They care about all people in the world, especially those who are poor and powerless. Like Christ, they are shepherds who speak out for justice and mercy and are willing to suffer for their flock. They encourage us to use our gifts to serve those who are poor and who suffer injustice.

Because we love Christ and our Catholic faith, we pray for and follow the guidance of the pope and bishops. We accept their teaching and try to live according to it.

Priest, Prophet, and King

Indicate whether each example describes a bishop sharing in Jesus' ministry as priest, prophet, or king. Write *a* for priest, *b* for prophet, or *c* for king.

_____ **1.** The pope today issued a letter teaching that . . .

_____ **2.** Next week Bishop Ramirez will be at our parish to celebrate Confirmation.

_____ **3.** During Lent, the bishop will visit a number of parishes to hear confessions.

_____ **4.** The United States Conference of Catholic Bishops is calling upon all states to make the process for adopting children easier.

_____ **5.** In response to the controversial new movie about Jesus, the bishops of the United States have issued a letter clarifying what Catholics believe about Jesus.

_____ **6.** The new bishop has announced that his first act will be to serve at a soup kitchen.

A Moment with Jesus

As a baptized Catholic, you share in Christ's ministry as priest, prophet, and king. Take a moment now to thank Jesus for the gift of his grace you received in Baptism. Ask him to help you celebrate the sacraments, learn and help others to learn about the teachings of the Church, and care for the people of the world, especially those who are poor, vulnerable, and powerless.

Popes of Recent History

Read how these popes have led the Church. After each description, write the name of the pope.

Leo XIII (1878–1903)

Saint John Paul II (1978–2005)

Pius XI (1922–1939)   Pius XII (1939–1958)

Benedict XV (1914–1922)   Francis (2013–)

Saint John XXIII (1958–1963)   Paul VI (1963–1978)

Benedict XVI (2005–2013)

- In 1891 he wrote an encyclical upholding the dignity of human beings, who are made in God's image.

  _____

- During World War I, this pope helped prisoners of war and refugees and set up a missing-persons bureau for victims of war. He pleaded for peace.

  _____

- Nazi leaders controlled Germany in 1933. They believed their race was superior. This pope denounced dictators who take away rights.

  _____

- This pope helped refugees during World War II. He spoke out courageously against communism.

  _____

- In 1961 this pope wrote an encyclical called *Peace on Earth*. He called us to live the teachings of Jesus so that all people can exercise their rights.

  _____

- This pope visited mission countries. In 1966 he wrote about poverty in developing countries.

  _____

- This pope, who declared 2000 a jubilee year, asked people your age to act as followers of Christ.

  _____

- In 2006 this pope issued his first encyclical. It taught people that love of God and love of neighbor cannot be separated.

  _____

- He became the first Jesuit pope in 2013 and called for Catholics to serve those who are poor.

  _____

Act Apostolic

You are apostolic when you act as a follower of Christ. Use the words in the box to list the ways you can take action in your home, school, parish, and world.

Participate	Pray	Speak
Act	Read about	Use

1. _____ for your pope, bishops, classmates, neighbors, and the whole world.

2. _____ your bishop so that you can get to know him, and support him by being a faithful follower of Christ.

3. _____ in the liturgy and the sacraments.

4. _____ your gifts and talents to serve others.

5. _____ positively about the Church and other people.

6. _____ with justice and mercy.

Summary

Remember

What makes the Catholic Church apostolic?

Jesus sent the apostles forth to share in his mission. The Catholic Church is apostolic because it is rooted in the teachings of the apostles and because it continues their mission. The pope and bishops are successors of the apostles and are faithful to what they taught.

Words to Know

bishop
collegiality
diocese
infallibility
pope

Respond

Read the fourth point under the section Act Apostolic on page 82. List in your reflection notebook three gifts God has given you. Then write someone's name next to each gift. Surprise each of these people today by using your gifts to serve them. Later write how you felt after you performed this service. Recognize your ability to serve as Jesus did.

Reach Out

1. Ask your parents or guardians to take you to a Sunday liturgy at a cathedral. Tour the cathedral afterward. Describe the visit to your classmates.

2. Read a biography of one of the popes mentioned in this book. Write a book report and display it.

3. With your parents or guardians visit the Vatican Web site at www.vatican.va. You can take a virtual tour of the Sistine Chapel and other beautiful and historic locations in the Vatican.

4. Find out more about the pope. How is he chosen? How does he get his name? What are some symbols of his office? What does he do each day? What does the papal flag look like?

5. Do a research project on how your diocese is governed. How is it organized? Who are the leaders? What are the newest departments?

6. Read Catholic newspapers and periodicals to find out what the pope and bishops are doing to promote social justice. Report to your class.

7. Obtain a copy of the TV miniseries *Peter and Paul*, starring Anthony Hopkins as Saint Paul and Robert Foxworth as Saint Peter. Watch the film as a family to learn about how the early Church overcame obstacles to proclaim the Gospel of Jesus under the leadership of Saint Peter.

Review

Analyze the Analogy An analogy is a comparison. For example, the Old Testament is to the Jewish people as the New Testament is to Christians. Finish these analogies.

1. Peter is to the apostles as _____ is to the bishops.

2. A Church leader is to the Church as a _____ is to a flock.

3. Apostles are to the early Church as _____ are to today's Church.

4. Washington, D.C., is to the president what _____ is to the Holy Father.

5. A priest is to celebrating the Eucharist as a prophet is to _____ .

6. Making mistakes is to human beings as _____ is to the pope when speaking officially on matters of faith and morals.

Two Sets of Three Answer the following questions.

What three responsibilities are yours as a member of the Church?

1. _____ **2.** _____ **3.** _____

What three roles of service do Church leaders have?

1. _____ **2.** _____ **3.** _____

Infallibility Check Write + if each statement is true and − if it is false.

_____ **1.** Church leaders are to be servants like Christ.

_____ **2.** The pope and bishops can never make mistakes.

_____ **3.** We are apostolic because what we believe comes from the apostles.

_____ **4.** The pope and the bishops adapt the message of Jesus to new ages.

_____ **5.** The pope is the Bishop of Rome.

_____ **6.** The teaching authority of the Church is called infallibility.

_____ **7.** The more you know your faith, the more apostolic you are.

_____ **8.** A diocese is the territory governed by a bishop.

CHAPTER 9

Unit 2 Review

Fill in the crossword puzzle.

Across

1. *Holy* is one of the four _____ of the Church.

4. The effort to unite all Christians. _____

8. Unity makes our Church _____ .

9. The territory a bishop is responsible for. _____

10. The Church takes into consideration the differences of various _____ around the world.

11. In celebrating the sacraments, the bishops share in Christ's ministry as _____ .

12. Saint _____ showed Christ's love to people with leprosy in Hawaii.

15. The Church is _____ because it is rooted in the teachings of the apostles.

16. The pope's teaching is _____ when he teaches officially on matters of faith and morals.

17. Inspired by the _____ , the pope and bishops govern the Church.

Down

2. All members of the Church are unified in our celebration of these. _____

3. Saint Angela Merici had this gift. _____

5. Pope John Paul II named her blessed in 2003. _____

6. The word *apostle* comes from the word meaning this. _____

7. Spiritual leader of the Church. _____

10. The bishops together form the _____ of bishops.

13. _____ unites us with Christ and one another.

14. The Church recognizes this in all people. _____

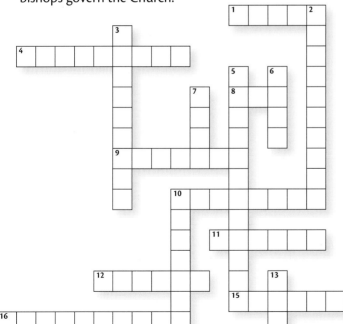

Celebrating

Church

Opening Song

Leader: Let us begin our prayer:
In the name of the Father
and of the Son
and of the Holy Spirit.
Amen.

The night before he died, Jesus prayed for his apostles and for his Church.

Reader: "I pray not only for them, but also for those who will believe in me through their word, so that they may all be one, as you, Father, are in me and I in you, that they also may be in us, that the world may believe that you sent me." (John 17:20–21)

Leader: We pray today for our Church, for ourselves. Father, Son, and Holy Spirit, keep us one.

All: Let us be one in what we believe, one in our government, one in our worship, and one in love.

Leader: Father, Son, and Holy Spirit, keep us holy.

All: Make us resemble Jesus, our head, more and more.

Leader: Father, Son, and Holy Spirit, keep us catholic.

All: Never let us be too small to include others and their gifts.

Leader: Father, Son, and Holy Spirit, keep us apostolic.

All: Help us be true to the faith that comes from the apostles and our leaders.

Leader: We pray to the Spirit, our sanctifier, to understand and live what we are called to be as Church.

Side 1: We are the Body of Christ.

Side 2: May our love for him and one another grow.

Side 1: We are the vine and the branches.

Side 2: May we never be separated from Christ.

Side 1: We are the temple.

Side 2: May we be worthy of Christ's presence in us.

Side 1: We are the sheepfold.

Side 2: May we always be grateful to the Good Shepherd, who gave us life by his Death.

Side 1: We are the bride of Christ.

Side 2: May we respond to his love by giving ourselves totally to him.

Side 1: We are leaven.

Side 2: May the kingdom be more present in the world through our influence.

Side 1: We are children of Mary, Mother of the Church.

Side 2: May we be like her in opening ourselves to your will for us.

Leader: As members of the Church, let us present one another with a symbol of our oneness in Christ.

(Students exchange stones, plants, bread, or cards with quotations as a reminder of their membership in the Church.)

Intercessions

Leader: Let us pray for Church members and those who are joined to us. After each group is mentioned, respond, "Bless them, Lord."

(Students name various groups.)

Leader: Let us spend a few moments praying silently for those people we wish to remember.

(Time for silent reflection)

All: God our Father,
by the promise you made
in the life, Death and resurrection
of Christ your Son,
you bring together in the Spirit
from all the nations
a people to be your own.
Keep the Church faithful to its
    mission;
may it be a leaven in the world,
renewing us in Christ,
and transforming us into your
    family.
Grant this through Christ
    our Lord. Amen.

(from Votive Mass for the Church)

Closing Song

Viewing the Spirit's Gifts

Fill in the titles of each numbered DVD with the Gift of the Holy Spirit described in its matching sentence.

1. Saint Angela Merici taught poor girls about Christ and his teachings.

2. Father Solanus gave people advice on Christian living.

3. Saint Catherine of Siena practiced what she believed.

4. Saint John Chrysostom recognized the importance of piety, a gift of the Holy Spirit that helps us love and worship God.

5. Blessed Miguel Pro served the Church in Mexico despite danger.

6. Saint Thomas More made decisions pleasing to God because he knew God's truth so perfectly.

7. Saint Francis of Assisi's awe of God and God's creation made him dread ever displeasing God.

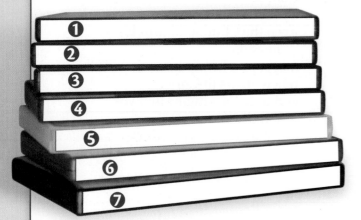

Looking Back

To belong to the one, holy, catholic, and apostolic Church is a challenge. By living those words from the Nicene Creed, you are letting people know that you are proud to be a follower of Christ, a member of the Church. You and other members of the Church are to love and believe the truths that have been handed on to you by the pope, the bishops, and the Christian community. You are to show what it means to be faithful. Your words and actions are to give hope to others by showing them that they can find happiness in Jesus. His message is important. His kingdom is in our midst. This unit, The Marks of the Church, has been a call to action for you. With the help of the Spirit, you are to lead others to Jesus. You can worship, believe, and serve. You can let everyone know that you are the Church!

As you complete this unit, ask yourself these questions.

1. What has this unit taught me about how the Holy Spirit helps me be a faithful member of the Church?

2. How have I grown as a friend and follower of Jesus?

3. What practical steps can I take to show others that I love my faith and am proud to be a member of the Church?

Images and Insights

Match each image of the Church from Scripture with the insight it gives into the mystery of the Church.

_____ 1. **vine and branches**

_____ 2. **temple**

_____ 3. **the sheepfold**

_____ 4. **the Body of Christ**

_____ 5. **Mary, Mother of the Church**

_____ 6. **leaven**

_____ 7. **bride of Christ**

a. Jesus loves us very much.

b. All those who have faith in Christ and his Church are under his care.

c. The power of Christ spreads slowly through Christians who do God's will and evangelize.

d. We can bear the fruit of love for God and others only through our union with Christ.

e. To be a follower of Christ calls for us to say yes to God's will.

f. God dwells in us.

g. We are united with one another.

Gather and Go Forth

Know and Proclaim

The truths of our Catholic faith have been handed down from the apostles. By proclaiming the Gospel, we continue Jesus' mission.

We Know Our Faith	We Proclaim Our Faith
The teaching of the Church is rooted in the teachings of the apostles, and the Church continues their mission.	Catholics pray the Apostles' Creed, which is the oldest formulation of the teachings of the Church.
The Church transmits a living faith through its teachings, life, and worship.	Catholics read pastoral letters issued by the bishops in the United States that clarify the Church's position and beliefs about issues that affect the nation.
Through the Church's teaching authority, called the Magisterium, the Church transmits a living faith.	Catholics often begin formal religious education outside the home by attending faith formation classes. Catholics continue to study the *Catechism of the Catholic Church* throughout their lives.

Test Your Catholic Knowledge

Fill in the circle that best completes the sentence.

The visible leader of the Catholic Church throughout the world is the pope, who is the successor of:

- ◯ Jesus.
- ◯ Saint Luke.
- ◯ Saint Peter.
- ◯ John the Baptist.

We are the community of disciples. We are the Church. We follow in the steps of the apostles and share in the roles of priest, prophet, and king.

They devoted themselves to the teaching of the apostles and to the communal life, to the breaking of the bread and to the prayers.

Acts of the Apostles 2:42

A Catholic to Know

Catherine was born in Siena, Italy, in 1347. She is remembered as one of the Church's great mystics and spiritual writers. One day when she was meditating, Jesus said to Catherine, "The only way you can serve me is in service of your neighbor." When she emerged from meditation, Catherine cared for those who were sick or poor, prisoners, and plague victims. She acted as a mediator between feuding families and pleaded with the pope to return the papacy from France to Rome. Catherine's ministries attracted many disciples, particularly those that resulted in miraculous healings. She is a companion for all who journey toward Christ in faith. We celebrate Saint Catherine of Siena's faith witness on April 29.

Saint Catherine of Siena

Witness and Share

These sentences describe what Catholics believe. Listen carefully as they are read. Ask yourself, "How strong are my Catholic beliefs?"

My Way to Faith

- I am aware of major events in Church history.

- I look to the pope as the spiritual leader of the Church.

- I include the pope and bishops in my prayers.

- I know and recite the Apostles' Creed.

- I share the faith of the Church with others as taught by the pope and my bishop.

Share Your Faith

Consider the ways in which you live your faith. Do your words reflect Jesus' values? Do your actions reflect your words? Write your witness on the lines below. Invite a relative or friend to discuss how he or she "gives life" to what he or she believes.

_____

_____

_____

_____

The History of the Church: Part I

"And behold, I am with you always, until the end of the age."

Matthew 28:20

Family Feature

Celebrate the Diversity of Our Church

> For in one Spirit we were all baptized into one body, whether Jews or Greeks, slaves or free persons, and we were all given to drink of one Spirit.
>
> 1 Corinthians 12:13

When the Holy Spirit descended upon the apostles at Pentecost, it quickly became apparent that the message of Christ knew no boundaries. The apostles emerged from the upper room speaking in tongues and carrying the Gospel to all who would listen. Just as it did in the early Church, the message of Jesus continues to speak to people of all cultures around the world, regardless of economic or social status.

We experience unity in the Church through the Holy Spirit, and this unity is manifested in a healthy variety of ways. How we express our universal faith depends on cultural background, local customs, historical conditions, and personal experience. During the next few weeks, look for ways to deepen your family's awareness and appreciation of the diversity of the Church and for ways to extend the love of Jesus across all boundaries.

Faith Connections

Following are practical ways to make faith connections with your family.

Diverse Appreciation

One simple but powerful way to deepen your family's appreciation of the Church's rich diversity is to visit the Maryknoll Missionaries at http://home.maryknoll.org. Let the images and stories inspire you. Pick a story and share it with your family at dinner.

Inclusive Conversation

Inclusion is one of Jesus' primary values. Jesus did not limit his attention to those considered acceptable by society. Throughout his ministry he went out of his way to gather with people who were despised or ignored by society. Choose a night at dinner to talk about what it means to follow Jesus' example.

- Parents: Talk about times you felt excluded or left out and what others did—or did not do—to reach out.
- Students: Where do you see people being excluded or ignored in your community, school, workplace, neighborhood, and parish?
- All: In what ways is diversity present in your school, workplace, or parish? Do you experience diverse cultures, income levels, ages, or political views?

After the conversation, name one thing you will do as a family to help someone feel more included and welcomed.

Visit **www.christourlife.com** for more family resources.

The First Years

When you go to the library to take out a biography about a famous person, you will notice that books such as these usually follow a typical pattern. They begin with the early years of the person's life. Imagine that a biography was being written about you. How would the early years of your life be described?

_____

_____

_____

From George Washington to the Beatles, from Michael Jordan to Oprah Winfrey, the stories of the early years of people's lives often tell us a lot about how they eventually reached their achievements.

The Beginnings of the Church

The same is true of the Church. For us to understand how the Church got to be the way it is today, it is helpful to look back at the early years of the Christian community. Before we do that, however, it is important to remember how the Church got started. It is not as if some followers of Jesus got an idea and said, "Hey, let's start a Church!" The Church began because Jesus wanted it to be so. The Church is both the means and the goal of God's plan. Jesus selected Peter to lead the apostles, and it was upon him that the Church was founded. Jesus instructed his apostles to carry on his

mission of bringing the good news of salvation to the ends of the earth. He taught them that, since God is our Father, we are all brothers and sisters.

A small band of disciples went forth on Pentecost, led by the Holy Spirit and bound together out of love for the Lord. The first Christians longed to touch the hearts of all people with their message about him. They journeyed to different towns and proclaimed this message: "Jesus is risen. Be baptized and be saved."

Some people listened and joined the Christians. Others covered their ears. During those early years, the Church had joys, sorrows, successes, failures, and conflicts. It had heroes and villains. Through everything, the message was kept alive. The Spirit was with the community, and the Church was strong.

In this chapter you will meet some of the leaders of the early Church. You will find out what they went through to keep the community one and to make it grow.

The Story of the Early Church

The Acts of the Apostles teaches us about the first years of the Church and its movement from Jerusalem to Rome. This book of the Bible is a continuation of Luke's Gospel. It opens with Jesus' promise to send the Spirit and the fulfillment of this promise on Pentecost. Then it follows the ministry of two great figures in the Church: Peter, the first leader of the Church, and Paul, the apostle to the Gentiles. Sixty percent of the Acts of the Apostles is about Paul and his missionary adventures. However, the Holy Spirit also plays a major role in the Church in the Acts of the Apostles. The Spirit is so important, in fact, that the book is often referred to as the Gospel of the Holy Spirit.

Letters written to the early churches and individual Christians also give us insights into the early days of the Church. About half of these letters, or **epistles,** in the Bible were written by Paul or attributed to him. The letters written by Paul were the first writings of the New Testament.

Read the quotations on the right—from New Testament letters—to get an idea of how early Christians spoke about faith in Jesus. Put an asterisk next to the ones you find most interesting.

Romans 12:9
[H]ate what is evil, hold on to what is good.

1 Corinthians 16:13–14
[S]tand firm in the faith, be courageous, be strong. Your every act should be done with love.

Ephesians 3:20–21
Now to him who is able to accomplish far more than all we ask or imagine, by the power at work within us, to him be glory.

Philippians 3:8
For his sake I have accepted the loss of all things and I consider them so much rubbish, that I may gain Christ.

Colossians 3:24
[B]e slaves of the Lord Christ.

Philippians 4:13
I have the strength for everything through him who empowers me.

Jude 1:21
Keep yourselves in the love of God and wait for the mercy of our Lord Jesus Christ that leads to eternal life.

In the Name of Jesus

One day Peter and John were going into the Temple. At the gate, a man who was crippled begged them for alms. Peter replied, "I have neither silver nor gold, but what I do have I give you: in the name of Jesus Christ the Nazorean, [rise and] walk." (Acts of the Apostles 3:6) The man immediately leaped up and walked into the Temple with them, jumping and praising God. The people were astonished to see him. They listened to Peter's speech about Jesus, whose name brought healing and in whose name they continued to act. (based on Acts of the Apostles, chapter 3)

A Moment with Jesus

Peter and John had compassion for the man who was crippled. Take a moment to ask Jesus to help you reach out to those who are in need, especially those who are poor. Ask Jesus to help you treat all people with dignity.

Overcoming Obstacles

The Jewish leaders, disturbed by the commotion, arrested Peter and John. The next day they freed Peter and John with a warning not to speak about Jesus again. Obeying God rather than men, Peter and John continued the mission that Jesus had given them. Then all the apostles were put in jail. But an angel opened the gates that night, and the apostles went back to preaching.

The next time the apostles were arrested, Gamaliel, a wise Pharisee, persuaded the officials not to kill them. He argued, "[I]f this endeavor or this activity is of human origin, it will destroy itself. But if it comes from God, you will not be able to destroy them." (Acts of the Apostles 5:38–39) The Sanhedrin, the senate of the Jewish people, had the apostles whipped and then let them go. Urged on by the love of Christ, they continued to proclaim the Good News with great joy. (based on Acts of the Apostles, chapters 4–5)

Saint Stephen.

> **Read Acts of the Apostles 5:40–42 and write how the apostles responded to their sufferings.**
>
> _____
>
> _____

The Life of the Community

The early Church is described in great detail in the Acts of the Apostles. We learn from this book that prayer was an important part of the life of the early Christians. In fact, they prayed with such intensity that, we are told, "the place where they were gathered shook." (Acts of the Apostles 4:31) The book goes on to tell us that they shared everything in common, making sure that no one was in need. Most importantly, it tells us that the apostles "bore witness to the resurrection of the Lord Jesus." (Acts of the Apostles 4:33) From their example, we learn to make prayer an important part of our lives and to care for those in need. We also learn to promote the well-being of all and to give witness to Jesus through our words and actions. (based on Acts of the Apostles, chapter 4)

Deacon and Martyr

Stephen was one of the first seven **deacons,** men chosen to minister to the needs of the community. An enthusiastic and Spirit-filled preacher and miracle worker, he angered the Jewish leaders by accusing them of not observing God's law. As a result, they threw him out of the city and began to stone him. (based on Acts of the Apostles, chapters 6–7) As they were stoning him, Stephen cried out in a loud voice, "Lord Jesus, receive my spirit . . . Lord, do not hold this sin against them." (Acts of the Apostles 7:59–60)

By dying for Jesus, Stephen became the first martyr. A **martyr** is someone who sacrifices his or her life out of witness to Jesus. The martyrs teach us that it is our duty to take part in the life of the Church and to act as witnesses of the Gospel. With the gift of courage, we are able endure the challenges that come with living as followers of Jesus.

Today deacons, men ordained through the Sacrament of Holy Orders, continue to serve the Church. They assist priests and bishops by serving in charitable practices of the Church. They help by proclaiming the Gospel, preaching, and assisting at the Liturgy of the Eucharist. Deacons also celebrate Baptism, witness marriages, and preside at funerals. The word *deacon* comes from a Greek word meaning "to serve." To follow Jesus is to serve others, especially those who are poor, as he did.

Read Acts of the Apostles 6:8–15 and 7:51–60. Imagine that you have just witnessed the death of Stephen. A reporter is interviewing you. Write your answers to the following questions based on what you have read:

Reporter: I heard that Stephen gave a long speech before he died. What accusations did he make against the Sanhedrin?

You: _____

_____

_____

Reporter: What vision did Stephen see before he died?

You: _____

_____

Reporter: How was Stephen killed?

You: _____

Reporter: What were Stephen's last words?

You: _____

_____

Reporter: What do you think might happen to the Christians now?

You: _____

After the death of Stephen, there was an all-out persecution against the Christians. Most of the Jerusalem community fled to the countryside of Judea and Samaria and as far as Antioch. Would the Church be able to survive through these difficult times?

Remember

Which books of the New Testament give us our understanding of the early Church?

The Acts of the Apostles and the letters give us our understanding of the early Church.

What are some of the experiences of the early Church?

Peter and John healed a man who was crippled. The Jewish leaders were angry because Peter, John, and all the apostles were healing and preaching in the name of Jesus. The apostles were arrested and jailed but were set free.

Why is Stephen called the first martyr?

Stephen was one of the first seven deacons of the early Church, and he angered the Jewish leaders by enthusiastically preaching about Jesus. He is called a martyr because he sacrificed his own life in witness to Jesus Christ.

Words to Know

epistle
deacon
martyrs

Respond

Choose one of the quotations from the New Testament letters on page 94. Think about it and then write about it in your reflection notebook. Record what it means to you and how it applies to your life.

Reach Out

1. Make a photo album of the Acts of the Apostles. Cut out magazine pictures or draw the "photos" and put captions under each. Include scenes from each phase of the Church's growth: Jerusalem, Judea and Samaria, and Asia Minor and Europe.

2. Read the Acts of the Apostles or one of the letters in the New Testament. Write a book review of it.

3. Interview some or all of the members of your family, asking them what they know about the New Testament letters and the Acts of the Apostles. Then write a brief report based on their information. Check the facts and then present the report to your family.

4. Research the Internet or a library to track the travels of Saint Paul. Print out or copy a map that shows the routes he took. Then in your reflection notebook, write down what Paul's travels mean to you about proclaiming God's Word.

5. Spend some time in prayer with your family this week. Thank God for the gift of the Church and its leaders, particularly the early leaders who risked their lives to spread Jesus' message. Make sure each family member has the opportunity to share something about the Church for which he or she is grateful.

Know That Term! Underline the term that matches each description.

1. Book of the Bible that tells about the early days of the Church

   Book of Revelation   Church History

   Acts of the Apostles

2. Letters in the Bible that were written to early Christian churches and individuals

   encyclicals   epistles   testaments

3. Someone who witnesses to Jesus through death

   deacon   missionary   martyr

4. Role that Stephen had of ministering to the needs of the Church

   Pharisee   bishop   deacon

5. The first martyr was

   Stephen   Peter   Paul

6. Person whom Jesus selected to lead the Church

   Stephen   Peter   Paul

7. Wrote about half the letters to the early Christian churches

   Paul   Matthew   Mark

8. Had great importance to the lives of early Christians

   Hebrew Scriptures   the Sanhedrin   prayer

9. People ordained in the Sacrament of Holy Orders in today's Church

   deacons   lectors   acolytes

10. Stephen's vision before death

    Abraham   heavens opening   Mount Sinai

Yesterday and Today Complete the sentences with key words from the past and present of the Church.

> Good News   Gospel   Spirit   wonders
> Jesus   deacons   letters   Luke

1. The Church began because of _____ .

2. Martyrs teach us to act as witnesses to the _____ .

3. _____ celebrate Baptism, witness marriages, and preside at funerals.

4. The first parts of the New Testament to be written were Paul's _____ .

5. The Acts of the Apostles continues from the Gospel of _____ .

6. The _____ was with the early Church and is with the Church today.

7. Christ's love helped the apostles to continue to proclaim the _____ .

8. The disciples were able to work _____ in the name of Jesus.

In Your Words Imagine you were alive at the time of the apostles. Write a letter to the officials in power, telling them why they should not persecute the apostles.

Dear Sirs:

_____

_____

_____

_____

_____

_____

_____

_____

                    Sincerely,

                    _____

Saint Stephen.

Gather and Go Forth

Know and Proclaim

We learn the truths of our Catholic faith so we can proclaim our beliefs with our lives.

We Know Our Faith	We Proclaim Our Faith
The Church is both the means and the goal of God's plan. Jesus selected Peter to lead the apostles.	Catholics honor Saint Peter as the first leader of the Church and the first Bishop of Rome by celebrating the Feast of Saint Peter and Saint Paul on June 29.
The Acts of the Apostles and the Letters provide us with a portrait of the early Church.	Catholics use a variety of resources for daily reflection on the Gospel to live their lives according to Jesus' teachings.
Stephen was one of the first seven deacons. He sacrificed his life in preaching the Gospel and is the first Christian martyr.	Taking inspiration from the martyrs, Catholics set aside their needs and work to build the faith community and spread the Word of God even when it is difficult to do so.

Catholics receive the gifts of fortitude and courage from the Holy Spirit. With these gifts, we can proclaim Christ's truth to all the earth, no matter what challenges and obstacles we face.

"I have told you this so that you may have peace in me. In the world you will have trouble, but take courage, I have conquered the world."

John 16:33

Test Your Catholic Knowledge

Fill in the circle that best completes the sentence.

The story of the early Church and ministries of Peter and Paul are told in:

○ the Historical Books.

○ the Acts of the Apostles.

○ the Book of Psalms.

○ the Gospel of Luke.

A Catholic to Know

In 202, the Emperor Severus issued an edict forbidding anyone from being baptized. Perpetua, a 22-year-old catechumen, was arrested along with five others. Perpetua was tried and sentenced to be executed in the Roman amphitheater. Her father pleaded with her to offer sacrifices to the pagan gods so that she could escape death. She told him, "Father, do you see this water jar, or whatever it is, standing here? Could one call it by any other name than what it is? Well, in the same way I cannot be called by any other name than what I am—a Christian." She was baptized as she was awaiting her execution. We honor Saint Perpetua's courageous witness to Christ on March 7.

Saint Perpetua

Witness and Share

These sentences describe what Catholics believe. Listen carefully as they are read. Ask yourself, "How strong are my Catholic beliefs?"

My Way to Faith

- I know that Peter was the first pope.

- I practice my faith even when it is not popular to do so.

- I am an active member in the faith community of my parish.

- I make sacrifices willingly to live my faith.

- I am grateful for the gift of the Church in my life.

- I am inspired by Saint Perpetua and the sacrifice she made.

Share Your Faith

Consider ways in which sacrifices can lead to a deeper understanding of what you are called to be as a disciple of Jesus Christ. Write your ideas on the lines. Invite a family member or friend to talk with you about sacrifices he or she has made for his or her faith.

_____

_____

_____

_____

The Church Grows

Saul of Tarsus was a tentmaker and a Roman citizen. As a Pharisee attempting to defend the Jewish faith, Saul joined with zeal in the persecutions of the Christians. He was present at the stoning of Stephen (Acts of the Apostles 7:58) and sought to rid the Jewish faith of all followers of Jesus. Then, in a flash of light, he saw the truth, and it changed his life. Saul the persecutor became Paul the apostle. Such a change of heart is called a conversion. Conversion is turning away from yourself and toward Jesus.

Closer to Jesus

Unlike Paul's experience, most conversions happen gradually over time. Think of a way in which you are closer to Jesus today than you were a year or two ago. How did this conversion come about?

_____

_____

_____

Think of a way in which you would like to grow closer to Jesus. Who or what can help you?

_____

_____

_____

One Story, Four Accounts

The New Testament has four accounts of Paul's conversion:

* **Acts of** the Apostles 9:1–22 (Luke describing Paul's experience)
* Acts of the Apostles 22:2–16 (Luke describing Paul's telling of his conversion to the crowd in Jerusalem)
* Acts of the Apostles 26:9–18 (Luke describing Paul's telling of his conversion to King Agrippa)
* Galatians 1:15–17 (from Paul, talking about his own conversion)

Look up each of these passages and make a list of the key "facts" in each passage. Then, compare and contrast the different versions.

Your Own Call to Conversion

In Baptism, we undergo a conversion to become disciples of Jesus. To live like his disciples and as brothers and sisters to one another, we are called to ongoing conversion. When we turn away from Jesus, we can return to him through the Sacrament of Penance and Reconciliation (commonly called Reconciliation), the sacrament of conversion. To return to the Lord, we must be sorry for our sins and must resolve to avoid sin in the future.

A Worldwide Audience

At first, the Christians were considered a Jewish sect, or branch. They followed the Jewish laws and did not mix with Gentiles, non-Jews. Then, in a vision, the Spirit led Peter to see that Baptism was also for the Gentiles. While Peter was thinking about the vision, men came who were sent by a Gentile named Cornelius. They invited Peter to Cornelius's house. When Peter arrived at Cornelius's house the next day, he learned that a messenger of God had told Cornelius to send for Peter. That day Peter baptized Cornelius and his relatives and friends. The Church began to be catholic, or universal. It did so because it recognized that because God is our Father, we are all brothers and sisters with the responsibility to care for one another.

based on Acts of the Apostles, Chapter 10

On the Road

Antioch was one of the world's greatest cities at the time. The Church there was made up of Gentile and Jewish communities. Here the disciples were first called Christians. Paul, Barnabas, and John Mark left Antioch for their first mission. They went to evangelize Cyprus and Asia Minor (in present-day Turkey). Their plan was to preach first in synagogues to their Jewish brothers. If rejected, they would then preach to the Gentiles.

Paul made three other journeys and started churches all around the Mediterranean Sea. In his Second Letter to the Corinthians, he listed some of the things he endured.

Five times at the hands of the Jews I received forty lashes minus one. Three times I was beaten with rods, once I was stoned, three times I was shipwrecked, I passed a night and a day on the deep; on frequent journeys, in dangers from rivers, dangers from robbers, dangers from my own race, dangers from Gentiles.

2 Corinthians 11:24–26

Paul's Travels and Letters

After his conversion, Paul journeyed throughout the Roman Empire, proclaiming Jesus Christ as Savior. Paul traveled more than 6,000 dangerous miles in what are now Turkey, Greece, Albania, Italy, Syria, and Lebanon. In these places, he founded Christian communities in cities such as Corinth, Ephesus, and Philippi. He kept in touch with these communities through his epistles, or letters. His epistles further instructed the communities he began, correcting their faults and praising their faith. According to tradition, Paul arrived in Rome as a prisoner and was executed during the Roman emperor Nero's persecution of the Church in A.D. 65.

All together, there are 13 epistles that bear Paul's name as the author. However, scholars do not believe that he wrote all of them. Paul himself was the author of the following letters:

- 1 and 2 Thessalonians
- Galatians
- Philippians
- 1 and 2 Corinthians
- Romans
- Philemon
- Colossians

The epistles to the Ephesians, Titus, and 1 and 2 Timothy bear Paul's name, but it is believed that they were written after his death. The writers of these letters were disciples of Paul who wanted to continue his teaching. These writings have been accepted as inspired by the Holy Spirit and are part of the New Testament.

A Moment with Jesus

Paul teaches that the love of God has been poured out to us through the Holy Spirit. The Spirit is the source of all love. He creates a bond between ourselves and God, like children bound to a father. Even though we are weak, the Spirit helps us live faithfully within our relationship with God. Through the Spirit, we can live in love with all people. Take a moment to ask Jesus to fill you with his Holy Spirit. Thank the Spirit for helping you live faithfully in relationship with God and others.

The Early Centers of Christianity

Few have done more for the Church than Paul. His journeys total a distance equal to three trips across the United States. On the map below, circle Rome and Antioch, the two centers of Christianity at the time of Paul.

The First Church Council

Around the years A.D. 48 to 49, some Jewish Christians demanded that the Gentile Christians keep the Jewish traditions. Paul and Barnabas disagreed and decided to speak with the apostles in Jerusalem. The argument was settled when they met with Peter, James, and others at the **Council of Jerusalem.** (Acts of the Apostles, Chapter 15) The Holy Spirit helped the council clarify the essential teaching of Jesus: to be a Christian, a person needs faith in Jesus and Baptism. Following all Jewish laws was not necessary. The Church made this decision because it was sent by Christ to teach us what to believe and to nourish our faith. Our faith is a gift of God and is necessary for our salvation.

The Council of Jerusalem is known as the first Church council. Since then the Church has held 21 worldwide, or **ecumenical, councils.** The most recent was the Second Vatican Council, from 1962 to 1965.

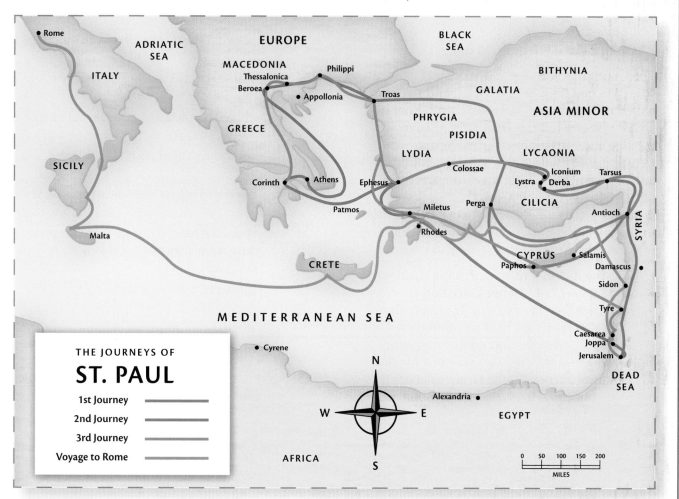

THE JOURNEYS OF
ST. PAUL

1st Journey
2nd Journey
3rd Journey
Voyage to Rome

Called to Witness

Like Stephen, Peter, Paul, and the other early disciples, you too can witness to Jesus and help spread his Church. When you were baptized, the same Holy Spirit who came to the first believers at Pentecost came upon you. The Spirit enables you to witness each day of your life in truthful words and deeds. Through our Baptism, we have the responsibility to witness to Jesus by promoting the well-being of all people.

Testify for Jesus

When we witness to Jesus, we set an example for other Christians to follow. Pretend you are a witness in a legal case about whether you have set a good example for others. Fill in the gavel if you have given witness in that way.

believed in the teachings of the faith

participated in Sunday liturgies

prayed regularly alone and with others

shared time and talent generously

obeyed teachers and others in authority

told others about Jesus' life and love

offered to help others who were in need

showed respect for people who are poor, have disabilities, and are elderly

spoke out against injustice

stood up for the values of Christ when peers disagreed

other: _____

Facing the Trials Ahead

The Council of Jerusalem united and strengthened the Church. Unity and strength were needed to face the trials ahead. Roman soldiers destroyed the Temple in A.D. 70, causing the Christians of Jerusalem to flee. Many of the Jewish Christians found acceptance in the Christian communities of cities such as Antioch, Corinth, and Rome. Because of the missionary work of the apostles in these Gentile lands, there were Christians to welcome the exiles.

During the movement away from Jerusalem, Rome became the center of Christianity. Peter was the first Bishop of Rome. Tradition claims that there both he and Paul were martyred. All the apostles were martyred except John. With the death of John, who was in exile on the island of Patmos in the Greek islands, the apostolic era came to an end around A.D. 95.

Remember

How did the Church begin to become more catholic, or universal?

At first, the Christians were considered a Jewish sect, or branch. They followed the Jewish laws and did not mix with Gentiles, non-Jews. Then, in a vision, the Spirit led Peter to see that Baptism was also for the Gentiles.

What did the Council of Jerusalem decide?

The Council of Jerusalem decided that Gentile Christians had to believe in Jesus and be baptized. They did not have to follow all Jewish laws.

What contributions did Paul make to the early Church?

Paul began many churches, preached to the Gentiles, and wrote letters that are included in the Bible.

Words to Know

Council of Jerusalem
ecumenical council

Respond

We bless ourselves with holy water when we enter and leave a Catholic church as a way of reminding ourselves of our Baptism and our call to ongoing conversion. In your reflection notebook, write some thoughts about how you need to change to follow Jesus more closely. Keep this in mind the next time you bless yourself with holy water.

Reach Out

1. Go with your parents or guardians to your parish church. Bring a small, empty plastic bottle and fill it with holy water. Place the holy water in a receptacle where you and members of your family can bless yourselves each day as a reminder of your Baptism and your call to ongoing conversion. Take turns refilling the holy-water receptacle.

2. Look at a map of your state and identify where you would travel if you were Saint Paul, spreading the Gospel message.

3. Research the first 13 epistles. When you are finished, write a brief summary of what they have in common. Focus on one or two themes that reappear throughout these epistles.

4. Because Mary Magdalene was the first to see the risen Lord, she is called the "apostle to the apostles." Women played an important role in the early Church. Read about Dorcas in Acts of the Apostles 9:36–42, Mary and Rhoda in 12:6–17, and Lydia in 16:11–15, 40.

5. Ask your parents or guardians to tell you a story about a time in their lives or in the lives of a relative when they or the relative had an experience of conversion—of turning their mind and heart toward God.

Firsts, Mosts, and Bests Write the names of the people or places that deserve the following awards.

1. Most letters written to early churches _____

2. First Bishop of Rome _____

3. Best supporter of the early Church _____

4. First martyr of the Church _____

5. First place where the disciples were called Christians _____

6. Most churches established _____

7. First Gentile to be baptized _____

8. Best recorder of early Church history _____

9. Most missionary journeys _____

10. Chosen by Jesus to lead the Church _____

Know That Term Underline the term that matches the description.

1. Church leaders held this meeting to make decisions about Gentile converts.

   Council of Rome   Council of Jerusalem

   First Vatican Council

2. This period in the Church ended with the death of John.

   persecution years   apostolic era   Gospel times

3. Paul's second letter to them described some of the struggles he endured.

   Galatians   Philippians   Corinthians

4. The Second Vatican Council was one of these.

   ecumenical council   encyclical   epistle

5. During the movement away from Jerusalem, this became the center of Christianity.

   Antioch   Corinth   Rome

6. All the apostles were martyred except him.

   John   Peter   Thomas

Gather and Go Forth

Know and Proclaim

We can renew our faith by learning the truths that the Church teaches. Renewed in faith, we can proclaim our beliefs to others.

We Know Our Faith	We Proclaim Our Faith
Conversion is a change of heart; it is the turning away from sin and toward Jesus.	As Catholics, we practice an examination of conscience as part of our ongoing conversion. We understand that conversion has to be renewed daily.
To live as disciples of Christ, we are called to live as brothers and sisters to one another.	Catholics celebrate the Sacrament of Penance and Reconciliation as an opportunity to move away from sin and grow closer to God and others.
The Council of Jerusalem was the first ecumenical council. The Holy Spirit helped the council clarify the essential teachings of Jesus.	Many Catholics study the documents of the Second Vatican Council to understand what it means to be a follower of Jesus. As Catholics, we seek to know and understand the intellectual tradition of the Church.

Test Your Catholic Knowledge

Fill in the circle that best completes the sentence.

At the Council of Jerusalem, the Church decided that:

○ to be a Christian, a person needed faith in Jesus and Baptism.

○ Paul's letters were accepted as part of the New Testament.

○ Gentile Christians must keep all Jewish traditions.

○ Peter would become the Bishop of Rome.

Because of our Baptism, we are called and sent forth to give witness to Jesus Christ. Our witness enables others to believe in Jesus Christ.

"Those who never have been
   told of him shall see,
and those who have
   never heard of him shall
understand."

Romans 15:21

A Catholic to Know

Ignatius was a convert to Christianity. When he was named the second bishop of Antioch, Syria, Ignatius became a successor of Saint Peter. In A.D. 107, Emperor Trajan tried to force Christians to renounce their religion. Ignatius allowed soldiers to bind him in a rickety cart and lead him to Rome for martyrdom. On the journey, Ignatius wrote seven letters to the churches that he left behind. He insisted that the people obey their bishop. "Wherever the bishop is," he wrote, "there let the people be, for there is the Catholic Church." Ignatius wrote that Christ is present in the Church, in each member, and in the Blessed Sacrament. He was devoured by wild beasts in the Roman amphitheater.

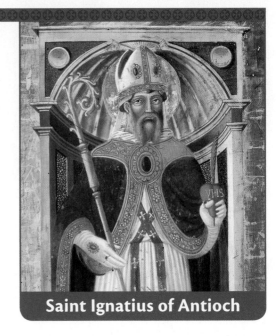

Saint Ignatius of Antioch

Witness and Share

These sentences describe what Catholics believe. Listen carefully as they are read. Ask yourself, "How strong are my Catholic beliefs?"

My Way to Faith

- I practice an examination of conscience to help me have a change of heart.

- I participate in the Sacrament of Penance and Reconciliation as part of my efforts to turn away from sin.

- I study Church documents to learn and understand Jesus' teachings.

- I have a responsibility to bear witness to Jesus by treating others as brothers and sisters.

- I believe that my Baptism calls me to a life of ongoing conversion.

Share Your Faith

Consider ways in which your faith has grown over the years. On the lines below, write examples of how you have grown in your faith recently. Invite family members to share how their faith has grown.

_____

_____

_____

_____

A House Built on Rock

Games often imitate life. Think of the following example: Imagine you are on the basketball team and the game has come down to the final shot. You are standing on the free-throw line in front of hundreds of noisy fans. Since you are playing at the other team's gym, most of the fans are trying to distract you. They are doing whatever they can to make you miss the shot. Will you be able to stand the pressure?

Although that example is taken from a game, the game imitates life. We may find ourselves in situations in which we need courage and strength to act in the face of opposition. As followers of Jesus, this is often true. People may try to distract us from keeping our focus on Jesus. We need courage to stand firm in what we believe and to accept our responsibility to stand up for what is right. Luckily for us, we can look to many people in our Church history for examples of standing firm in the face of pressure and even danger.

The Witness of the Martyrs

Jesus had warned his followers: "If they persecuted me, they will also persecute you." (John 15:20) We have already learned about the persecutions that the early Church faced at the hands of Saul. After encountering the risen Jesus, Saul courageously proclaimed the Good News even in the face of persecution. The worst, however, was yet to come.

In A.D. 64, great persecutions began under Nero, the Roman emperor. Nero knew that many Romans distrusted the Christians because they were different. The Christians refused to pay homage to the Roman gods and refused to serve in the military. Building on this distrust, Nero blamed Christians for a great fire that destroyed much of the city of Rome, and he began to kill them. Under Nero, Peter and Paul were martyred.

Some emperors ignored Christians; other emperors did not. In the last Roman persecution, which began in A.D. 303, Diocletian planned to remove every trace of Christianity from the world. Throughout these dangerous times, bishops, such as Ignatius of Antioch, wrote letters to strengthen Christian communities. Others, such as Bishop Cyprian, were killed in front of their people for openly following Christ.

As unbelievers saw the courage of these Christians, some were inspired to turn to God and be baptized. The martyrs teach us to never be ashamed of being a witness in our words and deeds on behalf of Jesus. In doing so, we become like the martyrs who sacrificed their own well-being to proclaim the Gospel. Through the Sacrament of Confirmation, the Holy Spirit strengthens our bonds with Jesus and the Church. The Spirit helps us bear witness to the Catholic faith and live together as brothers and sisters of the one Father.

Through the witness of the martyrs, God's plan unfolded. The Church grew and spread.

Sister Dorothy Kazel: A Martyr in Our Day (1939–1980)

In the 20th century, there were more martyrs than in all other centuries combined. In many countries, Christians are still persecuted for their faith. As the Church was born through the sacrifice of Christ on the Cross, so it continues to grow through the sacrifice of its martyrs.

Dorothy was a smart, fun-loving young woman. It was a surprise when she broke off her engagement with her fiancé and joined the Ursulines, a religious order. As a high school business teacher, Sister Dorothy had a heart for those who were poor. She longed to be a missionary. In 1974 her dream came true. She was chosen for the Cleveland mission team traveling to El Salvador in Central America.

In El Salvador, Sister Dorothy helped people learn Catholic doctrine and celebrate the sacraments. She also worked on projects to educate those who were poor and to promote their health. In a letter she wrote,

And so we continue, living through earthquakes, eating beans and tortillas in the cantones, taking attempted suicide victims to the hospital, walking in dust or water up to our ankles . . . building houses, demolishing and rebuilding churches, enduring the heat and mosquitoes . . . and just generally having a great time in the name of the Ursulines and the Christ who is Lord!

While the Church worked for those who were poor, the government backed wealthy landowners. Acts of violence against priests, sisters, and lay leaders increased. Archbishop Romero and hundreds of innocent people were murdered. The missionaries ministered to the victims of violence and lived in fear. In December 1980, Sister Dorothy, two Maryknoll sisters, and a lay missionary were returning home from the airport. They never arrived. The next day a milkman discovered their bodies in a ditch. Sister Dorothy herself fulfilled the words she wrote in her last letter home:

The steadfast faith and courage our leaders have to continue preaching the Word of the Lord even though it may mean "laying down your life" for your fellow man in the very real sense is always a point of admiration and a most vivid realization that Jesus is here with us.

You, a Martyr

You do not have to go to a distant land to witness to your Catholic faith. Read the following statements. Circle the letter of the ending that tells how to respond as a witness of Christ.

1. When I see a student ridiculing a young child in the playground, I
   a. defend the child.
   b. join in the ridicule.
   c. feel uncomfortable but say nothing.

2. When a friend criticizes someone in authority, I
   a. add more criticism.
   b. try to say something good about them.
   c. feel uncomfortable but say nothing.

3. When someone in class announces that it is stupid to help those who are poor, I
   a. continue to help.
   b. agree and stop helping.
   c. keep others from helping.

4. When I find out a friend is starting to take drugs, I
   a. feel uncomfortable but say nothing.
   b. join my friend in trying drugs.
   c. warn my friend about the danger of drugs.

EMPEROR CONSTANTINE PROCLAIMING

IN HOC VINCES

NIKA

LIBERTY OF RELIGION

EDICT OF MILAN 313 AD

From Persecution to Peace

In the early fourth century, Constantine was the Roman emperor. For several hundred years, Christians had been practicing their faith and spreading their message. By the time Constantine became emperor, there were Christians in nearly every part of the empire. Christian communities were becoming highly organized under the leadership of bishops, the successors of the apostles.

Constantine was very concerned about the divisions that existed in the Roman Empire between Christians and those who opposed them. He himself was gradually drawn to Christianity. As he headed into battle at Milvian Bridge in Italy in A.D. 312, Constantine placed a Christian symbol on the shields of his soldiers. When his army won the battle against a much larger force, Constantine took it as a sign that the Christian God was supporting him. As a result, in 313, Constantine decided to issue a decree—the Edict of Milan. In this decree, he declared that Christianity was no longer a forbidden religion. The time of persecutions had past. Within a short time, Christianity went from being forbidden to becoming the official religion of the Roman Empire.

Making Headlines

Newspaper headlines capture the key events of an era. The Roman headlines below reflect how the Church benefited when Emperor Constantine let Christians worship freely.

> **In this list of improvements for the Church, put the number of the headline next to the sentence that it matches.**

_____ Christian leaders influence the government.

_____ Martyrs get public recognition.

_____ Being a Christian is legal.

_____ New prayer forms are used in the Mass.

_____ Government provides places of worship for Christians.

_____ Christian art aids in praising God.

6
AMBROSE APPROVES RESPONSORIAL PSALM

2
BISHOP GOVERNS CITY

3
GOLD MOSAICS DECORATE CHURCH

4
EMPEROR BUILDS CHURCH OF ST. IRENE

1
PERSECUTION ENDED

5
ROMAN CAPITAL DEDICATED TO MARTYRS

A Different Kind of Witness

In the fourth century, when the persecutions had ended, Christians continued to realize that through their Baptism they were called to lives of holiness. They also realized that they had the responsibility to call others to holiness in a world that was not always supportive of the Christian way of life. Some Christians wanted to make a powerful statement about how each of us is called to uproot sin in the world. So, through the practice of self-denial, they went to live in the desert to continue the witness of the martyrs.

Imagine yourself wandering through the deserts and mountain caves in the fourth century. In your travels, you might meet a person who lives alone as a hermit, imitating the early life of Saint Anthony of Egypt. This hermit eats very little food each day and appreciates silence. He spends many hours in prayer, does penances, and makes sacrifices. His life is a sign to all people that we are called to pay attention to the interior life so that our relationship with Jesus may deepen. Like the martyrs, the life of the hermit showed that sacrificing one's own well-being for the sake of Jesus is a powerful way of preaching the Gospel.

You might meet someone who joined Saint Anthony, the founder of a community of his followers. Each follower, known as a monk, practices monasticism and lives alone in a hut. He joins the other monks in prayer and in the celebration of the Eucharist. He helps those who are poor by making and selling mats, ropes, and baskets.

From the earliest times, men and women banded together in religious communities. These groups needed a common rule to follow. Saint Pachomius wrote a rule of life for monks and nuns in Egypt. Saint Basil wrote one for religious communities in the Near East. They prayed at scheduled times and read Scripture. They also performed physical labor or mental labor such as copying manuscripts. They consecrated themselves to Jesus by publicly professing to live lives of **poverty,** chastity, and obedience within a stable community that was recognized by the Church.

Your Family's Rule

The rule that monks and nuns followed was designed to help them follow the teachings of Jesus. Think about your family's guidelines, or "rule," that help you follow Jesus' teachings. Make a list of at least five guidelines that are followed in your family. (Examples: Attend Sunday Mass together. Do all your homework without complaining.)

1. _____

2. _____

3. _____

4. _____

5. _____

Confusion from Within

When persecution was no longer a problem, another threat arose. This threat, known as **heresy,** was caused by Christians themselves. Heresies began to create confusion and doubt in Christian communities. A heresy is a false teaching that rejects a truth that has been revealed by God and taught by the Church. A person who believes or teaches a heresy is a heretic.

One very harmful heresy was started by a priest named Arius. He convinced many people that Jesus was not God but was a created being who existed before the world was created. In stating this, the Arian heresy denied that Jesus was both human and divine. The Church believes that only because Jesus is God could he redeem us, promise us eternal life, and send the Spirit upon us.

Saint Basil.

Settling Matters

To stop the Arian heresy, local bishops gathered for meetings called synods. They discussed ways to present the truth to confused Christians. But the Arian heresy continued to spread. Finally Emperor Constantine called a general meeting in the city of Nicaea in 325. Because every Catholic bishop in the world was invited, this meeting was called an ecumenical council. Present were both the bishops who taught Arianism and the bishops who opposed it. They wanted to settle one question for the whole Church: Is Jesus both God and man?

An important result of the Council of Nicaea was the creed the bishops began to compose. The Nicene Creed clearly expresses that Jesus is true God and true man. According to the teaching of the Council of Nicaea, Jesus is not a creature made by God. He is God's own Son and is God just as much as his Father is God. This is important for us because it means that, in Jesus, God took on human flesh. It is another reason why we believe that all human life is sacred and that all people must be treated with dignity.

In 381 the Council of Constantinople expanded the creed that was begun at Nicaea. It also defined the divine nature of the Holy Spirit, whose mission is inseparable from the Son's mission.

Another heresy was taught by Nestorius. He believed that Jesus was two persons. To Nestorius, Mary was the mother of the human Jesus but not the Mother of God. This heresy was refuted in 431 at the Council of Ephesus. There the bishops declared that Jesus was one person with two natures: one divine and one human. The Council also declared that Mary was the Mother of God since she was the mother of Jesus, the Son of God, who is God himself.

Fathers of the Church

In the early Church, the Holy Spirit called forth courageous leaders to explain the message of Jesus. These thinkers and teachers are Church Fathers. They wrote letters, homilies, and books about the faith. They also defended the Gospel against heresies. Because of Saints Athanasius, Basil, Ambrose, Augustine, and other Church Fathers, Christians gained a deeper understanding of their faith and became more strongly committed to Christ. Through the Church Fathers, the Holy Spirit did what he continues to do today: build, strengthen, and give life to the Church.

A Moment with Jesus

To survive the struggles of the early centuries, the Church put its total trust in God. To trust in God is to know that God will be with you and will help you no matter what the future may hold.

Take a moment to thank Jesus for always being with you. Ask him for the strength and courage of the Holy Spirit so that you can stand firm in your faith even in the face of challenge. Pray the words of this Psalm:

God alone is my rock and salvation,
my secure height; I shall never fall.

Psalm 62:3

Council	Year	Heresy	Doctrine Confirmed
Nicaea	325	Arian	Jesus' divinity, Nicene Creed
Constantinople	381	Arian	Holy Spirit's divinity, Nicene Creed
Ephesus	431	Nestorian	Jesus is one divine person. Mary is the Mother of God.

Your Rock

God is like a strong rock you can cling to in storms. Mark each statement with the letter that best describes your response.

S = Seldom   **O = Often**   **U = Usually**

_____ When sorrow makes things seem hopeless, I rely on God for help.

_____ When events do not go the way I want, I still trust that God cares about me.

_____ When others ignore me, I still trust that God loves me very much.

_____ Because I trust that God wants me to be happy, I obey God's laws.

_____ I spend more time praying than I do complaining or worrying.

_____ I trust that God listens to my prayers and will do what is best for me.

_____ When someone I love is ill, I trust that God will take care of him or her.

_____ I believe that God will guide my life as God guided the early Christians.

_____ I trust that God helps me overcome my sins and weaknesses.

_____ When I am in trouble, I pray.

Saints in the Early Church

Ignatius Ignatius was bishop of Antioch in A.D. 110. While being taken to Rome to be martyred, he wrote letters to Christian communities. He told the people of these communities to stay close to their bishops, to love one another, and to rejoice in dying for Christ.

Anthony Anthony spent much of his life alone in prayer and penance in the Egyptian desert. He taught other monks.

Ambrose A strong, popular bishop, Ambrose defended the Church against heretics and wrote much to uphold the faith.

Athanasius Bishop Athanasius skillfully defended the truth of Jesus' divinity against the Arian heresy.

Basil As a Greek Father of the Church, Basil tried to improve the relationship between the Eastern and Western Churches.

John Chrysostom John was nicknamed "golden-mouthed" because of his inspiring sermons.

Jerome Working tirelessly in a monastery, Jerome translated most of the Bible from the original Hebrew and Greek into Latin. His translation is called the Vulgate.

Monica Monica prayed constantly that her son, Augustine, would become a follower of Christ.

Augustine After a long search for truth, Augustine became bishop of Hippo and an outstanding Christian teacher, writer, and theologian. Augustine was led to the faith through the preaching of Ambrose.

Remember

How do martyrs contribute to the mission of the Church?

Martyrs, who choose to suffer and die for love of Christ and their belief in his teachings, inspire people to join the Church.

How do those who live a monastic life give witness to the mission of the Church?

Those who lead a monastic life show us how to build up the Church through prayer, penance, and service to those who are poor.

Why was the Council of Nicaea important to the Church?

The Council of Nicaea defended the truth that Jesus is true God and true man. Christians proclaim this truth in the Nicene Creed, which is prayed at Sunday Mass.

Words to Know

heresy
poverty

Respond

Saint John Chrysostom once wrote, "Never forget that God has made you his friend." Spend a few moments thinking about this statement. Then answer these questions in your reflection notebook: How has God shown great love for me? How can I show my love for God today?

Reach Out

1. **Write an original story about how someone might be persecuted today for being Christian. Or find an example of Christians being persecuted today and bring it to class.**

2. **Do research on a modern-day saint. Write a report.**

3. **Discuss how people today can be holy in ways other than by becoming hermits.**

4. **The Church in Korea began with a group of laymen. Find out about them and about the Korean martyrs.**

5. **Talk with your parents or guardians about where it is hard for them and for you to live as a Catholic. Ask them to tell you about their experiences at work and in the community. Talk to them about your experiences at school and with your friends.**

6. **You can learn from the lives of hermits the importance of spending time alone with God and paying attention to your interior life. Talk to your parents or guardians about your need to spend time alone. Tell them it will help you grow closer to Jesus. Ask them to help you identify a time and place to be alone with God.**

Diego Velazquez, *Saint Anthony Praying and Saint Peter as the First Hermit*, 1634.

The Secrets of Holy Men and Women Even though you are not a monk, aspects of the monastic life can influence your life with God. The following items were important to members of monastic communities. Check (✓) three items that you see as most important for yourself. Star (☆) items that are contrary to how the world thinks today.

_____ finding a quiet place to pray

_____ giving away money and possessions

_____ talking less and listening more

_____ getting along peacefully with others

_____ obeying the person in authority

_____ setting aside time for prayer

_____ making special sacrifices for God

_____ appreciating silence

_____ enjoying the beauty of nature

_____ recognizing Jesus in each person

_____ praying with Christ in the Eucharist

_____ being pure in thought, word, and action

Go to the Experts What type of person described in this chapter would you consult about the following:

1. Courage in witnessing to Christ despite suffering and death _____

2. How to live a deep spiritual life alone in silence and prayer _____

3. How to grow in prayer and spiritual life by living in a religious community _____

4. Deeper meanings of the Christian faith _____

5. What it feels like to believe and teach something contrary to the Church's teaching _____

Good Guys and Bad Guys Draw a halo over the names of people who helped the Church. Mark an *X* on the names of enemies of the Church. Then write a phrase identifying each person.

1. Arius _____

2. Anthony of Egypt _____

3. Nero _____

4. Constantine _____

5. Basil _____

6. Athanasius _____

7. Ambrose _____

8. Augustine _____

9. Nestorius _____

10. Cyprian _____

Gather and Go Forth

Know and Proclaim

Knowing the truths of our Catholic faith enables us to proclaim our beliefs with courage and conviction.

We Know Our Faith	We Proclaim Our Faith
Martyrs, monks, and hermits witness the Christian way of life. They sacrifice their own well-being for Jesus.	Many Catholics join religious communities and take vows of poverty, chastity, and obedience.
The Nicene Creed expresses our faith in the Three Persons of the Trinity: God the Father, God the Son, and God the Holy Spirit.	When the Nicene Creed is prayed during Mass, Catholics bow at the words "and by the Holy Spirit was incarnate of the Virgin Mary and became man."
The Church Fathers were early Church leaders called forth by the Holy Spirit to teach Jesus' message.	As Catholics, we study the writings of the Church Fathers to help us understand what the Church teaches and believes.

Our Church turns to God for safety and strength. The heroism of the Church's early members inspire us to witness Christ with courage and conviction.

*My soul rests in God alone,
    from whom comes my
        salvation.
God alone is my rock and
    salvation,
    my fortress; I shall never fall.*

Psalm 62:2–3

Test Your Catholic Knowledge

Fill in the circle that best answers the question.

Which of the following resulted from the Edict of Milan?

◯ Diocletian declared that Christianity was illegal.

◯ An ecumenical council declared that Mary was the Mother of God.

◯ Constantine declared that Christianity was no longer forbidden.

◯ An ecumenical council defined the divine nature of the Holy Spirit.

A Catholic to Know

Living in the 300s, Saint Basil described his conversion at age 30 as "waking from a profound sleep." He joined a monastic community and became known for teaching about the Holy Trinity and the social responsibilities of living the Gospel. He composed a rule of life for monks, allowing them to operate hospitals and guesthouses outside of the monastic community. As a champion of social justice, he challenged those who were wealthy to care for those who were poor and share their resources with them. Basil also clarified the Church's teachings about the Holy Trinity and the Incarnation. His writings place him as one of the greatest teachers of the Christian faith.

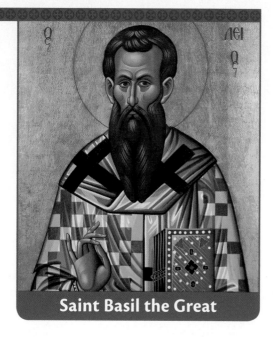

Saint Basil the Great

Witness and Share

These sentences describe what Catholics believe. Listen carefully as they are read. Ask yourself, "How strong are my Catholic beliefs?"

My Way to Faith

- I consider the call to join a religious community as a possible vocation.

- I believe that the Trinity is consubstantially one God in three distinct Persons related to one another as God the Father, God the Son, and God the Holy Spirit.

- I know the teachings of the Church.

- I stand up for my Catholic beliefs.

- I believe that all people should be free to practice and express their faith.

Share Your Faith

Consider ways in which your faith gives you strength and confidence. How have you inspired people to act with strength and courage? Write one of your faith experiences on the lines below. Invite a friend or relative to share his or her stories of courage.

_____

_____

_____

_____

CHAPTER 13

A Light in Darkness: Part I

On the morning of September 11, 2001, people in the United States awakened to frightening scenes on their TV screens. Terrorists had hijacked jet airliners and slammed them into the twin towers of the World Trade Center in New York City and the Pentagon in Washington, D.C. As the towers of the World Trade Center came toppling down, people in New York were on the brink of panic. Within a short time, however, officials from the city, state, and national government took to the airwaves to assure people that a response to the emergency was in place. Someone was in control. Despite the chaos and devastation of that terrible morning, people were able to get on with their lives because leaders stepped forward to respond. People need someone in authority in order to get through difficult times and to grow and develop as a community.

Imagine if a tragedy such as 9/11 was followed by no response from leaders. What if officials, police and firefighters, and emergency workers fled and left New Yorkers on their own? Fortunately this did not happen. People living in the Roman Empire in the early Middle Ages—around the fifth century—were not so fortunate. Imagine reading a newspaper article such as the one to the right.

Germanic Tribes Invade
Rome Falls

GAUL – Warriors attacked the borders of Gaul. The Rhine River was filled with armed Germanic tribes on swimming horses and floating tree trunks. The riders came wearing dyed red furs and bronze two-horned Gothic helmets. By evening, these warriors had plundered and burned shops and homes. The Roman army was defenseless before them. Most soldiers abandoned their posts in fear. Authorities claim, "Rome's soft lifestyle and undisciplined society are not prepared to withstand the invasion."

One invader was quoted as saying, "We have come for land and food. We are running from the Hun army led by Attila."

A state of emergency has been declared for all of the Roman Empire. Already many people are starving. People are afraid to harvest their crops. Law and order are gone. All communication between the provinces has been shut down. A reliable source reported that people everywhere have turned to the Church for aid and are going to the monasteries for protection. What will happen to civilization when these invaders are in control? A renowned scholar calls these times in the Roman Empire a "darkened age."

bishops also ran the cities when civil authority broke down. They took care to protect the true teaching of the Catholic faith.

The Light of Missionaries

Pope Saint Gregory the Great (540–604) led the Church in these difficult times. He organized Rome, gave generously to those who were poor, negotiated peace, and wrote letters to instruct Catholics. Nine hundred of his letters are preserved in libraries. Pope Gregory is also known for reforming the liturgy and compiling Church music. Most important, Pope Gregory sent monks to every land to evangelize the invaders and to preach the Good News to all people.

Besides proclaiming the Good News, the monks made laws; taught people to read, write, and count; and showed people how to cultivate the land and set up trade. The monks also hand-lettered copies of ancient manuscripts, preserving culture, doctrine, and the Bible. In these ways, the Church guided the world through the Dark Ages.

Western Monasteries

The waves of invasion that took place in the early Middle Ages meant that people could not live stable lives. They lived in fear for what the future might bring. At Monte Cassino, Italy, in 520, Saint Benedict established a way of life that provided stability. It was based on the values of work and prayer. From Monte Cassino, Benedictine monks went forth to establish monasteries all over Europe. Because of their vow of stability, the Benedictines provided a way of life that was much needed by nomadic tribes. Many historians credit the monastic tradition with saving Western civilization when much could have been lost forever.

A Beacon of Light

The fifth-century invasion by Germanic tribes threw all of Europe into a state of chaos. Many historians refer to the period between A.D. 500 and 1000 as the Dark Ages. The Roman Empire, with its sense of order and discipline, fell apart. The invaders who flooded into central and southern Europe were accustomed to tribal living. They opposed the highly organized and centralized form of government in the Roman Empire. Often they settled their disputes with bloodshed, and they worshiped the pagan gods Wotan and Thor. Most could neither read nor write. They had no schools for art, music, and science. They knew little of how to cultivate the land or organize a government. It seemed the whole world was in darkness and despair.

In the midst of this difficulty, the Church was a beacon of light. The Church brought God's peace and the power of God's Word. The Church worked to protect innocent people, preach the Gospel to the invaders, and build a new society. Bishops assumed authority and used it to protect the people from tax collectors who wanted to steal from them. They were at times successful in negotiating with tribal leaders to protect the people in the cities. The

Disciples' Duties

The Rule of Saint Benedict outlines the duties that each member of a monastery is to undertake to live as a follower of Jesus. Use your Bible to locate the following passages. Then describe some of the duties that Jesus is asking of us.

John 13:1–15 _____

Luke 17:3–4 _____

Matthew 5:43–48 _____

Luke 10:29–37 _____

Matthew 6:25–34 _____

Mark 9:33–37 _____

Luke 11:9–13 _____

Matthew 9:10–13 _____

Matthew 28:16–20 _____

John 13:34 _____

A Moment with Jesus

Taking responsibility is not always easy. As a disciple of Jesus, you have a responsibility to share in his mission. Take a moment to ask Jesus for the grace you need to accept responsibility. Thank him for giving us an example in himself so that we know what it means to truly serve others.

Conquering the World with Virtue

The Germanic tribes conquered the Roman Empire through physical force. As followers of Jesus, we are sent to conquer the world with a very different kind of force: **virtue.** Virtues lead us to live in a close relationship with Jesus.

Virtues are like habits. They need to be practiced. They can be lost if they are neglected. The three most important virtues—faith, hope, and charity—are called Theological Virtues because they come from God and lead to God.

Faith—We are called to be people of faith, who believe in the one God, in God's Revelation, and in the salvation brought by Jesus Christ.

Hope—We are called to be people of hope, who expect the coming of God's kingdom and eternal life.

Charity (love)—We are called to be people of charity, who love God above all else and love our neighbors as ourselves.

There are four other virtues that we refer to as the cardinal virtues—prudence, justice, fortitude, and temperance. These are human virtues acquired by education and good actions. *Cardinal* comes from the Latin word for "hinge" (*cardo*), meaning "that on which other things depend." The cardinal virtues call us to be prudent in our decisions, just in our dealings with others, strong in our determination to do what is right, and temperate in our use of things.

Holy Men and Women

Read about some Church leaders who spread God's kingdom. Write the letter of the Scripture reference that best matches each underlined description.

a. Matthew 10:19–20
b. Luke 12:22–31
c. Matthew 28:19–20
d. Galatians 6:9–10
e. Mark 10:42–45

_____ Augustine of Canterbury was sent by Pope Gregory the Great to England to preach the Gospel. On the way, he and his fellow monks became so frightened they wanted to turn back. Pope Gregory encouraged them. Later Augustine spoke courageously and converted King Ethelbert. Then he helped the people become strong Christians.

_____ Benedict was a man others wished to follow. He wrote a rule that included community living, prayer, fasting, and manual work. Pope Gregory encouraged the monks to move beyond the Alps. Benedictine monasteries became centers of learning and prayer. The monks turned swamps into golden meadows. They did good to all.

_____ Winifred was a brilliant and holy Benedictine monk. Pope Gregory II changed his name to Boniface, which means "one who does good," and sent him to Germany. There Boniface preached the Gospel and baptized many at the risk of his own life. He knew the Lord was with him.

_____ Margaret was married to the king of Scotland. She converted him, gathered women to study the Bible, gave money and food to those who were poor, and built hospitals. Like Jesus, she served others.

_____ The brothers Cyril and Methodius were monks who were missionaries to Russia and the Slavic nations. They evangelized the people and translated the Gospels into the Slavic language. They trusted God in everything.

Giants of the Age

One powerful leader trained by the monks in the Middle Ages was Charlemagne. He was crowned emperor by the pope in 800, with much of Europe under his rule. He governed wisely and firmly. Charlemagne also protected the pope and the Church, made laws that supported the Church, and established schools. Through him, many people became Christian. All Europe was linked to the Church.

Charlemagne divided his empire into counties, each administered by an official called a count. Royal agents, usually a churchman and a layman together, were appointed to travel through the counties and check on local affairs. These agents directed the government of both Church and state.

For all the good that Charlemagne did, some problems developed because of his form of government. The difference between the Church and the empire became unclear. As Church leaders became more and more involved in government, they sometimes forgot about their role as servants of God. Some members of the clergy grew rich and powerful. They began to rule like kings, acting proud and greedy. They forgot that they were called to be spiritual leaders, living according to Gospel values.

In his providence, God called forth strong and holy leaders. They reminded the erring members of the Church of their responsibility to defend the faith. One such leader was Pope Gregory VII. He was a reformer, someone who got the Church back on track and refocused on its mission. As spiritual leader of the Church, the pope was to lead God's people. He told rulers that the pope—not the king—should appoint bishops. Pope Gregory VII started the reform, but it took 300 years and many struggles before kings realized that they did not control the Church and that all true authority comes from God.

Charlemagne.

Remember

What happened to the Roman Empire in the early Middle Ages?

Invading armies threw all of Europe into a state of chaos. The Roman Empire, with its sense of order and discipline, fell apart.

In what ways did the monks of the sixth century spread the light of faith?

The monks became missionaries who educated people and preached the Good News. They copied manuscripts of the Scriptures and guided the world through the Dark Ages.

How are Christians called to "conquer" the world?

As followers of Jesus, we are sent to conquer the world with virtue. Virtues lead us to live in a close relationship with Jesus.

Word to Know

virtue

Respond

The saints of the Middle Ages were great givers, lovers, and pray-ers. Write in your reflection notebook how you can give at school, show love at home, and one way you could make an effort to pray more often in your daily life.

Reach Out

1. During the Middle Ages, monks copied the Bible in decorative printing called calligraphy. Select a quotation from Scripture. Print it neatly and illustrate the space around it. Find out more about the art of calligraphy.

2. Search the Internet for information about the Benedictines and their spiritual heritage. Report what you have learned to a friend or family member.

3. Find ways you can help those who are poor. If you have clothes or toys you no longer use, ask your parents or guardians if you may give them to the Society of St. Vincent de Paul.

4. Pope Gregory the Great had Church music written down and organized. Research Gregorian chant and try to obtain a CD. Listen to the CD.

5. With your family, discuss how the monks of the Middle Ages brought God's Word to others. Brainstorm ways that you can proclaim the Gospel message to today's world.

6. Pope Gregory wrote hundreds of letters to help Catholics. Write an encouraging letter to someone in need. This person could be someone you know or someone in an assisted-living center, for example.

7. Like the people of the Middle Ages, we can learn from the monks of our time. Many Catholics today visit monasteries as a way of quieting themselves and drawing closer to God. Discuss with your family the possibility of visiting a monastery or making a retreat. Contact your local diocese for information.

Thanks to the Monks
List ways that the monks helped humanity after the fall of the Roman Empire.

1. _____

2. _____

3. _____

In Search of Virtue
Find and circle the following words:

CARDINAL
FAITH
FORTITUDE
HOPE
JUSTICE
LOVE
PRUDENCE
TEMPERANCE
THEOLOGICAL
VIRTUE

```
L F M F H G B Y D Y R P L W B
J A A J I R D Q X O R O I K Z
A A C I I L A B E U X R X L F
S H D I T H Q H D K M U O Q W
V E W B G H O E T V C D P F P
H Q F T X O N P S G I X U D X
N J G H I C L J E I A R M A J
J I C K E O D O S W O L T D U
J U S T I C E K E W A A I U R
F O R T I T U D E H P N G M E
T E M P E R A N C E T I E T A
F E K D Y W V O N T S D V W J
T I B C H W D Z F M K R O Y G
Y M S K J U L N H L K A L D C
E W T M S K A I E E Q C W U W
```

Gregory the Great
What did Pope Gregory the Great do to lead the Church during difficult times?

_____

_____

_____

_____

_____

_____

_____

Gather and Go Forth

CHAPTER

13

Know and Proclaim

Living the truths of the Catholic Church helps us live in virtue and proclaim the light and truth of Jesus Christ.

We Know Our Faith	We Proclaim Our Faith
Faith, hope, and charity are called Theological Virtues because they come from God and lead to God.	When Catholics pray the Rosary, they pray a Hail Mary for each of the Theological Virtues.
Prudence, justice, fortitude, and temperance are the Cardinal Virtues that are acquired by education and good actions.	Catholics develop the virtue of justice when they respect the rights of others and fulfill their responsibilities to one another and to society.
The Church guided society during the Dark Ages. Monasteries became centers of religion, art, education, culture, and trade.	The Catholic Church supports and operates many universities throughout the world. These schools are centers of learning and research.

The light of Christ overcomes the darkness to illuminate the love of God for his people. By our Baptism, we are called to be the light that illuminates the world.

Jesus spoke to them again, saying, "I am the light of the world. Whoever follows me will not walk in darkness, but will have the light of life."

John 8:12

Test Your Catholic Knowledge

Fill in the circle that best completes the sentence.

The desire and expectation of eternal life is the virtue of:

- ○ humility.
- ○ hope.
- ○ faith.
- ○ love.

A Catholic to Know

Saint Wenceslaus lived during the 900s in what is now the Czech Republic. He was the grandson of Saint Ludmilla and the son of a duke. Wenceslaus worked to end the persecution of Christians and promoted the education of people. Wenceslaus set an example all could follow. He brought back exiled priests and rebuilt churches, he gave alms, practiced justice, and visited those who were imprisoned. When Wenceslaus's brother lost his claim to the throne upon the birth of Wenceslaus's son, the brother conspired to kill the duke during a religious festival. Before he died, Wenceslaus asked God to show his brother mercy. The patron of the Czech Republic, Wenceslaus remains a symbol of Czech independence.

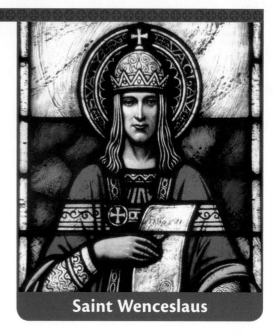

Saint Wenceslaus

Witness and Share

These sentences describe what Catholics believe. Listen carefully as they are read. Ask yourself, "How strong are my Catholic beliefs?"

My Way to Faith

- I hope in God and trust in his love.

- I practice the Cardinal Virtues in my everyday life. I pray to increase the Theological Virtues received in Baptism and make acts of faith, hope, and charity.

- I will continue my faith formation after Confirmation.

- I practice charity toward others, especially those who are poor.

- I bring the light of Christ to others, especially those who are in need and in despair.

Share Your Faith

Consider ways in which you can bring Jesus' light to others in your home, school, or parish community. Write your ideas on the lines, and invite a family member or friend to be a light for someone else.

_____

_____

_____

_____

A Light in Darkness: Part II

Working on the school newspaper used to be fun for Colleen. Everyone on the team got along very well. They did not always agree, but they shared ideas and made decisions together. Colleen and everyone else knew that Josh was the editor and a good leader. Everything changed, however, when a new teacher, Mr. Tracy, became moderator of the school paper and appointed Linda, a new student, as the editor. The problem was that Linda had no experience with the newspaper. All the veteran members of the team continued to look to Josh for leadership, while the new members looked to Linda. This led to a power struggle between Josh and Linda.

> **What effect do you think this power struggle had on the quality of the school newspaper?**
>
> _____
>
> _____

Losing and Regaining Focus

Between A.D. 500 and 1000, the Church became involved in a serious power struggle that hurt the Church's ability to carry out Jesus' mission. Because there were no political structures to hold society together, bishops assumed many of the responsibilities once held by government leaders. This was in keeping with the Church's mission of safeguarding the dignity of all people. When Church leaders became political leaders, however, abuses crept in. A bishop appointed by the king became responsible to the king, not to the pope. This practice of having political leaders assign jobs to bishops and priests is called lay investiture. Under lay investiture, it was easy for bishops to become rich landowners and to forget about being spiritual leaders.

The Holy Spirit called forth saints to bring the Church back to holiness and to its spiritual responsibilities. Pope Gregory VII knew that the pope alone has full authority to care for souls and that he alone should appoint bishops, make Church laws, and form dioceses. He fought to end lay investiture. King Henry IV of Germany defied Pope Gregory and continued to name bishops. The pope told the king that he would no longer be a member of the Church if he continued to interfere in Church government. King Henry IV visited the pope, stood barefoot in the snow, dressed in monk's robes, and begged forgiveness. The pope forgave him, and for a while King Henry IV obeyed the pope. But then the struggle continued.

Pope Gregory VII forgiving King Henry IV.

own letter of excommunication of the pope in Rome. The Eastern Church became known as the Orthodox Church, while the Western Church became known as the Roman Catholic Church. This tragic separation is called the Great Schism. A **schism** is a split or division.

Present-day popes and Orthodox Church leaders have met to discuss reconciliation. In 1965 the excommunications between the Bishop of Rome and the Patriarch of Constantinople were removed. Every January during the Week of Prayer for Christian Unity, we pray that the oneness of Christ's Church will be proclaimed more effectively through reconciliation. We also pray that Jesus' prayer that we "may all be one" (John 17:21) will be realized.

A Serious Break

While Christians in western Europe were occupied with the invasion of Germanic tribes, communication had been cut off with the Church in the East. Over the centuries, differences began to divide the eastern and western parts of the Church. The Church in the East used Greek and other languages for the liturgy. The Church in the West used Latin. Eastern priests were permitted to marry, while those in the West were not. The Christians in the eastern and western parts of the empire tended to think differently about some important issues, such as Original Sin, the use of pictures and statues, the place of the Holy Spirit in the Trinity, and the authority of the Bishop of Rome. There was another thing pulling them apart: the political rivalry between the two great cities of Constantinople in the East and Rome in the West.

Both Churches became suspicious and fearful of each other. Finally, in 1054, a serious break happened between the East and the West. While the Patriarch of Constantinople prepared for the celebration of liturgy, an ambassador from the pope arrived and placed on the altar a papal letter of **excommunication** of the Patriarch of Constantinople. Excommunication means that a person is separated from the Church, especially from the Eucharist. A few days later the Eastern bishop responded with his

The Crusades

At the end of the 10th century, the spread of Islam had slowed, and a period of generally stable relations among Jews, Christians, and Muslims existed. Although Muslims were in control of the Holy Land, Christians were generally able to safely make pilgrimages to sacred sites. This came to an end when the Turks, who were aggressively expanding in the Byzantine (Eastern) Empire, began to ambush Christians who made pilgrimages to the Holy Land. Desperate for help, Byzantine emperor Alexius asked Pope Urban II for assistance. As a result, the Crusades began. The Crusades

Pope Urban II announcing the first Crusade.

were expeditions, "holy wars," to regain the Holy Land. There were eight Crusades over 200 years. The Crusaders were only able to regain control of the Holy Land for a short time (1099–1187) before the Muslims took control again.

On the one hand, the Crusades stirred up enthusiasm for the Christian faith and opened the doors between East and West. Pilgrimages were promoted, as was a renewed devotion to the passion and Death of Jesus. Likewise, the Way of the Cross was introduced to Europe. On the other hand, many atrocities were committed by both Christians and Muslims during the Crusades. Some participated only to get rich. The Crusades led to suffering and death for many. During one Crusade, Western Christians attacked Eastern Christians in Constantinople. This caused further damage to the already strained relationship between the Roman Church and the Eastern Orthodox Church.

In 2000, Pope John Paul II issued an apology for the wrongs committed by some members of the Church during the Crusades.

A Moment with Jesus

During the Middle Ages, the Church often served as a beacon of light in the darkness. Jesus told his followers: "You are the light of the world . . . your light must shine before others." (Matthew 5:14,16) Take a moment to thank Jesus for these words. Ask him for the strength you need to be a light to others who are experiencing darkness.

In Search of Heretics

Jesus taught us that the first and greatest commandment is to love God "with all your heart, with all your soul, and with all your mind." (Matthew 22:37) The First Commandment calls us to believe in God, to hope in him, and to love him above all else. When a baptized Catholic denies a truth about God that the Church teaches, we call that a heresy. During the Middle Ages, heresy was looked upon as a great evil, and heretics were considered traitors. Therefore, in some countries, heretics were put

on trial in hopes that they would change their minds. Those who did not were punished.

In the 13th century, the Church established an official Catholic court, the Inquisition, to examine, investigate, and sometimes punish those accused of heresy. Unfortunately, sometimes that punishment was excessive. The Inquisition was generally successful in halting heresies and protecting suspected heretics from more severe penalties by civil officials. However, the Church has expressed regret for the court's excesses.

Saint Dominic.

A Blend of Church and State

In medieval times, the Church influenced life greatly. All were governed by Church law, celebrated Church feasts, and attended Church schools. People looked to the Church to meet their material and spiritual needs. The Crusades brought more commerce and led to more people moving to the city and needing education. Two great men, Saint Francis of Assisi and Saint Dominic, helped the Church enlighten and guide the world.

A Light to Those in Need

Born in Italy in the late 12th century, Saint Francis of Assisi was a high-spirited, rich young man. He followed a call from God to give up his carefree life and live according to the Gospel. Francis sold everything he owned, wore a rough brown robe, and went about preaching, teaching, and caring for those who were poor. Many men were so impressed with his holiness that they joined him. They came to be known as Franciscans. Because Franciscans lived like Christ, without land or money, they were the first **Mendicant Order.** Francis's way of living reminded the Church to live the Gospel value of poverty and to be concerned for people who were poor.

In addition to the Franciscans, other new religious orders, such as the Dominicans, Carmelites, Capuchins, and Augustinians, came into existence. Like other religious communities, members of these orders took vows of poverty, chastity, and obedience. Unlike the Benedictine monks who seldom left their monasteries, however, members of these communities lived in the cities. These orders also were known as Mendicant Orders because they begged for their food. Their lifestyle made them available to help people in their daily lives. The Mendicant Orders serve as guides for **spirituality** and are good examples of how the Church adapts to the times.

Centers of Light: The Universities

Saint Dominic was a wealthy Spanish noble who became a priest. In the early 13th century, he became convinced of the need for scholars and preachers of the Gospel who lived poor and simple lives. Dominic gave the men who followed him an appreciation for study of the Gospel and Catholic teaching. This group of men later called themselves Dominicans. One holy Dominican teacher was Saint Thomas Aquinas, who lived in the 13th century. When Thomas was a student, he was very large and slow in giving answers. The other students nicknamed him the "dumb ox." But Thomas Aquinas went on to become one of the Church's greatest thinkers and writers. His brilliance showed itself in his 21-volume work, *Summa Theologiae* (Summary of Theology), in which he explained Catholic beliefs. Through the Dominicans, many universities were founded to teach the faith.

The University of You

Universities often have mission statements that briefly explain who they are, who they serve, and why they exist. If you were to found a university to teach people about God and the Catholic faith, what would be your mission statement? Keep in mind that your university is dedicated to charity as well as education.

_____

_____

_____

_____

_____

_____

_____

_____

_____

Summary

Remember

How did some leaders in the Church lose their focus during the Middle Ages?

When Church leaders became political leaders, abuses crept in. A bishop appointed by the king became responsible to the king, not to the pope.

How was the Church a light during medieval times?

The Church was a light through saints who explained and lived the teachings of Christ.

What are some of the reasons that led to the Great Schism between the East and the West?

Over the centuries, differences in beliefs and practices began to divide the eastern and western parts of the Church. Likewise, there was a political rivalry between the two great cities of Constantinople in the East and Rome in the West.

Words to Know

excommunication
Mendicant Order
schism
spirituality
Summa Theologiae

Respond

The saints of the Middle Ages influenced others in positive ways. In your reflection notebook, write ways that you can be a positive influence on your friends, classmates, family members, and others.

Reach Out

1. Go grocery shopping with your parents or guardians and pay attention to the quantity of food they buy. When you get home, talk about what it must be like for members of Mendicant Orders to beg for their food.

2. With a parent or guardian, search the Internet for information about the spiritual heritages of the Benedictines, Franciscans, and Dominicans. Report your findings to another person.

3. Write a report on Islam. Include how it started, what Muslims believe, and how they practice their faith.

4. Visit the Web site of the Catholic University of America to gain an awareness of how Catholic universities continue to be centers of light.

5. Together with your family, learn the Peace Prayer of Saint Francis. Pray this prayer together regularly as a family.

6. Ask your parents or guardians to describe who has been a beacon of light for them during moments of darkness.

Spot the Flaw Correct the word or phrase that makes each sentence untrue.

1. In 1054 the Church experienced the Great Schism, when the Eastern churches joined the Western Church.

2. The Crusades were intended to regain Rome for Christians.

3. The Inquisition was meant to change the lives of thieves.

4. The Benedictines were the first Mendicant Order.

5. Thomas Aquinas founded the Dominicans, an order of preachers.

People of Note Match each name with its description.

_____	**1.** Saint Gregory VII	**a.** Was convinced of the need for scholars and preachers
_____	**2.** Pope Urban II	**b.** Founded the first Mendicant Order
_____	**3.** Saint Francis of Assisi	**c.** Sought to end lay investiture
_____	**4.** Saint Dominic	**d.** Become one of the Church's greatest thinkers
_____	**5.** Saint Thomas Aquinas	**e.** Called for the first Crusade

Theology Detective Find the missing information and use it to complete the sentences.

1. _____ was the practice in which political leaders assigned jobs to bishops and priests.

2. Eight _____ took place over a span of 200 years.

3. _____ impressed so many people with his holiness and example of Gospel living.

4. The Church established an _____, known as the Inquisition, to halt heresies.

5. _____ issued an apology for the wrongs committed by some members of the Church during the Crusades.

Unit 3 Review

A Beacon of Hope Color the flames of the candles that represent people or things that helped the Church remain a light of faith and truth.

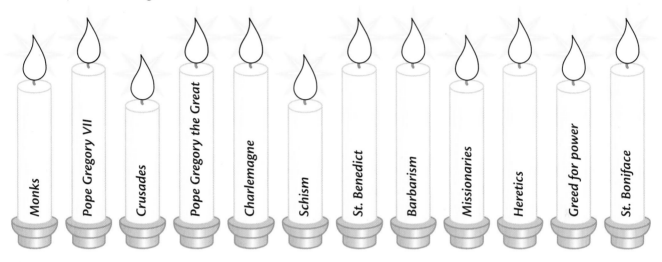

Monks | Pope Gregory VII | Crusades | Pope Gregory the Great | Charlemagne | Schism | St. Benedict | Barbarism | Missionaries | Heretics | Greed for power | St. Boniface

Key Concepts Match the key terms with the words that describe them or are related to them.

_____ **1.** monasticism

_____ **2.** schism

_____ **3.** Theological Virtues

_____ **4.** excommunication

_____ **5.** Mendicant Order

_____ **6.** conversion

_____ **7.** poverty

_____ **8.** *Summa Theologiae*

_____ **9.** spirituality

_____ **10.** ecumenical council

_____ **11.** heresy

_____ **12.** virtue

_____ **13.** Council of Jerusalem

_____ **14.** Baptism

_____ **15.** Dominicans

a. Leads us to live in a close relationship with Jesus

b. Meeting in which the Church clarified Jesus' teaching that to be a Christian, a person needs faith in Jesus and Baptism

c. Saint Basil wrote about religious communities that lived lives of chastity, obedience, and this.

d. Living alone and joining other monks for prayer

e. Saint Thomas Aquinas wrote this brilliant work.

f. In 1054 the leaders of the Eastern and Western Churches exchanged this type of letter.

g. A member of this begged for his food.

h. The most recent was the Second Vatican Council.

i. Mendicant Orders serve as guides for this.

j. A false teaching that rejects a truth revealed by God.

k. Faith, hope, and charity

l. Turning away from yourself and toward God

m. A split or division

n. They have a particular appreciation for studying the Gospel and Catholic teaching.

o. Through this, we have the responsibility to promote the well-being of all people.

Celebrating

Your Light

Opening Song

Leader: Let us begin our prayer:
In the name of the Father
and of the Son
and of the Holy Spirit.
Amen.

Jesus gathered his disciples around him and began to teach them.

Reader 1: "You are the light of the world.

Reader 2: A city set on a mountain cannot be hidden.

Reader 3: Nor do they light a lamp and then put it under a bushel basket;

Reader 4: it is set on a lampstand, where it gives light to all in the house.

Reader 5: Just so, your light must shine before others,

Reader 6: that they may see your good deeds and glorify your heavenly Father."

Matthew 5:14–16

Leader: We pray today that we may learn to let our light shine before others. Let us pause for a few moments in silence to think about all the people who are experiencing darkness in their lives.

(Pause for a minute of silence.)

Leader: To the following petitions, please respond, "May our light shine before others."

For those who are suffering in poverty, that we may care for their needs, we pray:

All: May our light shine before others.

Leader: For those who are experiencing unemployment, that we may build a society in which all people can work and earn a decent wage, we pray:

All: May our light shine before others.

Leader: For those who are suffering from illness, that they may be comforted, we pray:

All: May our light shine before others.

Leader: For those who are the victims of war, that we may learn how to live together in peace, we pray:

All: May our light shine before others.

Leader: For those who are experiencing the loss of a loved one either through death or the end of a relationship, that they may know they are not alone, we pray:

All: May our light shine before others.

Leader: Let us remember that our light comes from the Lord and that we are merely reflecting his light to others.

Let us pray the words of Psalm 27:

Side A: The LORD is my light and my
    salvation;
    whom do I fear?
The LORD is my life's refuge;
    of whom am I afraid?

Side B: When evildoers come at me
    to devour my flesh,
These my enemies and foes
    themselves stumble and fall.

Side A: Though an army encamp
    against me,
    my heart does not fear;
Though war be waged against me,
    even then do I trust.

Side B: One thing I ask of the LORD;
    this I seek:
To dwell in the LORD's house
    all the days of my life,
To gaze on the LORD's beauty,
    to visit his temple.

Side A: For God will hide me in his shelter
    in time of trouble,
Will conceal me in the cover of his
    tent;
    and set me high upon a rock.

Side B: Even now my head is held high
    above my enemies on every side!
I will offer in his tent
    sacrifices with shouts of joy;
    I will sing and chant praise to
    the LORD.

Side A: Hear my voice, LORD, when I call;
    have mercy on me and answer
    me.

Side B: "Come," says my heart,
    "seek God's face";
    your face, LORD, do I seek!

Side A: Do not hide your face from me;
    do not repel your servant in
    anger.
You are my help; do not cast me off;
    do not forsake me,
    God my savior!

Side B: Even if my father and mother
    forsake me,
the LORD will take me in.

Side A: LORD, show me your way;
    lead me on a level path
    because of my enemies.

Side B: Do not abandon me to the will
    of my foes;
    malicious and lying witnesses
    have risen against me.

Side A: But I believe I shall enjoy the LORD's
    goodness
    in the land of the living.

Side B: Wait for the LORD, take courage;
    be stouthearted,
      wait for the LORD!

Leader: Let us pray. Heavenly Father, thank
you for giving us your Son, Jesus,
to be the light of the world. Fill us
with the Holy Spirit so that we may
have the strength, courage, and
compassion to be a light to those who
are experiencing darkness.
We ask this through Christ, our Lord.
Amen.

(Offer one another the sign of peace.)

Closing Song

Scriptural Trios

Underline the Scripture passage from which each quote, message, or event comes.

1. "If they persecuted me, they will persecute you."

   Galatians 1:15–17   **Luke 11:9–13**

   John 15:20

2. Take up your cross and follow Christ.

   Mark 8:34–38   **Acts of the Apostles 9:1–22**

   John 15:20

3. Trust in God.

   Mark 9:33–37   **Luke 11:9–13**

   Matthew 6:25–34

4. Pray with perseverance.

   Luke 11:9–13   **Acts of the Apostles 26:9–18**

   John 15:20

5. Paul's conversion

   Luke 11:9–13   **Acts of the Apostles 9:1–22**

   Matthew 6:25–34

6. "[O]n frequent journeys, in dangers from rivers, dangers from robbers, dangers from my own race, dangers from Gentiles. . . "

   John 15:20   **Mark 8:34–38**

   2 Corinthians 11:26

7. Love others as Jesus loves us.

   John 8:1–11

   John 13:34

   Matthew 5:43–48

8. Avoid judging others.

   John 8:1–11

   Matthew 9:10–13

   Luke 17:3–4

Historical Trios

Underline the name of the person from Church history that fits each statement.

1. He organized Rome, gave generously to those who were poor, negotiated peace, and wrote letters to instruct Catholics.

   Benedict   **Elizabeth of Hungary**

   Pope Gregory the Great

2. She was prayerful and extraordinarily charitable to people in need.

   Gertrude   **Margaret of Scotland**   **Hedwig**

3. This pope was a reformer who refocussed the Church on it mission.

   Saint Gregory VII   **Urban II**   **Saint John Paul II**

4. These monks evangelized Russia and the Slavic nations and translated the Gospels.

   Gregory and Benedict   **Cyril and Methodius**

   Augustine and Ethelbert

Looking Back In this unit, you have discovered how Christ has remained with his Church through all times and difficulties. You have become aware of how the Holy Spirit has guided the Pilgrim People of every age to accept the challenges of Christianity. You have witnessed what the holiness and courage of the saints can do, not only for the Church, but for the world. Like an Olympic torch, the flame of Christianity is being passed on to you. Accept the challenge! Run swiftly toward Christ! Hold the torch of your faith higher!

As you complete this unit, ask yourself these questions:

1. Do I understand how the Holy Spirit guides my life as well as the life of the Church?

2. In what way have my recent actions shown that I love my faith?

3. What steps can I take to imitate Jesus and live a holy and courageous life as the saints did?

Gather and Go Forth

Know and Proclaim

With the truths of the Catholic Church to guide us, we follow the light of Jesus Christ and witness him by what we say and do.

We Know Our Faith	We Proclaim Our Faith
During the Middle Ages, the Church faced many challenges, including power struggles with kings, the Great Schism, and the Crusades.	Catholics practice a devotion called the Way of the Cross that originally began in the Middle Ages as an actual pilgrimage to the Holy Land. Catholic churches display the Stations of the Cross.
Mendicant orders like the Franciscans and the Dominicans helped reform the Church by serving those who were poor and by teaching the faith.	Some Catholics go on retreats to hermitages run by religious orders. Retreats and hermitages allow Catholics to seek spiritual renewal by devoting all their attention to God in a place of silence and solitude.
The Inquisition was established by the Catholic Church as an attempt to guard against heresy.	Catholics bishops review books and other teaching materials to make sure they are free from error in matters of faith.

Men and women of faith, inspired by the Holy Spirit, are lights leading our Church in the best and the worst of times. We bring the light of Christ through our actions.

"Just so, your light must shine before others, that they may see your good deeds and glorify your heavenly Father."

Matthew 5:16

Test Your Catholic Knowledge

Fill in the circle that best completes the sentence.

Saint Dominic and Saint Francis of Assisi helped the Church enlighten the world by:

○ preaching the Gospel and living simple lives.

○ living in monasteries and studying theology.

○ becoming political leaders responsible to kings.

○ leading Crusaders to regain control of the Holy Land.

A Catholic to Know

Gregory guided the Church after the fall of the Roman Empire in the 400s. As a government official, he helped rebuild Rome. When his father died, he turned the family home into a monastery and built six other monasteries. As pope, Gregory made peace with the invading Lombards and avoided famine by reorganizing the Church's food supplies. He sent Augustine of Canterbury to England to teach the people there the faith, earning him the title "Apostle of England." He promoted choral music known as Gregorian chant. Despite all his truly great accomplishments, Saint Gregory the Great preferred the humble title "servant to the servants of God."

Saint Gregory the Great

Witness and Share

These sentences describe what Catholics believe. Listen carefully as they are read. Ask yourself, "How strong are my Catholic beliefs?"

My Way to Faith

- I have participated in the Way of the Cross.

- I learn from those who live in religious orders such as the Franciscans, Benedictines, Ursulines, Notre Dames, and Dominicans.

- I work at faithfully understanding and expressing the teachings of the Catholic faith.

- I look for opportunities to serve others in need rather than seeking positions of power.

- I am a positive influence and sign of Jesus' love to others.

Share Your Faith

Consider ways in which you can serve others without seeking or attracting attention for yourself. Write your ideas on the lines, and invite a family member, friend, or classmate to serve with you.

_____

_____

_____

_____

The History of the Church: Part II

I urge you, brothers, in the name of our Lord Jesus Christ, that all of you agree in what you say, and that there be no divisions among you, but that you be united in the same mind and in the same purpose.

1 Corinthians 1:10

Family Feature

Living in the Light of the Second Vatican Council

At times in the life of the Church, popes have convened councils of bishops to address issues of the faith. In 1962, Pope John XXIII convened the Second Vatican Council, expressing the hope that the Council would "open a window" to let fresh air into the Church.

The Council brought together more than 2,600 bishops, advisers, consultants, and observers from around the world. One focus of Vatican II was to raise awareness of the crucial role of lay people in the Church. This meant calling each and every person to share in the Church's mission by making the love of Christ present in his or her family and community.

Faith Connections

Here are ways your family can make connections with key teachings of the Second Vatican Council. Look them over and act on one that you think would be most beneficial.

The People of God

Vatican II taught that the Church is the People of God. Everyone is called to holiness and to take responsibility for the life of the community.

> In what way are you responsible for your community of faith? Do something to strengthen your parish connection.

Full, Active Participation

The Council encouraged full, active participation of the community in the liturgy.

> Name one thing your family will do to make your participation in the liturgy more meaningful. For example, read the Scripture readings the night before Mass, talk about the homily after Mass, or sit in a different place and meet someone new.

Scripture

The Council encouraged Catholics to read Scripture.

> Take turns choosing an excerpt from the Sunday readings to display on your refrigerator. Take time at dinner or while riding in the car to talk about what that excerpt means to each family member.

The Laity

Vatican II called upon the laity to carry out the mission of the Church in the world.

> Set aside one night this week to talk with your family about the gifts and talents each of you has and the ways you are using those talents to serve others. Begin by asking everyone to write down responses to the questions below. Then take turns sharing your responses. Be sure to ask all members for their feedback. Often, others can see gifts and talents in us that we don't always see in ourselves.
>
> *What gifts and talents have you received from God?*
>
> *How has God blessed you?*
>
> *What are you doing—or what would you like to do—to share your talents with others and to bring Christ's love to the world?*

CHAPTER 15

The Church Faces Challenges

Should I join the team or not? Which high school should I attend? Who would make the best class president? We are constantly faced with decisions. Our choices make us what we are, and we must live with the consequences of our choices. Complete the following activity on a separate sheet of paper.

> **Describe a decision you made that turned out well.**
>
> **Describe a decision that did not turn out well.**
>
> **Describe what you learned from these decisions.**

Led by the Spirit

Sometimes our decisions turn out well, and sometimes they do not. Sometimes our mistakes have long-lasting consequences. Hopefully we learn from our mistakes and move on. The history of the Church reveals many human decisions—some that turned out well and others that did not. It is important to remember, however, that the Church is both human and divine. This means that, even when there are bad decisions, weak leaders, or evil events in the Church, we can trust the Holy Spirit to lead us so that God's saving plan can be carried out. We know this because Jesus promised the Spirit and his presence in the Church and in our lives too. We can have faith so unshakable that no matter what happens, the Holy Spirit is with us. As we try to follow Jesus, we can pray to the Spirit to guide and strengthen us and the Church every day.

> **Locate the following passages in the Bible and briefly summarize what Jesus promises.**
>
> Matthew 28:20
>
> _____
>
> _____
>
> Matthew 16:18
>
> _____
>
> _____
>
> John 14:16
>
> _____
>
> _____
>
> John 14:26
>
> _____
>
> _____

Too Many Popes

The Church had many problems in the 14th century. A Frenchman who was elected pope moved to Avignon, France. There he and his six successors were under the rule of the French king for 70 years. This caused many problems for people and rulers of other countries. They knew that the Catholic Church was meant to be universal and not tied to one people, one country, or one time. Through the guidance of the Holy Spirit, leaders in Italy and the people of the Church turned to Saint Catherine of Siena for help. Catherine was a young woman whose holiness and charity were well known. She wrote many letters and visited the pope in Avignon, urging him to return to Rome. Finally she was able to persuade him to return to Rome in 1378.

The problems, however, were not over. The next pope insulted the French cardinals. They declared his election invalid and elected their own pope in France. As a result, there were two men claiming to be pope: one in Rome and one in France! Christians were confused. Nations took sides, and Church leadership was in a state of confusion. For a short time, there were even three men claiming to be pope. This internal division in the Church is called the Great Western Schism. It took 39 years before a Church council restored the authority of the true pope.

To this day, Vatican City is an independent sovereign nation, the smallest in the world. This prevents any country from claiming ownership or authority over the papacy. Rather, the pope alone enjoys full authority in the care of souls. Because of Vatican City's independence, the Church can be truly catholic, sent out to all peoples.

The Black Death

Another crisis emerged during the 14th century: an epidemic called the Black Plague, or the Black Death. The disease caused swollen glands and brought death within a few hours. At least a third of Europe's population died in this plague, which raged for 50 years. Priests, sisters, and others treated with dignity those who were sick, bringing them food and clothing and burying those who died from the disease. Many of the stricken people were comforted by the thought that Jesus had suffered too. Because of the extreme suffering that people endured during this time, their thoughts and prayers turned to the passion and Death of Jesus, the sorrows of Mary, his mother, and the concepts of death and judgment.

Anointing of the Sick

Sickness and suffering have always been a part of the human condition. In the face of serious illness, people come face to face with their own powerlessness and limitations. Some people experience great sadness, anxiety, and a loss of dignity as a result of serious illness. During these times, many people's thoughts and prayers turn to God. The Gospels provide many stories of Jesus demonstrating his compassion to those who were sick and in need of healing.

Through the Sacrament of the Anointing of the Sick, Jesus continues to reach out to those who are seriously ill. Through this sacrament, those who are suffering from serious illness receive a special grace. Using the Oil of the Sick, blessed by a bishop, a priest may anoint the sick person on the forehead and the palms of the hands. Through the Sacrament of the Anointing of the Sick, those who are sick unite their own suffering to the suffering of Jesus. They are strengthened and given courage, peace, and dignity to endure their suffering in a Christian manner. The person also experiences spiritual healing and, in some circumstances, physical healing.

The Vatican, Rome.

A New Age

By the 16th century, a new challenge faced the Church. This challenge came from a new way of thinking and living called the Renaissance, or "rebirth." Some people began to emphasize human achievement rather than the divine presence in the world. Although there was renewed interest in the classical culture of ancient Greece and Rome, there was less interest in religion. New ideas spread quickly because of the recently invented printing press, and people began to ask questions about their faith and about the role of the Church. At the same time, new nation-states emerged. Some of the kings of these nation-states wanted to take away the power that the Church inherited when the Roman Empire and its system of government collapsed.

Because of their positions of authority in society, many bishops lived the lifestyle of Renaissance princes. As a result, they often neglected their spiritual duties or performed them badly, taking advantage of people they were responsible for serving, namely those who were poor and vulnerable. In response, people began to challenge not only the lifestyles of the Church leaders but also the teachings of the Church.

A Call for Change

In the early 16th century, a serious public challenge to the Church came from a priest named Martin Luther. He was a professor of theology and Scripture in Wittenberg, Germany. As a young monk, Luther wondered what he needed to do to earn salvation. He concluded that salvation cannot be earned and that faith alone saves us.

While the Church teaches that faith is necessary for salvation, it also teaches that faith cannot be separated from good works. At the time Martin Luther stressed the importance of faith, the Church stressed the importance of good works. Some people even thought that their good works, especially donations to the Church, would "buy" heaven for them and their loved ones. Some Church leaders took advantage of this way of thinking and began selling **indulgences**—the remission of temporal punishment due to sins

Martin Luther posting his 95 objections on the Castle Church door.

that have been forgiven—to gain riches for themselves and the Church.

Disturbed by abuses in the Church, Luther posted a list of 95 objections on the door of the Castle Church in Wittenberg, Germany, in 1517. Unfortunately some of Luther's ideas departed from Church teachings in significant ways. The Church teaches that God speaks through Scripture and Tradition, but Luther believed that Scripture alone should guide us. He accepted only those sacraments found directly in Scripture: Baptism and the Eucharist. He did not accept the teaching authority of the Church, the priesthood, religious life, or acts of penance.

The pope forbade Luther to preach and write about his objections. Because Luther continued his protest, the pope excommunicated him. Martin Luther gathered followers who sought to correct the abuses in the Church. Princes and other nobles backed Luther for political reasons. Eventually, although Luther still considered himself Catholic, the Lutheran Church was formed. Its creed, the Augsburg Confession, was written in 1531.

Division in the Catholic Church spread rapidly, and large communities became separated from full communion with the Catholic Church. The appearance of these separate Christian communities is called the **Protestant Reformation.**

Progress Toward Reconciliation

Although the Catholic Church and the Lutheran Churches remain separated today, much progress has taken place toward reconciliation. In 1999, the Catholic Church and the Lutheran World Federation signed a Joint Declaration on the Doctrine of Justification. This document expressed that both Lutherans and Catholics accept the notion that we are saved—justified—by God's grace through faith in Jesus Christ and, as a result, are called to do good works.

Your Advice

Write an e-mail to today's leaders of the Catholic Church and the Lutheran World Federation. Advise them on how to build unity among Christians.

To: _____

Subject: _____

_____

_____

_____

_____

_____

A Friend Turned Foe

At the beginning of the 16th century, England was loyal to the pope. King Henry VIII had even received the title Defender of the Faith from the pope for his writings in support of the Church against Luther. But then the king's wife was unable to bear him a son to inherit his throne. He asked the pope to grant him an **annulment**—declare his marriage invalid—so that he could marry another woman, Anne Boleyn. When the pope refused his request, Henry declared that the Church in England was to be under him rather than the pope. Anyone who did not take an oath acknowledging him as head of the Church was put to death.

King Henry VIII's Church of England, the Anglican Church, is now organized in over 40 countries. In some of those countries, such as the United States, it is known as the Episcopal Church.

Remember

What are some of the challenges the Church faced during the 16th century?

The Church faced the Great Western Schism, the Black Death, the Renaissance, Martin Luther's protest, the Protestant Reformation, and the challenge of England's King Henry VIII.

How does the Holy Spirit guide the Church?

The Holy Spirit makes all things work for the good of the Church so God's saving plan can be carried out.

What is Christ's promise to the Church?

Jesus said, "And behold, I am with you always, until the end of the age." (Matthew 28:20)

Words to Know

annulment
indulgence
Protestant Reformation

Respond

We sometimes think that we have to do something in order to earn salvation. Although it is wonderful to know that salvation is offered to us as a gift and that all we need is faith in Jesus, that does not mean we do not have to "do" anything. Accepting salvation through Jesus causes us to change our lives. In your reflection notebook, write how you feel about how your life will change as a result of accepting Jesus' invitation.

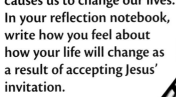

Reach Out

1. Use the Internet or a library to research Vatican City. Find pictures and statistics about Vatican City that you can share with your class.

2. Talk to your parents or guardians about important decisions they have made in their lives. Ask them to tell you about decisions that have turned out well and others that have not turned out well.

3. Find statistics about different Christian denominations today. Share these with your class.

4. St. Peter's Basilica and the Vatican have been the center of Christianity for years. At the base of the dome of St. Peter's is Matthew 16:18. Find out what this text is and why it is used. Then find a Scripture text for your parish church. Write an essay explaining why it fits your parish.

5. Ask your parents or guardians about relatives or friends who are Protestant. Find out which Christian denominations they belong to and gather information about those denominations.

6. The Black Death killed nearly a third of Europe's population. Today, AIDS is killing millions of people in Africa. Visit the Web site of Catholic Relief Services (www.crs.org) and find out how you can stand in solidarity with your brothers and sisters in Africa.

7. Ask your older relatives if they have ever received the Sacrament of the Anointing of the Sick or were present when someone else was anointed. Ask them to describe what they saw and felt.

Trying Times **Complete the sentences with key words from the chapter.**

1. In the 14th century, the pope moved from Rome to Avignon in _____ .

2. At the worst of the Great Western Schism, _____ men claimed to be pope.

3. A third of Europe's population died in the _____ Death epidemic.

4. Renaissance people were more interested in the _____ than in the divine.

5. _____ , a German priest, protested certain Church practices.

6. Luther stressed that _____ alone saves us.

7. The beginning of new Christian churches in the 16th century is called the _____ Reformation.

8. Some Church leaders abused their position and began to sell _____ to people who thought they could "buy their way into heaven."

9. The Church of England was begun by _____ .

10. The Anglican Church is known in the United States as the _____ Church.

Struggles and Strides **Write + if the statement is true and – if it is false.**

_____ 1. A woman was responsible for persuading the pope to return to Rome from Avignon.

_____ 2. During the plague, people thought more about the passion of Jesus and Judgment Day.

_____ 3. Kings of new nation-states did not want to have anything to do with the Church.

_____ 4. There was no reason for Martin Luther to post objections against the Church.

_____ 5. Catholics and Lutherans have made progress in working toward reconciliation.

Bringing Words to Life **Use the Glossary to look up the definitions for the Words to Know in this chapter: annulment, indulgences, Protestant Reformation. Then use each of the words in a sentence.**

1. _____

_____

2. _____

_____

3. _____

_____

Gather and Go Forth

Know and Proclaim

Knowing the truths of our Catholic faith helps us proclaim the Good News of Jesus Christ while respecting other faith traditions.

We Know Our Faith	We Proclaim Our Faith
The Holy Spirit gives the Church the strength to overcome the sorrows caused by divisions that exist in Christianity.	Some Catholics participate in Taizé prayer, a form of ecumenical prayer designed to foster peace and reconciliation among all people.
Through the Sacrament of the Anointing of the Sick, Jesus continues to reach out to people who are sick.	All Catholics are responsible for the care of those who are sick. Many Catholics do this by volunteering at hospitals.
Christians are united by their common baptism in Christ.	Catholics recognize any Christian baptism as long as it is performed only once by an authorized minister. The baptism must use flowing water and the Scriptural Trinitarian formula of Father, Son, and Holy Spirit.

The Holy Spirit is continually at work in the Church to guide the community of disciples, even in the face of great challenges. As Catholics, we trust that the Holy Spirit is always renewing the Church.

"The Advocate, the holy Spirit that the Father will send in my name – he will teach you everything and remind you of all that [I] told you."

John 14:26

Test Your Catholic Knowledge

Fill in the circle that best answers the question.

What was the Protestant Reformation?

○ the claims of two men as pope in the 14th century

○ the organization of the Church of England under King Henry VIII

○ the separation of large Christian communities from full communion with the Catholic Church

○ the emphasis of human achievement rather than the divine presence of God in the world

A Catholic to Know

Ignatius, a soldier in the army of the Spanish king during the early 1500s, never thought much about his faith. While he was recovering from an injury he suffered in battle that had shattered one leg and broken the other, Ignatius read about the lives of the saints. This began his conversion. After much reflection, including mystical visions, Ignatius wrote his Spiritual Exercises as a guide to Christian living. With six other men, Ignatius founded a religious order—the Company of Jesus—dedicated to serving the pope, social justice, and teaching. Today, the Company is known as the Society of Jesus, or the Jesuits.

Saint Ignatius of Loyola

Witness and Share

These sentences describe what Catholics believe. Listen carefully as they are read. Ask yourself, "How strong are my Catholic beliefs?"

My Way to Faith

- I pray for Christian unity.

- I pray for people who are sick.

- I respectfully encourage other Catholics who are seriously ill to celebrate the Sacrament of the Anointing of the Sick.

- I see Protestants as my brothers and sisters in Christ.

- I rely on the Holy Spirit to help me make difficult decisions.

- I believe that God has given me the gift of salvation freely and that I have done nothing to earn it.

Share Your Faith

Consider ways in which you can share the light of Jesus with someone who is sick or injured. Write your ideas on the lines. Invite a friend or classmate to join you in brightening someone's day.

_____

_____

_____

_____

A fresco painting of the Council of Trent, Vatican, Rome, 1512.

Reforming the Church

Jenny and Alicia had been friends since kindergarten. They enjoyed each other's company and could always count on each other. That is why their recent disagreement was so difficult for both of them. Jenny felt hurt that Alicia had gone out with some other friends without inviting her to go along. Alicia tried to explain that circumstances prevented her from calling. For a whole week, they did not speak to each other. Finally Alicia cornered Jenny and said, "Look, this whole thing was a misunderstanding. Can we just sit down and talk it out? Let's start over again." Jenny agreed and the two sat down to talk things over. In the end, Jenny came to see that it was all a misunderstanding. They agreed to some new rules for their friendship so that they would have better communication. Their friendship started over again, stronger than before.

Describe an experience in which you were able to start over at something.

_____

_____

Catholic Reformation

The Catholic Church experienced many challenges during the first part of the 16th century. The Church was able to respond to these challenges because the Holy Spirit is always building the Church, giving it life, and making it holy. Through the tragic events of this age, the Holy Spirit helped Church leaders see the need for reform—a way of "starting over." It was time for the Church to come to a deeper understanding of herself. The Council of Trent (1545–1563) finally brought reform.

Guided by the Holy Spirit, the bishops of the Church met in Trent—present-day northern Italy—to reexamine Catholic beliefs and traditions and identify ways of more effectively speaking about them. The doctrines and decrees of the Council stressed the Church's belief in the seven sacraments. They taught that the Mass is Christ's saving work extended through all time. The bishops also confirmed which books Catholics recognize as belonging in the Bible.

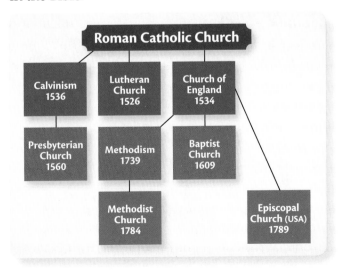

Roman Catholic Church

- Calvinism 1536
  - Presbyterian Church 1560
- Lutheran Church 1526
  - Methodism 1739
    - Methodist Church 1784
- Church of England 1534
  - Baptist Church 1609
  - Episcopal Church (USA) 1789

The Council of Trent: A Closer Look

The Catholic Church responded to the challenges of Luther and others at the Council of Trent. The bishops who met at the Council defended the Mass and the Eucharist as well as the rest of the seven sacraments. They emphasized that the sacraments are signs, instituted by Jesus and given to the Church, through which we receive grace.

The bishops also took steps to end abuses that had crept into the Church's practices, defended the ordained priesthood, and established seminaries for the proper training of priests. They preserved the Catholic understanding of the Scriptures but said that the Bible must be read within the context of the traditions of the living Church. In other words, they taught that Sacred Scripture and Sacred Tradition are not separate but are part of one single source of God's Word.

The Council of Trent was a strong response that inspired the renewal of Catholic life and the founding of new communities such as the Oratorians and the Jesuits. Renewed in their faith, Catholics addressed the issues raised by the Protestants. Through their efforts, two-thirds of the Christians in Europe remained Catholic. The teachings of the Council of Trent formed the Church into the 20th century.

A Teacher

Saint Charles Borromeo played a major role in the Council of Trent. After the Council was over, he made sure that its work would not be lost. Charles worked tirelessly to see that the liturgy was restored and that those who were poor and sick were cared for. Under his guidance, a catechism based on the Council was completed, and parish priests were made responsible for the Catholic education of the young. He established seminaries in his diocese so that priests would be educated for their ministry. The catechism that Charles directed was the official catechism until 1992, when the *Catechism of the Catholic Church* was published.

Four Pillars

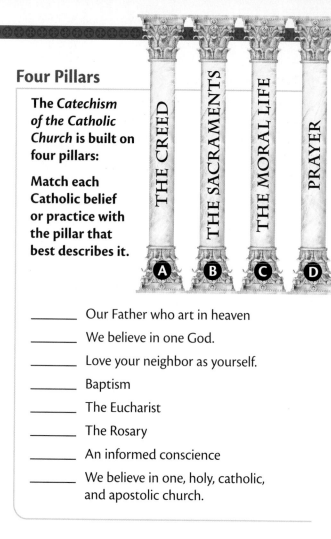

The *Catechism of the Catholic Church* is built on four pillars:

Match each Catholic belief or practice with the pillar that best describes it.

A THE CREED **B** THE SACRAMENTS **C** THE MORAL LIFE **D** PRAYER

_____ Our Father who art in heaven

_____ We believe in one God.

_____ Love your neighbor as yourself.

_____ Baptism

_____ The Eucharist

_____ The Rosary

_____ An informed conscience

_____ We believe in one, holy, catholic, and apostolic church.

A Mystic

Saint Teresa of Jesus was from Ávila, Spain. At age 20, she became a Carmelite sister. Sisters in her time (the 16th century) said their prayers but often spent much of their days on matters unrelated to spirituality or religion. After several years, Teresa decided to change her life and reform her community. She knew that serving God meant prayer, commitment, sacrifice, and courage.

Teresa devoted her entire life to prayer and penance for Christ and the Church. Because she was granted an experience of direct union with God, she is called a mystic. Through her life and her writings on Christian life and prayer, many people became better followers of Jesus. In 1970 Saint Teresa of Ávila and Saint Catherine of Siena both received the title Doctor of the Church.

Who have you known to have the qualities of a spiritual teacher or mystic? Briefly explain how this person has influenced your life.

_____

_____

Martyrs for Truth

Saint Thomas More, a Catholic layman, and Saint John Fisher, a bishop, defended the truths of the faith in England. A brilliant lawyer, Thomas was chancellor of England under King Henry VIII. Henry favored Thomas until Henry's conflict with the Church over his marriage. Bishop Fisher had once been Young Prince Henry's tutor. He had written eight books against heresy.

Thomas More and Bishop John Fisher refused to acknowledge Henry as head of the Church in England. They would not go against their consciences, even though all the bishops other than John Fisher decided to obey the king. Thomas and Bishop John Fisher remained loyal to the pope and trusted in the Lord, who promised his disciples that "I myself shall give you a wisdom in speaking that all your adversaries will be powerless to resist or refute." (Luke 21:15) Both men were imprisoned in the Tower of London for more than a year and then beheaded. Thomas told his executioner, "Don't be afraid for you send me to God." Then he said to the crowd, "I die the king's good servant, but God's first."

World Missionaries

Saint Ignatius of Loyola was a proud and adventurous soldier in Spain. After receiving a leg wound in battle, Ignatius was forced to spend long months recovering. During this time, he read about the life of Christ and the lives of the saints. As a result, his whole attitude toward life was changed, and he decided to become a soldier for Christ. When he recovered, he founded a new order of priests called the Society of Jesus, or the Jesuits. Ignatius wanted his order to do any work

Hans Holbein the Younger, *Sir Thomas More.*

or go anywhere in the world to serve the Church. That is why he placed his men at the service of the pope. The Jesuits taught, wrote, and advised kings and popes. Recognizing that all people are God's children, they went forth on missions to the farthest corners of the earth, just as Jesus had commanded, "Go, therefore, and make disciples of all nations." (Matthew 28:19)

Saint Francis Xavier was a Jesuit missionary who carried the Gospel to India and Japan. Another Jesuit, Saint Peter Claver, brought relief to Africans who were enslaved while living in South America. He knew that the moral law forbids the enslavement of human beings. So whenever a boat carrying enslaved people came into port at Cartagena in South America, Peter Claver would rush to the ship with medicine, fruit, vegetables, and clothing. Recognizing the dignity in all human beings, he would nurse the people to health and then teach them about Christ.

But the Jesuits were not alone in spreading the Good News of Jesus. By the 17th century, other priests such as the Franciscans also set out to the New World to evangelize. These missionaries built hospitals and churches, set up schools, and opened homes for those who were poor and aged. Through them, the Church reached out to teach all nations. The Holy Spirit guides the Church's missionary activity, which is driven by God's love for all people and his desire that all may find salvation in Jesus.

As if Talking to a Friend

The Holy Spirit teaches us how to pray. Guided by the Holy Spirit, Saint Ignatius of Loyola taught his followers a special way to raise their hearts and minds to God in prayer. He emphasized that, when talking to God, we can talk to him as if we were talking to a friend. Ignatius developed a simple form of **meditation** by which we can reflect on each day in a way that will help us recognize God's presence in our lives. This practice is often called the Daily Examen. Many people practice the Daily Examen before going to bed at night by following these simple steps.

Stillness: Recalling God's Presence
Relax in God's presence in your favorite prayer place and posture. Ask the Holy Spirit to help you to look honestly at your actions this day.

Gratitude: Expressing Thankfulness
Look over your day and give thanks to God for his gifts.

Reflection: Looking Back on Your Day
Review the events of the day and ask yourself when you were conscious of God's presence. Think about how you might change your actions in the future.

Sorrow: Asking for Forgiveness
Express sorrow for the times you failed to follow God's direction and ask him to be with you the next time you encounter a similar situation.

Hopefulness: Resolving to Grow
Ask God to help you as you look forward to a new day tomorrow. Resolve to cooperate and trust in God's loving guidance. Conclude with the Our Father, which comes to us from Jesus and is one of the most important prayers of the Church.

A Moment with Jesus

By practicing the Daily Examen, you will begin to recognize God's presence in your daily life.

Take a moment to review your day with Jesus by following the steps outlined above.

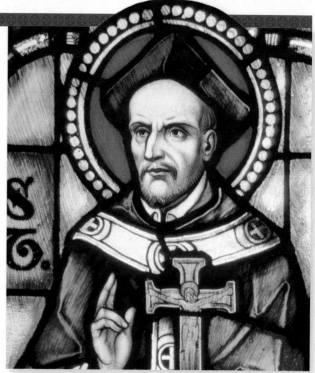

Saint Ignatius of Loyola.

It's Your Turn!

Write your responses to the following:

1. Why do you think a person could change his or her attitude toward life after reading about the lives of the saints?

   _____

   _____

   _____

   _____

2. Name two ways a person your age could serve others unselfishly at home or at school.

   _____

   _____

   _____

   _____

3. Name two things a person your age could do to help those in need.

   _____

   _____

   _____

   _____

Remember

What was the purpose of the Council of Trent?
> The Catholic Church responded to the challenges of Luther and others at the Council of Trent.

Name some of the who helped the reforms of the Council of Trent to take place.
> Saint Charles Borromeo, Saint Teresa of Ávila, Saint Thomas More, and Saint John Fisher

Name three Jesuit missionaries who carried the Gospel to the farthest corners of the earth.
> Saint Ignatius of Loyola, Saint Francis Xavier, and Saint Peter Claver

Words to Know
meditation

Respond

Many people who are serious about their spiritual lives set aside time each day to practice the Daily Examen. Practice the Daily Examen on your own, following the steps outlined on page 152. Afterward, write in your reflection notebook your thoughts about the experience.

Reach Out

1. The *Catechism of the Catholic Church* is available online. Visit the Web site and locate the four sections ("pillars") of the *Catechism*: the Creed (The Profession of Faith), the sacraments (The Celebration of the Christian Mystery), the moral life (Life in Christ), and prayer (Christian Prayer).

2. Go through family photo albums to identify photographs related to celebrations of any of the seven sacraments of the Church.

3. Rent or borrow the DVD *A Man For All Seasons* (1966), which tells the story of Saint Thomas More. Watch it together as a family.

4. The missionary spirit of the Jesuits lives on today. One of the ways that laypeople can participate in missionary efforts of the Jesuits is through the Jesuit Volunteer Corps (JVC). Visit the JVC Web site to gather information about the JVC and then report to your class.

5. Tell your parents or guardians about the Daily Examen that you learned. (See page 152.) Tell them when and where you plan to practice the Daily Examen so that they are aware of your need for private time. Encourage your parents or guardians and other family members to practice the Daily Examen.

6. Explore the lives of several of the saints included in this chapter. Prepare a report for your class.

Facts of Our Faith   Supply the missing words.

1. The Council of _____ reformed the Catholic Church.

2. Saint Ignatius of Loyola founded the _____, many of whom became great missionaries.

3. Saint Teresa of Ávila is called a _____, because she had an experience of direct union with God.

4. Saint Teresa of Ávila is also called a _____, because she excelled in guiding the Church.

5. Saint Ignatius developed a simple form of daily meditation called the _____ .

Important Events   Write *T* if the statement is true or *F* if it is false.

_____   **1.** The Council of Trent brought reform to the Catholic Church.

_____   **2.** Saint Charles Borromeo played a major role in the Council of Trent.

_____   **3.** The *Catechism of the Catholic Church* published in 1992 was the first catechism ever published by the Church.

_____   **4.** Saint Francis Xavier founded the Jesuits.

_____   **5.** Saint Teresa of Ávila reformed the Carmelites.

Saint Charles Borromeo.

Saints of Centuries Past   Draw a line to match the saint with his or her witness for the Church.

Peter Claver •	• Was a Jesuit missionary to the Far East and Asia
Catherine of Siena •	• Founded the Society of Jesus
Teresa of Ávila •	• Advised the pope and helped bring him back to Rome
Ignatius of Loyola •	• Was a mystic and wrote books on prayer
Thomas More •	• Brought physical and spiritual relief to enslaved Africans
Charles Borromeo •	• Was beheaded for his loyalty to the Church
Francis Xavier •	• Worked to put into effect the decisions of the Council of Trent

Council Quiz   Underline the correct answer for each statement about the Council of Trent.

1. The Church responded to his challenges.

Saint Charles Borromeo   **Martin Luther**   **Saint Thomas More**

2. Thomas More and this person refused to acknowledge King Henry as head of the Church in England.

Saint John Fisher   **Saint Francis Xavier**   **Saint Catherine of Siena**

3. The Council of Trent inspired the founding of this community.

Dominicans   **Franciscans**   **Jesuits**

4. The bishops defended the Mass and these.

devotions   **sacraments**   **rituals**

Gather and Go Forth

Know and Proclaim

Guided by the Holy Spirit, we proclaim the truths of the Catholic Church throughout the world.

We Know Our Faith	We Proclaim Our Faith
The Catholic Church responded to the challenges of the 16th century at the Council of Trent.	The *Catechism of the Catholic Church* includes many of the teachings from the Council of Trent. Catholics rely on the *Catechism* to help them better understand and articulate their faith.
The Council of Trent taught that Sacred Scripture and Sacred Tradition are not separate but part of one single source of God's Word.	Many Catholics study the documents of the Council of Trent, the Second Vatican Council, and papal encyclicals to better understand Sacred Tradition.
Many saints helped strengthen the Church by their example following the Protestant Reformation.	Many Catholics strengthen their faith by praying the Daily Examen, a meditation developed by Saint Ignatius of Loyola, who founded the Jesuits in the 16th century.

The Holy Spirit remains with the Church. Throughout history, the Church has relied on the Holy Spirit to guide holy men and women to renew the Church and one another in Christ.

Yes, brother, may I profit from you in the Lord. Refresh my heart in Christ.

Philemon 20

Test Your Catholic Knowledge

Fill in the circle that best completes the sentence.

The Council of Trent responded to the challenges presented by the:

○ conflict between King Henry VIII and the pope.

○ corruption within the Carmelite order.

○ Protestant Reformation.

○ Age of Enlightenment.

A Catholic to Know

John of the Cross entered the Carmelite order in 1563 at the age of 21. He had a special spiritual affection for Saint Teresa of Avila, the leader of the Carmelite reform movement during the Spanish Inquisition. As Teresa attempted to return her order to its original mission, John initiated reform in his community. The brothers in his community objected, removed John from his leadership position, and had him imprisoned. Even in the darkness of a small cell, John kept himself open to God's action. In confinement and in pain, John wrote his theology about suffering as a path for unity with Christ. Ignored during his lifetime, Saint John of the Cross is remembered as a saint for all times. His feast day is December 14.

Saint John of the Cross

Witness and Share

These sentences describe what Catholics believe. Listen carefully as they are read. Ask yourself, "How strong are my Catholic beliefs?"

My Way to Faith

- I refer to the *Catechism of the Catholic Church* in order to better understand my faith.

- I recognize God's Word in the Sacred Tradition of the Church.

- I spend time prayerfully reviewing my day.

- I support the missionary efforts of the Church.

- I celebrate the Sacrament of Reconciliation to help me reform myself.

Share Your Faith

Consider things you can do to renew and refresh your relationship with Jesus. Write your ideas on the lines, and choose to make one or more a priority beginning today. Invite a friend or family member to discuss your plan with you.

_____

_____

_____

_____

17

Galileo demonstrating his telescope.

In a Changing World

Did you know that, of all the billions of people on the earth, no two have the same fingerprints? Not even identical twins!

Take a close look at your own fingerprints and notice their complexity. On a separate sheet of paper, use a number 2 pencil to shade an area about an inch high and two inches wide. Rub a finger across the area. Tear off a one-inch strip of clear tape and place it on a table, sticky side up. Press your graphite-covered finger on the sticky side of the tape and press it down, gently rolling your finger back and forth, making sure you get your whole fingerprint on the tape. Remove the piece of tape from your finger and place it in the magnifying glass below.

Look at the complexity of your fingerprint. Notice the lines, loops, and arches that swirl in different directions. Think of how amazing it is that God pays attention to such minute details of our lives.

A Moment with Jesus

You are truly a unique person—one of a kind! Take a moment to thank Jesus for the gift of your uniqueness. Ask him to help you use your gifts and talents to serve others. Pray the words of Psalm 139, thanking God for making you unique.

You formed my inmost being;
    you knit me in my mother's womb.
I praise you, so wonderfully you made me;
    wonderful are your works!
My very self you knew;
    my bones were not hidden from you,
When I was being made in secret,
    fashioned as in the depths of the earth.
Your eyes foresaw my actions;
    in your book all are written down;
    my days were shaped, before one came to be.
How precious to me are your designs,
    O God;
    how vast the sum of them!

Psalm 139:13–17

New Ways of Thinking

In the 16th century, many people experienced shock and confusion over the discoveries of scientists such as Copernicus and Galileo. These men pointed out that the earth was not the center of the universe but that the planets revolved around the sun. This not only changed the way astronomers looked at the skies, but, for many people, it called God's role into question. Before these discoveries, most people believed that the earth was the center of the universe and God was making everything revolve around the earth. When science began to show that the planets were revolving around the sun and that gravity was causing this rotation, some people began to think that God's role in the universe was limited.

As time went on and scientific discoveries began to explain things that had been attributed solely to God's power, it began to seem as though God's role in the world was continuing to diminish. This period, the 1700s, became known as the Age of Enlightenment because of the many new ideas coming from the scientific revolution. During this time, it was suggested by some that God was not very involved in the world. Instead it was proposed that God created the universe and then sat back as it ran itself. As a result, many people began to see God as very distant. Jesus had shown us, however, that God is near to all people, especially those who need him most. As Catholics, we understand that the words "Our Father, who art in heaven" do not describe God as being in some distant place. Rather, they describe God's amazing presence in the hearts of those who live according to his law of love.

Serving Those in Need

Through his words and actions, Jesus was always near to those who were poor and in need. He taught us that by serving others, we help them to recognize that God is near to them.

During the 17th century, French leaders of the Church and the state lived in palaces and enjoyed great wealth. They were distant from the vast majority of people, who were peasant farmers and townsfolk who had to pay high taxes to support their leaders' lifestyles. Saint Vincent de Paul (1576–1660) did not imitate these leaders. Instead he gave an outstanding example of what it means to serve others with the mind and the spirit of Jesus.

Vincent was a talented young priest who lived a comfortable life in Paris, France, carrying out various religious duties for wealthy people. For a while, his life was somewhat shallow. Then, under the inspiration and influence of a holy priest named Peter de Bérulle, Vincent understood more deeply what it meant to be a Christian. He came face to face with his empty goals.

As Vincent became aware of God's love and his call to serve, he changed his life. He worked for a year in a small peasant parish. There he learned the meaning of poverty. Vincent realized that detachment from material goods is necessary in order to truly love God and others. He met people who sometimes had nothing to eat and who could not get hospital care when they were sick. He also witnessed a poverty of the spirit: people who had no understanding of their faith.

A practical man of enormous energy and love, Vincent decided to take action. He made the love of God real and visible to hundreds of suffering people. First, he organized charitable groups to provide food and clothing for those who were poor. At night, he searched the city for abandoned babies and found homes for them. He cared for people who had been made galley slaves on boats.

Vincent remained friends with many rich and influential people and involved them in his work with those in need. He wanted to be sure that the goods of God's creation were shared by all and not just by a few. He organized priests and sent them out to the peasant villages to preach to the people. Eventually this group of priests became the Congregation of the Mission. They are also known as the Vincentian Fathers.

Hospitals at this time were dirty and overcrowded. With the help of Louise de Marillac, Vincent founded the Daughters of Charity, sisters who cared especially for those who were sick and poor. Through their ministry, they taught that all human life is sacred and that all people must be treated with dignity.

Vincent believed it was a privilege to help those who were poor. He also recognized that those who lead have the responsibility to work for the common good of all. Because he loved every person as Christ, Vincent could inspire others to see Christ in those who were poor.

Saint Vincent de Paul.

Because of Vincent's faith, others came to recognize the dignity of each person and to see each person as God's child. They saw that Vincent did not limit his love. Those who were sick, aged, orphaned, mentally ill, imprisoned, or enslaved—all people found a friend in Vincent. Jesus was near to those who needed him most. Vincent de Paul followed Jesus' example.

Being of Service to Others

Vincent de Paul's life is a challenge to you! You are called to be of service to others, especially those who are most in need. By doing so, you help others to recognize that God is near to them.

> **Read Matthew 25:35–37. Then, in the story of Vincent's life on page 158, underline how he put into action what you read in Matthew.**
> **Now list three ways you have put into practice these teachings of Jesus.**
>
> 1. _____
>
> 2. _____
>
> 3. _____

Earthshaking Ideas

In the 18th century, the world was changing rapidly. New scientific discoveries and methods made people question old ways of thinking. Some people believed science had an answer for everything. They worshiped the human mind and thought that there was no need for faith or God. The lower and middle classes looked for more say in government and a greater share of the wealth. The time was ripe for change, and the French Revolution erupted in 1789.

The French Revolution attacked not only the existing government but also the Church, which supported the government. Monasteries, churches, and mansions were burned. Both rich and poor priests and religious went to the guillotine along with wealthy men and women of the ruling class. A state religion was introduced to replace the Catholic faith.

Fighting at the Hotel de Ville.

Finding Christ in the Poor

Saint Julie Billiart was a remarkable woman who founded a community dedicated to teaching children who were poor. As a young girl, Julie was present when someone shot at her father through a window. Although no one was struck by the bullet, the shock of the event affected her nervous system. For the next 20 years, she was paralyzed. Sometimes she could not even speak. This did not stop her from teaching about God. Julie recognized that all the baptized share in Christ's prophetic ministry and are called to be witnesses to Christ even in difficult situations.

After the revolution, the new government abused its authority by not allowing Catholics to practice their faith openly. Yet Julie gathered children to her bedside and taught about the goodness of God. She helped people get to Mass. One night an anti-Catholic mob gathered around the house where Julie was staying and demanded that she be burned alive. Friends hid her in a cart loaded with straw, and she escaped.

Women came to Julie for spiritual advice while she was in hiding. With them, she began the Sisters of Notre Dame. She opened schools and trained Christian teachers. After being miraculously cured of her paralysis at age 57, Julie Billiart did even more to teach the goodness of God.

The Second Vatican Council in St. Peter's Basilica.

The First Vatican Council

In the 1700s, many people began to think that we could solve all of humanity's issues by examining them scientifically. These people are called rationalists, and their philosophy is known as **rationalism.** Some people went as far as to reject or deny the existence of God. This way of thinking, called atheism, is a violation of the First Commandment.

At first, the Church saw these scientific developments as a threat. In 1864 Pope Pius IX issued a Syllabus of Errors condemning rationalism and other forms of modern thinking. In 1868 Pope Pius IX convened the 20th ecumenical council of the Church, now referred to as the First Vatican Council. More than 800 Church leaders attended the council at St. Peter's Basilica in Vatican City.

The pope called the Council to get confirmation of his Syllabus of Errors and to formulate a definition of the Church and its role in the rapidly changing world. At the time, many questions existed around the relationship between the Church and the state, or individual nations. Some people believed that the Church had no business interfering in government matters. Others felt that the pope had authority over kings and other state leaders. Those who supported the authority of the pope won out when the Council approved the doctrine of papal infallibility. The doctrine

states that when the pope solemnly and officially proclaims a teaching on faith or morals, that teaching is without error. At the time, however, the relationship of the bishops to the pope was not yet defined.

The Council was interrupted in 1870 by the Franco-Prussian War between France and Prussia. Since France was embroiled in war and no longer able to offer protection for the pope, the Italian states invaded Rome. The Council was suspended and never resumed. Finally in 1962, when Pope John XXIII convened the Second Vatican Council, a definition was established for the role of the Church in the world and the relationship between the bishops and the pope.

Although the Church was initially suspicious of scientific developments, it eventually learned that both faith and science come from God and that we do not have to choose one over the other. For Catholics, believing in science does not make God distant.

Legitimate Authority

The Fourth Commandment, *Honor your father and mother,* also calls us to respect legitimate authority. In a similar way, all communities need people in authority so that they might grow and develop. Those in authority are responsible for protecting the fundamental rights of all people. They use their authority legitimately when they are committed to the common good of all. As citizens, we are responsible for working with those in authority to build a society that is just and truthful and that provides all people with everything they need for human decency. At the same time, it is our obligation as followers of Jesus not to follow the orders of civil authorities when they are contrary to the Gospel.

Remember

What caused shock and confusion for many people in the 16th century?

The discoveries of scientists who pointed out that the earth was not the center of the universe and that the planets revolved around the sun caused shock and confusion. This not only changed the way astronomers looked at the skies, but, for many people, it called God's role into question.

How did Saint Vincent de Paul and Saint Julie Billiart help others to know that God is near to them?

Saint Vincent de Paul organized charitable groups to provide food and clothing for those in need. He also organized priests and sent them out to the peasant villages to preach to the people. He formed the Congregation of the Mission, also known as the Vincentian Fathers. Saint Julie Billiart formed a religious community, the Sisters of Notre Dame, dedicated to teaching children who were poor. She established schools and prepared teachers to staff them.

In the 17th century, how did the Church react to some of the discoveries of modern science?

At first, the Church saw these scientific developments as threats. Pope Pius IX issued a Syllabus of Errors condemning various aspects of modern thinking, and he convened the First Vatican Council to confirm the Syllabus.

Word to Know

rationalism

Respond

The principal end of our institute is the education of the poor. If we ever cease to help the poor, we shall no longer be fulfilling the work entrusted to us.

Saint Julie Billiart

In your reflection notebook, write about times when you served or remembered those who are poor and times when you did not. Then write down something that will help you remember to think of people who are poor.

Reach Out

1. Try to gain access to a microscope and examine a leaf under it. Look at all its complexity and realize how amazing it is that God pays attention to such detail. Or, if you have access to a telescope, look at the night sky on a clear night and praise God for the complexity of the universe and for his care of creation.

2. Out of gratitude for God's creation, work together as a family to protect creation and its many resources. Talk to your parents or guardians and family members about a way your family can make an effort to care for the environment.

3. Ask your parents or guardians to describe the ways you are different from your siblings and what makes you unique. If you are an only child, ask them to describe how you are different from them.

4. Research the lives of Copernicus and Galileo. Note how difficult it was for them to convince others to view all of reality in a new way. Then research the Papal States and pay attention to the issue of church-state relations. Finally find out what separation of church and state in the United States Constitution means and be ready to report to your class.

5. Find a Society of St. Vincent de Paul chapter in your area. As a family, go through all your clothing and find good clothes that you can share with those in need.

6. With your parents or guardians, look through newspapers to find examples of governments around the world that are not protecting the rights of their citizens or working for the common good of all. Pray for those governments and for the people governed by them. Find out if your family can contribute to an organization that helps these people.

Leadership Like Christ's Fill in the blanks.

1. _____ served the Church after the French Revolution by teaching God's love to others.

2. New ideas in the 17th and 18th centuries tempted some people to abandon their _____ .

3. _____ believed it was a privilege to help those who were poor.

4. The philosophy of _____ is based on the idea that all of humanity's issues can be solved by simply examining them scientifically.

5. Pope Pius IX called the First _____ Council to confirm his Syllabus of Errors.

6. The _____ Commandment calls us to respect legitimate authority.

Causes and Effects Match the causes with the effects by writing the letters on the lines.

a. the doctrine of papal infallibility

b. the French Revolution

c. Church leaders became spiritual leaders

d. some people began to think that God's role in the universe was limited

e. Syllabus of Errors

f. the persecution of the Church during the French Revolution

1. People who were not rich wanted a say in their government and a share of France's wealth. The result was _____ .

2. Church leaders who supported the authority of the pope dominated the First Vatican Council. The result was _____ .

3. Many of the clergy in France were wealthy and supported the ruling class. The result was _____ .

4. During the revolutions in Europe, Church leaders lost their political power. As a result, _____ .

5. Scientists such as Copernicus and Galileo pointed out that the earth was not the center of the universe. As a result, _____ .

6. At first, the Church was suspicious of scientific developments. This led to Pope Pius IX publishing a _____ .

Back in Time If you could go back in time, who would be the best person mentioned in this chapter to consult for the following information?

1. How to teach people about God while experiencing struggles of your own

   _____

2. An explanation of key scientific discoveries of the 16th century

   _____

3. A summary of the Second Vatican Council

   _____

4. How to work with Vincent de Paul to care for people who are sick and poor

   _____

5. The purpose of the First Vatican Council

   _____

6. How to inspire others to see Christ in those who are poor

   _____

Galileo Galilei.

Gather and Go Forth

Know and Proclaim

Knowing the truths of our Catholic faith brings us closer to God; proclaiming our beliefs brings other people closer to God.

We Know Our Faith	We Proclaim Our Faith
God is not in some distant place. He is present in the hearts of those who live his law of love. Both faith and science come from God.	Catholics believe that science and nature can help reveal God's truth. Catholics study science to recognize God's truth and work to ensure that scientific advances adhere to that truth.
In serving those in need, we help others recognize that God is close to them.	Catholics support organizations like the St. Vincent de Paul Society, which operates food pantries and thrift stores to assist people in need.
The Fourth Commandment calls us to respect our leaders and those in authority. People in authority are required to obey God's truth.	Catholics participate in civil society to help build a society that is just and truthful and serves the needs of all, especially those who are most vulnerable.

As part of God's creation, we share in his truth, beauty, and goodness. As disciples of Jesus, we help people recognize the power of God's love through our works of service.

"And the king will say to them in reply, 'Amen, I say to you, whatever you did for one of these least brothers of mine, you did for me.'"

Matthew 25:40

Test Your Catholic Knowledge

Fill in the circle that best completes the sentence.

Pope Pius IX called the First Vatican Council in response to:

- ◯ the French Revolution.
- ◯ the philosophy known as rationalism.
- ◯ an increase in the number of people who were poor.
- ◯ the discoveries of Copernicus and Galileo in the 16th century.

A Catholic to Know

Marie-Rose Durocher was a living saint—the goodness she showed while working in her brother's parish earned her the title "the saint of Boloeil," a village not far from Montreal, Canada. Bishop Bourget of Montreal, who was also her spiritual director, encouraged her to found a teaching community. At first, she was against the idea, but with two friends, she began a boarding school for 13 girls. In 1843, she founded the Sisters of the Holy Names of Jesus and Mary. Marie-Rose remained steadfast in her concern for children who were poor and their education. Today her order continues her work and is concerned with educating and empowering people in need.

Blessed Marie-Rose Durocher

Witness and Share

These sentences describe what Catholics believe. Listen carefully as they are read. Ask yourself, "How strong are my Catholic beliefs?"

My Way to Faith

- I see God at work in the wonders and discoveries in nature.

- I participate in parish efforts to help people in need.

- I respect people in positions of authority.

- I feel that God is close to me; he strengthens and sustains me.

- I follow God's truth when I am in a position of leadership.

Share Your Faith

Consider how scientific discoveries complement your faith in God. Where do you see God in the natural world? How does nature reveal God's loving action? Write your ideas and invite family members and friends to share their experience of finding God in the natural world.

_____

_____

_____

_____

Pope Leo XIII recording Benediction c. 1880s.

Signs of the Times

Today technological advances occur at a remarkable rate. New electronic devices for communication and entertainment are rapidly changing the way we live our lives. What are some examples of electronic devices that are popular right now? Which of these would you most like to have?

_____

_____

Seeking Justice, Mercy, and Peace

The beginning of the Industrial Revolution in the 19th century created inhuman working conditions. Untrained workers labored 14 hours a day for little pay. People had to crowd into slums to live. Children were forced to work. Workers were denied the rights of fair pay and decent working conditions. They had neither time nor money for education. Family members felt the strain of having too little time together.

The Church Speaks Out

How could the Church keep silent when people were suffering from injustice? Pope Leo XIII believed that each person has dignity as well as rights and duties. He also recognized that those in authority must be committed to the common good and must support conditions that allow

people to develop and reach fulfillment. To teach the world the Christian view of labor, Pope Leo XIII wrote an **encyclical** on social justice. In his letter, called *Rerum Novarum (On New Things),* he taught the following:

- Every worker should receive a fair wage.
- Employers should treat workers fairly.
- Workers should form organizations to defend their rights.

Every pope since Leo XIII has called the world's attention to the need for justice, love, and mercy.

Judging Justly

The following statements reflect Church teachings on justice. Check (✓) the ones you think are most important.

☐ Richer nations are responsible for helping poorer nations.

☐ People have the right to develop their talents.

☐ You must respect every person, even if you do not like that person.

☐ Giving to people who are poor is not only an act of charity but an obligation.

☐ Everyone should work for laws that protect those who are elderly, have disabilities, and are unborn.

☐ Students who live in poor areas have as much of a right to a good education as those who live in wealthy areas.

Catholic Social Teaching

Since the publication of *Rerum Novarum*, the Church has developed a large body of teaching on social justice issues. The Church makes judgments about economic and social matters that relate to the basic rights of individuals and communities. The Church's social teaching is a rich treasure of wisdom about how to build a just society and live holy lives amid the challenges of the modern world. In the story of the Good Samaritan (Luke 10: 29–37), Jesus makes clear our responsibility to care for those in need. The Church teaches this responsibility in the following themes of Catholic Social Teaching:

Life and Dignity of the Human Person
All human life is sacred and must be respected and valued over material goods. We are called to ask whether our actions respect or threaten the life and dignity of the human person.

Call to Family, Community, and Participation
Participation in family and community is central to our faith and to a healthy society. Families must be supported so that people can participate in society, build community spirit, and promote the well-being of all.

Rights and Responsibilities
Every person has a right to life as well as a right to those things required for human decency. As Catholics, we have a responsibility to protect these basic human rights in order to achieve a healthy society.

Option for the Poor and Vulnerable
In our world, many people are very rich while many are extremely poor. As Catholics, to make an option for the poor means that we are called to pay special attention to the needs of those who are poor by defending and promoting their dignity and by meeting their immediate needs.

The Dignity of Work and the Rights of Workers
The basic rights of workers must be respected: the right to productive work, to fair wages, to private property, to organize, to join unions, and to pursue economic opportunity. Catholics believe that the economy is meant to serve people and that work is not merely a way to make a living but an important way in which we participate in God's creation.

Solidarity
Because God is our Father, we are all brothers and sisters with the responsibility to care for one another. Solidarity is the attitude that leads Christians to share spiritual and material goods. Solidarity unites rich and poor, weak and strong, and helps to create a society that recognizes that we all depend upon one another.

Care for God's Creation
God is the Creator of all people and all things, and he wants us to enjoy his creation. The responsibility to care for all God has made is a requirement of our faith.

A Moment with Jesus

Read the story of the Good Samaritan (Luke 10:29–37). Take a moment to ask Jesus to help you to recognize your neighbor and to reach out to those who are in need. Thank Jesus for the people in your life who reach out to you when you are in need. Ask Jesus for the strength you need to work for the well-being of all people.

The Quest for Peace

During the 20th century, the world underwent two world wars. The world witnessed the sufferings people endured through Nazi and Communist governments and saw those who were poor oppressed by those who were wealthy. Then and now, the popes and bishops have reminded Church members to treat one another as Jesus taught. Church leaders have pointed out that greed is the root of all war and that greed robs people of their human dignity and rights. They have challenged nations, families, and all people to show justice and mercy. Church leaders have asked us to make sure that every person has food, clothing, medical care, and education. They have called us to contribute to peace by living Gospel values and growing in truth.

Fresh Air

Saint John XXIII.

One way the Church grows in truth is through ecumenical councils. There have been 218 Church councils. The most recent one was called by Pope John XXIII in 1962.

John XXIII became pope in 1958 at age 77. People did not expect him to do much. But John XXIII remembered that the First Vatican Council (Vatican I), which Pope Pius IX began in 1869, had to adjourn suddenly and was never finished. Vatican I had pronounced the Church's teaching on papal infallibility, but it had not studied the role of bishops in the Church. Saint John XXIII also recognized that the life and mission of the Church needed renewal. For these reasons, he called the Second Vatican Council. He explained that he was "opening a window to let in fresh air."

About 2,600 bishops came from all over the world. Because Saint John XXIII believed strongly in Christian unity, he invited other churches to send observers. When the Second Vatican Council (Vatican II) opened, the pope was confident that the Holy Spirit would lead the Church in truth. Sadly, John XXIII died in the course of Vatican II. Pope Paul VI was elected and continued the council. He brought it to a close in 1965. Pope Francis canonized Pope John XXIII in April of 2014.

Models of Holiness

Saint Thérèse of Lisieux (also known as Thérèse of the Child Jesus) In 1888, at age 15, Thérèse entered the Carmelite convent in Lisieux, France. She became a saint by doing ordinary things extraordinarily well. This was what she called her Little Way. Her example has inspired many others to follow this way to gain eternal life.

Saint Francis de Sales As the bishop of Geneva (in modern-day Switzerland) in the early 1600s, Francis had great patience and gentleness in helping people grow in their spiritual lives.

Saint Jane Frances de Chantal In 1610, aided by Francis de Sales, Jane founded the Order of the Visitation in France to educate and care for girls.

Saint Margaret Mary Alacoque Margaret Mary, a Visitation nun in France, spread devotion to the Sacred Heart of Jesus in the mid-to-late 1600s.

Saint John Bosco John had a gift for helping boys, especially those who were poor and in trouble, to know God. In Italy in 1854, he founded the Salesians to help boys know God and learn a trade.

Saint Thérèse of Lisieux.

Living in Truth

A powerful wind blew through Saint John XXIII's open window. Vatican II touched on all areas of Christian life and produced 16 documents. Becoming familiar with the thinking of the bishops at the Council will help you understand the Church today. Read the messages of Vatican II and write your responses on a separate sheet of paper.

1. The Second Vatican Council said that the Church is the People of God, a community of believers. Everyone, not only bishops and priests, is called to holiness and is responsible for the community's life. Name a way your parish community supports its members.

2. The Council pointed out the need for collegiality, or shared decision making, among the bishops and the pope. For example, this means that the pope should consult with the bishops. Representatives of the bishops meet periodically with the pope to discuss important issues. This meeting is called a synod. What issues do you think a synod should address today?

3. Vatican II encouraged participation in the liturgy. It replaced Latin with the language of the people at liturgical celebrations. Describe what it means to fully participate in the Mass.

4. The Council promoted Christian unity. Instead of avoiding people of different Christian traditions, we are to discuss, work, and pray with them. The Church teaches that we should have a healing and forgiving spirit toward all people. Why is this a good attitude to have?

5. The Council encouraged people to read Scripture. How do you think reading the Bible at home and at school or hearing it read at Mass can help you live a better Christian life?

6. Vatican II taught that every member of the Church is responsible for sharing the faith and for standing up for the dignity of every human being. Who are people who share their faith with you?

7. Vatican II called upon the laity to take their rightful role in the Church, to live lives of holiness, and to carry on the work of the Church in the world. How can laypeople bring about change in the world?

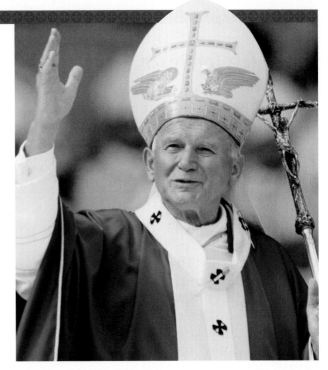

Saint John Paul II.

The Polish Pope

For 456 years—from 1522 to 1978—all the popes were Italian. Then in 1978 the cardinals of the Church gathered in Rome and selected Karol Wojtyla of Poland to take the chair of Peter. Wojtyla, who took the name John Paul II, became the 264th pope. Saint John Paul II led the Church for almost 27 years until his death in 2005. He was instrumental in bringing about the fall of Communism in Eastern Europe. John Paul II also had great concern for those who were poor and spoke out against war, violence, and capital punishment. He emphasized the universal call to holiness and called Catholics to engage in what he called the New Evangelization. After John Paul II died, he was succeeded by German Cardinal Joseph Ratzinger in 2006, who took the name Benedict XVI. In 2011, Pope Benedict beatified Pope John Paul II, naming him Blessed. In 2013, Pope Benedict XVI retired from the papacy, citing failing health. As a retired pope, he took the title Pope Emeritus. Pope Francis was elected by the College of Cardinals on March 13, 2013, as the 266th successor of Saint Peter. Pope Francis canonized Pope John Paul II in April of 2014.

Remember

How did the Industrial Revolution change society, and how did the Church respond?

The growth of industry created inhuman working conditions. To teach the world the Christian view of labor, Pope Leo XIII wrote an encyclical on social justice.

How did the Second Vatican Council change our view of the Church?

The Second Vatican Council taught that the Church is more than an institution. It is the People of God. Everyone, not only bishops and priests, has a call to holiness and the responsibility to live and spread the Christian faith.

What were some of the things that Saint John Paul II supported and opposed?

Saint John Paul II spoke out for the dignity of human life. He emphasized the universal call to holiness and called Catholics to engage in what he called the New Evangelization. He spoke out against war, violence, and capital punishment. He was a defender of the dignity of human life, and he spoke out against a "culture of death."

Word to Know

encyclical

Respond

It is up to you to begin it [peace] by being truthful and just, merciful, and peace-loving, for we can expect peace from others only if we live it ourselves.

Saint John Paul II

In your reflection notebook, write a letter to Jesus, explaining how you can be a leader for peace at home and at school.

Reach Out

1. The Industrial Revolution resulted in many changes in society and in how people lived and worked. In a similar way, we are currently experiencing a technological revolution. Talk to your parents or guardians about how technology has changed life for them since they were children.

2. Work together as a family to make a Catholic Social Teaching family plan. Brainstorm and identify ways that you can do the following: As a family, what can we do to

   - show respect for all human life?
   - strengthen our family and participate in the community?
   - assume our responsibility to make sure that all people have what they need?
   - address the needs of those who are poor and vulnerable?
   - support family members and relatives who work?
   - show solidarity with others around the world?
   - care for God's creation?

3. Talk to relatives or others who might remember the Catholic Church and the Mass before the Second Vatican Council. Ask them to describe the differences.

4. Research the life of Saint John Paul II and report your findings to your class. Search for a DVD on the life of Saint John Paul II and watch it together as a family.

5. Look for information on Saint Thérèse of Lisieux's Little Way and talk to a parent or guardian about ordinary things you can each do at home in extraordinary ways.

Pope Francis. At right is Cardinal Agostino Vallini, Vicar General of Rome.

Something New Check (✓) the things that the Second Vatican Council brought about.

_____ **1.** Laity involvement in Church government through parish councils

_____ **2.** Latin as the language of the Eucharistic celebration

_____ **3.** Synods in which the pope consults bishops on important issues

_____ **4.** Statements condemning theological errors of Protestants

_____ **5.** The idea that people should read the Bible at home or at school

Agents of Change Write *L13* (for Pope Leo XIII), *V2* (for the Second Vatican Council), or *JP2* (for Saint John Paul II) for the person or council that caused or influenced each change described below.

_____ **1.** Catholics are to discuss, work, and pray with members of other Christian traditions.

_____ **2.** The fall of Communism in Eastern Europe

_____ **3.** Renewed emphasis on life and opposition to a culture of death

_____ **4.** Workers should be treated fairly and should form organizations to defend their rights.

_____ **5.** Every member of the Church is responsible for sharing the faith.

Just Facts Draw lines through the statements that are not part of the Church's teaching on justice.

Richer nations are responsible for helping poorer nations.

People should be concerned primarily with their own well-being and should only help others if they are completely secure themselves.

The Holy Spirit empowers you to proclaim the Gospel and work for peace.

You must respect every person, even if you do not like that person.

In special circumstances—such as when someone has offended you—you are not obligated to respect certain people.

Students who live in poor areas have as much of a right to a good eduction as those who live in wealthy areas.

Workers have the right to productive work, fair wages, and private property.

It is OK to take from others as long as doing so will help you to get ahead.

Pope Leo XIII.

Gather and Go Forth

Know and Proclaim

Knowing the truths of our Catholic faith enables us to support one another in the proclamation of our beliefs.

We Know Our Faith	We Proclaim Our Faith
Catholic Social Teaching is a rich treasure of wisdom about how to build a just society and live holy lives.	Many Catholics support and participate in the efforts of the Catholic Campaign for Human Development, an instrument of the Church to carry out Jesus' mission of serving people in need.
Pope John XXIII called the Second Vatican Council in order to renew the life and mission of the Church.	Catholics live the principles of the Second Vatican Council by taking a more active role in the life and mission of the Church.
Every member of the Church is responsible for sharing the faith and for standing up for the dignity of every human being.	Catholics work against a "culture of death" by supporting efforts that protect human life and oppose abortion, euthanasia, the death penalty, and war.

The Church works for the eternal welfare of all people. Although much has changed, the Church meets the challenges of the modern world with a constant faith.

Indeed someone might say, "You have faith and I have works." Demonstrate your faith to me without works, and I will demonstrate my faith to you from my works.

James 2:18

Test Your Catholic Knowledge

Fill in the circle that best answers the question.

Which of the following was encouraged by the Second Vatican Council?

○ participation of the laity in the liturgy of the Church

○ a New Evangelization in Europe and North America

○ opposition Communism

○ obedience to the pope

A Catholic to Know

Joseph reminds us of the importance of labor in building up the Body of Christ. Through his trade as a carpenter, Joseph honored God and continued the act of creation. The Church teaches with pride that Jesus' human father, Joseph, taught Jesus his trade as a carpenter. Jesus must have learned both the satisfaction and difficulty of human work. The Church recognized that workers needed a patron saint. Pope Benedict XV named Joseph the protector of workers, and in 1955 Pope Pius XII proclaimed May 1 as the feast of Saint Joseph the Worker. We can ask Saint Joseph to pray for those people who want and need to work but cannot find jobs.

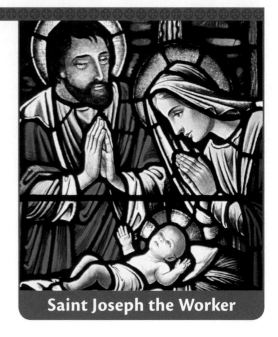

Saint Joseph the Worker

Witness and Share

These sentences describe what Catholics believe. Listen carefully as they are read. Ask yourself, "How strong are my Catholic beliefs?"

My Way to Faith

- I support laws that protect the most vulnerable in society.

- I believe that prosperous nations have a responsibility to poorer nations.

- I look to the teachings of the Second Vatican Council to help me lead a holy life.

- I respect the dignity of every person, even if I do not like him or her.

- I participate fully, actively, and consciously in the celebration of the liturgy.

Share Your Faith

Do you respect life? Think about the ways in which you show respect for life. Write your ideas on the lines and invite a friend or family member to share what he or she does to demonstrate respect for life.

_____

_____

_____

_____

The Church in North America

There are tens of thousands of museums in the United States. Each year hundreds of millions of people visit museums of all types: science and technology, botanical, railway, children's, art, ethnic, sports, communications, natural history, and more. People like museums because they preserve and display things that have great scientific, historical, or artistic value. Describe your most recent visit to a museum and the exhibit you enjoyed most.

_____

_____

_____

Those Who Went Before Us

Museums teach us about things we might otherwise take for granted. Some things we take for granted are the result of the dedication, labor, and suffering of many people. Consider the freedom you have compared to people in some other countries. Our ancestors worked hard and even gave their lives so that you could enjoy this gift.

Something else that it is easy to take for granted is our Catholic faith. We need to know the story of how Catholicism was brought to our country and preserved by strong, active believers. Then we will better appreciate it as a precious heritage.

A Walk Through Time

Imagine that you are in a museum of the Catholic Church in North America. The items you see in the displays represent the adventures and milestones of the Church in North America. Through them (as presented on the following pages), you will trace the growth of the Church from its beginnings in the New World to the present.

The Good News in a New World

When Columbus made his second journey to the New World in 1493, twelve Spanish Franciscans sailed with him. Recognizing that the Word of God is meant for all people, they started missions in Cuba, Puerto Rico, Florida, Mexico, and Texas.

Thousands of Native Americans were introduced to Christ and his teachings. One of them, Saint Juan Diego of Mexico, had a vision of Our Lady in 1531. According to the story, Mary appeared dressed in native clothes and spoke to Juan in his native language. Mary sent him to the bishop to ask that a shrine be built in her honor. When the bishop asked for a sign, Mary had Juan pick roses from the hill where she appeared and where none grew, especially in December. Standing before the bishop, Juan opened his cloak and let his miraculous roses spill out. There on the cloak was an image of the Blessed Virgin as she had appeared to him. She has come to be known as Our Lady of Guadalupe. In 1945 the pope made her patroness of the Americas.

The first firmly established Spanish settlement in the United States, Saint Augustine in Florida, was built in 1565. In 1609 the second Catholic settlement, the town of Santa Fe, New Mexico, was founded.

New World Martyrs

Jesuits from France came to minister to the Native American nations in the Great Lakes region in Canada and the United States. These Jesuits learned the Native American languages and lived in the wilderness. They were in constant danger of being attacked by enemy tribes. The tribes they lived among sometimes blamed them for disasters and turned on them.

Six Jesuits and two lay missionaries were martyred between 1642 and 1649. They became known as the North American Martyrs and were canonized in 1930. The most famous is Saint Isaac Jogues, who worked with the Hurons. Once he was held captive by Mohawks for 14 months. They tortured him, mutilated his hands, and made him a slave. After Father Jogues escaped, he was sent to France. There he begged to return to Canada. When he did return, he was martyred. Through the bravery and love of the missionaries, Native Americans such as Saint Kateri Tekakwitha, a Mohawk, came to know and love God.

The Word of God Spreads

Jacques Marquette was a Jesuit who worked at different missions. He learned many Native American languages and was known for his courage. In 1672 he was sent by the governor and by his superior to explore the Mississippi River with a layman named Louis Joliet. They traveled 2,500 miles, sometimes encountering bad weather and hostile native peoples. The maps and journal of Father Marquette helped settlers in America.

Jacques Marquette.

Carmel Mission, California.

The California Missions

In Luke 9:1–6, Jesus sends his twelve apostles out on a mission, telling them to proclaim the Kingdom of God. The Catholic Church, by its very nature, is missionary. This means that the Church is sent to all people. Many of California's large cities, such as San Diego, San Francisco, and Los Angeles, began as missions. Nine of the twenty-one California missions were founded in the 1700s by Blessed Junípero Serra, a Franciscan. He named his missions after the saints who were honored on the island off Spain where he was born. After dangerous mission work in Mexico, Junípero was sent to begin missions along the whole Pacific coast. At 56, hampered by a diseased leg, he planned and directed communities of Native Americans. These missions taught Native Americans to farm and to build. They were introduced to European art, writing, music, and to Christ's love for them.

> If you had been a missionary in early America, what would you have found most difficult?

Oppression and Growth in the Colonies

The Protestants from England who settled the 13 colonies resented Catholics. Therefore, in all the colonies except Pennsylvania, Catholics were persecuted and forbidden to practice their faith. They were not allowed to own property or to vote, and they were barred from public office. Maryland originally was owned by a Catholic and granted freedom of worship to all, but it eventually passed anti-Catholic laws as well. When Great Britain granted religious freedom to French Catholics in Canada in 1774, the Protestant colonists were angry.

Feelings toward Catholics improved in the colonies when many Catholics supported the Declaration of Independence and served in the Revolutionary War. The United States Constitution of 1789 ensured that the government would not be identified with or favor any one religion. Because the Constitution also granted freedom of religion, Catholicism was allowed to flourish. Since then the Catholic Church has grown from less than 1 percent of the population to 25 percent, or more than 70 million Americans.

The First American Bishop

John Carroll.

For at least 150 years, Catholics in the colonies had no bishop. They were anxious to have their own American bishop, a successor of the apostles. After negotiations carried on with the help of Benjamin Franklin, the Vatican let the 26 available U.S. priests vote for a bishop. In 1789 they elected John Carroll, a Jesuit priest from Maryland, who was then appointed bishop of the diocese of Baltimore. Under Bishop Carroll, the Catholic Church in America was organized. In 1789 he helped found Georgetown College (University), the first Catholic university in the country. In 1791, he established the first U.S. seminary, St. Mary's, in Baltimore. At one time Bishop Carroll's diocese was the entire United States, including the Louisiana Purchase. Now there are more than 200 dioceses in the country.

The First Native-Born American Saint

Saint Elizabeth Ann Seton.

Elizabeth Ann Seton was a young widow with five children. She became a Catholic to the dismay of her upper-class friends and relatives. In 1808, with Bishop Carroll's encouragement, Elizabeth established the first Catholic parish school in America for girls. Then in 1809 she founded the first American religious community, the Sisters of Charity. At Emmitsburg, Maryland, you can visit the place she lived and see the rock she sometimes sat on as she taught. This shrine has become more popular since 1975, when Elizabeth was canonized the first native-born American saint.

A Dedicated Bishop

Saint John Neumann.

In the early years of our country, Catholics saw a priest only a few times a year. Priests rode for miles on horseback, going from home to home and encouraging people to pray and to live Christ's teachings. John Neumann was a short, quiet priest born in Bohemia. He knew nearly a dozen languages. Hardworking and responsible, John Neumann became bishop of Philadelphia. He was responsible for the building of 50 churches, and he also began construction on a cathedral. Neumann opened nearly 100 schools, resulting in the increase of Catholic school students from 500 to nearly 10,000. His devoted care for more than 100 parishes helped a growing Church. He was canonized in 1977, the first American man and the first American bishop to be named a saint.

> How is the Catholic Church present in your community today? What institutions (such as schools or hospitals) and services does the Catholic Church provide in your community?
>
> _____
>
> _____

Catholic Immigrants

Saint Frances Cabrini.

From 1820 to 1920, nine million Catholics immigrated to the United States. These Catholics often wanted to worship in their own language and with their own traditions. Ethnic parishes sprang up in many cities.

An outstanding woman came to minister to Italian immigrants. To care for orphans, Frances Cabrini started a community in Italy called the Missionary Sisters of the Sacred Heart. Mother Cabrini had always dreamed of being a missionary in China. But Pope Leo XIII told her, "No, not to the East, but to the West." Frances and her sisters sailed to the United States in 1889. There they were often without food and money. But in 35 years Frances founded 70 institutions for those who were poor, abandoned, and sick. She was canonized in 1946, the first American citizen to be declared a saint.

Anti-Catholicism

As the number of Catholics in the country increased, Protestants feared that soon the United States would be under the rule of the pope. Anti-Catholic feeling grew. Catholics were persecuted and their churches were burned. Three anti-Catholic groups formed. The Know-Nothing party was a political party that tried to suppress Catholicism. The Ku Klux Klan, which still exists, was against Catholics, Jews, and African Americans. The American Protective Association was an organization that spread anti-Catholic propaganda.

In Defense of Workers

Many immigrants were poor and uneducated. Often they worked long hours under terrible conditions for little pay. Workers who tried to organize into unions were fired. Secretly many Catholics joined a union known as the Knights of Labor, founded in 1869. When some bishops in Canada and the United States condemned this union, the archbishop of Baltimore, James Cardinal Gibbons, spoke and wrote to Rome on its behalf. The matter was settled when Pope Leo XIII wrote his encyclical *Rerum Novarum* in defense of workers. This was the first of many judgments the Catholic Church would make about economic and social matters as they pertain to the fundamental rights of people. Later Cardinal Gibbons became a peacemaker among Catholic groups in America. He was popular and respected by Catholics and world leaders.

James Cardinal Gibbons.

The *Baltimore Catechism*

At the Council of Baltimore in 1884, the U.S. bishops decided that every parish should have a Catholic school. They also commissioned the *Baltimore Catechism*, a book that would be the religion text for all Catholic children through the 1950s. The goal of this catechism was to faithfully transmit to each generation the Catholic Church's beliefs and teachings.

As early as 1774, French settlers in Quebec were allowed to practice their Catholic faith. Other provinces were mostly Protestant. When the Dominion of Canada was formed in 1867, there was no separation of church and state. The government helped each church to operate its schools. By 1900, Catholics made up about 40 percent of Canada's population.

What immigrant peoples today need help and understanding as they strive to become Americans?

_____

_____

_____

Coming of Age

Until 1908 the United States was considered a mission country under the Roman Congregation for the Propagation of the Faith. Three years later, two American priests founded America's own missionary association, the Catholic Foreign Mission Society of America. They opened a foreign mission seminary on a hill in New York, which they named Mary Knoll. The Society became known as Maryknoll. In 1918 the first Maryknoll missionaries left for China.

To carry out the social teachings of the Church, the American bishops set up the National Catholic Welfare Conference in Washington, D.C., in 1919. Now it is called the United States Conference of Catholic Bishops.

Also in Washington is the National Shrine of the Immaculate Conception. Mary, under the title of the **Immaculate Conception**, was declared patroness of the United States in 1847. The shrine was dedicated in 1959. In the beautiful white marble building are individual shrines in honor of Mary, representing the nationalities of people in the United States.

National Shrine of the Immaculate Conception, Washington, D.C.

A Catholic in the White House

Alfred E. Smith, a Catholic, ran for president of the United States in 1928. His defeat was largely caused by an anti-Catholic attitude in the country. In 1960 the election of John F. Kennedy, the first Catholic president, was a sign that Catholics were generally accepted by other Americans. Today there are a number of Catholics in the Congress and on the Supreme Court.

The Catholic Worker

The Church in America continued to address social issues in a number of ways. Dorothy Day, with Peter Maurin, founded the Catholic Worker movement and began the *Catholic Worker,* a newspaper that explains Catholic social thought. They also opened a house for homeless people in New York. Dorothy Day often joined demonstrations for civil rights and social justice. She spent her life showing love for her neighbor.

In which of today's social justice issues should Catholics become most involved and why?

_____

_____

_____

Popes Visit the United States

On October 4, 1965, Pope Paul VI became the first pope to visit the Western Hemisphere, addressing the United Nations General Assembly in New York. In October 1979, Pope John Paul II visited the United States, making stops in six major U.S. cities over six days. He visited again in 1987, 1993, 1995, and 1999. Pope Emeritus Benedict XVI visited the United States for six days in April 2008. He spoke with a large number of diverse groups.

A New Catechism

In 2006 the United States Conference of Catholic Bishops published the *Compendium of the Catechism of the Catholic Church*, a 200-page summary of the 1992 *Catechism of the Catholic Church*. The *Compendium* consists of 598 questions and answers, similar to the format used in the *Baltimore Catechism* discussed earlier. Another guide authored by the United States Conference of Catholic Bishops is *The United States Catholic Catechism for Adults.* In 2010 Pope Benedict XVI spread *YouCat: Youth Catechism of the Catholic Church,* a resource for young people to learn about the Catholic Faith.

Summary

Remember

Which missionaries first brought the Catholic faith to North America?

The Jesuits from France brought the Catholic faith to the Great Lakes region in Canada and the United States. The Franciscans from Spain brought the faith to Mexico and California.

What did Bishop John Carroll do for the Church?

As the first bishop of the United States, John Carroll organized the Church in America. He founded the first seminary and the first Catholic college. He encouraged Elizabeth Ann Seton to start the first parish school and the first American religious community, the Sisters of Charity.

Who is the patroness of the United States?

Mary, under the title of the Immaculate Conception, is the patroness of the United States.

Word to Know

Immaculate Conception

Respond

You can be proud of the Catholics who made the Church in America what it is today. In your reflection notebook, write a prayer thanking God for ways that the American Church has been blessed. Include the example and accomplishments of some of the people you studied in this chapter.

Reach Out

1. Find out more about a person or an event mentioned in this chapter. Write a report and draw a picture to accompany it.

2. Research the lives of other people who figured into the history of the Catholic Church in America, such as Fray Marcos, the North American Martyrs, Stephen Badin, John Dubois, Catherine de Hueck, John England, Thomas Frederick Price, James Anthony Walsh, Charles Carroll, Sister Angelica, Venerable Frederick Baraga, Benedict Joseph Flaget, Simon Brute, Augustine Tolton, Elizabeth Lange, Pierre-Jean de Smet, and Fulton J. Sheen. Present your findings to the class. You might make a puppet of your person and have it tell his or her own story.

3. Interview a senior citizen to find out what it was like to be a Catholic when he or she was young.

4. Make a map that shows a phase of the Church in America. For example, indicate the missions of the North American Martyrs, the California missions, the parish school of Elizabeth Ann Seton, the journey of Jacques Marquette, or key places like St. Augustine, Baltimore, and Washington, D.C.

5. Discuss with your family some of the important contributions of Catholic missionaries. Establish a time each month to pray together for missionaries serving throughout the world.

6. Talk to your family about how Catholics in the original 13 colonies were persecuted. Then pray together for the religious freedom of all Catholics in the world today.

7. Share with a parent or guardian what you have learned about John Carroll, the first American bishop. Then ask your parent or guardian to share what he or she knows about your own bishop. Finally pray together for this bishop and for all Church leaders.

Tough Questions   Write *yes* or *no* to answer the following questions:

_____   **1.** Were there Catholics in the United States in 1565?

_____   **2.** Did Isaac Jogues give up missionary work after he was tortured?

_____   **3.** Was the Mississippi River explored by a Jesuit priest?

_____   **4.** Did Junípero Serra work with the North American Martyrs?

_____   **5.** Did San Diego, San Francisco, and Los Angeles begin as missions?

_____   **6.** Did Catholics probably celebrate Mass with the pilgrims on Thanksgiving Day in the early years of the 13 colonies?

_____   **7.** Was John Carroll the first bishop in the United States?

_____   **8.** Did Elizabeth Ann Seton teach from the *Baltimore Catechism?*

_____   **9.** Did Pope Leo XIII show concern for the problems of the Catholic Church in the United States?

Father Marquette approaches the Native Americans with a peace pipe.

_____   **10.** Was the United States considered a mission country at the beginning of the 20th century?

Who's Who?   Match the descriptions with the correct terms.

_____   **1.** First Catholic president of the United States

_____   **2.** Highly respected Catholic who did much to promote social justice for workers

_____   **3.** Founder of the first Catholic parish school

_____   **4.** First American citizen to be canonized

_____   **5.** Franciscan who founded nine missions in California

_____   **6.** First American bishop who organized the Church in the United States

_____   **7.** Founder of the Catholic Worker Movement

_____   **8.** Jesuit missionary to the Native Americans who was martyred

a. Cardinal James Gibbons

b. Saint Frances Cabrini

c. Saint John Neumann

d. Blessed Junípero Serra

e. John Carroll

f. John F. Kennedy

g. Dorothy Day

h. Alfred E. Smith

i. Saint Isaac Jogues

j. Saint Elizabeth Ann Seton

What's What?   Match the descriptions with the correct terms.

_____   **1.** First Catholic university in the United States

_____   **2.** Document that granted Catholics freedom of religion

_____   **3.** First diocese in the United States

_____   **4.** Anti-Catholic organization

_____   **5.** Organization that carries out the Church's social teaching in the United States

_____   **6.** Patroness of the United States

_____   **7.** First religious community in the United States

a. United States Constitution

b. The Immaculate Conception

c. *Rerum Novarum*

d. Ku Klux Klan

e. Maryknoll

f. Baltimore

g. United States Conference of Catholic Bishops

h. Pennsylvania

i. Georgetown University

j. Sisters of Charity

✳ HALL OF FAME ✳

Read the description of the saint or historical figure and write his or her name in the box.

1 She was an American saint who founded the first Catholic parish school in the United States.

2 She spread devotion to the Sacred Heart of Jesus in the mid-to-late 1600s.

3 He was the pope who opened the Second Vatican Council.

4 She taught children about God and believed that all baptized people are called to share in Christ's ministry.

5 He played a major role at the Council of Trent. He established seminaries in his diocese and helped write a catechism.

6 He was the first bishop of the United States.

7 He began the First Vatican Council in 1869.

8 She persuaded the pope to return to Rome from Avignon.

9 He served as bishop of Geneva in the 1600s and had great patience in helping people with their spiritual lives.

10 He founded the Society of Jesus.

11 He wrote the first major social encyclical, *Rerum Novarum.*

12 He brought the Second Vatican Council to a close in 1965.

13 He defended the dignity of human life and opposed the "culture of death."

14 He was chancellor of England. He remained loyal to the pope and the universal church during the time of Henry VIII.

15 She founded the Order of the Visitation in France to educate and care for girls.

16 He was a friend of those who were poor, sick, orphaned, aged, imprisoned, and enslaved. He founded the Vincentian Fathers.

17 He criticized the abuses in the Church in the 16th century and then formed his own church, starting the Protestant Reformation.

18 He was a Jesuit missionary who brought the Gospel to India and Japan.

19 She was a mystic who reformed the Carmelites and brought about a renewal of prayer in the Church.

20 She was the first American citizen to be canonized.

Celebrating

The Church Filled with the Spirit

Song and Procession with Bible and Candle

Leader: Together we begin our prayer:
In the name of the Father
and of the Son
and of the Holy Spirit.
Amen.

The Church is Christ with us
through the power of the Spirit.
We are called to put our trust and
confidence in Christ and his Church.

Reading and Response

Leader: The Holy Spirit is the soul of the
Church. The Spirit gives us true
understanding of the teaching of
Christ and his Church. Let us listen
now to God's Word and hear what
the Spirit brings us.

Reader 1: A reading from Paul's letter to the
Galatians.

(Galatians 5:22–25 is proclaimed.)

The Word of the Lord.

All: Thanks be to God.

Leader: Let us pray.

All: Let us choose always to allow the
Holy Spirit to work in us. Then we
can bring a spirit of reconciliation,
mercy, and unity to the Church.
We know that when we are filled
with the Spirit, we can reach out
to others in love.

Song

Presentation of Symbols

*(If symbols have not been made,
participants may sign each other with
the Sign of the Cross in place of the
Presentation of Symbols.)*

Leader: We bring these symbols as signs of
our desire to be open to the power
of the Spirit working in us. We pray
that our witness to the Spirit will
draw others to greater love of the
Church.

(Symbols are placed on the table.)

Litany to the Spirit

Reader 1: Let us praise and thank the Spirit and ask for continued guidance. Our response is Lord, send us your Spirit.

Reader 2: That we may love Christ and grow in deeper friendship with him through prayer, we pray, (*All respond.*)

Reader 3: That we may bring joy by keeping a positive attitude toward life, we pray, (*All respond.*)

Reader 4: That our words and actions may bring peace at home, we pray, (*All respond.*)

Reader 5: That we may be patient with ourselves as we try to imitate Jesus, we pray, (*All respond.*)

Reader 6: That our dealings with one another may be marked by goodness and kindness, we pray, (*All respond.*)

Reader 7: That we may continue to trust in God no matter what happens, we pray, (*All respond.*)

Reader 8: That we may develop the self-control to make the right decisions, we pray, (*All respond.*)

Silent Prayer

Leader: During this time of silent prayer, let us consider how we need to rely on the Holy Spirit. You may wish to write your thoughts in a prayer.

Holy Spirit, guide me _____

_____

_____

Leader: Let us go now to build up the Church by proclaiming the Good News through our words and the faithful witness of our lives.

All: Thanks be to God.

Closing Song

History Mystery Match the terms.

_____ **1.** Saint John XXIII   **a.** Syllabus of Errors

_____ **2.** Council of Trent   **b.** King Henry VIII

_____ **3.** Jesuits   **c.** More interest in the human than in the divine

_____ **4.** Pope Pius IX   **d.** Second Vatican Council

_____ **5.** Pope Leo XIII   **e.** First American bishop

_____ **6.** Saint Isaac Jogues   **f.** Defender of life

_____ **7.** Saint Elizabeth Ann Seton   **g.** World missionaries

_____ **8.** Renaissance   **h.** North American Martyr

_____ **9.** The Church of England   **i.** First American-born saint

_____ **10.** Blessed Junípero Serra   **j.** *Rerum Novarum*

_____ **11.** John Carroll   **k.** Reform

_____ **12.** Saint John Paul II   **l.** California missions

First Things First Number each set of events from 1 to 3 in the order in which they occurred.

1. _____ Industrial Revolution   **4.** _____ Protestant Reformation

_____ Renaissance   _____ Council of Trent

_____ French Revolution   _____ Great Western Schism

2. _____ Great Western Schism   **5.** _____ Founding of the Daughters of Charity

_____ Council of Trent   _____ Founding of the Jesuits

_____ Second Vatican Council   _____ Founding of the Sisters of Notre Dame

3. _____ *Baltimore Catechism*   **6.** _____ *Catechism of the Catholic Church*

_____ First Vatican Council   _____ *Baltimore Catechism*

_____ Second Vatican Council   _____ U.S. Constitution

Looking Back In this unit, you have discovered how Christ has remained with his Church through all times and difficulties. You have become aware of how the Holy Spirit has guided the pilgrim people of every age to accept the challenge of Christianity. You have witnessed what the holiness and courage of the saints can do, not only for the Church but for the world. Now the torch of Christianity is being passed on to you. Accept the challenge, run swiftly toward Christ, and hold high the torch of your faith. Let your love for Christ and others shine outward. You are the Church! As you complete this unit, ask yourself these questions:

1. Do I understand how the Holy Spirit guides my life as well as the life of the Church?

2. In what way have my recent actions shown that I love my faith?

3. What steps can I take to imitate Jesus and live a holy and courageous life as the saints did?

Gather and Go Forth

Know and Proclaim

We proclaim the truths of Jesus as we bring the Catholic faith to life among all peoples and nations.

We Know Our Faith	We Proclaim Our Faith
The Catholic Church was brought to North America by missionaries from Europe who traveled with explorers and settlers.	Catholics today continue the missionary activity of the Church. Many Catholics volunteer to visit areas of poverty in the United States and other countries to assist communities in need.
Catholic immigrants set up parishes in the United States where they could worship in their own language and with their own traditions.	Many Catholic parishes offer Masses in various languages and celebrate festivals that reflect the cultural traditions of their parishioners.
The Blessed Virgin Mary is the patroness of the United States and of the Americas.	Catholics celebrate the feast of Our Lady of Guadalupe, which commemorates the appearance of the Blessed Virgin Mary to Juan Diego.

As Catholics, we trust in God's goodness and live by his laws. We pray that our nation can be a light to others.

And he put all things beneath his feet and gave him as head over all things to the church, which is his body, the fullness of the one who fills all things in every way.

Ephesians 1:22–23

Test Your Catholic Knowledge

Fill in the circle that best completes the sentence.

The establishment of Catholic missions throughout the world illustrates that:

○ all religions are the same.

○ only immigrants need churches.

○ the Word of God is meant for only a few people.

○ the Word of God is meant for people of all nations.

A Catholic to Know

Isabel de Flores was born April 20, 1586. Gaspar de Flores and his wife, Maria de Olivia, were proud of their daughter. One day, a maid said Isabel looked just like a rose. Isabel's mother declared that this child would be called "Rose" from then on, and Isabel took Rose as her Confirmation name. When her family experienced financial difficulties, Rose gave up her plans to enter a convent and helped support her family by doing needlepoint and gardening. Her desire, however, was to live for God alone, and she joined the Third Order of Saint Dominic. She set up a room in her parents' house as a free medical clinic for the elderly and children who were poor. Rose gained a reputation for holiness throughout the city of Lima, Peru.

Saint Rose of Lima

Witness and Share

These sentences describe what Catholics believe. Listen carefully as they are read. Ask yourself, "How strong are my Catholic beliefs?"

My Way to Faith

- I appreciate the heritage and history of the Catholic Church in America.

- I respect the cultural differences within the Catholic Church.

- I respect and support religious freedom for all people.

- I know the history of my own parish faith community and local diocese.

- I present the truth and beauty of the Catholic Church to non-Catholics.

Share Your Faith

Consider ways in which you can show your devotion to Mary, the patroness of the Americas. Write your ideas on the lines, and invite a family member or friend to participate in that devotion to Our Lady with you.

_____

_____

_____

_____

The Witness of the Church

[L]ive in love, as Christ loved us.

Ephesians 5:2

Family Feature

The Church: Parish Communities

The Holt family realizes that the Catholic faith is practiced and flourishes within the communities known as parishes. That is why, after they moved, they registered at St. Mary's parish as soon as possible and investigated the opportunities their new parish offered. Before long, Mrs. Holt was a choir member, and Mr. Holt was a member of the Holy Name Society and an usher at the 9:00 A.M. Mass on Sunday. Although Judy Holt is only an eighth grader, she volunteered to help with religious education sessions on Monday nights. Now, through working with the first graders, she feels more a part of the parish.

Fifteen-year-old Alex Holt is excited that his new parish has a Life Teen program just as his old parish had. His first project with the group will be to help repair a house for an elderly couple in the neighborhood. Alex has also become a lector at Mass.

The next-door neighbors, the Durants, invited the Holts to join their prayer group. They explained that the group had been together for two years and that all the group's members found the support for their daily life invaluable. Mr. Durant remarked that when he was unemployed, he wouldn't have managed to pull through so well without the group's love and concern.

The Holts also discovered that St. Mary's parish has a vibrant RCIA (Rite of Christian Initiation for Adults) process for preparing adults for Baptism, the Eucharist, and Confirmation. Last year 15 people received the Sacraments of Initiation at the Easter Vigil. Mr. and Mrs. Holt are considering becoming involved in the RCIA, although they have never done anything like this before. They like the idea of being companions to others on the journey of faith and sharing the gift of faith with them.

Last Sunday the Holts learned that St. Mary's is paired with another parish as a sister parish. The communities hold various activities together, such as a special Lenten lecture program. They also sponsor projects together, such as an upcoming silent auction, the proceeds of which will benefit Catholic Charities. Mrs. Holt is already planning what to donate to the auction.

The faith thrives and spreads because of Catholics who make time to live their faith. Your family might think about how you can take a more active role in your parish. Not only will others benefit by your commitments and generosity but you will find the experiences rewarding.

Visit **www.christourlife.com** for more family resources.

CHAPTER 20

The Way of Holiness

More is said, written, and sung about love than about anything else. Love is central to our lives. As you grow older, you see love in various ways. Your understanding grows. You become more aware of the importance of love.

> **If you were asked to count all the people you love, how many names would you list?**
>
> _____
>
> **Who was the very first person who loved you?**
>
> _____
>
> **Write three reasons why people love you.**
>
> _____
>
> _____
>
> _____

Sharing Love

Long ago, you received the gift of love. God was the very first one to love you. God has loved you with an everlasting love. God called you into being and surrounded you with his love. Because God loves you, you become lovable! Look around you. People sitting next to you, people walking down the street—all are loved by God. And all are lovable, as hard as that may be to believe at times!

How do we thank God for this gift of love? We share it, especially with those who have not found it. Because God and others love you, you can give love to others. Love is the best gift you can give. It is one gift you can share with many people and still have enough for many more. When you give your love away, you become richer, not poorer. Love is shown through actions. Whenever you protect the dignity of others, show compassion for those who are poor and vulnerable, show care for God's creation, or treat all people as brothers and sisters, you show that you realize how much God loves you.

According to Scripture, "God is love." (1 John 4:8) It makes sense then that the more you love, the more you are like God. To be holy does not mean to act like something you are not. Being holy is being loving in the ways that God is loving. And love is the greatest thing we know.

The Covenant: A Way of Love

The Israelites learned much about God's love for them through the Exodus. God brought them out of slavery. Because he had done so much for them, they wanted to show their love and gratitude. They did this by using their God-given freedom responsibly.

God made a covenant with the Israelites in which they pledged him their love and loyalty. They received the Ten Commandments, which spelled out how to love. By living out their covenant, the Israelites witnessed to the world that they were the people of the Lord.

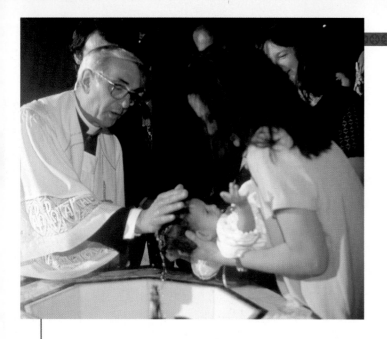

things in common. Jesus had said that to inherit eternal life, we must keep the commandments. In addition, he had given his followers a new commandment: "As I have loved you, so you also should love one another." (John 13:34) The first Christians kept this commandment so well that, according to third-century Church Father Tertullian, people remarked, "See how these Christians love one another."

In his letters, Saint Paul referred to the living members of the Church as saints. He recognized that they were holy, filled with love.

We also entered into a covenant with God at Baptism. Through Jesus, we have been saved from the slavery of sin. Like the Israelites and the early Christians, we try to show love for God and for one another. We show this love through the Eucharist, in which we thank God for saving us through Jesus. We also demonstrate this love by living like him: showing care and concern for those who are in need. We know that real freedom and happiness are found by living God's Way. When we love, God dwells in us, and we also are saints.

The New Covenant in Jesus

The early Christians were also people of the Covenant. They lived a pattern of life that they called "the Way." This meant that they followed Christ, who said, "I am the way." (John 14:6) They lived according to his example and his teachings. The early Christians recognized one another as brothers and sisters and shared all

Saint Isidore

Saint Isidore the farmer was one man who lived the Way. He was born in Spain in 1070. As a poor peasant boy, he began working for a landowner named John de Vergas. Isidore spent the rest of his life plowing the earth, feeding animals, and harvesting crops for this man. Isidore's wife, Maria, is a saint too. They had one son, who died at a young age.

Isidore loved God. He spoke to God and the saints as he labored on the farm. Sometimes he was late getting to the fields because he lingered to pray after morning Mass. Despite this delay, Isidore did his share of the work and did it well.

There is a story that jealous coworkers complained that Isidore often arrived late.

One morning John de Vergas hid in some bushes to observe his workers. Isidore did arrive late, but then on either side of him and his plow was an angel with a plow!

Both Isidore and Maria shared with those who had less than they had. Isidore was also kind to animals. It is said that one winter day on the way to grind corn into flour, Isidore passed some starving birds. He poured out half of his grain for them. Men who were with Isidore mocked him, but when they got to the mill, Isidore's sack was full and yielded twice as much flour as one sack usually held.

Saint Isidore is the patron of farmers. He is also a good patron for one who combines work and prayer.

Two Ways

One of the oldest known Christian writings is the *Didache*, or the *Teaching of the Twelve Apostles.* This document describes two ways to live: the Way of Life and the Way of Death. It says that the Way of Death is a life of sin and evil but that the Way of Life is to love the God who made you and love your neighbor as yourself. This Way leads to God. In this unit, you will study the Ten Commandments, the guidelines God gave to show us the way to love. These reflect the natural law written in our hearts as a result of being made in God's image. Natural law expresses our dignity and forms the basis of our rights and duties.

Read Psalm 1. What is a good person like?

_____

a wicked person?

_____

God's guidelines and the Church help us follow the way of Christ. Yet we still sin, or fail to love God and others. The obstacles in our path make it difficult to avoid sin.

The Deadly Sins

Vice is one obstacle to Christian happiness and growth in Christ. Vice is a habit or tendency toward evil that all of us experience in some way. It is an ease in sinning that can be acquired by repeating a sinful act. Seven vices are called the **capital sins** or deadly sins. These are actually evil tendencies rather than sins. They are called *capital* because they can kill the life of God within us. The capital sins are listed below.

Pride is excessive love for one's self, an exaggerated opinion of one's own excellence. It leads us to think that we are better than others or that we deserve more than others. It is often referred to as the root of all sin. People who are proud fail to realize that all their gifts come from God.

Avarice (covetousness or greed) is an excessive desire for wealth and possessions. It may lead to lying, cheating, neglecting people who are poor, or being wasteful and extravagant.

Lust is an excessive desire for or indulgence in sexual pleasure. It is also the use of other people to satisfy one's own desire for such pleasure.

Wrath (anger) is an emotion that urges a person to repel anything displeasing. It leads to quarreling, hatred, and violence. Uncontrolled anger causes unhappiness to the one who is angry and to all those around him or her.

Gluttony is an excessive liking for or use of food or drink.

Envy is sadness at or resentment of another's success. A person who is envious may be happy about another's failure or misfortune.

Sloth is laziness, an unwillingness to do anything, particularly to fulfill one's religious obligations. Sloth leads to a neglect of social and personal duties.

Good Habits

A virtue is a habit or tendency that helps you do what is morally good. It helps you avoid evil and follow the way of Christ, living as a good Christian. It takes more than one action to make a virtue. Although virtue is a gift from God, it must be developed through practice until it becomes easy to do.

You have learned about the Theological Virtues of faith, hope, and charity and the cardinal virtues of prudence, justice, temperance, and fortitude.

> **Seven other important human virtues help you grow closer to Christ and express your love for him. These virtues are the opposites of the vices. Below are descriptions and stories for each virtue. Read them and, on a separate sheet of paper, answer these questions for each story.**
>
> 1. What vice seems to be most evident?
> 2. How would the situation be different if the corresponding virtue was developed in the people?

Generosity leads you to give freely of your time, talents, or money for the good of others, especially those who are in need. It helps you realize that the goods of the earth are meant to be shared.

> Elizabeth was hard-working and ambitious. She was in the band, on the swim team, and in the drama club. She wore designer clothes and always looked great. Recently a lay missionary addressed her class. He pointed out that some people were poor because the wealthy people in their countries owned the land and the workers received very low salaries. In the class discussion that followed the talk, Elizabeth was furious. "If poor people want a better life, they should work for it! And farmer workers should be grateful—at least they have jobs!"

Chastity controls our sexual desires by conforming them to right reason and the Christian faith. A chaste person is modest and respectful of the dignity of others.

> Bao knew that his parents would be upset with the magazines he was buying, so he sneaked them into his room. At first he bought them out of curiosity. Now he found his mind filled with the images of the women pictured in them. His own attitude toward the girls he knew was changing. He also noticed that he did not pray as he used to.

Humility, or Christian self-esteem, leads you to have a truthful opinion of yourself. You are able to give credit to God for your success and talents. A humble person depends on God and expresses this attitude in gratitude and prayer. A humble person recognizes that we are all brothers and sisters.

> Elena and Kyle were popular, and they knew it. Both were class officers, earned good grades, and were attractive. As head of the yearbook committee, Elena posted a notice asking for volunteers to help with the project. As she arranged the names of the volunteers into groups, she made sure she did not have to work with Mark. No one liked him, and she did not want to get stuck with him in her group. Instead she assigned Kyle and her closest friends to the project.

Meekness, mildness, gentleness, or Christian courage, leads you to be gracious and peaceful with others. A meek person can protect others and do what is right with calm courage. A meek person can control anger, bear sufferings, and accept responsibility without complaining.

"Would you go away and leave us alone!" Diego yelled at his little sister. It seemed as though every time he had a friend over, Ana would pester him. "Mom said I could watch TV with you and Antwan," she replied.

Diego felt anger well up inside as he thought of all the times he had to drag Ana along when he wanted to be with his friends. He heard Antwan groan, "What a brat."

"Get out of here, Ana," Diego shouted.

"No! I'll tell Mom!"

Diego could not stand her whining any longer. He jumped up and started toward her. Ana bolted for the door, and Diego swung it shut with all his might—on Ana's hand. He heard Ana's scream and his mother's footsteps on the stairs.

Temperance, or moderation, leads you to make sensible use of food and drink. It leads you to consume that which you need to sustain your health, avoid selfish use or overindulgence, and recognize the need to share with others.

Everyone was having a great time at Clare's party. Josh had just defeated Ben in a contest to see who could eat more. Suddenly in walked four classmates who had lost the directions to Clare's house. The new arrivals were hungry. Josh quietly walked into the kitchen. He saw that there were only three pieces of pizza left, and he took one more piece for himself.

Love of others and joy at their success helps you recognize the giftedness of others. This love promotes peace, harmony, and community and is proved through your prayers, acts of kindness, and encouraging words for others.

Judine had practiced for weeks for the cheerleading tryouts. She knew that stiff competition would come from Renée and Laura. After Judine did her routine, she felt good about it. "That will show them," she thought.

Laura was visibly nervous as she began her cheers. She lost her balance several times. At the end, there were tears in her eyes. "Good! For once she knows what it's like to lose!" Judine thought.

Renée's performance was flawless. Both Judine and Renée made the team. As the students left the gym, someone remarked how well Renée had performed. Judine snapped, "Of course they picked Renée! Her older sister is a cheerleader. She gets everything just because her sister is popular!"

Diligence helps you work hard and devote the time needed for any task. It leads you to faithfulness and the joy of persevering to the end.

Jim yelled at his brother for waking him so early. He had been up late the night before watching TV. He could hear his family getting ready for Mass. "Tell Dad I'm sick. Maybe I'll go to a later Mass." For a moment, he felt guilty. He could not even remember the last time he had prayed. Then he thought, "Why should I care? Lots of people don't pray."

A Moment with Jesus

Through Baptism, we have new life in the Holy Spirit, who helps us to make good choices. The Word of God guides us down the right path as long as, through faith and prayer, we put it into practice. Take a moment to ask Jesus for the grace you need to practice virtue and to combat the vices. Thank Jesus for the gift of the Holy Spirit who helps you and guides you.

The Choice Is Ours

God leaves us free to accept or reject love. We can choose to live a good life, cherishing and taking care of our world and the people in it. Or we can make bad choices and harm ourselves and others. For an act to be morally good, these three elements must be good: the act itself, the intention, and the circumstances. Whatever we choose to do, we will leave our mark on this world. At the end of our life, we will be judged on how we have loved. Then we will either enjoy love forever in heaven or suffer eternally without it in hell. This is the teaching of Jesus and his Church.

Tactics for Christian Growth

You are made for love. Sin stunts your growth and warps you. Through God's grace and with your cooperation, you can grow in all that is good and holy. Living the Christian way demands sacrifice and courage, but it promises you deep peace and happiness—now and for eternity. Plan your growth in these ways:

- In quiet prayer, examine your life and habitual ways of acting. Choose an area in which you want to improve.

- Decide on a virtue you need in order to accomplish your goal and grow closer to Christ. Select a way or two to practice it.

- Pray, especially through the Mass, Holy Communion, and the Sacrament of Reconciliation. Depend on God for the strength you need.

- Read about God's love in the Scriptures. Remember that God is always with you and understands that there will be many times you will fall. God looks to your heart and your desire to love and serve him.

- Read about the lives of the saints. See how they grew in love for God and others.

- Examine your life every day in prayer.

- Participate in works of service and charity to and for others, especially those who are in need.

Remember

What is a virtue?
A virtue is a habit or tendency that helps us do what is morally good. It helps us avoid evil and follow Christ.

How do virtues help us live as Christians?
Virtues help us grow closer to Christ and express our love for him. Although virtue is a gift from God, it must be developed through practice.

What does the Christian life demand, and what does it promise in return?
The Christian life demands sacrifice and courage, and it promises peace and happiness now and for eternity.

Words to Know

capital sins

Respond

Record in your reflection notebook one or two virtues you want to acquire. Note several occasions when you will have the opportunity to practice them.

Reach Out

1. Make a booklet entitled Guide to Christian Living. In it, list the virtues you have studied, their definitions, and original prayers for each. Collect stories and articles from books, magazines, and newspapers about people who possess these virtues.

2. With your family, design a covenant of love. List the benefits you all enjoy as members of your family. List ways each member can show gratitude and love for the others. Include each member's responsibilities for the care of the household.

3. Memorize the Ten Commandments and the theological and cardinal virtues.

4. Find a way to show love to someone who is considered "unlovable" in your neighborhood or school.

5. Choose a sentence from this chapter that you would like to remember. Write it on a card and keep it where you will see it.

6. Use a Bible to search the Book of Exodus. Locate references to God's covenant with the Israelites. Study one or more of these sections. Reflect on their significance to your life.

7. Research the life of Saint Isidore. Share some of your findings with another person. Then discuss with that person what can be learned from Isidore's way of living.

8. Use the Internet or a library to find information about some of the main teachings of the apostles contained in the *Didache*. Record in your reflection notebook anything that might help you in your spiritual journey.

9. Study the lives of various saints to find a different saint to represent each of the seven human virtues. Reflect on your findings and then pray to God, thanking him for his gift of the saints. Finally write in your reflection notebook any insights you have gained by studying these saints.

Virtue Versus Vice For each vice, write the letter of its opposite virtue.

_____ **1.** envy

_____ **2.** lust

_____ **3.** covetousness

_____ **4.** gluttony

_____ **5.** anger

_____ **6.** pride

_____ **7.** sloth

a. meekness

b. humility

c. temperance

d. love of others

e. diligence

f. generosity

g. chastity

True or False Write *T* if the statement is true and *F* if it is false.

_____ **1.** There are some people whom God does not love.

_____ **2.** Holiness is easy.

_____ **3.** You must be perfect to be a saint.

_____ **4.** Everyone has some vice.

_____ **5.** A virtue can be lost.

_____ **6.** We are free to be good or bad.

_____ **7.** Holiness is being loving.

_____ **8.** God helps us to make right choices.

Growing into Sainthood List five ways to grow in holiness.

_____

_____

_____

_____

_____

Virtues and Vices Find and circle:

AVARICE	CHASTITY	DILIGENCE
ENVY	HUMILITY	GENEROSITY
LUST	GLUTTONY	TEMPERANCE
PRIDE	MEEKNESS	LOVE OF OTHERS
SLOTH	WRATH	

```
L X A J U W O Y S X Y B N S T
H O C H A S T I T Y P V E Q F
K H V R A I P J A U D I N J Y
C F U E L Z L B Q H F X T E X
M Y G I O S U P E K A U E M Q
U I M R X F R H T O L S M A V
W U W N N I O N O K L K P D F
H M R A D H C T B S F M E U D
I B A E I W G F H K K U R O Y
A J T J T U X U P E G N A X K
J V H X B N W E C C R A N H K
J B A X M S N C M H U S C J R
F A A R Z N J H X G T G E X S
F K T K I E C N E G I L I D S
D Q K U G C X N T G J H V Q E
O R X W V O E S O P T R H X N
T N S H X R B B T P H J Z J K
J A O B O Y G T S N B C E T E
E R Y S C J N J U B K U G K E
T U I K R X N O L S K F Q P M
E T M D J L K R T I D W Y R V
Y Y M E D R M O D T Q D Q I B
X C R A M L W C M Y U Z W V F
J H D U N P J Y O D Y L Y V V
S J P N P U H X G P S K G Z G
```

In Need of Virtue Write the virtue most needed by the people who are described.

1. A person who eats an entire box of chocolates in a day _____

2. Someone who puts down classmates who excel _____

3. A person who screams at another driver in traffic _____

4. Someone who brags about being a great basketball player _____

Gather and Go Forth

Know and Proclaim

By living our Catholic faith, we share in God's holiness. We proclaim the love of God through our lives.

We Know Our Faith	We Proclaim Our Faith
We enter a covenant with God at Baptism. We show our love for God in the way we live our lives.	Catholics keep their covenant with God by obeying the Ten Commandments. Many Catholics reflect on the Ten Commandments before celebrating the Sacrament of Reconciliation.
The virtues are habits and tendencies that help us do what is morally good.	Catholics prayerfully review their thoughts and actions in order to better practice virtues and avoid vices.
The Christian life requires courage and sacrifice. Through God's grace, we can grow in holiness.	Catholics develop their spiritual life and grow in holiness through daily prayers and meditations, Scripture, and service to others.

The path to God and to holiness is the path that Jesus walked. As Catholics, we rely on the strength of the Holy Spirit to follow Jesus.

Jesus said to him, "I am the way and the truth and the life. No one comes to the Father except through me."

John 14:6

Test Your Catholic Knowledge

Fill in the circle that best completes the sentence.

A habit that helps you work hard and that leads to faithfulness and perseverance is:

- ◯ chastity.
- ◯ diligence.
- ◯ meekness.
- ◯ temperance.

A Catholic to Know

Augustine struggled to find God. He was a brilliant but restless student who searched for the meaning of love and life. None of the answers he found satisfied him. His mother, Saint Monica, prayed for his salvation, but nothing changed. Augustine was 33 years old when a voice called him to read Scripture. He opened the Bible and read Romans 13:13–14, a passage about turning from sin and toward Jesus. His subsequent conversion eventually led him to become the bishop of the city of Hippo in 396. Augustine's many sermons, letters, and books reflect an ever-deepening love for God. His spiritual autobiography, *Confessions*, written in the fifth century, continues to inspire and influence Christians today.

Saint Augustine

Witness and Share

These sentences describe what Catholics believe. Listen carefully as they are read. Ask yourself, "How strong are my Catholic beliefs?"

My Way to Faith

- I ask God for help in developing good habits and tendencies.

- I love others with the love of Jesus, regardless of the cost.

- I look up to virtuous people as role models.

- I examine my thoughts and actions in times of quiet prayer.

- I depend on God for the strength I need to accept responsibility without complaining.

Share Your Faith

Consider ways in which you can develop your Christian virtues through prayer, study, and good works. Write your ideas on the lines, and make a plan for your spiritual growth. Invite a family member or a friend to support you.

_____

_____

_____

_____

The Way of Faith

If you love someone, your actions will show it. There are a variety of ways you can show love and respect for the people you care about.

Check (✓) the boxes that show ways you love the following:

	obey	help	play	respect	pray
parents/ guardians	☐	☐	☐	☐	☐
best friend	☐	☐	☐	☐	☐
brother or sister	☐	☐	☐	☐	☐
teacher	☐	☐	☐	☐	☐
God	☐	☐	☐	☐	☐

A Loving God

God loves you! You see God's love in his creation, which we are called to care for. You see it in Jesus, who redeemed you. God greatly desires our love in return. He created you so that you could live in a relationship with him.

Once a Pharisee asked Jesus what the greatest commandment was. Read Matthew 22:37. What was Jesus' response?

_____

_____

_____

The first three commandments direct you to give your love completely to God. Loving God means putting your faith in God's promises and goodness and doing God's will.

> **FIRST COMMANDMENT**
> **I, the Lord, am your God.**
> **You shall not have other gods besides me.**

The First Commandment calls us to believe in God, to hope in him, and to love him above all else. It forbids worship of "other gods," or idols. An **idol** is anyone or anything you think is more important than God. The neighbors of the Israelites worshiped objects as gods. They prayed and sacrificed to things in nature and to statues they made. The Israelites knew the one true God, revealed to them as the only God, the almighty one who made all of creation. God was not made by human hands.

We can act foolishly today when we substitute other things for God. No, you are not likely to worship a tree or a statue. (Praying before a statue is not idolatry because we do not pray to it but to the holy one it represents.) But you might find yourself believing that your ultimate happiness comes from people or things besides God, such as the latest game or gadget. God invites you to believe and trust in him and not in the power of human beings or in material things. God's love will last forever, and God alone can make you happy. As Saint Augustine said, "Our hearts are restless, Lord, until they rest in you."

Dishonor

A person who loves God would not be likely to sin against the First Commandment by committing a sacrilege. A **sacrilege** is a violation of and irreverence toward a person, a place, or an object that is sacred because of public dedication to God. For example, stealing a consecrated vessel from a church, defacing church property, or showing disrespect for the Eucharist are examples of sacrilege. Attacking or harming a priest or a male or female religious is a sacrilege.

Playing with Fire

In society today, some people have an unhealthy and harmful fascination with the occult. The occult refers to beliefs and practices that are not divine but seek to control powers beyond human nature. By involving themselves with the occult, people try to use their own power to manage the forces of good and evil, something that only God can do. They do not trust God and try to control their own lives. People who do this fail to honor and trust in God. By attempting to use powers to control the lives of others, they show a lack of respect for the life and dignity of people. They fail to believe in God, to hope in him, and to love him above all else.

Following occult practices could seriously harm a person's friendship with God. These practices are a form of idolatry because they take a person away from the true worship owed to God.

- **Astrology:** Belief that the sun, moon, planets, and stars control our lives. A horoscope, the map of the heavens at the time of our birth, is thought to determine our temperament and what will happen to us. Astrology is against our belief in our free will and in God's providence. God alone knows the future.

- **Spiritualism:** Attempting to contact (and thus have power over) the souls of the dead or spirits of the other world by means of seances or Ouija boards. The Church forbids this because these practices represent a desire for power that God alone has. Our faith teaches us that, through the

Andreas Cellarius, *The Celestial Atlas.*

Communion of Saints, we are already in prayerful contact with those who have died in Christ. Through prayers of intercession, which know no boundaries, we can pray for the souls in purgatory who await eternal happiness with God.

- **Witchcraft:** The attempt to use magical formulas such as spells or chants by people who desire to exercise power that belongs only to God.

- **Satanism:** Worship of the devil, or worship of that which is contrary to God. Through Satanism, people seek to join forces with the power of evil. Turning from God who loves them and gave them life, they look to Satan to satisfy their needs and commit serious crimes for him. They are blind to the fact that the way of evil leads only to death, eternal death.

Cults

Cults can also threaten the worship of the true God. A cult is a system of misguided religious beliefs that centers around a strong religious leader. Sometimes sincere and good people are lured into joining a dangerous cult. They are brainwashed and led to do strange things. An extreme example is the one in which 937 people, including children, followed their leader to Guyana, South America, where they committed mass suicide in 1978. As Catholics, we have no need to belong to a cult because we believe that we are all brothers and sisters with the responsibility to care for one another.

Other Sins

The First Commandment is related to the Theological Virtues of faith, hope, and charity. If we truly acknowledge who God is, then it follows that we will believe in, hope in, and love God. A sin against faith is atheism, which rejects or denies the existence of God. One sin against hope is despair, in which people do not have enough trust in God's goodness and mercy. Another sin against hope is presumption, in which people either presume to be able to save themselves or assume that God will forgive them even if they do not repent from their sins.

Worshiping in Prayer

Jesus teaches you how to love God and put God first in your life. If you follow his example, you will share your deepest thoughts and desires with God. Prayer is the way you talk to God.

> **Read the following Scripture passages and complete each phrase.**
>
> **Matthew 6:6**
> [W]hen you pray, go
>
> _____
>
> _____
>
> **Matthew 18:20**
> [W]here two or three are gathered together in my name,
>
> _____
>
> **Matthew 21:22**
> Whatever you ask for in prayer with faith,
>
> _____
>
> **Mark 11:25**
> When you stand to pray, forgive
>
> _____
>
> _____
>
> _____
>
> **Luke 18:1**
> [P]ray
>
> _____

> Prayer is our humble answer to the inconceivable surprise of living.
>
> Rabbi Abraham Heschel

A Moment with Jesus

You never grow tired of talking to your closest friends. God wants to be your best friend. As you grow in faith, you discover more fully how to love God through prayer. Some types of prayer include the following:

Adoration—praising God and telling God of your love

Contrition—telling God you are sorry for your sins

Thanksgiving—being grateful for all of God's gifts

Supplication—petitioning or asking God for help for yourself or others

Take a moment now to silently adore God and all of his greatness. Tell him that you love him. Talk to Jesus and tell him that you are sorry for your sins. Tell him what you are thankful for. Ask the Holy Spirit for the help you need for yourself and others.

Sacrifice

A **sacrifice** is a gift given to God. It is a sign of all of the attitudes of prayer mentioned above. A sacrifice can be large or small. It can be doing something difficult or giving up something we like. We can offer our entire lives and all our actions to God with the perfect sacrifice of Christ offered on the Cross. We can do this every day in a morning offering. We can do it especially when we celebrate the Eucharist. The Eucharist contains all forms of prayer and is the ultimate sacrifice.

The Power of God's Name

> **SECOND COMMANDMENT**
> **You shall not take the name of the Lord, your God, in vain.**

Do you know why your parents or guardians gave you your name? Do you know its meaning? Names are important because they show respect for the uniqueness and dignity of each individual. In Scripture, a person's name often was a clue to his or her character. The name of God, Yahweh, was so great that the Israelites never said it aloud and instead used the word *Lord.* God revealed to them the holy divine name and its power. Calling on God's name meant calling on God's great goodness and power. God taught the people to bless rather than curse. God wanted his people to heal and care for one another through the power of his name. God asked them to use the divine name with reverence and to speak to and of others with love.

Speaking with Love

The Second Commandment directs us to honor God's name by using it with love and respect. When we use God's name, we should have an honorable reason for using it. Two serious and reverent uses of God's name are vows and oaths. A **vow** is a free promise made to God to perform a good act not required for salvation. Religious usually take vows of poverty,

chastity, and obedience. An oath is calling on God to witness to the truth of what one says. Anyone who lies under oath asks God to witness a lie. This is the sin of perjury.

Christians respect all names. Sacred names are to be given special reverence. A person could hurt friendship with God in these ways:

- Careless, casual, and inappropriate use of God's name is profanity.
- Words that insult the goodness of God or show hate for God are blasphemy.
- Calling on God to bring evil or harm to someone or something is cursing.
- Cursing and language that insults God are commonly called swearing.

Some people confuse cursing and swearing with vulgar language, offensive and "dirty" words that show irreverence and disrespect for the human body. Sometimes vulgar words are used in anger and involve the careless use of God's name. They show disrespect for God and others. They mark a person as crude and unfeeling. Your words reflect who you are. As a Christian, honor God with your words. Praise and encourage others. Respect all people, because when you honor them, you honor God.

Remember

How do the first two commandments help us love and honor God?

The First Commandment tells us to love God above all and to put God first in our lives. The Second Commandment tells us to honor God's name and use it with love and respect.

What are some types of prayer?

Some types of prayer include adoration, contrition, thanksgiving, and supplication.

Words to Know

sacrifice
sacrilege
vow

Respond

In Psalm 46, we hear God say, "Be still and confess that I am God!" Spend a few minutes trying to realize who our God is. Think about God's greatness and goodness. In your reflection notebook, write a short prayer of adoration to God.

Reach Out

1. Find a place in your bedroom for a prayer corner. Put a table there with your Bible and a candle. You might wish to keep your reflection notebook there too. Decide on a regular prayer schedule.

2. Pray or make up a litany of praise honoring God by many names. Offer your prayer to make up for disrespect of God's name.

3. Watch TV for one night and pay close attention to commercials. Make a list of things that commercials suggest will bring us happiness. Write a brief script for a TV commercial that reminds people that true and lasting happiness is found only in God.

4. Imagine that you have been asked to design a Web site to convince young people not to get involved in the occult or cults. Make an outline of the information you would provide.

5. Talk to your parents or guardians about relatives and friends who have died and are joined to you through the Communion of Saints. Ask about good qualities that these people had that can serve as an inspiration to you. In your prayer, ask these people to intercede for you so that you might grow in your relationship with Jesus.

6. Begin your day and the important activities of your life by praying the Sign of the Cross. Ask God to help you honor his name through your words and actions. Remind yourself, as you participate in various activities throughout the day, that you are doing so in the name of the Father, and of the Son, and of the Holy Spirit. At the end of the day, review your day and ask yourself whether or not your words and actions brought honor to God's name.

7. Talk to your parents or guardians about why they chose to name you as they did. Talk about the significance of their names and the names of other family members.

False Gods For each set of words, find the correct heading from the list below and write it on the line.

idols   astrology   spiritualism   occult   prayer
witchcraft   Satanism   honoring God   cult

1. _____

magic
chants
spells

2. _____

sun
money
golden calf

3. _____

horoscope
sun and stars
the future

4. _____

the dead
seances
Ouija board

5. _____

adoration
contrition
supplication

6. _____

spiritualism
witchcraft
Satanism

7. _____

First Commandment
Second Commandment
Third Commandment

8. _____

the devil
power of evil
crime

9. _____

strong leader
brainwashing
suicide

Prove It Wrong For each statement, write a reason to show that it is not true.

1. People today do not have idols.

_____

_____

2. Ouija boards are harmless fun.

_____

_____

3. God does not want us to pray, because God already knows what is on our minds.

_____

_____

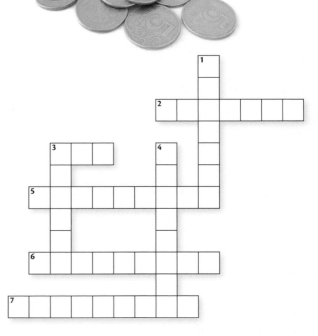

Word Power Fill in the puzzle.

Across

2. Calling down evil on someone or something

3. A free promise made to God to perform a good act not required for salvation

5. Words that insult the goodness of God or show hate for God

6. Careless, too frequent, and inappropriate use of God's name

7. Violation of and irreverence toward a person, a place, or an object that is sacred because of public dedication to God

Down

1. Lying while under oath; asking God to witness a lie

3. Describes offensive or "dirty" words, which show disrespect for people

4. Taking an oath

Gather and Go Forth

Know and Proclaim

We can proclaim our Catholic faith because we love God with all our heart, soul, and mind.

We Know Our Faith	We Proclaim Our Faith
God loves us and greatly desires our love in return. Loving God means putting faith in God's promises.	Adoration is a devotion to Jesus by which Catholics praise God while in the presence of the Blessed Sacrament—the Eucharist. Many parishes have adoration chapels.
The First Commandment calls us to believe in God, to hope in him, and to love him above all else.	Catholics fast one hour before receiving Holy Communion. This practice reminds them that they are to worship God with their entire mind, body, and spirit.
We honor God's name with love and respect when we follow the Second Commandment.	Catholics pray prayers called litanies in which God is praised and honored by many names.

God gave us the first three commandments to unite himself with us. True and lasting joy is found in observing God's laws.

"You shall love the Lord, your God, with all your heart, with all your soul, and all your mind."

Matthew 22:37

Test Your Catholic Knowledge

Fill in the circle that best answers the question.

Which of the following is an example of honoring the Second Commandment?

○ substituting other things for God

○ wishing harm on another person

○ honoring God with your words

○ going to Mass every Sunday

A Catholic to Know

Saint Hilary was a friendly and charitable man.
Following his conversion to Christianity, the people
of Poitiers, France, chose Hilary as bishop in 353. He
protested Arianism, a heresy that denied Christ's
divinity. Emperor Constantius II, who followed the
heresy, demanded that Hilary condemn Saint Athanasius,
a great defender of the faith. Hilary refused and was
banished. While in exile, Hilary challenged the Arians
to debate. Hilary's arguments and writings show that he
was fierce in defending the faith, but he always showed
charity to the bishops who had succumbed to the heresy,
showing them their errors. Although the emperor
called him a "disturber of the peace," Saints Jerome
and Augustine praised him as "teacher of the churches."

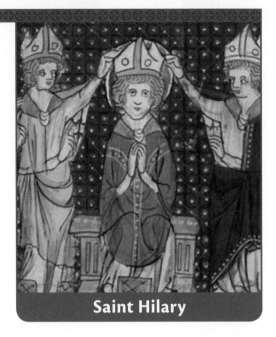

Saint Hilary

Witness and Share

**These sentences describe what Catholics believe. Listen carefully as they are read.
Ask yourself, "How strong are my Catholic beliefs?"**

My Way to Faith

- I pray before the Blessed Sacrament during Eucharistic Adoration.

- I abstain from eating anything one hour before receiving Holy Communion.

- I honor God with my words by respecting and encouraging others.

- I keep the promises I make to others.

- I put God first in my life.

Share Your Faith

**Consider ways you can put God first in your life. Write your ideas on the lines, and
invite a family member and friend to support you.**

_____

_____

_____

_____

The Way of Worship

Take a look at how you spend your time on Sundays. Answer the following questions.

Did you attend Mass last weekend? If so, which Mass did you attend and where?

_____

What meal or meals did your family share together last Sunday?

_____

What was one activity you did last Sunday to relax?

_____

What was an activity your family did together last Sunday?

_____

What would you like your family to do together on Sundays?

_____

Why is it good to have one day when your family can be together?

_____

The Lord's Day

Sunday is special. It is the **Lord's Day**—a day to be together with those you love and to join with them in worshiping God.

> **THIRD COMMANDMENT**
> **Remember to keep holy the Lord's Day.**

The Third Commandment guided the people of Israel to set aside the seventh day for rest. The day was called the **Sabbath.** The word itself means "rest." In the Creation story of Genesis, God rested on the seventh day and made it holy. On the Sabbath, the Israelites remembered God's great act of Creation. They gave thanks and praise to God for his goodness. Honoring the Sabbath was part of their covenant with God. It was a sacred obligation. The Sabbath was a day on which to read the Scriptures, pray, serve a festive meal, and offer special blessings.

The early Christians celebrated their Sabbath by joining together for the Eucharist. Like the Jewish people, they worshiped by listening to God's Word. They also shared bread and wine transformed into the Body and Blood of Jesus. They changed their Sabbath from Saturday to Sunday, the traditional day of the Resurrection and of Pentecost. By joining together as a community they grew in love for God and for one another. Today, we continue to observe Sunday as the Lord's Day by celebrating the Eucharist and resting from work. We also strive to avoid making demands on others that might hinder them from observing the Lord's Day. Work is an important way in which we participate in God's creation. The same dignity that comes with work also comes with resting from work. All workers are entitled to rest.

A Weekly Celebration of Easter

As a member of the Church, you are responsible for keeping Sunday as a day for celebration. On the Lord's Day we celebrate the Paschal Mystery of Jesus together at Mass on the day itself or the evening before. Every Sunday is a little Easter, a celebration of the new life won for us by Christ.

Sunday is a special day for loving God. You can show you are grateful for God's love and care when you worship. By dressing appropriately and going to Church, by joining in the prayers and songs at the eucharistic liturgy, and by receiving Holy Communion, you proclaim "I love God. I am God's follower."

Sunday is a day of rest, relaxation, and joy. On Sunday, you let go of your everyday problems. You avoid unnecessary work and take time to relax. You thank God for creation and for the gift of life God has given you. One way to thank God for life is by taking care of your health. Relaxing on Sunday renews you in body, mind, and spirit and prepares you for sharing and serving others during a new week.

Sunday is a day for strengthening community and family life. Followers of Jesus take time to appreciate one another. The Eucharist reminds us that we are all brothers and sisters, called to care for one another. Likewise, time together with your family is important. When you share family fun or meals, you get to know the members of your family. You grow to love them. When you worship together as a family, you are making God an important part of your family life.

Home is where we first hear the Word of God proclaimed. For this reason, we can call our family home the domestic church—a community of grace and prayer. Our home is like a school where we learn good habits or virtues that help us to follow Jesus more closely.

A Foretaste of Heaven

The Eucharist is the very heart of Catholic life and the greatest prayer we can offer God. During Mass, the redeeming acts of Christ are made present for us to share in. We offer Jesus and ourselves to the Father. In the Eucharist, Jesus strengthens us for our spiritual journey.

The Eucharist is a time of both community and personal prayer. This gift from Jesus nourishes and strengthens the community of believers by word and sacrament. The Word of God proclaimed at Mass challenges us to love and serve others. Receiving the Body and Blood of Christ transforms us into him, unites us, and energizes us to live as Christ's followers. The Eucharist makes us what we are—the Church, the Body of Christ.

At the Eucharist, we are most completely the Church. We are God's people, celebrating God's goodness, being redeemed, and sharing God's love. We proclaim our faith in the Creed, witness to our belief in Jesus by offering the Eucharist, and are sent out to proclaim the Good News by word and by actions. Christ, the head of the Church, is with us during the Eucharist in a special way. He is present

in the people gathered in his name,

in the priest who represents him in offering the sacrifice and presiding over the meal,

in the Word that is proclaimed,

and under the appearance of bread and wine that has been consecrated.

Mass is a foretaste of heaven where it is always Sunday ("eternal rest"!) and where all the saints are united in love and glorify God. Through the liturgy, we are united with the Church in heaven, with the Blessed Virgin Mary, and with the saints.

Why Bother?

Here are reasons some young people might give for not going to Mass and Christian responses to them:

I get nothing out of it. The Mass is not a form of entertainment that we passively watch, as though attending a play or a concert. It is a ritual action that we participate in. We do not attend a birthday celebration to get something out of it. We do so to express our love for the person being honored. The Mass is a way of expressing that we are totally dependent on God and desire to be united with him. Praising God is what we were made for. God thinks of us, keeps us in existence, and loves us seven days a week. In response, we offer praise and thanks and ask him for his continued presence in our lives. And, of course, we actually *do* get something out of the Mass every time: Jesus!

I can pray better in my own room or while walking outside. Of course, God is present in our rooms and in the woods. In the Eucharist, however, Jesus Christ is present in a real and substantial way, under the appearances of bread and wine. In Holy Communion, we receive into our lives the Real Presence of Jesus Christ, his Body and Blood. Walking in the woods is a nice personal activity, but it does not teach us to love our enemies, to pray for our persecutors, or to love our neighbor as ourselves. We need to hear the Word of God proclaimed to us so that we can change our lives and grow closer to him. Likewise, the Mass is a communal prayer that reminds us that we are all brothers and sisters with the responsibility of caring for one another.

I know people who go to Mass every Sunday and who do not live like Christians. The Christian community, like any family, is not perfect. We are all sinners in need of God's grace. We often have difficulty living up to Christ's standards. The bottom line is that we all need salvation. Through the Eucharist, we obtain forgiveness for venial sins and strength to improve. Each of us could be worse without the graces of the Mass. The Mass reminds us that we are all in need of God's grace, and we pray for one another that we may live lives of holiness.

It's always the same. Rituals, by their nature, are actions that are performed in the same manner over and over again. Imagine what it would be like if every birthday celebration was completely different from the previous one. We would not know what to do. The ritual of the Mass provides us with a structure and a rhythm that allow us to express praise and thanksgiving to God. Because the Mass is a ritual, we can even celebrate the Eucharist in another language and fully participate because of our recognition of the parts of the Mass.

Your Ritual

As a Catholic, your daily ritual should include prayer. Check (✓) the boxes of the things that are part of your morning ritual. If prayer is not a part of your morning routine, resolve to include it.

☐ hitting the snooze button

☐ praying

☐ showering

☐ listening to music

☐ watching the news

☐ eating breakfast

☐ working out

☐ walking the dog

A Moment with Jesus

In the Eucharist, Jesus offers us the gift of himself. Take a moment to thank Jesus for giving himself to you in the Eucharist. Ask him to help you recognize your need to be strengthened by the weekly celebration of the Mass. Ask the Holy Spirit to help you participate fully in the Mass as a way of expressing your gratitude for God's wonderful gifts.

A Christ Calendar

Sunday is the most important day of the week, when we celebrate Christ's Resurrection. In a sense, every Sunday is a celebration of Easter. Sunday, then, is the foundation of the **liturgical year,** which revolves around the life, Death, and Resurrection of Jesus Christ.

The Church begins the liturgical year by preparing for the coming of Jesus in the season of Advent. We celebrate his coming at Christmas and then ponder this mystery of the Incarnation during the weeks after Christmas. In Lent we prepare to celebrate Jesus' passion, Death, and Resurrection. We celebrate it on Easter and reflect on it during the weeks after Easter. During Ordinary Time, we continue to celebrate the Paschal Mystery of Jesus by considering the many wonderful events in Jesus' life.

As a maturing Catholic, you try to make prayer a part of your everyday life. A good way to do this is to reflect on the Scripture readings for each upcoming Sunday Mass. As you learn more about Jesus, you will become aware of God acting in your life. You will talk to God more often. You will love and care about others more deeply. Your love of God and others will help you grow in grace, in friendship with Jesus.

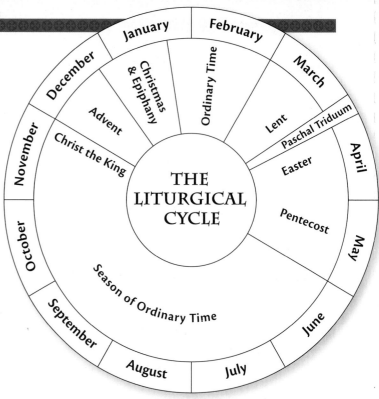

Shade in or leave blank the liturgical seasons on the graphic. Use the appropriate symbolic colors:

Advent and Lent—purple, for penance

Ordinary Time—green, for life and hope

Easter and Christmas—white, for glory

Holy Days of Obligation

Solemnity of Mary, Mother of God: January 1

Ascension: forty days after Easter (Many dioceses celebrate the Ascension on the seventh Sunday of Easter. Check with your diocese.)

Assumption: August 15

All Saints' Day: November 1

Immaculate Conception: December 8

Christmas: December 25

Celebrating Special Feasts

Certain days in the Church year commemorate special people or events. These days are called **holy days of obligation.** The Church calls everyone to celebrate these days in a grand way by participating in the Eucharist. These days are decided by the bishops of each country, who may dispense with the obligation if circumstances call for it. The holy days of obligation for the United States are described on page 295.

Throughout the year, along with celebrating Jesus, the Church celebrates the Paschal Mystery of Jesus through the lives of Mary and the saints in the liturgy. This shows we are united with the liturgy of heaven. Usually saints are celebrated on the date of their death, their "birthday" into eternal life. The Eucharist on that day has prayers to them and in their honor. Some people name their children for the saint on whose feast they are born.

Prayers in the Liturgy of the Hours, the Prayer of Christians, correspond to the liturgical calendar and the feast days of the saints. Through the liturgy of the Eucharist and the Liturgy of the Hours, at all hours of the day and night, the Church is praising God somewhere in the world.

Remember

How does the Third Commandment help us worship God?

The Third Commandment tells us to make Sunday a day of worship by celebrating the Eucharist, avoiding unnecessary work, and strengthening community and family life.

What is the purpose of the Church's liturgical calendar?

The Church year revolves around the Paschal Mystery—the life, Death, Resurrection, and ascension of Jesus Christ. We also celebrate the Paschal Mystery of Jesus through the lives of Mary and the saints.

Words to Know

holy days of obligation
liturgical year
Lord's Day
Sabbath

Respond

In your reflection notebook, set up a schedule for yourself that makes Sunday a day of prayer and relaxation, a day for deepening community and family life. Keep your schedule practical. Then try to follow it.

Reach Out

1. After Mass next Sunday, in your reflection notebook, write your reflections on the Scripture readings or homily.

2. Make Sunday a special day by doing some of the following:

   - Wear clothes that express how important this day is.
   - Participate in Mass with your family.
   - Lead an original prayer before meals.
   - Spend extra time with your family.
   - Contribute money to the collection.
   - Read a brief section of the Scriptures.
   - Suggest that your family go on an outing or visit relatives.
   - Read the Sunday church bulletin.
   - Become involved in a parish activity.

3. **To worship the Father through Jesus, you need to develop attitudes that help you love him. Select two from the list below and, on a sheet of paper, describe how they can help you keep the Third Commandment.**

attention	humility
respect	prayerfulness
willingness to listen	gratitude
reverence	love
faith	unselfishness
trust	forgiveness

4. **With other family members, explore how people of other faith traditions worship.**

5. **Celebrate a feast of Mary or of a saint in a special way in your class or at home.**

6. **Talk to your parents or guardians about family rituals. Identify how your family celebrates special occasions and holidays through rituals: actions that are performed in the same manner over and over again. Talk about which family rituals are your favorite. The next time you go to Mass, pay attention to the ritual of the Mass. Ask yourself how the "sameness" of the Mass helps you and the community to celebrate together.**

CHAPTER 22 Review Activities

| SUNDAY | MONDAY | TUESDAY | WEDNESDAY | THURSDAY | FRIDAY | SATURDAY |

Sunday: A Day for R and R Complete these statements with a word that begins with *r*.

1. The word *Sabbath* means r _____ .

2. After creating all things, on the seventh day, God r _____ .

3. Christians observed the Sabbath on Sunday, the day of the R _____ .

4. Relaxing on Sunday r _____ you in body, mind, and spirit.

5. In the Eucharist, we share in the r _____ acts of Christ.

6. R _____ the Body and Blood of Christ unites us and makes us the Church.

7. The priest r _____ Christ during the Eucharist.

8. We celebrate the Eucharist because at the Last Supper, Jesus said,

"Do this in r _____ of me."

Reasons to Worship Check (✓) the six most positive reasons for worshiping at the Eucharist.

_____ **1.** You owe God thanks and praise.

_____ **2.** Your parents or guardians will be angry or hurt if you do not.

_____ **3.** God tells us to.

_____ **4.** You might go to hell if you do not.

_____ **5.** The Church is united there with Christ and with one another.

_____ **6.** It is the highest form of prayer.

_____ **7.** People will think better of you.

_____ **8.** You participate in the Paschal Mystery of Christ.

_____ **9.** It makes you feel good.

_____ **10.** You witness to your faith.

Living Liturgically Match the liturgical seasons with their scriptural themes.

a. Advent

b. Christmas

c. Ordinary time

d. Lent

e. Easter

_____ Its readings are filled with alleluias, hope, and excitement because Christ is risen and he will come again.

_____ Its readings help us in prayer and in service to others by reflection on Christ's teachings and public ministry.

_____ Its readings help us prepare joyfully for the coming of Christ's birth and his coming at the end of time.

_____ Its readings call for conversion of heart to become followers of Christ. They teach us about the courage we need to let go of sinful ways so we can rise to eternal life.

_____ Its readings tell of Christ's birth and his revelations about himself.

Gather and Go Forth

Know and Proclaim

We seek to know the truths of our Catholic faith and proclaim them in our worship.

We Know Our Faith	We Proclaim Our Faith
Sunday is the Lord's Day, a day to gather and worship God as a community.	As Catholics, we celebrate the Lord's Day by going to Mass on Sunday to celebrate the Paschal Mystery of Jesus. Every Sunday is a celebration of the new life won for us by Christ.
The Eucharist nourishes and strengthens the community of believers by Word and sacrament.	Catholics celebrate the seasons and feasts of the liturgical year in their homes with traditional meals and customs.
The liturgical year revolves around the life, Death, and Resurrection of Jesus Christ.	Catholics mark each season of the liturgical year with different colors. During Advent and Lent, the color purple symbolizes penance. During Ordinary Time, green symbolizes life and hope. During Christmas and Easter, white symbolizes glory.

We kneel before the God who made us. With hearts overflowing, we respond to God's goodness and love by participating in the eucharistic feast.

*Enter, let us bow down in
    worship;
  let us kneel before the LORD
    who made us.
For he is our God,
  we are the people he shepherds,
  the sheep in his hands.*

Psalm 95:6–7

Test Your Catholic Knowledge

Fill in the circle that best completes the sentence.

The foundation of the liturgical year is the:

- ◯ mystery of the Incarnation.
- ◯ celebration of the witness of the saints.
- ◯ ministry of Saint Peter as bishop of Rome.
- ◯ life, Death, and Resurrection of Jesus Christ.

A Catholic to Know

Paul was born in Italy in 1694, the second of 16 children. At age 15, his awareness of Christ's suffering for him led him to perform acts of penance. He slept on the floor and denied himself favorite foods so he could focus exclusively on Jesus. Later in his life, God called him to form a group of men called Passionists who were dedicated to preaching parish missions. Paul developed a method for giving parish mission talks that involved lay people. He was so powerful when he preached and so gentle in confession that he brought many people back to the Lord. We celebrate Saint Paul's gifts of prophecy and healing on October 20.

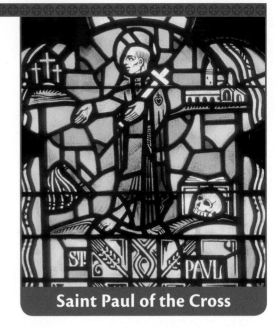

Saint Paul of the Cross

Witness and Share

These sentences describe what Catholics believe. Listen carefully as they are read. Ask yourself, "How strong are my Catholic beliefs?"

My Way to Faith

- I observe the Lord's Day by going to Mass and refraining from unnecessary work.

- I am nourished and energized by the Eucharist.

- I recognize the true and real presence of Jesus in the Eucharist.

- I reflect on the Scripture readings in preparation for Sunday Mass.

- I follow the seasons and feasts of the Church's liturgical calendar.

Share Your Faith

What is one act of service that you can offer as a sacrifice to the Lord? How does this sacrifice help you follow Christ more closely and share in his passion and Death? Write your ideas on the lines. Invite a family member or friend to join you in your service.

_____

_____

_____

_____

The Way of the Family

"Happy birthday," Ann's mother said with a hug. "Have some yogurt and toast."

"Please, Mom, not today," begged Ann. "I just have time for juice."

"You better put on a warmer jacket," advised Mom. "It's supposed to get cold today."

"I'll be OK," said Ann, running out the door, saying to herself that Mom had been bugging her all week, especially about studying for the English test.

"Be careful crossing the street, and remember to come home right after school," Mom called after her.

Ann hurried down the street. Although the sign at the corner read Don't Walk, Ann darted across the street. A car appeared from nowhere and brakes screeched. Horrified, Ann realized that she was almost killed on her birthday.

She was still shaking as she sat in English class and stared at her vocabulary test. Why hadn't she studied a little every day as her mother had suggested? Ann turned in her test, knowing she had failed. She brightened, though, when she was seated next to Roberto in history class. Suddenly, her stomach rumbled! Her face burned as she turned red with embarrassment.

After school, Ann met Sue and Rose, two older girls. "We're going to the mall," said Sue. "Want to come?" Mom said to come right home, but it had been a hard day and she needed some fun. "I'd love to go," Ann replied.

Four hours later, Ann walked into her house, feeling miserable. The bus had been late, and she was cold and hungry. "Happy birthday!" came a chorus of voices. The living room was filled with her friends. "Where have you been?" someone asked. "Your party is almost over!"

Ann burst into tears and ran to her room. When Dad came in, she sobbed on his shoulder. "Everything went wrong today. This was not a happy birthday at all."

"We'll talk about it later," said Dad. "Right now, why don't you wash your face and get something to eat?" Ann stopped crying and joined her guests. When Ann and her parents did discuss the day, she realized that obeying her mother would have been helpful.

Ann has a right to enjoy herself and make some decisions on her own. However, she also has a responsibility to obey her parents. In the story you just read, underline the mishaps that Ann would have prevented by obeying. How did Ann's parents show their love?

_____

_____

_____

_____

Authority, a Gift of Love

> **FOURTH COMMANDMENT**
> **Honor your father and your mother.**

The Fourth Commandment calls for obedience. The word *obey* comes from a Latin word that means "to listen." To obey God is to listen and to do what God says. God's voice comes through the commandments, the Gospels, and other people. Parents and others in authority have been entrusted by God with the responsibility of caring for you and making sure you have everything required for human decency. In other words, they represent God's authority.

Your parents or guardians and those who care for you love you and want what is good for you. In return, you have the responsibility to show them gratitude, respect, and obedience. **Obedience** enables you to do what those with rightful authority ask of you. Your parents or guardians ask you to do certain acts and to avoid other things so that you can fulfill your potential. By obeying them, you are obeying God. You are returning God's love.

To Obey Is to Love

All creation follows God's plan. With your free will, you can cooperate with God's plan. When you serve God in faith by obeying those in authority, you praise and love God. Love for God should impel you to do God's will gladly. Often small acts are hardest: cleaning your room, taking your brother or sister with you, turning down the stereo, taking out the garbage. Each act of obedience is not the burden of a slave but the gift of one who loves. In doing God's will, you will find joy and be united with God in a love that never ends.

To Obey Is to Be Free

When we obey the right people, we do not give up our freedom, but rather, we find the freedom to grow as we should. Think of it this way. If you wanted to excel at playing the piano or playing tennis, you might enlist the help of a teacher or coach. Without help, you are not free to enjoy this new skill as you would like. If you obey your teacher or coach and learn the skills you want to learn, you will be free to enjoy that new skill.

Whenever people live together, they need rules to help them enjoy and protect their freedom. Imagine what would happen without traffic laws. You could drive on the left-hand side of the street—but you would land in the hospital.

Laws are made for the good of all. When you follow them, you add to everyone's well-being, including your own. When you do not obey lawful authority, you let some other power rule you. If your parents or guardians tell you not to smoke and your friends talk you into it, you let your friends run your life. Often disobedience makes you a slave to a fault—it takes away your true freedom. For example, when you refuse to obey your teacher, you are probably giving in to your pride, anger, or laziness. Obedience frees you from these evil tendencies.

Mature adults choose to obey. To win a game, an athlete follows the coach's direction. Likewise, you must listen to those whom God places in your life to guide you. Only then will you be free to realize your full potential.

> **Your parents or guardians have probably told you to stay away from drugs. How will obeying them make you free?**
>
> _____
>
> _____
>
> _____
>
> _____

A Moment with Jesus

Because Jesus loved his Father, he obeyed him. He became the son of Mary and Joseph and "was obedient to them." (Luke 2:51) The words of Jesus to his Father the night before he died were his life's motto: "Not my will but yours be done." (Luke 22:42) Take a moment to thank Jesus for being a model of obedience for you. Ask him for the grace you need to obey your parents or guardians and others in authority.

To Obey Is to Do God's Will

Those who govern receive their authority from God to promote the common good and to protect the dignity of human life. The Fourth Commandment calls you to respect those in authority as long as their efforts are intended to improve the conditions of human life. You are not bound to follow unjust laws—laws that contradict one of God's laws. Authority should be committed to the common good and should use morally acceptable means. If it does not, "We must obey God rather than men." (Acts of the Apostles 5:29) It is your duty to work and pray that unjust laws be changed. Citizens should work with civil authority to build a society of truth, justice, oneness, and freedom.

Before you decide to disobey orders, however, be sure those orders are contrary to God's law. In general, the laws of those who care for you are what God in his love wants for you. You should obey promptly and cheerfully. To argue, to challenge, or to ignore the directions

of those who lawfully command you shows little love for them or for God.

Parents are not perfect. They make mistakes. Do you still owe them obedience? Yes. Despite their faults, those who take the place of God in your life speak for him. You should pray for them, obey them, and work together with them to maintain a healthy environment in your family.

To Obey Is to Be Open

Describe how Paul can question a family rule in a loving, respectful way.

Paul is invited to a party that goes beyond his curfew. He decides to ask his father to extend his curfew time. For what should Paul pray?

_____

_____

What time and place should Paul choose to approach his father?

_____

_____

_____

With what attitude should Paul speak?

_____

_____

_____

Obedience could become more difficult as you grow older, make more decisions on your own, and become more independent. Obedience requires more effort, sacrifice, humility, and trust. You can grow in obedience through practice. Obedience is easier if communication lines are open. By talking with your parents or guardians, you learn to know each other. Communication fosters friendship and love. It is not so hard to obey someone you love.

Remember, of these parents you were born; what can you give them for all they gave you?

Sirach 7:28

Called to Give Honor

The Fourth Commandment is worded "Honor your father and your mother." (Deuteronomy 5:16) To honor means to show gratitude, respect, and love. You honor your parents or guardians by being proud of them and by not offending them. How else can you honor your parents or guardians?

_____

Your duty toward your parents does not end when you turn 18 or 21. The Fourth Commandment requires that you provide for your parents in their old age. Adults show gratitude to their parents by caring for them when they can no longer care for themselves.

All senior citizens deserve your respect. They have a right to those things that are required for human decency. Their experience, accomplishments, wisdom, and virtue make them precious gems in your life. You share in the responsibility we all have to make sure that senior citizens are cared for and that their human dignity is protected.

Name an elderly person who means a lot to you.

_____

What does he or she add to your life?

_____

What have you added to his or her life?

_____

God's Gift of Life

Life is a wonderful gift from God. Our Creator is so good and loving that he made us in his own image. We can think and love. We are holy; we have dignity. God even sent his Son to die for us so that we can live forever. How precious we are in God's sight! To safeguard the sacred gift of life, God gave us the Fifth Commandment.

FIFTH COMMANDMENT
You shall not kill.

This law obliges us to respect human life, from the moment of conception, by protecting and nurturing it. We are called to support institutions that improve the conditions of human life. The Fifth Commandment commands us to avoid whatever would harm or destroy life. In gratitude for life, you care for it. By showing love for God's gift, you show love for God.

Jesus' Love for Life

The mission of Jesus was to bring God's life to all people. He healed those who were sick, blind, deaf, and paralyzed. He raised the dead to life. When he met those who were wounded in spirit, such as Zacchaeus and Mary Magdalene, he made them whole. He reached out to children and lepers. He treated everyone with gentleness, reverence, and compassion.

Jesus taught respect for life. His new commandment was to "[L]ove one another as I love you." (John 15:12) He explained it in the parable of the Good Samaritan. (Luke 10:29–37) In that parable, a man attacked by thieves is rescued by a Samaritan, an enemy. Jesus asks his followers to love even their enemies.

Cherishing Your Own Life

Not so long ago, God called you out of nothingness. Out of millions of possibilities, God gave you life. At Baptism, God adopted you as his son or daughter. The Trinity began to dwell within you. In Holy Communion, Jesus himself comes to live in you. Your destiny is to live forever with God and all the saints. You learn to treasure and take care of your life and the lives of others because life is sacred, a gift from God.

Check (✓) any of the following acts by which you have seen people hurt or destroy their lives.

- ☐ overeating
- ☐ suicide
- ☐ unnecessary use of drugs
- ☐ immoderate use of alcohol
- ☐ dangerous sports
- ☐ smoking
- ☐ little exercise
- ☐ wrong use of medication
- ☐ not getting enough sleep
- ☐ not eating the right food
- ☐ reckless driving
- ☐ taking life-threatening risks unnecessarily
- ☐ joining a gang

Nurturing Life in Everyone

Each person is unique, special, and loved by God. Each one is a reflection of God. The Fifth Commandment calls you to nurture life in everyone, beginning with your family, friends, and neighbors. When you foster life, you share in God's work of creation. You serve God's kingdom of peace and love. This means seeing that people have what they need to grow. They need material goods such as food, clothing, and shelter. They also require human support—praise, encouragement, understanding, and sympathy.

Murder is the most hideous sin against life. Everyone has the right to life, including those who are unborn, mentally disabled, sick, or aged. Robbing another person of life is assuming power that belongs to God alone. In particular, abortion—the direct taking of the life of an unborn child—is a serious crime. From his or her conception, a child has a right to life. The unborn are to be treated as any other person: defended, cared for, and healed.

Other sins against life—many of which stem from the vice of anger—are hatred, fighting, revenge, cruel words, hurtful criticism, prejudice, and using people. These sins harm life, and anything that does so is evil.

Violence is justified only when it is in defense against an unjust aggressor. Defense is a duty for those who are responsible for others or for the common good. War, however, causes evil, injustice, and suffering. The buildup of military arms, for instance, inflicts great harm on those who are poor. Therefore, war should be avoided whenever possible. Moral law, the law of nations, must be followed during war.

It is possible to harm another person's spiritual life. Scandal is leading others to sin by bad example. The next time you are tempted to do wrong, consider who else's spiritual growth you may be damaging.

When you work to make life flourish, you are like Christ. He said, "I came so that they might have life and have it more abundantly." (John 10:10) Those who respect and defend human life will experience life to the full and receive everlasting life.

The Church Respects Life

Since God is the author of all human life, the Church respects and defends the dignity of life. The Church speaks out and acts to defend people whose lives are endangered. As a member of the Church, you are called to be concerned about life issues. Commit yourself to finding out about them and doing what you can to help others live better.

Volunteers serve breakfast at a soup kitchen serving the poor and disenfranchised.

Taking a Stand

Many Church members give more than money for the cause of life. People are justly angry that every year in the United States millions of babies are legally murdered through abortion—the direct taking of the life of an unborn child. They protest this crime by participating in nonviolent actions that draw attention to this tragedy. They encourage others to join them. When people take a stand against abortion, capital punishment, or unjust military aggression, they risk being arrested and imprisoned. To them, it is worth it. What do you think? How else can crimes against life be prevented?

Defending Life

One way to defend life is to voice your concerns to those in power. Write a letter to a government official, explaining why he or she should work to support the lives of one of the following groups:

those who are poor, aged, disabled, unborn, or victims of war or other violence.

Dear _____ ,

_____

_____

_____

_____

_____

_____

Sincerely,

_____

Campaign for Human Development

Every year since 1970, the Catholic Church in the United States has held a Campaign for Human Development. The money collected in this campaign is used to improve the lives of people who are poor and oppressed in the United States. The mission of the Catholic Campaign for Human Development (CCHD) is to promote and support grass-roots organizations and education that address the root causes of poverty in the United States. The CCHD strives to empower those who are poor through participation and education for justice. The goal of the CCHD is to build solidarity between people who are poor and those who are not. The money collected each year is awarded to organizations dedicated to economic development and education for justice. Visit the CCHD Web site to learn more.

Remember

What does the Fourth Commandment oblige us to do?

> The Fourth Commandment obliges us to obey and honor all those who have lawful authority over us because they take the place of God in our lives.

How can we revere life as a sacred gift from God and keep the Fifth Commandment?

> We can revere life as a sacred gift from God by protecting and nurturing it and by avoiding whatever would harm or destroy it.

Word to Know

obedience

Respond

In your reflection notebook, write a thank-you letter to God the Father for specific people and things that make your life rich. Think of one thing that keeps you from living fully. In your letter, ask God for help in dealing with the difficulty.

Reach Out

1. Suppose a family conflict arises in deciding which TV program to watch. Write ways that this problem can be resolved.

2. With your class, plan an Appreciation Day for certain people in authority in your school or parish. Invite them to your classroom and present to them a thank-you award or certificate.

3. Friendship promotes life. Doing things with and for others makes us and them feel loved and more human. It makes us happier and holier. Begin to cultivate a new friendship today.

4. Collect newspaper clippings related to life issues. Mount the articles and write on the sheets of paper how each one shows respect for life or lack of respect for life.

5. Find needs in your family and fill them. Your family should be the people you serve first and foremost. You cannot be completely responsible for your family, but perhaps you can do more than you think.

   - Think of a special need each member of your family has right now. For instance, your brother might be having a hard time in physics class and need quiet time to study; your mother might have the flu and need extra rest; your baby sister might need someone to play with. Find a way that you can put your love into action and help fill these needs.

   - Make a chart on a sheet of paper or in your reflection notebook. Write the name of each family member and under it write "Need" and then "My action." Fill in the chart.

   - Choose one action to put into practice immediately.

6. Write a letter to influence a person with power to help out in a situation in which people are oppressed or threatened.

7. Ask your parents or guardians to talk about their experience of obeying their parents or guardians when they were your age. Ask them to tell you about what they learned by obeying and about any difficulties they may have had in doing so.

CHAPTER 23 Review Activities

Good and Bad Fill in the blanks to make the sentences correct.

1. _____ is leading others to sin by bad example.

2. Those who govern receive their authority from _____ .

3. _____ is a virtue that enables you to do what others with rightful authority ask.

4. The worst sin against life is _____ .

5. We have a duty to work to change _____ laws.

6. By obeying people with rightful authority, you are obeying _____ .

7. You can grow in obedience through _____ .

To Obey or Not to Obey Fill in the star before each situation that calls for obedience according to the Christian way of life.

☆ 1. An older friend tells you to help him or her with a paper route.

☆ 2. The librarian tells you to stop talking in the library.

☆ 3. Your aunt is caring for you, and she tells you it is time to go to bed.

☆ 4. Your uncle tells you to skip school to watch the baseball game.

☆ 5. Your mother seldom cleans house. She tells you to clean your room.

☆ 6. Your coach tells you to cheat in order to help the team win.

☆ 7. Your mother tells you to mow the lawn.

☆ 8. You think that your father is telling you to do something that is unfair to you.

Live and Let Live Write an example for each of the following.

1. Caring for your own life _____

2. Jesus' respect for life _____

3. A sin against life other than murder _____

4. A group of people who are not able to live fully _____

5. A way to give life to those who are not able to live fully _____

_____

Gather and Go Forth

Know and Proclaim

We proclaim the truths of our Catholic faith by supporting the family and human life and dignity.

We Know Our Faith	We Proclaim Our Faith
By serving God and obeying those in rightful authority, we praise and love God.	Catholics consider the family to be the domestic church in which parents are entrusted by God with authority and responsibility and deserving of obedience from their children.
Laws are made for the good of all. By obeying them, we add to the well-being of all.	As Catholics, we take our responsibility as citizens seriously. We make sure that laws do not offend God or human dignity and work to change those that do.
Life is a wonderful gift from God. We have dignity and are called to be holy because we are created in God's image.	Catholics defend life by voicing their opinions and concerns to those in power. Many Catholics work to protect the lives of the unborn or those who are poor, aged, disabled, or victims of violence.

As Catholics, we honor God when we make our families a source of love and virtue.

For this reason I kneel before the Father, from whom every family in heaven and on earth is named . . . that Christ may dwell in your hearts through faith.

Ephesians 3:14,17

Test Your Catholic Knowledge

Fill in the circle that best completes the sentence.

We obey the laws of the Church and society in order to:

○ gain greater authority and responsibility.

○ contribute to the common good.

○ keep from being arrested.

○ achieve sainthood.

A Catholic to Know

Francis had many opportunities for a career. He was a skilled swordsman, an expert horseman, and a superb dancer. He also held a doctorate in both civil and canon law. Francis's father wanted him to marry, but Francis chose the priesthood and was ordained in 1593. He preached and wrote weekly essays to explain the faith in simple and clear language, winning many hearts for God during a period of religious warfare. As bishop of Geneva, Switzerland, he took an active interest in training men for the priesthood, and he trained laypeople to teach catechism. Francis showed that everyone can grow in holiness. Francis was declared a Doctor of the Church and is the patron saint of journalists and writers.

Saint Francis de Sales

Witness and Share

These sentences describe what Catholics believe. Listen carefully as they are read. Ask yourself, "How strong are my Catholic beliefs?"

My Way to Faith

- I respect and obey my parents and other people in authority.

- I show respect for all human life, beginning with the unborn and continuing to those who are elderly.

- I show respect for the life God has given me by eating healthful foods and getting enough sleep.

- I help others act in ways that obey God's laws.

- I respond to anger by showing patience, mercy, and forgiveness.

Share Your Faith

Consider ways in which you can share your faith by living a healthier lifestyle. Why does living a healthy lifestyle honor God? Write your ideas on the lines, and invite family members and friends to join you in being healthy.

_____

_____

_____

_____

The Way of Human Dignity

Who are you?

That is not an easy question to answer. You are a very unique and complex person. You are a special gift of God in our world.

1 Physical Level
Your appearance: your hairstyle, height, weight, gender, unique physical characteristics

_____

_____

2 Cultural Level
The way you dress, act; your manners, personality, talents, charms

_____

_____

3 Personal Level
Your ideas, ideals, values, desires, goals, principles; things that make you angry, sad, happy

_____

_____

4 Faith Level
Your friendship with God, the life of grace, sharing in God's life, living according to Gospel values

_____

_____

God wants you to become a whole person and to achieve your full potential. To do so, you must know yourself. Expressing yourself is one way that you learn about who you are. You express yourself on various levels: physical, cultural, personal, and spiritual.

All of your relationships involve these four levels to some extent and involve many choices. When it comes to expressing yourself on these levels, you are faced with many choices. You are free to choose your hairstyle, the way you dress, your goals in life, and the extent to which you wish to have a relationship with God. Some choices are easy. Other decisions will have lifelong consequences and are thus more difficult to make.

Some young people are desperate to find an answer to the question "Who am I?" So they rush into sexual relationships, mistakenly thinking that a sexual relationship will answer this question for them. It is important for you to know yourself if you want to truly develop a relationship with someone else. It is also important to be aware of the choices that you make in relationships. The choices you make now in your relationships may lead to lifelong consequences and responsibilities.

A Gift for Love and Life

Sexuality includes all the human qualities that characterize a person as male or female. Your sexuality touches all four levels of your person. The gift of sex is a very good and important part of your whole person. God has given you the gift of sex for two reasons:

• Through sex, you express and deepen your love for your marriage partner.

• Sex enables you to share in God's creative love and to cooperate with God in bringing new life into the world.

God wants you to understand and appreciate the gift of sex and its relationship to your whole being. God wants you to respect your own sexuality and the sexuality of others.

Men and women were created equal but different. One sex is not better than the other, but each has its own strengths, weaknesses, and characteristics. Both sexes have dignity. Men and women are to acknowledge and accept their sexual identity. The two sexes complement, or complete, each other. They need each other. This is especially true in marriage.

Catholic Facts of Life

> **SIXTH COMMANDMENT**
> **You shall not commit adultery.**

> **NINTH COMMANDMENT**
> **You shall not covet your neighbor's wife.**

The Sixth and Ninth Commandments protect love and family life. They guide you in making decisions that involve the gift of sex. According to God's plan, this gift is to be used only in marriage. In marriage, one man and one woman vow to love only each other in a special way until death. They make a total, free, and permanent gift of themselves to each other. They celebrate their love by acts that give

pleasure to each other and that may produce a new human being in whom their individual traits are united forever. Sexual love is the language, the expression, of their total self-giving and their permanent commitment. This is why sex outside marriage is seriously sinful. It does not have the tremendous meaning that God intended for sex.

In particular, adultery, unfaithfulness on the part of a husband or wife, is very wrong and against the laws of God and the Church. In adultery, a person gives to another person the special love promised only to his or her marriage partner. Adultery is a sin against love, against vows, and against the partner who has given himself or herself completely to the other.

Essentials of Marriage

Because marriage establishes a man and woman in a public state of life in the Church, it is best if the wedding is public, within the liturgy, and before the priest (or witness authorized by the Church), the witnesses, and the faithful.

Three basic characteristics of true marriage are unity, permanency, and openness to conceiving children. In view of these, polygamy, having more than one spouse, is wrong. Divorce and remarriage while one's lawful spouse is still living is not permitted in the Catholic Church. Divorced and remarried Catholics still belong to the Church, but they cannot receive Holy Communion unless they have received an annulment. An annulment is a declaration that the marriage was not valid and sacramental in the first place because an essential element for marriage was missing. If the Church decides that an annulment is in order, then the person is free to marry again and to receive Holy Communion.

God Knows Best

God's laws are always for our own good. Misuse of the gift of sex leads to all kinds of sadness. It destroys families, damages people psychologically and emotionally, creates distrust, and spreads disease. Another evil effect of sex outside marriage is that it may result in an abortion or in a child who is not loved and cared for. We will be more likely to use sex in the right way and avoid these problems if we practice **chastity.** This virtue integrates and controls our sexual desires by conforming them to right reason and Christian faith. Chaste people love God more than themselves or others. They do God's will by using or controlling their sexual desires. They follow Christ, who is the model of chastity.

Sometimes young people engage in sexual activity, which rightfully belongs in marriage, believing that there is no harm in it. On the other hand, people your age may fear sex and think that anything having to do with it is evil. Both of these ways of thinking are incorrect. Sexual love is beautiful and good, but it belongs only to those who are married.

When you practice chastity, you see others the right way—as people made in the image of God. You remain respectful of others in your thoughts, words, and desires. Your respect shows in your speech and in your actions. It guides what you choose to read, look at, or listen to. Chastity keeps you from using people and robbing them of their human dignity. It helps you to be a balanced person, a whole person, the person God wants you to be. Chastity, however, calls for self-mastery.

The Sacrament of Matrimony

The Bible begins with God creating Adam and Eve in his likeness and telling them to be fruitful and multiply. Their love for each other is an image of the love that God has for us. Whenever the authors of the Old Testament wanted to show how beautiful was the relationship between the Israelites and their God, they would often compare it to a marriage. In marriage, a man and woman become one flesh in a union that cannot be broken.

Marriage is a vocation that comes from the Holy Spirit, who calls the couple together. While it is their personal commitment to each other, it is also a commitment to build up the People of God. For this reason, the Sacrament of **Matrimony** is called a Sacrament at the Service of Communion. The husband and wife are the ministers of this sacrament to each other. The priest or deacon is there as a witness for the Church. In the Sacrament of Matrimony, the man and woman must both want to marry, must both promise to remain faithful to each other for life, and must both be open to having children. Their promise has to be made freely and publicly and before a witness for the Church—a priest or deacon.

Truly Chaste

Some people think that being chaste means being a prude and never having any fun. For each pair of situations, check (✓) the response you might find in a person who practices the virtue of chastity.

You explain why you like a new TV show, which happens to feature little sex or violence, and a classmate responds,

_____ "Only losers like that show."

_____ "That's interesting—I never thought of it that way."

You show your new cell phone to a friend, who says,

_____ "I'll call you tonight."

_____ "That's great—if you're into last year's model."

You share how you are really enjoying your science project, and someone responds,

_____ "That's one of the coolest projects I've heard about."

_____ "You need to get a life."

You find a sweater at the mall that fits your style, and your friend says,

_____ "You're never going to get any attention in that. You need something that shows off your body."

_____ "You look great in that sweater."

A Precious Gift

If your sexuality is precious to you, if you want to use it someday to show a unique, deep, love for one special person, you will not take chances with it. You will avoid people, places, and situations that may tempt you to be untrue to yourself—and perhaps untrue to a person God has planned to be your lifelong partner.

A Moment with Jesus

By your Baptism, you have become a temple where God dwells and a member of the Body of Christ. You are to live as a courageous follower of Christ. In all of your desires, words, and actions, you are to follow this principle: In all things, act like Christ. Take a moment to thank Jesus for dwelling within you. Ask him for the grace you need to act like him in all of your desires, words, and actions.

A Saint for Purity

The Goretti family worked as tenant farmers for the landholder Serenelli in Rome. To Maria Goretti, not quite 12 years old, 18-year-old Alessandro Serenelli was like her big brother. She was terrified when he suddenly made sexual advances toward her. Maria struggled and begged him to stop, crying out, "It is a sin, God does not want it." Because she resisted, Alessandro stabbed her 14 times. Even in her fear and pain, Maria forgave him before she died the next day, July 6, 1902. In prison, Alessandro had a dream that Maria offered him

14 lilies, saying, "Alessandro, I forgive you, and one day you will be here with me." He repented. Released after 27 years in prison, he went to beg forgiveness from Maria's mother. She forgave him, and he died a holy man.

God does not ask us to die rather than to submit to someone sexually. If Maria had been forced to have sex, she herself would not have sinned. In an extreme way, Saint Maria Goretti teaches us how precious God's laws are. She did not want her friend to sin. She was a true namesake of the Blessed Virgin Mary, the woman called "Mother most pure."

Making Responsible Choices

You can control what you do by making responsible choices. You can become a whole and holy person by making choices based on what Jesus teaches you. With his help, you can make responsible choices. Jesus teaches you that to be a whole and holy person is to be unselfish in all your choices. He challenges you to make responsible choices about love and the gift of sex.

Read the following Scripture passages, and then answer the questions.

1. Jesus teaches us that we must love people, not use them. What does Jesus teach us about our desires? (Matthew 5:27–28)

   _____

   _____

2. What guidance does Jesus give us for how we are to love other people? (John 15:12)

   _____

   _____

3. Jesus teaches us that sacrifice is a part of love. What does he say? (John 15:13–14)

   _____

   _____

Obstacles to Wholeness

Jesus gave us directions for the use of sex so that we may become whole and holy people. But we can choose not to live up to our human dignity. We can be self-centered and fail to make Christian choices in matters of sex and love. We can use drugs and alcohol, which dull our human power to make and carry out good choices. We can make wrong choices so often that we become numb to the evil in them.

Two attitudes toward sex are particularly dangerous: using sex selfishly and considering sex as entertainment. Some people use sex selfishly. They want to enjoy sexual pleasure without the total gift of selfless love in marriage. A sin such as fornication—engaging in the sexual act before marriage—is seriously wrong. Masturbation—self-stimulation to arouse sexual pleasure—and homosexual activity— sexual activity with someone of the same sex—are also not permitted by the Church.

Some people see sex as entertainment. TV, videos, the Internet, advertising, and movies often give the impression that sex is meant just for fun. Casual sex is far from the intention of God. As long as sex is seen as entertainment, serious evils such as pornography and prostitution will continue in our society.

As God Intends

Discuss the following examples. How can these people use sexuality as God intends?

1. Ashley goes out with Jim every weekend. Few eighth-grade girls are "going with" anyone. Her friend Lisa tells Ashley she is getting too serious.
2. Armando's new friends are a fast crowd. When he joins them in obscene talk and drinking, he feels in control. However, his father sees that Armando's grades have dropped and that his attitude is changing for the worse. Armando's father tells him that he is not to associate with these boys. Armando thinks, "What right does he have to determine who my friends will be?"
3. Lucy and Rosa go to a party at Esteban's house when his parents are out of town. Some of the boys from their class suggest that they play strip poker.
4. Kirsten's friend Leah confides in her that a man in the neighborhood has abused her sexually since she was a child. Leah is filled with guilt and does not know what to do.

Look to Jesus

Jesus gave us the greatest, most unselfish example of love possible. His life and Death show us what it means to be a Christian who really loves and cares about others. We cannot give our lives as generously as Jesus did. But we can be unselfish in our actions, in our choices, and in our relationships with others. Making sacrifices by thinking of others rather than ourselves is the way to start.

Helps to Wholeness

Growing up whole and holy is a great challenge. Here are some hints.

1. Develop real friendships. Friendship is a gift freely given. You have the right to choose your friends. Your choices should be wise ones.
2. Read about great men and women. Their ideals, example, and experience can inspire you and help you find meaning in your life.
3. Involve yourself in service to others. People who make their lives worthwhile and reach out to assist others are really happy. They are less tempted to use others, especially sexually, than people whose lives are centered on themselves.
4. Be modest in dress and behavior. You are constantly giving unspoken messages by the way you act and dress.
5. Watch your thoughts. Sin begins in our minds. Thoughts lead to action. If an impure thought comes into your mind, replace it with a pure one.
6. Develop a relationship with Jesus. He is not only your model but your truest and best friend. You need to devote time to getting to know Jesus. You need to share with him your dreams and desires and to give him your love. You can do this through prayer.
7. Celebrate the sacraments regularly. The Eucharist can make you strong in combating temptation and living up to the examples of Jesus. Should you fail to act like Christ, admit your sins and celebrate the Sacrament of Reconciliation. Jesus will always help and heal you.
8. Pray to Mary, most pure, and to the saints. They can help you practice chastity. Mary is always the friend of young men and women who want to become like her Son.

Remember

How do the Sixth and Ninth Commandments direct us to treat ourselves and others?

These commandments direct us to treat ourselves and others with respect in our thoughts, words, desires, and actions.

What is chastity?

Chastity is the virtue that controls our sexual desires by conforming them to right reason and Christian faith.

Words to Know

chastity
Matrimony

Respond

Think of a time when you were loved and appreciated. Thank God for the experience of being loved. Ask God to enable you to share this love with others. Write your thoughts in your reflection notebook.

Reach Out

1. Read about Saint Maria Goretti, Saint Norbert, Saint Agnes, Saint Jerome, Saint Thomas Aquinas, or Saint Charles Lwanga. Find out how these men and women struggled and overcame their temptations against chastity. Try to imagine the kind of people they were by studying their relationship with God and others.

2. Call the American Red Cross to see if there are services for which you and your friends can volunteer.

3. Talk to a married couple about how they met. Ask about some of the struggles and joys they had in the early days of their life together. If they have family pictures of these years, talk about them together.

4. Make a list of good biographies for people your age to read. Post your list or give a report so that your friends can learn from the people in these books how to be whole and holy.

5. List five important qualities a Catholic should show in relationships with others. Give reasons for your choices.

6. Make a scrapbook of your friends. Collect pictures of them at different ages. Under each person's picture, write how he or she has enriched your life. Create a prayer asking God to give each friend a quality or an experience that you think he or she needs or wants.

7. Spend time thinking about and reflecting on the four levels of self-expression (see page 225). Identify things in each category that you are happy about as well as things that you would like to improve.

8. Watch an hour of prime-time television and keep a log of the number of times that sex is referred to directly or indirectly. Then summarize the attitudes concerning sex that you see portrayed.

About Love Fill in the puzzle.

Across

2. A Christian dresses and acts with _____ .

5. In order to develop a relationship with Christ, we must _____ .

6. The virtue a person practices who uses his or her sexual powers according to God's plan

7. The power to express love and create new life

10. An agreement to love with total, permanent, and self-giving commitment

13. Christians follow the principle: Act like _____ .

14. The saint of purity is Maria _____ .

Down

1. The most pure saint who can help us use our sexuality the right way

3. A sacrament that helps you combat temptation

4. What you should develop with Christ and others to become a whole person

8. We are to _____ sex in ourselves and in our relationships with others.

9. Unfaithfulness to one's marriage partner

11. Something that dulls our human power to make correct choices

12. A commandment that protects love and life

15. Adultery and fornication are serious _____ .

Love That Is for Real Put a heart in front of each phrase that shows sex used the way God intends.

_____ **1.** As entertainment

_____ **2.** As a way to thank someone after a date

_____ **3.** As an expression of total, permanent commitment

_____ **4.** As a means to bring new people into the world

_____ **5.** As a way to make ourselves feel good when we are lonely, sad, or bored

Gather and Go Forth

Know and Proclaim

We learn the truths of our Catholic faith and proclaim our beliefs with love and respect.

We Know Our Faith	We Proclaim Our Faith
God wants us to respect the gift of sex, our own sexuality, and the sexuality of others.	Catholics moderate and control their sexual desires by practicing the virtue of chastity. Chastity helps Catholics see one another as people made in the image of God.
Marriage is a vocation that comes from the Holy Spirit to help build up the People of God.	Catholics treat sex as a precious gift to express a unique, special, and deep love between a married man and woman.
Jesus gives us the greatest example of unselfish love. His life and Death show us what Christian love means.	Catholics look to the saints as role models and inspiration. The lives of the saints model how people in various times and states of life show Christian love and service.

Test Your Catholic Knowledge

Fill in the circle that best answers the question.

Which of the following virtues helps us control our sexual desires?

- ⦿ chastity
- ⦿ humility
- ⦿ modesty
- ⦿ prudence

As Catholics, we value the virtue of chastity, which enables us to love unselfishly, as Christ loves us.

Do you not know that your body is a temple of the holy Spirit within you, whom you have from God, and that you are not your own? For you have been purchased at a price. Therefore, glorify God in your body.

1 Corinthians 6:19–20

A Catholic to Know

Thomas More had to choose between two people he loved—his friend, King Henry VIII of England, or the pope. King Henry wanted a divorce, but the pope refused the king's request. King Henry then asked Thomas to approve the divorce he wanted. Thomas had to make a decision. The king wanted Thomas to be on his side. After all, the king had promoted Thomas to several government posts, including chancellor. Thomas decided to stay faithful to the Church. He resigned rather than approve Henry's request. As a result, he was imprisoned, his family was disgraced, and he was beheaded for treason in 1535. Saint Thomas sacrificed his life to follow his conscience and remain God's obedient servant.

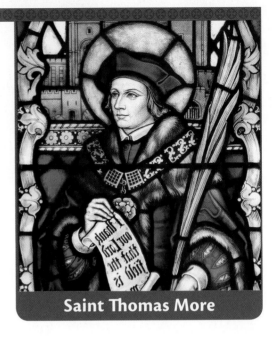

Saint Thomas More

Witness and Share

These sentences describe what Catholics believe. Listen carefully as they are read. Ask yourself, "How strong are my Catholic beliefs?"

My Way to Faith

- I practice the virtue of chastity.

- I respect my sexuality and the sexuality of others.

- I believe marriage is a vocation that builds up the People of God.

- I believe that sex is a gift reserved for marriage.

- I look to the saints for inspiration to be like Jesus in my desires, words, and actions.

Share Your Faith

Write a brief description of a book that promotes chaste living through the plot and how the characters interact with one another. Tell a friend about the book and invite him or her to read it.

_____

_____

_____

_____

The Way of Justice and Truth

JESUS

Can you see the word above? If not, hold the book at a distance and focus on the blue. You should be able to recognize the name *Jesus.*

With the eyes of faith, you can see Jesus in people. You can respond to them with love. You can avoid harming them. With the eyes of faith, you can also see creation as it really is. Everything on earth glorifies God and shows what God is like. Everything is a gift from God to be cared for and used according to God's plan. Through honest work, we participate in God's work of creation.

Correct vision is what the Seventh and Tenth Commandments are all about. They call for respect. The word *respect* comes from a word that means "to look at." The Seventh Commandment, "You shall not steal," calls us to respect others by looking at their possessions as their gifts from God and by not taking what rightfully belongs to them. The Tenth Commandment, "You shall not covet anything that belongs to your neighbor," tells us not even to desire what belongs to others. Both commandments protect the ownership and the use of private property. We will obey these commandments if we see things and people as God does.

> **SEVENTH COMMANDMENT**
> **You shall not steal.**

> **TENTH COMMANDMENT**
> **You shall not covet anything
> that belongs to your neighbor.**

A Broader Understanding

We sometimes tend to limit our understanding of stealing to the act of taking an object that belongs to someone else. The *Catechism of the Catholic Church,* however, offers a much broader understanding of what it means to violate the Seventh Commandment by including the following examples:

- work done poorly
- tax evasion
- forgery of checks and invoices
- excessive expenses and waste
- damaging property
- paying unjust wages

> **How can copying a friend's homework, even with his or her permission, be a violation of the Seventh Commandment?**
>
> _____
>
> _____

Looking Out for Human Rights

When you really care about others and see Christ in them, you want to keep them from the pain of being victims of injustice. The Seventh and Tenth Commandments challenge us to work for justice. All people possess the God-given human right to life, liberty, and the pursuit of happiness. Everyone has the right to food, clothing, shelter, and the opportunity to work and to share in the goods of the earth. The good of the human person should be the purpose of every social organization. Only when each person's rights are respected does the virtue of justice exist among people.

Sometimes people's vision becomes distorted. They see possessions as being all-important. Greed blinds them to the dignity of every human being. They no longer recognize the rights of others. Then there is injustice. As Catholics, we are to do what we can to promote justice.

The Role of the State

The role of political authority is to defend and promote the common good. The common good means social conditions that allow people to reach their fulfillment more fully and more easily. Society should promote virtue and justice. It should eliminate sinful inequalities that should not exist, because all people have equal dignity. Nations should work together for the common good of the whole human family.

Being a Person of Integrity

Cecilio Rodríguez, a city waste collector, once had an extraordinary truckload of trash. As the truck was being dumped, he found more than $11,500 in an old brown shoe. Immediately he had visions of Hawaii and a fancy car. But he knew the treasure had come from the home of the Boltons, a couple in their seventies. Instead of pocketing the money, Mr. Rodríguez did

what he knew was right and turned it in. For his selfless act, Mr. Rodríguez received the citizen of the month award.

Mr. Rodríguez had integrity. Integrity is righteousness. It comes from the word *integer*, which means "whole." An integer in math is a whole number. People of integrity see the whole picture and live life accordingly. They are just. When they have enough to live comfortably, they are content. If they have more than enough, they share. They do not envy others. They do not trample people's rights in order to have more for themselves.

Various forms of stealing show no respect for others or their property. When people do steal, they must restore their integrity by making restitution. This means to replace what was taken or to repair what was damaged. Restitution is made to the victims or their heirs. If that is impossible, the cash value can be given to a worthy cause.

Making Things Right

It is only by the grace and mercy of God that we are forgiven for our sins. We cannot do anything to earn God's forgiveness. At the same time, once we have allowed God's mercy into our lives, we are called to perform acts of penance to restore that which has been harmed by our sin. Performing acts of penance is a way of taking responsibility for a wrong that we have done and reestablishing the balance and harmony broken by sin. After confessing our sins to a priest in the Sacrament of Reconciliation, we are assigned acts of penance through which we make amends for the wrongs we have done. This act of penance brings about satisfaction for sins committed.

Caring for the World

It is important to take good care of our planet, not only for our neighbors today but for future generations. This means we do not litter, pollute our water and air, or waste our resources. We are called to show respect for the natural world—mineral resources, plants, and animals. God gave us his beautiful creation so that we might enjoy it and so that our needs may be met. All of the goods of creation are intended to be shared by the entire human race. God also asks that we assume responsibility to care for all that he has made. We are called to care for our own communities and for the world as a whole. How beautiful do you keep your corner of the world?

Your Lucky Day

The phone rings. It is for you. You are the lucky winner of $10,000. How will you spend it?

_____

Sharing the World

Did you think of using some of your winnings to relieve the suffering of those in need? The wealth of the world is for all people, but three-fourths of them go to bed hungry every night. Many parents helplessly watch their babies starve. The children shrink to skin and bones, and their stomachs swell. Then they die. This happens while we spend money on unnecessary things and waste our food.

To practice justice requires mercy, which is having a heart for those in need. When we help those who are starving, underpaid, oppressed, and considered worthless, we serve Jesus. His law of love demands that we have compassion for those who are poor. In Matthew 25:31–40, Jesus tells us that one day we will be judged on our response to the hungry, the thirsty, the stranger, the naked, the sick, and the imprisoned. What we do for them, our brothers and sisters, Jesus sees as done to himself.

Solidarity, oneness with others, involves sharing not only material goods but spiritual goods. What is one way you can share a spiritual good?

_____

What Can One Person Do?

Every Saturday, 15-year-old Eric Bryson takes a bus downtown. There he coaches basketball for children who are mentally disabled. At six-foot-four, Eric towers over the group, but with his help these children are learning to stand just as tall.

You can also help make a just world. Here are some ideas:

- Cultivate the attitude that all people are of equal importance, regardless of their sex, race, age, physical appearance, ability, or level of intelligence.
- Be content with what you have.
- Learn to share with your family, your friends, and your neighbors.
- Become informed about situations in which people are oppressed.
- Reach out to people in need.
- Pray that unjust systems and practices be changed.

What one thing will you do this week?

_____

The Value of Truth

Julie and Hannah entered a contest at their local library. They had to write answers to 20 questions about well-known books. As they walked home, Hannah said, "How did you do?"

"I think I got them all," replied Julie.

"Really?" Hannah asked. "Even the one about Huck Finn? Who was his friend, anyway? You can tell me now. The contest ends in an hour. I promise I won't go back to the library."

"Tom Sawyer was Huck's friend," Julie responded.

A few days later, Hannah came to Julie's house and announced excitedly, "Guess what? We won the contest! Our names are posted in the library window."

"We?" asked Julie. "How could that be?"

"I don't know," fibbed Hannah. "Maybe they counted the two highest papers as winners. Let's go pick up our prize."

1. Whom did Hannah deceive?

_____

_____

_____

2. Why did she do it?

_____

_____

3. What might be consequences of Hannah's act?

_____

_____

_____

_____

_____

Truthful in Word and Action

If you view all people correctly, you try to treat them with justice and love. Hannah acted unjustly by being false in words and actions and by misleading people. Knowing the truth is a basic desire and human right. When we unnecessarily keep back the truth, distort it, tell a lie, or break a promise, we deny people this right. Everyone has the right to a good reputation. The Eighth Commandment calls us to be truthful in word and action and to protect reputations.

> **EIGHTH COMMANDMENT**
> **You shall not bear false witness against your neighbor.**

The good of everyone depends on the truth. Imagine if you could not believe the mayor, your doctor, the newscaster, your best friend, or your mother. Untruth causes distrust, dislike, and confusion. Attempting to cover up lies leads to further untruth and other evils.

Truth in the Bible

Jesus, who called himself the Truth, refers to the devil as "a liar and the father of lies." (John 8:44) Jesus warns that "on the day of judgment people will render an account for every careless word they speak." (Matthew 12:36)

Saint James compares the tongue to a small flame that can set fire to a huge forest. (James 3:5–6) What does he mean?

_____

_____

Read Ephesians 4:15–16. What will happen if we live in truth?

_____

_____

Proverbs 6:16–19 lists things that God hates. Which does the Eighth Commandment forbid?

_____

_____

A Moment with Jesus

Read John 14:1–7 in which Jesus refers to himself as "the way and the truth and the life." Take a moment to ask Jesus to help you to be a truthful person. Ask him for the grace you need to see other people as God sees them. Thank him for the gift of the Holy Spirit, who shows you the way.

The Honest Truth

Outright lying, as well as stretching the truth or twisting it, is against the Eighth Commandment. "White lies" are still lies. You must speak the truth out of respect for other people as a habit. Then there will be no need to use phrases such as "I swear to God" and "honest to God," which Jesus said to avoid. Everyone will be able to depend on your word.

Certain lies do more harm than others. **Calumny,** or slander, is accusing a person of a wrongdoing when you know he or she is innocent. To spread this kind of lie is to ruin a person's reputation. Even if the person's name is cleared later, suspicion lingers. People are more apt to believe bad about someone than good. Cruel gossip is also a harmful violation of the Eighth Commandment. Its effects are long-lasting.

Common types of lies are flattery, boastfulness, and exaggeration. When would people resort to these forms of lies?

_____

_____

_____

Hypocrisy is lying through actions. Some people are phony because they try to appear to be what they are not. For instance, Joe is a model student in front of the teacher but cheats and criticizes the school with his friends.

To conceal the truth can be as dangerous as lying. Sometimes it may be necessary for the sake of the common good to reveal the wrongdoing of another. It is a serious injustice to let crime go unpunished, and it is worse to let an innocent victim be accused.

When Not to Speak

At times, it is wrong to reveal the truth.

- Talking about the faults and misdeeds of others is the sin of **detraction.** Like calumny, it is evil because it ruins another's name.

- People in public office and in certain careers are often obliged to keep information secret.

- Sometimes you accidentally gain confidential knowledge that you should not spread.

What do you do when you are asked about something you are bound to keep secret or when the truth would lead to harm? You keep silent, say "I can't tell you," or use mental reservation. Mental reservation is using words that mean something different in your mind from what they say. When a salesperson telephones and asks if your mother is at home, you and he might both know she is. If you answer no, you mean, "No, she isn't home *for you*," and he gets the point. Similarly, to keep a professional secret, someone may answer, "I don't know," meaning, "I don't know anything that I can say to you about it." Mental reservations are allowed when the listener can reasonably believe you are withholding the truth.

Promises and Secrets

Make a promise only when you are sure you can fulfill it. Going back on your word is a good way to ruin your own reputation. Likewise, when someone shares a secret with you, the right thing to do is to keep the secret. Respect for others will make you a person to be trusted.

Truth in the Media

We are continually exposed to an unending flow of information through magazines, TV, the Internet, and many other forms of communication. Even if we try to not pay attention, communication media, for better or worse, shape us and the society we live in.

The fact is that we have a right to information based on truth. All the communication media have the responsibility to communicate information honestly and fairly. Because of our commitment to honor the truth, we need to question the media we are exposed to, be it music, movies, or cable news. We then need to critically evaluate the messages we receive.

Your News

If you were an anchor for your school's newscast, how would you report the following story? Write your report below. Avoid calumny and detraction, and report only the facts.

Hundreds of dollars in athletic equipment was reported missing from the boys' locker room Wednesday afternoon. Among the items missing are basketballs, soccer balls, catcher's gear, and assorted floor hockey equipment. Some students suspect eighth-grader Bobby Johnson of stealing the gear, since Johnson was dismissed from Tuesday's sixth-period gym class for bad behavior.

"I didn't see anyone take anything, but the equipment seemed to disappear after my sixth-period class," gym teacher Paul McGowan said.

Kevin Phillips, a neighbor of Johnson's, said that Johnson recently spoke to him about needing a baseball mitt. Phillips added that Johnson always seems to be getting new equipment.

_____

_____

_____

_____

Remember

What do the Seventh and Tenth Commandments command us to do?

> They command us to respect others' rights by not taking or desiring what belongs to them.

What does the Eighth Commandment oblige us to do?

> It obliges us to be truthful in thought and action and to protect reputations.

Words to Know

calumny
detraction

Respond

Do you see as God sees when it comes to the earth's goods? Answer these questions in your reflection notebook as a personal checkup.

1. How much do I worry about my possessions and plan how to accumulate more?

2. Do I have more of some items than I need?

3. Do I share my things grudgingly or gladly?

4. When did I last donate my time or my money to help those who are poor?

5. Have I ever sacrificed something I wanted for something someone else needed?

6. Do I take care of my belongings?

7. Do I give gifts only when I expect something in return?

8. Am I unhappy when someone has something I do not have?

Reach Out

1. Discuss or write how these people are fighting injustice:

   - A young person decides on a career as a police officer.

   - A husband and wife adopt a baby girl who has cerebral palsy.

   - A young adult works at a home where people who are homeless are given a new chance.

   - A company sells oil cheaply to those who are poor.

   - A sister spends her days talking to young people involved with gangs.

2. Find a helping organization in your parish. Donate what you can to its activities, either your time or your possessions.

3. Think of a way your family can save money. At a family meeting, suggest that this practice be adopted. The money saved can be contributed to those who are poor.

4. Contact a charitable organization for information about those who are hungry and what you can do to help them.

5. Write a prayer or poem about being truthful. Display it in a prominent place.

6. Write the lyrics for a song about justice. You might work on it with a friend.

7. Research organizations dedicated to working for justice in the world. Introduce your family to one such organization's causes, and discuss how you can work together to help the cause.

DONATIONS
Please Help the Needy

Treasure Hunt Jesus said, "For where your treasure is, there also will your heart be." (Matthew 6:21) Find your way through the maze to the treasure. Write in the boxes the letters that your path crosses. They spell the way to reach heavenly treasure.

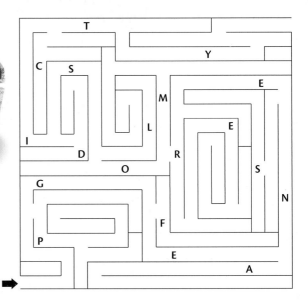

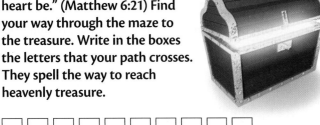

☐☐☐☐☐☐☐☐☐

Hidden Lies Be a human lie detector. Write *yes* before the situations in which you see a failing against the Eighth Commandment. Write *no* if you do not see a violation of the Eighth Commandment.

START ➡

_____ **1.** A newscaster is covering a political campaign. She is convinced that Mr. Anderson is a better candidate than Mr. Billings. In her report, she presents the good points of Mr. Anderson and almost ignores Mr. Billings.

_____ **2.** Mr. Gómez, a heart patient, is discovered to have cancer. His wife decides not to tell him right away.

_____ **3.** Nikki thinks she has done all her homework. When her dad asks if she has finished, she says yes. The next day she finds out that she forgot to do her math assignment.

_____ **4.** Juan sees Anthony carving something in the library table. When the teacher asks Juan if he knows who vandalized the table, he answers no.

_____ **5.** Taylor cannot stand Jasmine. When she thinks that she might have heard Jasmine using vulgar language, she tells the teacher.

_____ **6.** Jacob, a new boy, joins the class. Tom hears about the trouble Jacob caused at his old school and informs the rest of the class.

_____ **7.** Angie comes to school with a hairstyle that Emily thinks looks ridiculous. When Angie asks her how she likes it, Emily replies, "It's terrific. Wish my hair looked half as good."

Circle the Right Word Choose the best word for each definition.

1. Spreading lies about someone

detraction   calumny   mental reservation

2. Making up for damaged or stolen property

reservation   restitution   integrity

3. Greed

integrity   hypocrisy   avarice

4. Lying through actions

detraction   hypocrisy   calumny

5. Righteousness

covet   integrity   respect

Make It True Change the boldfaced words to make the statements true.

1. **No** lies do more harm than others.

2. It is **all right** to tell white lies.

3. We are obliged to help those who are **wealthy**.

4. It is **right** to let crime go unpunished by not telling what we know.

5. **Detraction** is making up for something that has been stolen.

6. The **Sixth** Commandment obliges us to take care of our own property and the world in which we live.

Praising God   The clouds of incense contain terms from this unit.
On the line, write the letter of the word that best completes each sentence.

1. A _____ is a promise made to God to do something good that is not necessary for salvation. Calling on God to bear witness to a lie is _____ . The _____ Commandment calls us to show reverence for God's name. Casual and inappropriate use of God's name is _____ .

2. The _____ Commandment forbids the worship of false gods called _____ . We give God the love and praise he deserves when we _____ . A _____ is a violation of and irreverence toward a person, a place, or an object that is sacred.

3. The highest form of worship we can offer God is the _____ . When we participate in it on Sunday, we keep the _____ Commandment.

4. The _____ has to do with seeking something beyond human nature from something superhuman that is not divine. An example is _____ , which is worship of the devil.

5. The _____ is the seasons of the Church's worship that center around the life of Christ. The first season is _____ , when we recall the anticipation of Christ's coming into the world and look forward to his second coming.

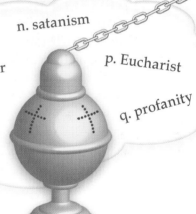

c. pray   h. astrology   a. occult   d. oath   m. sacrilege   k. perjury   n. satanism   e. First   o. idols   l. liturgical year   p. Eucharist   f. Second   g. Third   i. cults   b. vow   r. Lent   q. profanity   j. Advent

Decisions   On the lines after each situation, write the number(s) of the commandment(s) that each person is tempted to break. Then think about what you would suggest these teenagers do to be faithful and prove their love for God.

1. Michael's friends are going to the movies. They invite him to go along. He discovers that the show is rated NC-17. _____

2. Gina is failing history. The day before a major test, she notices that Ashley, the best student in the class, has left her notebook behind. _____

3. Luis senses that two of his classmates might be smoking in the restroom during lunch hour. He is not sure whether to report them. _____

4. Isabel used to be Madison's friend, but suddenly Isabel has joined a clique and has been avoiding Madison. Yesterday Madison was absent, and the teacher asks if someone would explain to Madison what she missed in English class. No one volunteers. _____

5. Ethan makes Matthew angry during lunch. Matthew loses control and starts a fight. The two boys are kept after school. When Matthew comes home, his mother asks where he was. _____

6. Abby is dying to know what her older sister is writing in her diary. One day Abby is the only one home. _____

7. Drew's mother tells him to take good care of his sweater. Drew knows he looks good in the sweater, so he does not want to take it off for art class, even though the class will be painting. _____

8. The father of the child whom Liz babysits is young and handsome. One night as he drives her home, she can tell his interest in her is more than it should be. _____

Celebrating

The Church's Witness

Opening Song

Leader: Let us begin our prayer:
In the name of the Father
and of the Son
and of the Holy Spirit.
Amen.

Jesus is counting on us, his Church,
to carry on his work of proclaiming
the kingdom and making it present.
When we follow the law that God
gave us and the guidelines that
Jesus gave us, we are Christ for the
world. We bring it peace, joy, love,
and salvation. Furthermore, we
ourselves are blessed, and we find
happiness. Let us praise God for the
gift of his law and ask God to help
us to live by it.

Side 1: Happy those whose way is blameless,
who walk by the teaching
of the Lord.

Side 2: Happy those who observe God's
decrees,
who seek the Lord with
all their heart.
They do no wrong;
they walk in God's ways.

All: How I love your law, O Lord!

Side 1: Open my eyes to see clearly
the wonders of your teachings.

Side 2: Your decrees are my delight;
they are my counselors.

Side 1: I cling to your decrees, Lord;
do not let me come to shame.

Side 2: Lead me in the path of your
commands,
for that is my delight.

All: How I love your law, O Lord!

Side 1: I will speak openly of your decrees
without fear even before kings.

Side 2: I lift up my hands to your
commands;
I study your laws, which I love.

All: How I love your law, O Lord!
(Psalm 119:1–2,18,24,31,35,46,48)

Readings

Leader: At their last supper together,
Jesus showed and explained to his
disciples the kind of love he asked
of them.

Reader 1: A reading from the Gospel of John
(John 13:3–5;12–15 is proclaimed.)

Reader 2: A reading from the Gospel of John
(John 13:34–35 is proclaimed.)

Reader 3: A reading from the Gospel of John
(John 14:21 is proclaimed.)

Leader: Before Jesus returned to his Father,
he commissioned his disciples to do
his work.

Reader 4: A reading from the Gospel of
Matthew (Matthew 28:19–20 is
proclaimed.)

(time for silent reflection)

Intercessions

Leader: Let us pray for the disciples of Jesus today who witness to him.

Reader 5: Our response is "Father, Son, and Holy Spirit, hear our prayer."

For our Church leaders, our Holy Father, bishops, and priests, that they may have the wisdom, courage, and zeal to inspire us and to help us meet the challenges of this age, let us pray to the Lord.

All: Father, Son, and Holy Spirit, hear our prayer.

For theologians, catechists, and those who spread the Word through the media, that through their lives and words many people may come to know and love God, let us pray to the Lord.

All: Father, Son, and Holy Spirit, hear our prayer.

For missionaries at home and abroad, that their labors may bring them much joy and bear much fruit, let us pray to the Lord.

All: Father, Son, and Holy Spirit, hear our prayer.

For all those who work for social justice and minister to those who are poor and oppressed, that their work may be crowned with success, let us pray to the Lord.

All: Father, Son, and Holy Spirit, hear our prayer.

For Catholic families, that they may grow together in faith and love and witness to Christ, let us pray to the Lord.

All: Father, Son, and Holy Spirit, hear our prayer.

For each of us, that we may be true to Christ our head, live by his teachings, and love as he loved, let us pray to the Lord.

All: Father, Son, and Holy Spirit, hear our prayer.

Leader: Let us conclude our prayer by giving praise to the Trinity.

All: Glory be to the Father, and to the Son, and to the Holy Spirit, as it was in the beginning, is now and ever shall be, world without end. Amen.

Closing Song

Looking Back

In this unit, you have made an in-depth study of the Ten Commandments, God's gift to his people. These are the laws Christ recommends to his followers. He explained how they were to be lived. You have seen what a guide and protection they are as you strive to be a witness to Christ in the Church. God's law shows you how to be your best self, to practice virtue, and to avoid vice. It enlightens you about the attitudes and actions needed in your relationship with God, with yourself, with others, and with created things. God does not force you to love and obey; God leaves you free. If you are wise, you will follow the way God has shown. Prayer helps you grow in your love for God and find the strength to make the right decisions.

Through obedience to the commandments and through prayer, you will make every day a chance to become a better member of Christ's Church:

> To see him more clearly,
> Love him more dearly, and
> Follow him more nearly.
> — Saint Richard of Chichester

As you complete this unit, ask yourself these questions:

1. How has this unit helped me become more like Christ?

2. What in my life is keeping me from giving God total love and obedience?

3. In what practical ways can I develop a virtue that is proposed by one of the Ten Commandments?

The Cost of Covenantal Love

Write *T* if the statement is true or *F* if it is false.

_____ 1. Christ's new commandment is to participate in Mass on Sundays.

_____ 2. Living according to the law of God frees us.

_____ 3. The seven capital sins are the source of all sin.

_____ 4. Sloth is another name for greed.

_____ 5. Envious people are sometimes happy at another's failure or misfortune.

_____ 6. Meekness is being cowardly.

_____ 7. Temperance is the virtue of controlling our temper.

_____ 8. The virtue of diligence enables us to be devoted to a task.

_____ 9. The First Commandment tells us to put our trust in God, not in human beings or material things.

_____ 10. It is OK to swear whenever we like.

_____ 11. Christians made the day of the Lord Sunday, the day of the Resurrection.

_____ 12. Sunday should be a day when we relax and rejoice.

_____ 13. We obey God when we obey lawful authority.

_____ 14. We are obliged not only to obey those with lawful authority, but to honor and respect them.

_____ 15. We must obey those with lawful authority even if they command us to sin.

_____ 16. The Fifth Commandment tells us to take care of the lives of others and not our own lives.

_____ 17. We may take a person's life if he or she is suffering very much.

_____ 18. God is against sex.

_____ 19. Because sex outside of marriage diminishes real love and harms individuals, God forbids it.

_____ 20. We should work to get as many possessions as we can for ourselves.

_____ 21. To replace stolen goods or to pay for them is called restitution.

_____ 22. Mental reservation is morally justified when the situation calls for it.

_____ 23. Detraction is the sin of talking about the faults and sins of others.

_____ 24. We are not bound to report any crime to authority.

_____ 25. We should treat all people with justice and love.

Gather and Go Forth

Know and Proclaim

We learn our Catholic faith to proclaim the truth of our beliefs to all creation.

We Know Our Faith	We Proclaim Our Faith
The Seventh and Tenth Commandments tell us that through honest work, we participate in God's gift of creation. We do not desire what belongs to others.	Catholics campaign to make sure workers receive a just wage for their labor. They work for laws to ensure that all people have what they need and deserve as a way to protect their human dignity.
Practicing justice requires mercy. Jesus' law of love demands compassion.	Catholics show compassion for one another by showing solidarity with people who are oppressed.
The good of everyone depends on the truth; the Eighth Commandment obliges us to be truthful and to protect reputations.	Catholics question information they hear in the media and critically evaluate the messages they receive. They often balance their consumption of media with programming and news from Catholic sources.

Love of God is best demonstrated in the way we love one another. As Catholics, we show our love for one another by working for justice.

"What you did not do for one of these least ones, you did not do for me."

Matthew 25:45

Test Your Catholic Knowledge

Fill in the circle that best answers the question.

Which commandment is violated when someone pays unjust wages?

◯ the Tenth Commandment

◯ the Ninth Commandment

◯ the Eighth Commandment

◯ the Seventh Commandment

A Catholic to Know

Louis IX became king of France in 1226 when he was 12 years old. As king, Louis had a great love of God and for the people of his kingdom. He showed this love in the advice he gave to his son, the future king of France. "Dear son," he wrote, "let your heart be gentle, compassionate, and charitable toward people who are poor, feeble, unfortunate, toward everyone you think is suffering in mind or in body . . . Maintain the good customs of your kingdom, suppress those which are bad. Do not covet your people's goods, and do not oppress them with taxes." Louis tried to follow his own advice until his death in 1270.

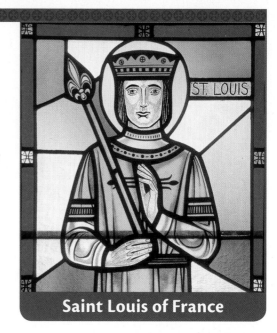

Saint Louis of France

Witness and Share

These sentences describe what Catholics believe. Listen carefully as they are read. Ask yourself, "How strong are my Catholic beliefs?"

My Way to Faith

- I respect the work and property of my friends and family as their share in God's creation.

- I always give an honest effort, even at those things I don't enjoy.

- I believe that all people share equal dignity because they are made in the image of God.

- I keep informed about situations in which people are in need and work to help them.

- I speak the truth while avoiding gossip.

Share Your Faith

Consider ways in which you can improve your ability to avoid gossip. Write your ideas on the lines. Invite your friends to join you in protecting the reputation of others.

_____

_____

_____

_____

Special Seasons and Lessons

The Year in Our Church

Advent
Christmas
Ordinary Time
Lent
Holy Week
Easter
Ordinary Time
Christmas
Epiphany
Ash Wednesday
Palm Sunday
Holy Thursday
Good Friday
Holy Saturday
Easter Sunday
Ascension
Pentecost
All Souls Day
All Saints Day
First Sunday
of Advent
Winter
Spring
Summer
Fall

Liturgical Calendar

The liturgical calendar highlights the seasons of the Church year. Various colors symbolize the different seasons.

1 | Feast of All Saints

> Indeed, for your faithful, Lord, life is changed not ended, and, when this earthly dwelling turns to dust, an eternal dwelling is made ready for them in heaven.
>
> *Preface I for the Dead*

This prayer from the funeral Mass clearly states our belief about God's promise of eternal life. The saints in heaven are signs to us that God's promise of eternal life is real and that its grace affects our lives in powerful ways. Each time we, the living, pray for those who have died, it is an example of the strength of the bond that unites us in the Communion of Saints. Christ himself is that bond of unity.

We are never alone. That's what the Communion of Saints tells us. Even when we face death, we are upheld in prayer by our family of faith. This family includes those in heaven, on earth, and in purgatory. If we journey through the period of purification, called *purgatory*, before standing in the presence of God, we are strengthened and aided by the prayers of the saints and by those still living on earth.

Saint Bernadette of Lourdes.

The Communion of Saints

In Heaven

On Earth

In Purgatory

Those who are already in the presence of God, the saints in heaven, intercede with God on behalf of the living and the souls in purgatory. One might even think of the saints as our cheering squad in heaven. Even in the most difficult of circumstances—perhaps especially then—we can call on our friends in heaven to help us.

Saint Joan of Arc.

Praying with the Saints

Our Catholic Tradition distinguishes the prayer and worship we offer to God from the veneration and honor given to Mary and the saints. Prayer and worship are only properly directed toward God. When we honor the saints, we ask them to intercede with God on our behalf. The effects of our devotion to the saints come from God's grace alone. Of all the saints, Mary is given a place of honor. We offer special devotion to her.

Archbishop Oscar Romero.

Saint Thérèse of Lisieux.

A Family of Faith

On All Saints Day (November 1) and All Souls Day (November 2), we celebrate this family of faith. On All Saints Day, we stand in the company of all of the faithful and praise God for the witness of the saints and for his grace, which is evident in their lives. We also pray that we, too, one day will be counted among the saints in heaven, sharing eternal happiness.

On All Souls Day, we pray for those on their way to God. We pray for those who have died, that they will soon share the joy of heaven.

All Saints Day and All Souls Day are days of hope. We look forward to the promise of eternal life. But these are also days that encourage us and strengthen us for daily living. We are not alone. Our family of faith, the Communion of Saints, journeys with us each and every day.

Saint Francis of Assisi.

2 | Advent

Occasionally, people use the word *O* (or *Oh*) when making a special appeal to someone. In the cartoon *It's the Great Pumpkin, Charlie Brown*, Charlie's friend Linus calls out in desperation, "O Great Pumpkin, where are you?"

During the final days of Advent, we call out in special appeal to God, relying on prayers called "O" Antiphons. The "O" Antiphons are used at Evening Prayer—before and after the Canticle of Mary (the *Magnificat*)—and at weekday Masses as the Alleluia verse. Some phrases from the "O" Antiphons are also used in the well-known Advent hymn "O Come, O Come, Emmanuel."

"O" Antiphons

Read the "O" Antiphons and then answer the questions. Color the symbols and think about what they mean. Pray the "O" Antiphons on the appropriate days of Advent.

DECEMBER 17
O Wisdom of our God Most High,
guiding creation with power and love:
come to teach us the path of knowledge!

DECEMBER 18
O Leader of the House of Israel,
giver of the Law to Moses on Sinai:
come to rescue us with your mighty power!

DECEMBER 19
O Root of Jesse's stem,
sign of God's love for all his people:
come to save us without delay!

Questions

What do we ask of God in the December 17 antiphon?

_____

What title do we use to address God in the December 18 antiphon?

_____

Who has been raised up as a sign of all people, the "flower of Jesse's stem"?

_____

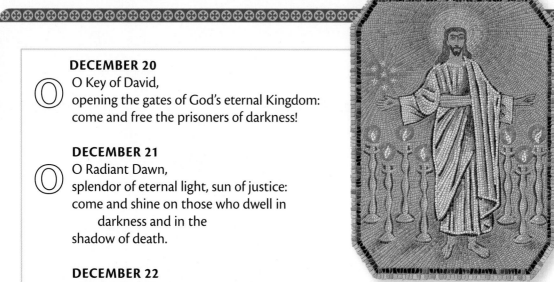

DECEMBER 20

O Key of David,
opening the gates of God's eternal Kingdom:
come and free the prisoners of darkness!

DECEMBER 21

O Radiant Dawn,
splendor of eternal light, sun of justice:
come and shine on those who dwell in
    darkness and in the
shadow of death.

DECEMBER 22

O King of all nations and keystone of the
    Church:
come and save man, whom you formed
    from the dust!

DECEMBER 23

O Emmanuel, our King and Giver of Law:
come to save us, Lord our God!

Questions

Whom do we ask God to lead to freedom?

_____

What title is God given in terms of his standing among all the nations?

_____

For whom is Emmanuel the Savior?

_____

Darkness of spirit is caused by suffering, temptation, and sin. What can people do to bring the light of Christ to people in need of hope?

_____

Read Matthew 1:22–23. What does the name *Emmanuel* mean?

_____

When Jesus is with us, he sets us free. What can we do to keep Jesus with us?

_____

_____

Which of the "O" Antiphons is your favorite? Why?

_____

_____

3 | Epiphany

Some occasions are so important and so festive that we cannot limit their celebration to one day. This is true of Christmas. Many of us celebrate Christmas as a single day, December 25, the day on which we commemorate the birth of Jesus. But to limit Christmas to a single day is to diminish the importance of what we are invited to celebrate during this nine-day season of celebration.

Yes, Christmas celebrates the birth of Jesus. But there is mystery behind this event. Throughout the Christmas season, we are encouraged to reflect on the truth that Jesus' birth revealed, the mystery of the Incarnation and the beginning of our salvation.

The Christmas Season

- The Christmas season begins on Christmas Eve, December 24. On Christmas Eve and Christmas Day, we hear the Gospels about the birth of Jesus (Matthew 1:1–25; Luke 2:1–14; Luke 2:15–20).
- We celebrate the feast of the Holy Family on the Sunday after Christmas.
- The Christmas season continues with the Solemnity of Mary, the Holy Mother of God, celebrated January 1.
- On the feast of the Epiphany of the Lord, celebrated on January 6 or the Sunday between January 2 and 8, we recall the Magi's journey to find the infant Jesus and their worship of him as King.
- The Christmas season ends on the Baptism of the Lord, the Sunday after the Epiphany.
- On the weekdays of the Christmas season, we celebrate a number of important feasts, including the feast of Saint Stephen, Martyr, the feast of Saint John the Evangelist, and the feast of the Holy Innocents.

At various times in Christian history and in many places today, Christmas Day has not carried the importance of the Christmas season as it does in American culture. Instead, the highlight of the season has been the feast of the Epiphany of the Lord.

The liturgical feast of the Epiphany recalls an event reported only in the Gospel of Matthew: travelers from the East followed a star, searching for a newborn king. The word *epiphany* means "manifestation" or "revelation." Among Christians in the Eastern traditions, the feast of the Epiphany is remembered as one of three important revelations about the identity and significance of Jesus, the Son of God. In these traditions, the feast of the Epiphany is celebrated along with the feast of the Baptism of the Lord and Jesus' first miracle at the wedding feast at Cana.

The Real Christmas Story

So you think you know the story of Christmas . . .

Check (✓) the details about Jesus' birth that can be found in the Gospel of Matthew.

_____ The Magi journeyed to Jerusalem before going to Bethlehem.

_____ There were three Magi.

_____ The shepherds and the Magi worshiped Jesus together at the stable.

_____ The Magi were kings.

_____ The Magi brought gifts of gold, frankincense, and myrrh.

_____ Herod sought to worship Jesus as did the Magi.

_____ The names of the Magi were Caspar, Melchior, and Balthasar.

_____ The Magi followed a star that they believed was a sign of the birth of the newborn king of the Jews.

Read Matthew 2:1–12. Then check your answers above to see how you did.

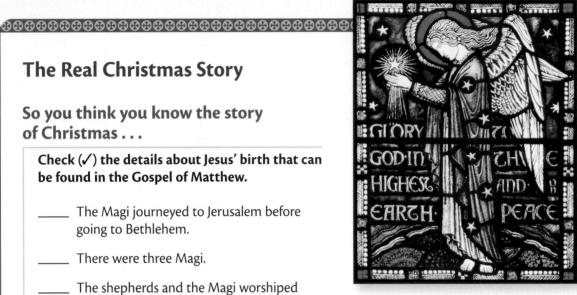

Gospel Details

Write three details that we learn about the Magi and Jesus' birth from this Gospel.

1. _____

_____

2. _____

_____

3. _____

_____

A First-Hand Account

Imagine you are one of the Magi returning to your home country. You decide to write a brief summary of your experience to share with others. Write a paragraph describing your impressions of this unusual journey and what it meant to you.

_____

_____

_____

_____

_____

4 | Lent

Look up each Scripture passage and identify the kinds of changes God wants us to make during Lent:

Ezekiel 36:25–26 _____

_____

Ephesians 4:22–24 _____

_____

Romans 6:3–4,10–11 _____

_____

Beginnings of Lent

Read this play and perform it with other members of your class. Then discuss the answers to the questions.

Narrator: The year is 350. The place is Rome. We are waiting with the rest of the Christian community that has gathered in the bishop's home. Today three catechumens will be allowed to enter the intense preparation for the Sacraments of Initiation. They will receive these sacraments at the Easter Vigil.

Deacon: Will the catechumens please step forward?

Bishop: Marcus, Celia, and Julius, you studied the Gospel of Jesus Christ and worked with the Christian community. Let us hear from those who sponsored you.

Sponsor 1: Marcus has tried to share the Good News with his family. He has visited those who are sick and done many other good works.

Sponsor 2: Celia is often at prayer. She has faithfully helped her neighbors and has given alms to those who are poor.

Sponsor 3: Julius has been fair in dealing with his workers. He has risked his life to bring others to Christ.

Bishop: Celia, Julius, and Marcus, the Christian community here in Rome trusts that God has chosen you to join his elect. As Jesus fasted and prayed in the desert for 40 days, so you now begin 40 days of preparation. Then you will be initiated into the Church of Jesus Christ.

Deacon: During this time you will meet for daily instruction in the faith. Each Sunday you will join the community to discover areas in your lives that keep you from following Christ and areas in which your virtue is growing and may be strengthened.

Bishop: Are you willing to enter this new phase, waiting for the moment when you will die to sin with Christ and rise to life with him, receiving a new heart and a new self?

Marcus, Celia, Julius: We are ready and willing.

Bishop: This time is very important for our catechumens. Members of the Christian community, how will you aid them on their journey toward initiation into Christ?

All: We will join in prayer with and for these catechumens whom God has chosen.

Stephen: We will fast from food on the days preceding the Easter Vigil, the time of initiation.

Lydia: We will reexamine our lives, once more renounce sin, and try harder to witness to the Lord Jesus.

Nicholas: Anyone who has fallen into serious public sin will do penance, wearing sackcloth and ashes.

All: As we gather for worship on Sunday, we will listen to special readings and celebrate the Eucharist for these chosen ones.

Narrator: Forty days from now, at the Easter Vigil, these three candidates will enter into the dying and rising of Christ through the waters of Baptism. They will receive the Holy Spirit in the Sacrament of Confirmation. And they will receive the Body and Blood of Christ for the first time, thus fully participating in the Eucharist.

Discussion Questions

1. What were the good works performed by the catechumens? How did these good works make them more like Jesus?

_____

_____

_____

_____

2. How did the members of the community aid the catechumens? Whom could you aid by your prayers, sacrifices, and acts of service during Lent?

_____

_____

_____

_____

3. How do you know that the catechumens appreciated the Sacraments of Baptism, Confirmation, and the Eucharist? How could you show greater appreciation for these sacraments?

_____

_____

_____

_____

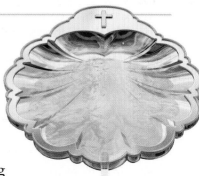

Renewing Our Commitment

How will you make this Lent a time to renew your commitment to living your Baptism?

5 | Holy Week

When we refer to something as *holy*, that means it is "set aside" for a special purpose. Holy water is not intended for drinking; it is a symbol of our Baptism. The week leading up to Easter is called Holy Week because it is set aside for recalling the suffering, Death, and Resurrection of Jesus. Three days during Holy Week are especially important: Holy Thursday, Good Friday, and Holy Saturday. These three days are called the Easter Triduum.

In the spaces below, list the events of Jesus' life that we remember on each day of the Easter Triduum. Then list the special ceremonies or rituals we use to celebrate these events.

Holy Thursday

Events _____

_____

_____

_____

Ritual _____

_____

_____

Good Friday

Events _____

_____

_____

_____

Ritual _____

_____

_____

_____

Easter (Vigil)

Events _____

_____

_____

_____

Ritual _____

_____

_____

_____

_____

_____

_____

A Commemoration and Celebration

The Easter Triduum

Fill in the blanks to make the sentences correct.

1. begins with the Mass of the Lord's Supper on

    _____.

2. continues with the celebration of the Lord's

    Passion on _____.

3. reaches its high point at the Easter Vigil on

    _____.

4. has many references and symbols related to the

    Jewish feast of _____.

5. recalls the Jewish celebration of Passover, when
   Jewish families celebrate a special meal called a

    _____.

List the ritual that commemorates each event.

1. Jesus eats the Last Supper with his disciples:

    _____

2. Jesus washes the feet of his disciples:

    _____

3. Jesus suffers and dies for us:

    _____

4. Jesus redeems us by his Death on the Cross:

    _____

5. Jesus rises from the dead:

    _____

In Your Words

Imagine that a friend or relative who is not
Catholic will be visiting you during Holy
Week. This person has sent you an e-mail
asking about Holy Week services at your
parish. In your reflection notebook, write what
you would say in response. Describe what he
or she can expect to see during Holy Week
services.

6 | Easter

Fill in the blanks to complete the story of Easter. The first letter of each missing word forms the acrostic to the left.

T Jesus was crucified and buried in the

_____ .

H The theological virtue we celebrate at

Easter is _____ .

E On the third day after Jesus died, women

found Jesus' tomb _____ .

L Sacrificial victim of the Old Testament,

as Christ is the sacrificial victim of the

New Testament _____ .

O To remind _____ that we should

be clothed with Christ, many people get new

clothes for Easter.

R The disciples did not know who had

_____ away the stone from

Jesus' tomb.

D The empty tomb was

discovered at

_____ .

H Just as the sun announces the day, Christ's

Resurrection announces, or _____ ,

a new day, a new life.

A An expression of joy meaning "Praise the Lord."

_____

S The _____ brings us from darkness

into light, just as Christ did by his Resurrection.

R By Christ's passion, Death, and Resurrection we

are saved, or _____ .

I Christ's Resurrection reminds us we will share

his everlasting, or _____ , glory.

S A lily is a _____ of purity, beauty, and

perfection.

E We can meet the glorified Christ daily in the

_____ .

N All Easter symbols remind us of the

_____ life Christ gives us.

261

Symbols of Easter

Below are symbols of Easter and Scripture passages related to them.
Find each Scripture passage and, in the space provided, write a word or
phrase from the passage that relates to the symbol.

1. Sun

John 1:3–5 _____

_____

Matthew 17:2 _____

_____

2. Lamb

Exodus 12:21–23 _____

_____

John 1:29 _____

_____

3. Eggs

John 11:38–44 _____

_____

John 20:1 _____

_____

4. Butterfly

1 Corinthians 15:42–43 _____

_____

Romans 8:11 _____

_____

5. New clothes

Galatians 3:27 _____

_____

Revelation 7:14 _____

_____

6. Lily

John 12:24 _____

_____

Philippians 3:21 _____

_____

7. Rabbit

John 10:10 _____

_____

Revelation 21:3–5 _____

_____

8. Alleluia

Psalm 118:24 _____

_____

Revelation 19:5–7 _____

_____

Words of the Risen Lord

Listen to the words of the risen Lord that we hear at Easter. To Thomas, Jesus says: "Do not be unbelieving, but believe." (John 20:27) To the women: "Go quickly and tell his disciples, 'He has been raised from the dead.'" (Matthew 28:7) To Peter: "Feed my lambs." (John 21:15)

The first words various people said when they met Jesus in his glorified body are beautiful prayers. Mary Magdalene said, "Rabbouni," which means "Teacher." (John 20:16) Thomas said, "My Lord and my God." (John 20:28) Peter said, "Yes, Lord, you know that I love you." (John 21:15) The two disciples on the way to Emmaus said to him, "Stay with us, for it is nearly evening." (Luke 24:29)

What would you say and do if you met Jesus face to face in his risen body? In your reflection notebook, write your prayer to Jesus, who comes to you glorified in the Eucharist.

7 | Pentecost

On the feast of Pentecost, celebrated 50 days after Easter, the Church gathers to give praise and thanksgiving for the work of the Holy Spirit throughout salvation history. We renew our commitment to live as Spirit-filled people who cooperate with the grace of God to serve the Kingdom of God.

As Catholics, we look back over the story of God's loving relationship with his people. We can identify three periods in salvation history. In each of these eras, we discover the presence and action of the Holy Spirit, who works with God the Father and God the Son for our salvation.

The Time of the Promises

The first period of salvation history, called "the time of the promises," includes all the time before the birth of Jesus. The Holy Spirit is with God from the beginning of time. With God's first act, Creation, the Spirit moved over the waters and was the breath that brought Adam to life. God led the Israelites from Egypt, parting the waters of the Red Sea and leading the Israelites by means of a pillar of fire. The Holy Spirit spoke through the prophets, announcing and preparing for the Messiah promised by God.

The Fullness of Time

The second period of salvation history, called "the fullness of time," is the time of Jesus' life and ministry on earth. It is the time of the fulfillment of God's promise of salvation. The Holy Spirit was active in the lives of the people who prepared for Jesus' birth—Mary, Joseph, and John the Baptist. Jesus himself identified his mission in union with the promises of the prophets when he announced his ministry. He used the words from the prophet Isaiah,

> "The Spirit of the Lord is upon me,
> because he has anointed me
>   to bring glad tidings to the poor.
> He has sent me to proclaim liberty to captives
>   and recovery of sight to the blind,
>   to let the oppressed go free,
> and to proclaim a year acceptable to the Lord."
>
> Luke 4:18–19

The work of Jesus for our salvation is a mission shared by the Son and the Holy Spirit.

The Time of the Church

The third period of salvation history is called "the time of the Church," or "the time of grace." This is the period of salvation history in which we live. It began with the outpouring of the Holy Spirit on the disciples at Pentecost and will continue until the end of time, when Christ returns in glory.

Read the following passages from the Acts of the Apostles. What does each passage reveal about the work of the Holy Spirit in this, the time of the Church?

Acts of the Apostles 4:23–31 _____

_____

_____

Acts of the Apostles 7:54–60 _____

_____

_____

Acts of the Apostles 10:44–49 _____

_____

_____

The Spirit in the Church Today

The Holy Spirit continues to guide the mission of the Church, working within us to make us bold witnesses to Christ. The Spirit strengthens us in the face of difficulties and builds the community of the Church, uniting us in the bond of love.

Identify one way you have seen members of the Church today

give bold witness to Christ.

_____

_____

_____

show strength in the face of difficulties.

_____

_____

_____

act as a community united in love.

_____

_____

_____

Prayer for the Work of the Holy Spirit

Response: Lord, send out your Spirit, and renew the face of the earth.

Bless the Lord, O my soul!
O Lord, my God, you are great indeed!
How varied are your works, O Lord!
The earth is full of your creatures;

May the glory of the Lord endure forever;
May the Lord be glad in his works!
Pleasing to him be my theme;
I will rejoice in the Lord.

If you take away their breath, they perish
And return to their dust.
When you send forth your spirit, they are created,
And you renew the face of the earth.

adapted from Psalm 104

When we, the members of the Church, cooperate with the work of the Holy Spirit, we serve the Kingdom of God and renew the face of the earth.

El Greco, detail of _Pentecost_.

8 | Reconciliation

Ryan made the eighth-grade honor roll at South Junior High. He captained the football team, and his coach encouraged him to prepare for the high school team. He was popular with his classmates. Usually he was the center of attention. Ryan was a good, honest kid. Then slowly, something began happening to him.

At first no one noticed. Then Diego, his best friend, asked, "Ryan, what's the matter? You missed practice twice. And you were really out of it in history yesterday. Are you OK?" Ryan just passed off the remarks with a strange smile.

Then the football coach noticed. "Ryan," he asked, "are you sick? You were out of breath after the first half hour of practice. You don't look healthy." Ryan just shrugged and walked away.

Ryan's parents began noticing that their son was spending a lot of time with Connor, a new boy in the neighborhood. Connor seemed older, but Ryan's parents never paid much attention to their son's friends.

The shock came when Ryan's mother was putting away laundry. What she found in the back of Ryan's drawer filled her with dread. There were all the items she had heard about! Could Ryan be on drugs? Then she remembered that some of her money had recently been missing. Other signs began to take shape—Ryan's lack of energy, the hours he spent at Connor's house, the loss of interest in his schoolwork and even in football.

Throughout the afternoon, Ryan's mother thought back over the past several years. She recalled that they had not attended Mass for a long time. Nor had they encouraged Ryan to do so. No one in their house prayed. Ryan did receive his First Holy Communion, but then he stopped going to religion classes. She and her husband had too many social obligations to take him. But she thought that she and her husband had given Ryan a good home and a chance to prepare for a career. Now he had let them down.

When Ryan's parents talked with him that night, the truth came out. Yes, he was taking drugs. Yes, he took the money, though he denied it at first. He said he did it because Connor insisted. Ryan's mother sobbed, "Ryan, didn't you know these things were wrong?"

Ryan looked down. He answered quietly, "How was I supposed to know?"

Discuss the following questions:

1. What should have helped Ryan make better decisions?

2. Why was Ryan's conscience unable to guide him?

3. Find reasons in the story for why Ryan's conscience was not formed. Explain.

Conscience: The Power to Decide

You know how to make decisions about right and wrong because you possess a special gift from God: a conscience. Conscience is the power of the intellect to decide whether an act is good or bad. An act's morality depends on the act itself, the intention, and the circumstances. Some acts are evil by nature. We may never do evil for a good purpose.

Underline the names of the students you think make a responsible decision.

- Brigid sees the new girl, Alyssa, come into the room. She snickers and whispers something rude about her to another student.

- Jackson needs money to download music he wants. He takes $10 from his dad's wallet.

- Christine's parents forbid her to spend a long time on the phone when she is babysitting her younger brother. When they are out, Christine gets a call from Renée. Christine promises to return the call when her parents get home.

- The librarian told the class that reference books may not be taken out of the library. Daniel needs an encyclopedia volume for a report due the next day. He sneaks the book out of the library because it is an emergency.

- Scott was in trouble at school for drinking. Gavin's mother knows about her son's friendship with Scott. She tells Gavin that she doesn't want him to go anywhere with Scott again. When Scott calls, Gavin excuses himself from going out.

- Kylie and Sydney work on props for the school play. They leave the room a mess. The next day, the teacher asks who was responsible. Kylie admits her part but becomes angry when Sydney does not. At lunch, when Sydney tries to join Kylie's table, Kylie tells her there is no room.

Though you were born with the potential for knowing the difference between good and evil, you were not born with an informed, responsible, Christian conscience. A conscience that remains in ignorance can lead you to wrong judgments. Your conscience develops with your spiritual growth. You develop an informed conscience by considering obligations and consequences before making a decision.

Obligations are the responsibilities you have because you are a follower of Jesus. You show your love for Jesus by the way you live, the example of your moral life. The guidelines for expressing your love for Christ are the Ten Commandments and the teachings of Jesus and his Church. You form a good conscience by repeatedly applying these guidelines to moral situations.

Christian Decisions

Rewrite the stories to show responsible Christian decisions.

Brigid: _____

_____

_____

Jackson: _____

_____

_____

Daniel: _____

_____

_____

Consequences are the results of choices. Sometimes before you make a decision, you can be sure of the consequences. Other times you cannot. Consequences are important to consider, however, because they affect your life and the lives of other people.

After considering obligations and consequences in the light of faith, a responsible Christian conscience makes a decision. You have the choice of following its judgment or ignoring it. This choice may require sacrifice and courage.

What may be the consequences of Kylie's unkindness to Sydney?

_____

_____

_____

The Peace of Christ

God will never force us to choose what is right. But Jesus promises that those who follow his way will be filled with joy and will find great peace. As a member of the Catholic Church, you can trust Christ and rely on him in making all your decisions.

Those who choose selfishly will be restless and uneasy. But the feeling of uneasiness is good because it warns us that we are not following our formed conscience or growing closer to Christ. If you find yourself feeling this way, make an act of contrition and promise to make an unselfish choice the next time.

Peace or Anxiety?

Read both Scripture passages. Did the people in these stories make choices that led to great peace? Explain your answers.

Luke 19:1–10 _____

_____

_____

_____

Luke 22:54–62 _____

_____

_____

_____

Peace Plan: An Examination of Conscience

You need a guide so that your choices lead you to live a holy life. Christ is your guide. He guides you when you make an examination of conscience. He enables you to form a responsible Christian conscience.

Through the practice of the examination of conscience, you take an honest look at yourself. You remember what God asks of you, and you see how you are responding. You know that through God's grace and your cooperation, you will grow to be a good and holy person.

To make a good examination of conscience, set aside prayer time to examine or review your life. During this time do the following:

- Try to see how God shows love to you in daily life.
- Ask yourself questions on how you have lived the Ten Commandments and the teachings of Jesus.
- Decide which is your greatest weakness and think of how you can improve in this area.
- Pray that Christ will help you remain open to his friendship, and cooperate with his grace working in you.

Many of the saints advised making an examination of conscience regularly. They knew the truth of Socrates' words, "An unexamined life isn't worth living."

Examine Your Life

Read the examples. See how these people could grow through an examination of conscience.

1 "I hate going to that stupid lake cottage!" screamed Rose as she stomped upstairs to her bedroom. She slammed the door to show her mother how mad she was. Every weekend, Rose's parents take the family out to spend time together. Rose would rather be with her friends than with her family. She made the weekend miserable for her family.

When Rose examines her conscience, what area might she work on?

_____

What is one way she could improve?

_____

_____

_____

2 At recess, the eighth-grade boys started a game the principal had forbidden them to play. When the teacher on playground duty asked them to stop, Charles sneered at her and continued with the game. Later, the teacher spoke to the boys about the incident, and Charles answered disrespectfully. Then he pretended not to listen to her advice.

When Charles examines his conscience, what area might he work on?

_____

What is one way he could improve?

_____

_____

3 Teresa was telling a group of eighth-grade girls about her weekend with her aunt. She described how exciting the shopping trip to the city had been. Suddenly, Cecilia started talking about the time she went shopping in the "really big stores in New York." Teresa's trip now sounded boring by comparison.

When Cecilia examines her conscience, what area might she work on?

_____

Think of one way she could improve.

_____

_____

_____

Conscience and Confession

A regular examination of conscience makes it easier to prepare for the Sacrament of Reconciliation. Find out when your parish offers the Sacrament of Reconciliation. Tell the priest honestly about your examination of conscience and the area you plan to work on to grow closer to Christ. Relate how you have sinned in this area and ask for suggestions on how to improve. Be open to the penance given you.

The Sacrament of Reconciliation is a powerful means of forming your conscience. It gives you the grace to come closer to Christ. It gives you peace of heart.

Your conversion will probably not be as dramatic as Saint Augustine's, whose story follows. But you are continually called to conversion. A Catholic is someone who is always turning toward the Lord, always converting.

The Restless Heart

Don't give up in your efforts to examine your conscience and grow more like Christ! Think of Saint Augustine. Through Scripture he experienced a change of heart that led to peace in Christ. Here is his story:

Saint Monica, Saint Augustine's mother, spent a lot of time worrying about her carefree and unsettled son. Augustine was born to his Christian mother and pagan father in A.D. 354. He was not baptized as a child but did receive a Christian education. Augustine was very intelligent, but at first school did not interest him.

As a young man, Augustine wanted to be famous and successful. He filled his mind with pleasure and comfort instead of unselfish things that could make him a better person. He did whatever he thought would make him feel good, regardless of whether or not it might hurt others. He joined a heretical religion. He lived with a woman and had a son by her. But this style of life did not satisfy him.

ST. AUGUSTINE

Many things influenced Augustine's conversion: the Baptism of his good friend, the preaching of the bishop Saint Ambrose, and his mother's prayers. One day, Augustine opened a Bible and read Romans 13:13–14. He saw his life in the light of the Scriptures and had the grace to change it. He became a confirmed Christian and, through daily effort, a saint!

The Dare

The girls leaned against the wall, tired from gym class. Mrs. Lynch blew her whistle. "Time's up, ladies. Out of the locker room!" She pushed open the door to see if anyone was left.

As soon as Mrs. Lynch was gone, Zoe began pressuring Maya. "Come on, I dare you to pull the fire alarm!"

"Good idea," laughed Jordan. "That would really scare Andrea. I bet she's still in the shower."

Maya shook her head, trying to ignore them. Anyhow, Andrea was her friend.

"You aren't scared, are you?" Amy said slyly.

Maya blushed. She hated the way Amy always seemed to control things. If only she could think of something to say. She made Maya feel so weak! Amy needled her further. "You always do what the teachers want."

Maya couldn't stand it. No one was going to make her look stupid. Without hesitation she pulled the alarm.

Maya's heart pounded as she hurried out of the building with the bewildered teachers and students. Sure enough, Jordan had been right. Andrea ran out of the locker room last. Zoe giggled nervously at the sight of the frantic girl, but Maya froze as she saw Andrea slip. Before she could see what followed, Maya was pushed with the crowd through the doorway.

It didn't take long for the principal to realize there wasn't a fire. It also wasn't difficult for him to find out which group pulled the prank. Maya's class, minus Andrea, was called to the office. The principal told them that as a result of the false alarm, Andrea had broken her leg. He wanted to know who was responsible. He began to call names.

"Amy?"

"No sir, I had nothing to do with it."

"Zoe?"

"No sir."

"Maya?"

"No sir." Maya fought hard to keep from crying. She hadn't thought all this would happen. She knew how much Andrea wanted to be in the track meet that week. Now there was no chance for that. Maya didn't want to lie. But she dreaded having her parents find out.

Maya soon learned that one lie leads to another. The days that followed were worse than ever. First, Maya's parents discussed how hard it must be for Andrea and her parents. "Practical jokes are never funny," her father said. "Do you know who did it?" her mother asked.

"No. But I bet whoever did it feels terrible," said Maya, avoiding her mother's look.

When Amy, Zoe, and Jordan went to visit Andrea in the hospital, Maya made up the excuse that she had to babysit. She also realized that Amy was telling people that Maya was responsible for the false alarm. Maya wondered how long it would be before the principal found out. Every day she hated herself more, and she hated Amy. Zoe and Jordan were avoiding her, too. Maya felt she would never forgive them for the dare.

Choices and Consequences

Sin is complicated. It affects our lives, and it affects the lives of others in the community. Sin doesn't just happen. We make the free decision to turn away from God. We are responsible when we hurt others. Answer the following questions.

1. What was Maya's sin?

_____

_____

2. How did sin affect her?

_____

_____

3. To cover up her mistake of pulling the fire alarm, what sinful decisions did she make?

_____

_____

_____

_____

4. How did Maya's pulling the fire alarm hurt another?

_____

_____

The Choice for God

Sin isn't the last word. God loves us very much. Through the power of the Holy Spirit, God calls us back to him and to others through reconciliation. The word *reconciliation* means "to renew a friendship after that friendship has been broken." Maya needs healing in her relationship with God and with others through the Sacrament of Reconciliation.

The First Step: Prayer

By Saturday, Maya knew she had to do something. Going to school hurt. At home she hurt because she knew she had lied to her parents. And she couldn't face Andrea. Maya decided to receive the Sacrament of Reconciliation. When she arrived at St. Paul's Church, she sat in the last pew, where no one could see her. Over and over she prayed. "Please give me the courage, Jesus, to go to confession. I'm really sorry for everything I did. I wish I hadn't lied or hurt anyone. Help me to know what I should do."

As Maya sat there, she thought back to religion class. Mrs. Gomez had said that God will forgive us when we make sinful choices. But we must be sorry and ask forgiveness of him and others.

Looking deeper. When we read Scripture and pray, we hear God calling us to turn away from sin and be faithful to the Gospel. This is conversion. It isn't easy. Conversion is a life-long work. It starts in the heart of a person. Conversion is to turn away from sin and to become like Jesus. As we grow more like Christ, we will be happier and more at peace. We will be living as we were meant to live.

Think about the meaning of *conversion* and answer these questions.

Why is "just being sorry in her heart" not enough for Maya?

_____

_____

_____

_____

How can Maya's feelings of guilt be a gift from God to help her begin a conversion of the heart?

_____

_____

_____

The Second Step: Examination of Conscience

As Maya sat in the church, she thought over what she had done and why. "I really want to be popular like Amy," she thought. "I'm afraid of what other kids will think of me. I guess I do things because I want people like Amy to admire me. Pulling the alarm got me into trouble. I lied to cover up because now I'm afraid of what my parents and teachers will think. I can't be myself because I don't think others will love me for who I am."

Looking deeper. Examination of conscience is an honest look at ourselves to see how and why we have sinned. When we examine our conscience, we ask ourselves questions, usually based on the commandments. We do this because we realize that God loves us more than anyone else loves us, and we want to be his friend. A daily examination of conscience can help us become open to God's love and grace. What time could you set aside for your own examination of conscience?

The Third Step: Contrition

Just thinking of her actions made Maya miserable. But she was really sorry and did not want to hurt her parents and friends any further. She wanted to be good. She wanted to be forgiven. And Maya was willing to take the consequences of her actions.

Looking deeper. Contrition is sorrow for sin. It goes on deep in the heart between God and you. Are you really sorry? Are you willing to take responsibility for your sins? Do you really trust that God will help you heal and be healed? With contrition, you make a firm resolution not to sin again.

> **Read the following Scripture passages. What signs of true contrition do these people show?**
>
> Luke 7:36–50
>
> _____
>
> _____
>
> _____
>
> _____
>
> Luke 15:11–24
>
> _____
>
> _____
>
> _____
>
> Luke 19:1–10
>
> _____
>
> _____
>
> _____
>
> Luke 22:54–62
>
> _____
>
> _____
>
> _____
>
> _____

Depiction of Luke 22:54–62.

The Rite of Penance and Reconciliation

The Fourth Step: Confession

The last penitent left. Maya opened the door to the reconciliation room and walked in.

"Hello, Father," she said nervously.

"May God bless you," Father Hanes answered. They made the Sign of the Cross. Father prayed that Maya would know her sins and trust in God's mercy. Then he read the story of the prodigal son. Now Maya really thought she knew what the son felt. Father Hanes closed the Bible and encouraged her to speak. She took a deep breath and began. Maya told him how she pulled the fire alarm because she was afraid of Amy. She explained that she had lied to the principal, her parents, and her friends to cover up. Maya asked, "What am I supposed to do now? I'm sorry I've hurt so many people. I'll try never to do anything like this again."

Father Hanes spoke gently. "It's good you are so open with God. What do you think was the wrong you did?"

Maya thought for a moment. Then she answered, "It was lying. I wasn't honest with anyone, not even myself. I also broke the rules and put other people at risk."

"What do you think you could do to show these people you are sorry?" Father asked.

"I suppose I have to tell the principal and my parents the truth and tell them I'm sorry," Maya answered.

"That would be a good penance," Father said. "Can you accept it? Be honest with your parents, teachers, and friends. They will respect you. You will be at peace with yourself because you are living the Gospel. I also think it would be a good idea to visit Andrea. Tell her the story and ask forgiveness. If you pray every day to be a strong and faithful Christian, you will have the courage to be your best self at all times."

Looking deeper. Penance enables us to convert our hearts by prayer or action and strengthens the bond of friendship with Christ. It reconciles us not only to God, but to all the people in the Church through the priest, their representative. Penance also helps keep us from falling into the same sin.

Underline Maya's penance. Why do you think Father Hanes gave Maya this penance?

_____

_____

The Fifth Step: Praise of God

Father Hanes said, "You have done a wonderful thing. Christ will now help you with his grace and power. Give thanks to the Lord for he is good."

Maya responded, "His mercy endures forever. Thanks, Father."

Answer these questions on a sheet of paper.

1. Why do you think Maya will be more at peace when she completes her penance?

2. What might happen when Maya tells the principal, her parents, and friends?

3. How do you think Andrea will respond when Maya comes to visit her?

4. After Reconciliation, what should Maya's attitude be toward Amy, Zoe, and Jordan?

5. How does regularly celebrating the Sacrament of Penance help spiritual growth?

Next, Father asked Maya to pray an act of sorrow for her sins. She could pray the Act of Contrition or use her own words. Maya said, "Jesus, I'm sorry for offending you and hurting my family and friends by lying. I know I didn't do what was right, and I'm going to try harder to give good example by being truthful. With your help, I want to live what I believe. I know you'll help me do this."

Maya expressed her sorrow to Christ through his representative, the priest. In the name of Christ, Father pardoned her sins, saying, "I absolve you from your sins in the name of the Father and of the Son and of the Holy Spirit." Maya answered, "Amen," accepting in faith Christ's forgiveness.

9 | Celebrating Eucharist

The cup of blessing that we bless, is it not a participation in the blood of Christ? The bread that we break, is it not a participation in the body of Christ?

1 Corinthians 10:16

Each week, as part of the Catholic Christian community, you gather together with others in the celebration of the Eucharist. The word *Eucharist* means "thanksgiving." *Thank* comes from the word *think*. To thank someone is to think of him or her and what he or she has done for us. People have been celebrating their thankfulness throughout history.

What exactly are we to be thankful for—to be thinking of—during Mass? What makes this celebration such a vital part of the life of Catholics and of your life, too? When we speak of the Eucharist as thanksgiving, we are referring to the redeeming acts of Jesus Christ. Through his Death on the Cross and his

Resurrection from the dead, he saved us from sin. He made it possible for us to return to the Father. This is the great act of love that we celebrate in our gathering and worshiping.

For which event would each of these people be thankful? Match the names and events, using the Scripture references if necessary.

a. Adam and Eve

b. Abraham

c. Jacob and his sons

d. Moses

e. All people

_____ God made him a leader and saved his people from slavery in Egypt. (Exodus 14:15–31)

_____ God promised to send the world a savior, born of a woman, to crush the power of evil. (Genesis 3:8–15)

_____ Jesus suffered and died on the Cross and then rose again. (1 Corinthians 15:3–8)

_____ God saved them from hunger through the efforts and kindness of Joseph. (Genesis 45:1–13)

_____ God promised to make his descendants many. God gave him a new land and made a covenant with him. (Genesis 17:1–8)

The Mass: Changing Yet Changeless

The celebration of our thankfulness is patterned after Jesus' own words and actions. He did the following on the night before he died:

> [H]e took the bread, said the blessing, broke it, and gave it to them, saying, "This is my body, which will be given for you; do this in memory of me." And likewise the cup after they had eaten, saying, "This cup is the new covenant in my blood, which will be shed for you."
>
> Luke 22:19–20

Our celebration of the Mass has changed over the centuries. But the basic truths about it do not change. At every Eucharist, the sacrifice of Jesus continues. At every Eucharist, bread and wine truly become Christ's Body and Blood. At every Mass, Christians are called to worship the Father with, through, and in Christ. They are called to be nourished by his Word and his Body and Blood. The community is made one and carries his love to others through service and support.

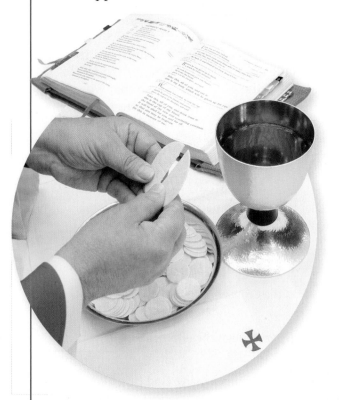

The Mass in the First Centuries

After Jesus returned to his Father, his followers gathered together in homes to pray. At a memorial meal, they offered again the sacrifice of Christ.

For the most part, in the early days Christians met in secret because they were being persecuted. The Mass was simple. During the Mass, the letters of the apostles or readings from the prophets were proclaimed. A sermon was given, and the people joined in prayer for the needs of others in the community. Gifts of bread and wine, made at home, were brought by the people to the altar as signs of their love and faith. A prayer of thanksgiving was offered, during which the bread and wine were consecrated and the people received Christ's Body and Blood in Holy Communion. Then a deacon would take Communion to the homes of those who were sick. Food was also given to those unable to provide for themselves.

> Underline similarities between the Mass in the first centuries after Christ and the Mass today.

Ritual Develops

When the persecutions ended, the Church openly celebrated the Eucharist. Large churches were built, and prayers were added to the Mass. Scripture readings, the prayer of thanksgiving called the Eucharistic Prayer, and the receiving of Holy Communion remained. But more responses of the people were included, candles were lit, incense was used, and the Creed was proclaimed. All these helped the priest and people celebrate this great mystery of faith in a dignified and joyful manner.

A Deeper Understanding

Throughout the centuries, the basic form and the essential mystery of the Mass have remained the same. But at various periods in history, changes in attitudes and culture affected people's understanding of the Mass. In the Middle Ages, people emphasized private prayer during the Mass. In the 16th century, some people were fearful of receiving Holy Communion because they felt unworthy. Today the Church calls us to pray together and to take part in the liturgy. It encourages devout reception of Holy Communion at every Mass because it is our food for life.

Names for the Eucharistic Celebration

We have many names for the celebration of the Eucharist. Each one reveals something about the mystery of what occurs during each Mass.

The Eucharist is a liturgy, the work of the whole Christ, head and body. There is a form, a flow, and a pattern to this public prayer. It is our common worship, and it reflects centuries of growth and faith. In the Eucharist, we bless and adore God the Father as the source of all the blessings of creation and salvation.

The Eucharist is the Mass. The word *Mass* comes from a Latin word meaning "dismissal." It refers to the Dismissal after the Final Blessing. With each Mass, we are sent to live our faith and to bring it to others with the Holy Spirit's help.

The Eucharist is a holy meal, a sacred banquet in which wheat bread and grape wine are essential. The Jewish people celebrated thanks for the Exodus with a Passover meal. They were brought from the slavery of Egypt to the freedom of the Promised Land. Through Christ, we have been brought from the slavery of sin to freedom as the children of God. We celebrate our thankfulness through a memorial meal that makes Christ's saving work present. We receive the Bread of Life and the cup of eternal salvation.

The Eucharist is the greatest sign of unity. Together we proclaim the truth of redemption. We are united with Christ and with one another in Christ. With others, we receive the risen Christ as food for our lives. We are sent to proclaim the saving message of Jesus in the world. The Eucharist, the Communion of Saints, represents and brings about our unity.

The Eucharist is also a sacrifice. The Eucharist is the sacrifice of Calvary made present today. It is the sacrament of our redemption. As on the Cross, Jesus is both priest and victim. As high priest, through the ministry of the priests, he offers the sacrifice to God. As victim, he offers himself and all of us to the Father. We are invited to receive him. On Calvary, Christ won for us the graces we need to reach heaven. At Mass, through the power of the Spirit, he now gives us these graces. At each Eucharist, the risen Christ is present in his glorified form.

The Mass and You

Check (✓) all the ways you are open to Christ in the Eucharist.

BEFORE GOING TO CHURCH

☐ I think about what is going to happen as I go to church.

☐ I take special care to dress neatly when I am going to church.

☐ I try to be loving and considerate of others.

☐ I fast from food for one hour before I expect to receive Holy Communion.

☐ I make sure I am not chewing gum or eating candy on my way to Mass or after I enter the church.

ARRIVING AT CHURCH

☐ I make the Sign of the Cross with holy water as I come into the church.

☐ I genuflect reverently before the tabernacle.

☐ I look over the readings for the Mass (if they are provided in the missalette or missal).

☐ I speak to God in my heart and ask for help to become as receptive as possible during the Mass.

DURING MASS

☐ I sing, respond, and listen attentively during the entire celebration.

☐ I pay special attention to the readings and homily and try to apply God's Word to my life.

☐ I recall and pray for those who are living and dead; I offer my prayers for all those in need.

☐ During the Eucharistic Prayer, I unite myself with the community and the priest, thanking God for his love and for Christ's saving action on the Cross.

☐ As I approach the altar to receive Holy Communion, I walk reverently, taking my time and speaking to Jesus in my heart. Before I receive the Eucharist, I make an act of adoration.

☐ After receiving Christ in the Eucharist, I return to my place and pray in thankfulness to Jesus, who is really present within me.

AT THE END OF MASS

☐ I take time to greet people as I leave.

☐ I do not rush, but try to be attentive to the needs of others.

☐ During the week, I try to recall all I experienced at the Eucharist and prepare to receive Christ again.

☐ I try to bring Christ's love and kindness to my family, friends, and others in all that I do during the week.

The more you come to understand the meaning of the eucharistic liturgy, the more your view of life and the world will change. You will begin to see life with a new vision of faith and will want to serve others. You will respond generously and act as a peacemaker. Your whole life will be an act of thanksgiving for all God has done for you.

What Catholics Should Know

(continued on next page)

(continued from previous page)

Prayer and How We Pray

God is always with us. He wants us to talk to him and listen to him. In prayer we raise our hearts and minds to God. We are able to speak and listen to God because through the Holy Spirit, God teaches us how to pray.

What Is Prayer?

Being a Christian requires that we believe all that God has revealed to us, that we celebrate it in the liturgy and the sacraments, and that we live what we believe. All this depends on a vital and personal relationship with the living and true God. This relationship is rooted in prayer. Prayer is a gift from God. We can pray because God seeks us out first and calls us to meet him. We become aware of our thirst for God because God thirsts for us. Prayer arises from our heart, beyond the grasp of reason. Only the Spirit of God can understand the human heart and know it fully. Prayer is the habit of being with God—Father, Son and Holy Spirit. This communion with God is always possible because through our Baptism we are united with Christ. By being united with Christ, we are united with others. Christian prayer is communion with Christ that branches out to all the members of his body, the Church.

Many Forms of Christian Prayer

The Holy Spirit, who teaches us to pray, leads us to pray in a number of ways. This conversation with God can take the form of adoration, blessing, contrition, petition, intercession, thanksgiving, or praise.

Adoration

In a prayer of adoration, we acknowledge God as Creator and Savior. In adoration we recognize how little we are in respect to God's greatness. Like Mary in the *Magnificat*, we confess with gratitude that God has done great things and holy is his name.

Blessing

To bless someone is to acknowledge the goodness of that person. The prayer of blessing is our response to God's goodness because of all the gifts he has given us. In the prayer of blessing, God's gifts and our acceptance of them come together.

Contrition

Contrition is the prayer of sorrow for sin along with a resolution not to sin again. If contrition is motivated by love of God alone, it is called perfect contrition. If contrition is motivated by fear of just punishment, it is called imperfect contrition.

Thanksgiving

Thanksgiving is characteristic of Christian prayer, especially in the Eucharist. The word *Eucharist* means "thanksgiving." Through his Death and Resurrection, Christ has reconciled us to God. His sacrifice is made present in every Eucharist. Every joy we experience, as well as our every need, can become an offering of thanksgiving in the Eucharist. In celebrating the Eucharist, the Church reveals itself as and becomes more fully a people of thanksgiving.

Praise

Praise is the form of prayer that recognizes that God is God and gives him glory. Praise goes beyond thanking God for what he has done for us. Praise gives him glory simply because he is. Praise embraces the other forms of prayer and carries them to God, who is the source of all that is.

We Meditate and Contemplate

To meditate is to think about God. We keep our attention and focus on God, using Scripture, prayer books, or religious images to help us concentrate and spark our imagination. To contemplate means that we rest quietly in God's presence.

We Get Ready to Pray

We can get ready for meditation by resting our bodies in a comfortable position, sitting with our backs straight and both feet on the floor. We can close our eyes, fold our hands in front of us, take a deep breath, and then slowly let it out. We can establish a rhythm by slowly counting to three while breathing in and slowly counting to three while breathing out. Concentrating on our breathing helps us quiet our thoughts.

Petition

Petition is much more than asking God for things we want or need. By prayers of petition, we express our relationship with God as our Creator. We depend on him, and we ask him for something for ourselves. Sometimes we sin and turn away from God. The first step in the prayer of petition is turning back toward him and asking for forgiveness. We can then ask God for what we need, confident that he knows what we need before we ask.

Intercession

In prayers of intercession, we ask something on behalf of another. As a prayer form, intercession is a prayer of petition that leads us to pray as Jesus did. Throughout his life on earth, Jesus interceded with the Father on behalf of all people. To pray in this way means that our hearts are turned outward, focused on the needs around us.

Prayers We Pray as Catholics

We can pray with any words that come to mind. Sometimes when we find that choosing our own words is difficult, we can use traditional prayers. Memorizing traditional prayers such as the following can be very helpful. When we memorize prayers, we take them to heart, meaning that we not only learn the words but also try to understand and live them. See the inside front and back covers of your book for the most frequently used prayers.

Act of Contrition

O my God, I am heartily sorry for having offended Thee, and I detest all my sins because of thy just punishments, but most of all because they offend Thee, my God, who art all good and deserving of all my love. I firmly resolve with the help of Thy grace to sin no more and to avoid the near occasion of sin.
Amen.

Act of Contrition (Prayer of the Penitent)

My God,
I am sorry for my sins with all my heart.
In choosing to do wrong
and failing to do good,
I have sinned against you
whom I should love above all things.
I firmly intend, with your help,
to do penance,
to sin no more,
and to avoid whatever leads me to sin.
Our Savior Jesus Christ
suffered and died for us.
In his name, my God, have mercy.
Amen.

Jesus Prayer

Lord Jesus Christ, Son of God, have mercy on us sinners.

Prayer for Generosity

Eternal Word, only begotten Son of God,
Teach me true generosity.
Teach me to serve you as you deserve,
To give without counting the cost,
To fight heedless of wounds,
To labor without seeking rest,
To sacrifice myself without thought of any reward
Save the knowledge that I have done your will.
Amen.

Peace Prayer of Saint Francis

Lord, make me an instrument of your peace.
Where there is hatred, let me sow love; where
there is injury, pardon;
where there is doubt, faith; where there is
despair, hope;
where there is darkness, light; and where there
is sadness, joy.
Grant that I may not so much seek to be
consoled as to console,
to be understood as to understand, to be
loved as to love;
for it is in giving that we receive, it is in
pardoning that we are pardoned,
And it is in dying that we are born to eternal
life.

Memorare

Remember, O most gracious Virgin Mary,
that never was it known
that anyone who fled to thy protection,
Implored thy help,
or sought thy intercession,
was left unaided.
Inspired by this confidence
I fly unto thee,
O Virgin of virgins, my Mother.
To thee do I come,
before thee I stand,
sinful and sorrowful.
O Mother of the Word Incarnate,
despise not my petitions,
But in thy mercy hear and answer me.
Amen.

Nicene Creed

I believe in one God,
the Father almighty,
maker of heaven and earth,
of all things visible and invisible.

I believe in one Lord Jesus Christ,
the Only Begotten Son of God,
born of the Father before all ages.
God from God, Light from Light,
true God from true God,
begotten, not made, consubstantial with
the Father;
through him all things were made.
For us men and for our salvation
he came down from heaven,
and by the Holy Spirit was incarnate of the
Virgin Mary,
and became man.

For our sake he was crucified under Pontius
Pilate,
he suffered death and was buried,
and rose again on the third day
in accordance with the Scriptures.
He ascended into heaven
and is seated at the right hand of the Father.
He will come again in glory
to judge the living and the dead
and his kingdom will have no end.

I believe in the Holy Spirit, the Lord, the giver
of life,
who proceeds from the Father and the Son,
who with the Father and the Son is adored
and glorified,
who has spoken through the prophets.

I believe in one, holy, catholic and apostolic
Church.
I confess one Baptism for the forgiveness
of sins
and I look forward to the resurrection of
the dead
and the life of the world to come.
Amen.

An Ancient Language of Prayer

From the beginning of the Church until the Second Vatican Council in the 1960s, the Church in the West used Latin as its common language. The Latin language was used in prayer, worship, documents, administration, and all areas of Church life. We have a rich and long tradition of hymns and prayers in Latin.

Even today there are parts of the Mass such as the Holy, Holy, Holy (*Sanctus*) and the Lamb of God (*Agnus Dei*) that are occasionally sung in Latin. Certain prayers that are shared by the universal Church can be learned in Latin and prayed as a sign of the universal nature of the Church.

Signum Crucis (Sign of the Cross)

In nomine Patris
et Filii
et Spiritus Sancti.
Amen.

*Gloria Patri** (Glory Be to the Father)

Gloria Patri
et Filio
et Spiritui Sancto.
Sicut erat in principio,
et nunc et semper
et in sae cula saeculorum.
Amen.

*Pater Noster** (Our Father)

Pater noster, qui es in caelis:
sanctificetur Nomen Tuum;
adveniat Regnum Tuum;
fiat voluntas Tua,
sicut in caelo, et in terra.
Panem nostrum
cotidianum da nobis hodie;
et dimitte nobis debita nostra
sicut et nos dimittimus
debitoribus nostris;
et ne nos inducas in tentationem;
sed libera nos a Malo.
Amen.

*Ave, Maria** (Hail Mary)

Ave, Maria, gratia plena,
Dominus tecum.
Benedicta tu in mulieribus,
et benedictus fructus ventris tui, Iesus.
Sancta Maria, Mater Dei,
ora pro nobis peccatoribus,
nunc et in hora mortis nostrae.
Amen.

Agnus Dei (Lamb of God)

Agnus Dei, qui tollis peccáta mundi: miserére nobis. (Lamb of God, you take away the sins of the world: have mercy on us.)

Agnus Dei, qui tollis peccáta mundi: miserére nobis. (Lamb of God, you take away the sins of the world: have mercy on us.)

Agnus Dei, qui tollis peccáta mundi: dona nobis pacem. (Lamb of God, you take away the sins of the world: Grant us peace.)

Sanctus (Holy, Holy, Holy)

Sanctus, Sanctus, Sanctus, Dóminus Deus Sábaoth. (Holy, Holy, Holy Lord, God of hosts.)

Pleni sunt caeli et terra glória tua. (Heaven and earth are full of your glory.)

Hósanna in excélsis. (Hosanna in the highest.)

Benedíctus qui venit in nómine Dómini. (Blessed is he who comes in the name of the Lord.)
Hosánna in excélsis. (Hosanna in the highest.)

*The English versions of these prayers are found on the inside front cover of this book.

The Rosary

The Rosary helps us pray to Jesus through Mary. When we pray the Rosary, we think about the special events, or mysteries, in the lives of Jesus and Mary.

The Rosary is made up of a string of beads and a crucifix. We hold the crucifix in our hands as we pray the Sign of the Cross. Then we pray the Apostles' Creed. Next to the crucifix, there is a single bead, followed by a set of three beads and another single bead. We pray the Lord's Prayer as we hold the first single bead and a Hail Mary at each bead in the set of three that follows. Then we pray the Glory Be to the Father. On the next single bead, we think about the first mystery and pray the Lord's Prayer.

There are five sets of 10 beads; each set is called a decade. We pray a Hail Mary on each bead of a decade as we reflect on a particular mystery in the lives of Jesus and Mary. The Glory Be to the Father is prayed at the end of each set. Between sets is a single bead on which we think about one of the mysteries and pray the Lord's Prayer.

In his apostolic letter *Rosary of the Virgin Mary,* Pope John Paul II wrote that the Rosary could take on a variety of legitimate forms as it adapts to different spiritual traditions and different Christian communities. "What is really important," he said, "is that the Rosary should always be seen and experienced as a path of contemplation." It is traditional in some places to pray the Hail, Holy Queen after the last decade.

We end by holding the crucifix in our hands as we pray the Sign of the Cross.

Hail, Holy Queen (*Salve Regina*)

Hail, Holy Queen, Mother of Mercy,
our life, our sweetness, and our hope.
To you do we cry,
poor banished children of Eve.
To you do we send up our sighs,
mourning and weeping in this valley of tears.
Turn, then, most gracious advocate,
your eyes of mercy toward us,
and after this exile,
show unto us the blessed fruit of thy womb,
Jesus.
O clement, O loving,
O sweet Virgin Mary.

PRAYING THE ROSARY

10. Think about the fourth mystery. Pray the Lord's Prayer.

9. Pray 10 Hail Marys and one Glory Be to the Father.

11. Pray 10 Hail Marys and one Glory Be to the Father.

8. Think about the third mystery. Pray the Lord's Prayer.

12. Think about the fifth mystery. Pray the Lord's Prayer.

7. Pray 10 Hail Marys and one Glory Be to the Father.

6. Think about the second mystery. Pray the Lord's Prayer.

5. Pray 10 Hail Marys and one Glory Be to the Father.

4. Think about the first mystery. Pray the Lord's Prayer.

13. Pray 10 Hail Marys and one Glory Be to the Father.

14. Pray the Hail, Holy Queen.

3. Pray three Hail Marys and one Glory Be to the Father.

2. Pray the Lord's Prayer.

15. Pray the Sign of the Cross.

1. Pray the Sign of the Cross and the Apostles' Creed.

Mysteries of the Rosary

The Church had three sets of mysteries for many centuries. In 2002, Pope John Paul II proposed a fourth set of mysteries—the Luminous Mysteries, or the Mysteries of Light. According to his suggestion, the four sets of mysteries might be prayed on the following days: the Joyful Mysteries on Monday and Saturday, the Sorrowful Mysteries on Tuesday and Friday, the Glorious Mysteries on Wednesday and Sunday, and the Luminous Mysteries on Thursday.

The Joyful Mysteries

1. **The Annunciation.** Mary learns that she has been chosen to be the mother of Jesus.
2. **The Visitation.** Mary visits Elizabeth, who tells her that she will always be remembered.
3. **The Nativity.** Jesus is born in a stable in Bethlehem.
4. **The Presentation.** Mary and Joseph take the infant Jesus to the Temple to present him to God.
5. **The Finding of Jesus in the Temple.** Jesus is found in the Temple, discussing his faith with the teachers.

The Luminous Mysteries

1. **The Baptism of Jesus in the River Jordan.** God proclaims that Jesus is his beloved Son.
2. **The Wedding Feast at Cana.** At Mary's request, Jesus performs his first miracle.
3. **The Proclamation of the Kingdom of God.** Jesus calls all to conversion and service to the kingdom.
4. **The Transfiguration of Jesus.** Jesus is revealed in glory to Peter, James, and John.
5. **The Institution of the Eucharist.** Jesus offers his Body and Blood at the Last Supper.

The Sorrowful Mysteries

1. **The Agony in the Garden.** Jesus prays in the garden of Gethsemane the night before he dies.
2. **The Scourging at the Pillar.** Jesus is lashed with whips.
3. **The Crowning with Thorns.** Jesus is mocked and crowned with thorns.
4. **The Carrying of the Cross.** Jesus carries the Cross that will be used to crucify him.
5. **The Crucifixion.** Jesus is nailed to the Cross and dies.

The Glorious Mysteries

1. **The Resurrection.** God the Father raises Jesus from the dead.
2. **The Ascension.** Jesus returns to his Father in heaven.
3. **The Coming of the Holy Spirit.** The Holy Spirit comes to bring new life to the disciples.
4. **The Assumption of Mary.** At the end of her life on earth, Mary is taken body and soul into heaven.
5. **The Coronation of Mary.** Mary is crowned as queen of heaven and earth.

Stations of the Cross

The 14 Stations of the Cross represent events from Jesus' passion and Death. Even before the Gospels were written down, the followers of Jesus told the story of his passion, Death, and Resurrection. When people went on pilgrimage to Jerusalem, they were anxious to see the sites where Jesus lived and died. Eventually, following in the footsteps of the Lord on the way to his Death became an important part of the pilgrimage.

The stations as we know them today came about when it was no longer easy or even possible to visit the holy sites in Palestine. In the 1500s, villages all over Europe started creating replicas of the way of the Cross, with small shrines commemorating the places along the route in Jerusalem. Eventually, these shrines became the set of 14 stations we now know.

The important point to remember about the stations is that they are a prayer. They are not an exercise in remembering events from the past. They are an invitation to make present the final hours of Jesus' life and to experience who Jesus is. It becomes a prayer when we open our hearts to be touched, and it leads us to express our response in prayer. Jesus wants to use any means available to move our hearts so that we know his love for us.

At each station we use our senses and our imagination to reflect prayerfully upon Jesus' suffering, Death, and Resurrection. The stations can allow us to visualize the meaning of his passion and Death and lead us to gratitude. They can also lead us to a sense of solidarity with all our brothers and sisters, especially those who suffer, who are unjustly accused or victimized, who are on death row, who carry difficult burdens, or who face terminal illnesses.

1. Jesus Is Condemned to Death.
Pontius Pilate condemns Jesus to Death.

2. Jesus Takes Up His Cross.
Jesus willingly accepts and patiently bears his Cross.

3. Jesus Falls the First Time.
Weakened by torments and loss of blood, Jesus falls beneath his Cross.

4. Jesus Meets His Sorrowful Mother.
Jesus meets his mother, Mary, who is filled with grief.

5. Simon of Cyrene Helps Jesus Carry the Cross.
Soldiers force Simon of Cyrene to carry the Cross.

6. Veronica Wipes the Face of Jesus.
Veronica steps through the crowd to wipe the face of Jesus.

7. Jesus Falls a Second Time.
Jesus falls beneath the weight of the Cross a second time.

8. Jesus Meets the Women of Jerusalem.
Jesus tells the women to weep not for him, but for themselves and for their children.

9. Jesus Falls the Third Time.
Weakened almost to the point of death, Jesus falls a third time.

10. Jesus Is Stripped of His Garments.
The soldiers strip Jesus of his garments, treating him as a common criminal.

11. Jesus Is Nailed to the Cross.
Jesus' hands and feet are nailed to the Cross.

12. Jesus Dies on the Cross.
After suffering greatly on the Cross, Jesus bows his head and dies.

13. Jesus Is Taken Down from the Cross.
The lifeless body of Jesus is tenderly placed in the arms of Mary, his mother.

14. Jesus Is Laid in the Tomb.
Jesus' disciples place his body in the tomb.

The closing prayer—sometimes included as a 15th station—reflects on the Resurrection of Jesus.

Formulas of Catholic Doctrine

The following formulas present the basic teachings of the Catholic Church. These are core teachings every Catholic should know.

The Great Commandment

The Ten Commandments are fulfilled in Jesus' Great Commandment: "You shall love God with all your heart, with all your soul, with all your mind, and with all your strength. You shall love your neighbor as yourself." (adapted from Mark 12:30–31)

The New Commandment

Before his Death on the Cross, Jesus gave his disciples a new commandment: "I give you a new commandment: love one another. As I have loved you, so you also should love one another." (John 13:34)

The Golden Rule

"Do to others whatever you would have them do to you." (Matthew 7:12)

The Beatitudes

The Beatitudes are the teachings of Jesus in the Sermon on the Mount. They can be found in Matthew 5:1–10. Jesus teaches us that if we live according to the Beatitudes, we will live a happy Christian life. The Beatitudes fulfill God's promises made to Abraham and to his descendants and describe the rewards that will be ours as loyal followers of Christ.

Blessed are the poor in spirit,
for theirs is the kingdom of heaven.
Blessed are they who mourn,
for they will be comforted.
Blessed are the meek,
for they will inherit the land.
Blessed are they who hunger and thirst
    for righteousness,
for they will be satisfied.
Blessed are the merciful,
for they will be shown mercy.
Blessed are the clean in heart,
for they will see God.
Blessed are the peacemakers,
for they will be called children of God.
Blessed are they who are persecuted
    for the sake of righteousness,
for theirs is the kingdom of heaven.

Precepts of the Church

The precepts of the Church describe the minimum effort we must make in prayer and in living a moral life. All Catholics are called to move beyond the minimum by growing in love of God and love of neighbor. The precepts are as follows:

1. To keep holy the day of the Lord's Resurrection. To worship God by participating in Mass every Sunday and every Holy Day of Obligation. To avoid those activities (like needless work) that would hinder worship, joy, or relaxation.

2. To confess one's sins once a year so as to prepare to receive the Eucharist and to continue a life of conversion.

3. To lead a sacramental life. To receive Holy Communion at least during the Easter season.

4. To do penance, including abstaining from meat and fasting from food on the appointed days.

5. To strengthen and support the Church—to assist with the material needs of the Church according to one's ability.

The Four Last Things

There are four things that describe the end of all human life.

death   judgment   heaven   hell

First is the death of the individual. Then immediately after death is the judgment by Christ. The result of this judgment is either heaven (perhaps with a time in purgatory) or hell.

The Ten Commandments

As believers in Jesus Christ, we are called to a new life and are asked to make moral choices that keep us united with God. With the help and grace of the Holy Spirit, we can choose ways to act that keep us close to God, help other people, and be witnesses to Jesus.

The Ten Commandments guide us in making choices that help us live as God wants us to live. The first three commandments tell us how to love God; the other seven tell us how to love our neighbor.

1. I am the Lord your God: you shall not have strange gods before me.

2. You shall not take the name of the Lord your God in vain.

3. Remember to keep holy the Lord's Day.

4. Honor your father and your mother.

5. You shall not kill.

6. You shall not commit adultery.

7. You shall not steal.

8. You shall not bear false witness against your neighbor.

9. You shall not covet your neighbor's wife.

10. You shall not covet your neighbor's goods.

Virtues

Virtues are gifts from God that lead us to live in a close relationship with him. Virtues are like habits. They need to be practiced; they can be lost if they are neglected.

Theological Virtues

The three most important virtues are called *Theological Virtues* because they come from God and lead to God.

faith   hope   charity

Cardinal Virtues

The cardinal virtues are human virtues, acquired by education and good actions. *Cardinal* comes from *cardo,* the Latin word for "hinge," meaning "that on which other things depend."

prudence   justice   fortitude   temperance

Gifts and Fruits of the Holy Spirit

The Holy Spirit makes it possible for us to do what God asks by giving us these gifts.

wisdom   understanding   counsel   piety

fortitude   knowledge   fear of the Lord

The Fruits of the Holy Spirit are signs of the Holy Spirit's action in our lives.

love	kindness	faithfulness
joy	goodness	modesty
peace	generosity	self-control
patience	gentleness	chastity

When we help others, we are performing works of mercy.

Works of Mercy

The Corporal and Spiritual Works of Mercy are actions we can perform that extend God's compassion and mercy to those in need.

Corporal Works of Mercy

The Corporal Works of Mercy are the kind acts by which we help our neighbors with their material and physical needs:

- Feed the hungry.
- Give drink to the thirsty.
- Clothe the naked.
- Shelter the homeless.
- Visit the sick.
- Visit the imprisoned.
- Bury the dead.

Spiritual Works of Mercy

The Spiritual Works of Mercy are acts of compassion by which we help our neighbors with their emotional and spiritual needs:

- Counsel the doubtful.
- Instruct the ignorant.
- Admonish the sinner.
- Comfort the afflicted.
- Forgive offenses.
- Bear wrongs patiently.
- Pray for the living and the dead.

Celebrating and Living Our Catholic Faith

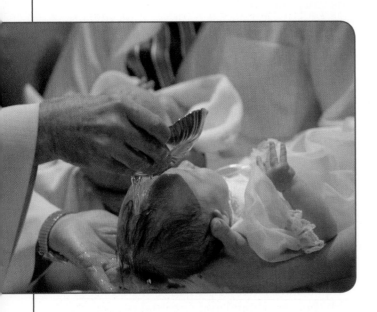

The Mystery of Faith Made Present

The Church was revealed to the world with the coming of the Spirit on Pentecost. This gift of the Spirit ushered in a new era in the history of salvation. This era is the age of the Church in which Christ makes present and communicates his work of salvation through the liturgy. The Church, as Christ's Body, is the first sacrament, the sign and instrument through which the Holy Spirit dispenses the mystery of salvation. In this age of the Church, Christ lives and acts through the sacraments.

The Seven Sacraments

Jesus touches our lives through the sacraments. In the sacraments, physical objects such as water, bread and wine, and oil are the signs of Jesus' presence.

Sacraments of Initiation

These sacraments lay the foundation of Christian life.

Baptism

In Baptism, we are born into new life in Christ. Baptism takes away Original Sin and makes us members of the Church. Its sign is the pouring of water.

Confirmation

Confirmation seals our life of faith in Jesus. The signs of Confirmation are the laying on of hands and the anointing with oil on a person's head, most often done by a bishop. Confirmation and Baptism are received only once.

Eucharist

The Eucharist nourishes our life of faith. We receive the Body and Blood of Christ under the appearances of bread and wine.

Sacraments of Healing

These sacraments celebrate the healing power of Jesus.

Reconciliation

Through Reconciliation we receive God's forgiveness. Forgiveness requires being sorry for our sins. In Reconciliation we receive Jesus' healing grace through absolution by the priest. The signs of this sacrament are the confession of sins, repentance and satisfaction, and the words of absolution.

Anointing of the Sick

This sacrament unites a sick person's sufferings with those of Jesus. Oil, a symbol of strength, is the sign of this sacrament. A person is anointed with the oil of the sick and receives the laying on of hands by a priest.

Sacraments at the Service of Communion

These sacraments help members serve the community.

Matrimony

In Matrimony, a baptized man and woman are united with each other as a sign of the unity between Jesus and his Church. Matrimony requires the consent of the husband and the wife as expressed in the marriage promises. The husband and the wife and their wedding rings are signs of this sacrament.

Holy Orders

In Holy Orders, men are ordained priests to serve as leaders of the community or as deacons to be reminders of our baptismal call to serve others. The signs of this sacrament are the laying on of hands and the prayer by the bishop asking God for the outpouring of the Holy Spirit.

Holy Days of Obligation

The holy days of obligation are the days other than Sundays on which we celebrate the great things God has done for us through Jesus and the saints. On holy days of obligation, Catholics attend Mass.

Six holy days of obligation are celebrated in the United States.

January 1—Mary, Mother of God

40 days after Easter—Ascension (in many U.S. dioceses the Seventh Sunday of Easter)

August 15—Assumption of the Blessed Virgin Mary

November 1—All Saints

December 8—Immaculate Conception

December 25—Nativity of Our Lord Jesus Christ

The Order of Mass

The Sabbath, the day on which God rested after creating the world, represents the comple-tion of creation. Saturday has been replaced by Sunday as the Sabbath for Christians because it recalls the beginning of the new creation through the Resurrection of Christ. Since it is the day of the Resurrection, Sunday is called the Lord's Day. The Sunday celebration of the Lord's Day is at the heart of the Church's life. That is why we are required to participate in the Mass on Sundays and other holy days of obligation. We also rest from work, take time to enjoy our families, enrich our cultural and social lives, and perform works of mercy. On Sunday, people from all over the world gather at God's eucharistic table.

The Mass is the high point of Christian life, and it follows a set order.

Introductory Rites

We prepare to celebrate the Eucharist.

Entrance Chant

We gather as a community, praising God in song.

Greeting

We pray the Sign of the Cross, recognizing the presence of Christ in the community.

Penitential Act

We remember our sins and ask God for mercy.

Gloria

We praise God in song.

Collect Prayer

It focuses the attention of all gathered.

Liturgy of the Word We hear the story of God's plan for salvation.

First Reading
We listen to God's Word, usually from the Old Testament.

Responsorial Psalm
We respond to God's Word in song.

Second Reading
We listen to God's Word from the New Testament.

Gospel Acclamation
We sing "Alleluia!" to praise God for the Good News. During Lent, we sing an alternate acclamation.

Gospel Reading
We stand to acclaim Christ present in the Gospel.

Homily
The priest or deacon explains God's Word.

Profession of Faith
We proclaim our faith through the Nicene Creed.

Prayer of the Faithful
We pray for our needs and the needs of others.

Liturgy of the Eucharist
We celebrate the meal Jesus instituted at the Last Supper and remember the sacrifice he made for us.

Presentation and Preparation of the Gifts
We bring gifts of bread and wine to the altar.

Prayer over the Offerings
The priest prays that God will accept our sacrifice.

Eucharistic Prayer
This prayer of thanksgiving is the center and high point of the entire celebration.

- *Preface Dialogue*—We give thanks and praise to God.

- *Holy, Holy, Holy (Preface Acclamation)*—We sing an acclamation of praise.

- *Institution Narrative*—The prayer over the bread and wine whereby, through the power of the Holy Spirit and the ministry of the priest, the bread and wine are transformed into the Body and Blood of Jesus Christ.

- *The Mystery of Faith*—We proclaim Jesus' Death and Resurrection.

- *Amen*—We affirm the words and actions of the Eucharistic prayer.

Communion Rite
We prepare to receive the Body and Blood of Jesus Christ.

- *The Lord's Prayer*—We pray the Lord's Prayer.

- *Sign of Peace*—We offer one another Christ's peace.

- *Lamb of God*—We pray for forgiveness, mercy, and peace.

- *Communion*—We receive the Body and Blood of Jesus Christ.

- *Prayer after Communion*—We pray that the Eucharist will strengthen us to live as Jesus did.

Concluding Rites
At the conclusion of Mass, we are blessed and sent forth.

Final Blessing
We receive God's blessing.

Dismissal
We go forth in peace to glorify the Lord by our lives.

Making Good Choices

Our conscience is the inner voice that helps us know the law God has placed in our hearts. Our conscience helps us judge the moral qualities of our actions. It guides us to do good and avoid evil.

The Holy Spirit can help us form our conscience. We form our conscience by studying the teachings of the Church and following the guidance of our parents and pastoral leaders.

God has given every human being freedom of choice. This does not mean that we have the right to do whatever we please. We can live in true freedom if we cooperate with the Holy Spirit, who gives us the virtue of prudence. This virtue helps us recognize what is good in every situation and make the correct choice. The Holy Spirit gives us the gifts of wisdom and understanding to help us make the right choices in life in relationship to God and others. The gift of counsel helps us reflect on making correct choices in life.

The Ten Commandments, the Beatitudes, and the two Great Commandments help us make moral choices. We also have the grace of the sacraments, the teachings of the Church, and the good example of saints and fellow Christians.

Making moral choices involves the following steps:

1. Ask the Holy Spirit for help.

2. Think about God's law and the teachings of the Church.

3. Think about what will happen as a result of your choice. Ask yourself, will the consequences be pleasing to God? Will my choice hurt someone else?

4. Seek advice from someone you respect, and remember that Jesus is with you.

5. Ask yourself how your choice will affect your relationships with God and others.

In making moral choices, we must take into consideration the object of the choice, our intention in making the choice, and the circumstances in which the choice is made. It is never right to make an evil choice in the hope of gaining something good.

The Morality of Human Acts

Human beings are able to act morally only because we are free. If we were not free to decide what to do, our acts could not be good or evil. Human acts that are freely chosen after a judgment of conscience can be morally evaluated. They are either good or evil.

The morality of human acts depends on

- the object chosen;

- the end in view or the intention;

- the circumstances of the action.

For an act to be good, what you choose to do must be good in itself. If the choice is not good, the intention or the circumstances cannot make it good. You cannot steal a digital camera because it is your father's birthday and it would make him happy to have one. But a good act done with a bad intention is not necessarily good either. Participating in a hunger walk, not out of concern for the poor but to impress a teacher from whom you want a good grade, is not necessarily a good act. Circumstances can affect the morality of an

act. They can increase or lessen the goodness of an act. Acting out of fear of harm lessens a person's responsibility for an act.

An Examination of Conscience

An examination of conscience is the act of looking prayerfully into our hearts to ask how we have hurt our relationships with God and with other people through our thoughts, words, and actions. We reflect on the Ten Commandments and the teachings of the Church.

My Relationship with God

- What steps am I taking to help me grow closer to God and to others? Do I turn to God often during the day, especially when I am tempted?

- Do I participate at Mass with attention and devotion on Sundays and holy days? Do I pray often and read the Bible?

- Do I use God's name and the names of Jesus, Mary, and the saints with love and reverence?

My Relationships with Family, Friends, and Neighbors

- Have I set a bad example through my words or actions? Do I treat others fairly? Do I spread stories that hurt other people?

- Am I loving toward those in my family? Am I respectful of my neighbors, my friends, and those in authority?

- Do I value human life? Do I do what I can to promote peace and to end violence? Do I avoid talking about others in ways that could harm them?

- Do I show respect for my body and for the bodies of others? Do I keep away from forms of entertainment that do not respect God's gift of sexuality?

- Have I taken or damaged anything that did not belong to me? Do I show concern for the poor and offer assistance to them in the ways I am able? Do I show concern for the environment and care for it as God has asked?

- Have I cheated or copied homework? Have I told the truth even when it was difficult?

- Do I quarrel with others just so I can get my own way? Do I insult others to try to make them think they are less than I am? Do I hold grudges and try to hurt people who I think have hurt me?

How to Make a Good Confession

An examination of conscience is an important part of preparing for the Sacrament of Reconciliation. The Sacrament of Reconciliation includes the following steps:

- The priest greets us, and we pray the Sign of the Cross. He invites us to trust in God. He may read God's Word with us.

- We confess our sins. The priest may help and counsel us.

- The priest gives us a penance to perform. Penance is an act of kindness, prayers to pray, or both.

- The priest asks us to express our sorrow, usually by reciting the Act of Contrition.

- We receive absolution. The priest says, "I absolve you from your sins in the name of the Father, and of the Son, and of the Holy Spirit." We respond, "Amen."

- The priest dismisses us by saying, "Go in peace." We go forth to perform the act of penance he has given us.

The Bible

God speaks to us in many ways. One way God speaks to us is through the Bible. The Bible is the most important book in Christian life because it is God's message, or Revelation. The Bible is the story of God's promise to care for us, especially through his Son, Jesus. At Mass, we hear stories from the Bible. We can also read the Bible on our own.

The Bible is not just one book; it is a collection of many books. The writings in the Bible were inspired by the Holy Spirit and written by different authors using different styles.

The Bible is made up of two parts: the Old Testament and the New Testament. The Old Testament contains 46 books that tell stories about the Jewish people and their faith in God before Jesus was born.

The first five books of the Old Testament—Genesis, Exodus, Leviticus, Numbers, and Deuteronomy—are referred to as the *Torah,* meaning "instruction" or "law." The central story in the Torah is the Exodus, the liberation of the Hebrew slaves as Moses led them out of Egypt and to the Promised Land. During the journey, God gave the Ten Commandments to Moses and the people.

A beautiful part of the Old Testament is the Book of Psalms. A psalm is a prayer in the form of a poem. Each psalm expresses an aspect or feature of the depth of human emotion. Over several centuries, 150 psalms were gathered to form the Book of Psalms. They were once sung at the Temple in Jerusalem, and they have been used in the public worship of the Church since its beginning. Catholics also pray the psalms as part of their private prayer and reflection.

The prophets were called by God to speak for him and to urge the Jewish people to be faithful to the Covenant. A large part of the Old Testament (18 books) presents the messages and actions of the prophets.

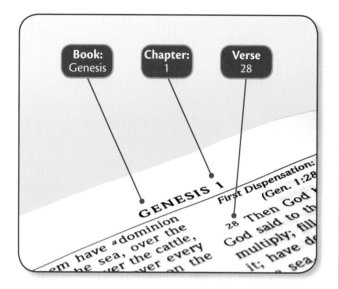

The New Testament contains 27 books that tell the story of Jesus' life, Death, and Resurrection, and the experience of the early Christians. For Christians, the most important books of the New Testament are the four Gospels—Matthew, Mark, Luke, and John. Many of the 27 books are letters written by leaders such as Paul.

How can you find a passage in the Bible? Bible passages are identified by book, chapter, and verse—for example, Genesis 1:28. The name of the book comes first. Sometimes it is abbreviated. Your Bible's table of contents will help you determine what the abbreviation means. For example, *Gn* stands for *Genesis.* After the name of the book, there are two numbers. The first one identifies the chapter, which in our example is chapter 1; it is followed by a colon. The second number identifies the verse or verses. Our example shows verse 28.

How the Old Testament and the New Testament Were Put Together

The Old and New Testaments developed in oral cultures, and much of the material was passed on by word of mouth before ever being written down. Stories from the prehistory of Israel were probably the first part of the Old Testament to be written down. These can be

King David.

found in parts of the 2nd through 11th chapters of Genesis. They would have been written by the court historian of King David around 1000 B.C. This writer always referred to God as Yahweh and spoke of God in human terms. It was this writer who wrote the story of God walking in the garden with Adam and Eve. Other stories developed in the northern kingdom of Israel and favor the religious sites of that region, such as Bethel.

The Old Testament as we know it today did not begin to take shape until the Babylonian Exile (587–537 B.C.). There members of the priestly class took many of the oral and written accounts of God's saving work and put them together in what we know as the Torah, the first five books of the bible—Genesis, Exodus, Leviticus, Numbers, and Deuteronomy.

The writers in Babylon also wrote the opening chapter of Genesis that tells of God's orderly creation of the world in six days and his rest on the seventh day.

The historical books were put together from the court accounts of various kings of Israel and Judah. The psalms were gathered from collections of prayers, and new psalms were written for the temple that was rebuilt after 537 B.C. Other Wisdom Literature was also gathered. Finally, the writings of the prophets were gathered together and collected by

their followers. They included prophets who preached and wrote from 150 years before the exile, such as the first Isaiah and Amos, to the second part of the book of Zechariah, which was probably written after 330 B.C. In the middle of the third century B.C., these books were translated from Hebrew into Greek in Alexandria, Egypt. In time a number of other books, such as First and Second Maccabees, were added to the Bible in Greek. By the end of the first century A.D., religious leaders in Israel decided which books would be in their Bible. They included only the Old Testament books written in Hebrew.

In about year 50, Paul wrote his first letter to the Thessalonians, followed by a second one later that year. This was more than 20 years after the Death and Resurrection of Jesus. Over the next 13 years, Paul wrote letters to other Christian communities as well as to the Christians of Rome, a city he hoped to visit. Meanwhile, Christians were passing on stories about Jesus—his message, his miracles, and others things he did. Probably the first stories to come together centered on his final days— his passion, Death, and Resurrection. This is why all four Gospels tell similar stories about Jesus' last days.

The first Gospel to be written was the Gospel of Mark. It was written in Rome during and after Nero's persecution in the second half of the 60s. In the 80s, the authors of the Gospels of Matthew and Luke, using Mark's Gospel as a starting point, wrote their own Gospels for their specific Christian communities. Matthew, Mark, and Luke, though writing about Jesus in different ways, tell stories that are similar enough to be read side by side. Because of their similarities, we call them the *Synoptic Gospels*. They also made use of a collection of Jesus' sayings. The Gospel of John was written in the mid-to-late 90s. It is very different in tone and theology. The last book of the New Testament to be written was Second Peter, shortly after the year 100.

Showing Our Love for the World

The Catholic Church has developed a large body of teaching on social justice issues, because action on behalf of justice and work to create a more just world are essential parts of preaching the Gospel. In the story of the Good Samaritan (Luke 10:29–37), Jesus makes clear our responsibility to care for those in need.

The major development of the social doctrine of the Church began in the 19th century, when the Gospel encountered the modern industrial society. There were new structures for the production of consumer goods, new concepts of society, new types of states and authorities, and new forms of labor and ownership.

Since that time the Church has been making judgments about economic and social matters that relate to the basic rights of individuals and communities. The Church's social teaching is a rich treasure of wisdom about how to build a just society and how to live holy lives amid the challenges of the modern world.

All human life is sacred, and all people must be respected and valued over material goods. We are called to ask whether our actions as a society respect or threaten the life and dignity of the human person. The Catholic Church teaches this responsibility in the following themes of Catholic Social Teaching.

Call to Family, Community, and Participation

Participation in family and community is central to our faith and to a healthy society. Families must be supported so that people can participate in society, build a community spirit, and promote the well-being of all, especially the poor and vulnerable.

Volunteers distribute free bottled water to survivors of Hurricane Jeanne, Florida.

Rights and Responsibilities

Every person has a right to life as well as a right to those things required for human decency. As Catholics, we have a responsibility to protect these basic human rights in order to achieve a healthy society.

Option for the Poor and Vulnerable

In our world, many people are rich while others are poor. As Catholics, we are called to pay special attention to the needs of the poor by defending and promoting their dignity and meeting their immediate material needs.

The Dignity of Work and the Rights of Workers

The basic rights of workers must be respected: the right to productive work, fair wages, and private property; the right to organize, join unions, and pursue economic opportunity. Catholics believe that the economy is meant to serve people and that work is not merely a way to make a living, but an important way in which we participate in God's creation.

Solidarity

Because God is our Father, we are all brothers and sisters with the responsibility to care for one another. Solidarity is the attitude that leads Christians to share spiritual and material goods. Solidarity unites rich and poor, weak and strong, and helps create a society that recognizes that we depend on one another.

Care for God's Creation

God is the Creator of all people and all things, and he wants us to enjoy his creation. The responsibility to care for everything God has made is a requirement of our faith.

A teen weeds a native habitat restoration site, California.

Glossary

A

Abba an informal word for *father* in Aramaic, the language Jesus spoke. It is like "dad" in English. When Jesus spoke to God the Father, he called him "Abba."

abortion the deliberate ending of a pregnancy that results in the death of the unborn child. The Church teaches that since life begins at conception, abortion is a serious crime against life and is gravely against the moral law.

Abraham the model of faith in God in the Old Testament. Because of his faith, he left his home and traveled to Canaan, where God made a covenant with him that promised him land and many descendants. He became the father of the Chosen People.

absolution the forgiveness we receive from God through the priest in the Sacrament of Penance and Reconciliation

abstain the practice of denying oneself food, drink, or other pleasures. Catholics over age 14 abstain from eating meat on Ash Wednesday and on the Fridays of Lent.

adore to worship God above all else because he is our Creator. The First Commandment requires us to adore God alone.

adultery an injury to the marriage bond covenant. It occurs when a man or a woman who are married to each other has sexual relations with another person. The Sixth Commandment forbids adultery because it undermines the institution of marriage and is harmful to children, who need the stability of their parents' marriage commitment.

Advocate Jesus' name for the Holy Spirit. The Holy Spirit comforts us, speaks for us in difficult times, and makes Jesus present to us.

Alleluia an acclamation meaning "praise God." Alleluia is sung before the Gospel except during Lent.

altar the table in the church on which the priest celebrates Mass, where the sacrifice of Christ on the Cross is made present in the Sacrament of the Eucharist. The altar represents two aspects of the mystery of the Eucharist. It is the place where Jesus Christ offers himself for our sins and where he gives us himself as our food for eternal life.

ambo a raised stand from which a person reads the Word of God during Mass

Amen a Hebrew word meaning "it is so" or "let it be done." It signifies agreement with what has been said. Prayers in the New Testament, in the Church's liturgies, and the Creed end with *Amen*. In the Gospels, Jesus uses *Amen* to reinforce the seriousness of what he is about to say.

angel a spiritual creature who worships God in heaven. Angels serve God as messengers. They tell us of his plans for our salvation.

Angelus a prayer honoring the Incarnation of Jesus. The *Angelus* is prayed in the morning, at noon, and in the evening.

annulment a finding by a Church tribunal that at least one essential element for a real marriage was not present on the day of the wedding. The Church can declare that the Sacrament of Marriage did not take place if at least one of the parties was not freely choosing to marry, had been married before and that marriage was not annulled, or was not open to having children. An annulment cannot be considered until after a person is divorced. Catholics who receive an annulment are free to marry in the Church and can receive Communion.

Annunciation the announcement to Mary by the angel Gabriel that God had chosen her to be the mother of Jesus. When Mary agreed, the Son of God became human in her. The feast of the Annunciation is celebrated on March 25, nine months before Christmas.

anoint to put oil on things or people to dedicate them to the service of God. The anointing of the kings of Israel was a sign that they were chosen to rule God's people.

Anointing of the Sick one of the seven sacraments. In this sacrament, a sick person has the oil of the sick applied and receives the strength, peace, and courage to overcome the difficulties associated with illness. Through this sacrament, Jesus brings the sick person spiritual healing and forgiveness of sins. If it is God's will, healing of the body is given as well.

apostle one of twelve special men who accompanied Jesus in his ministry and were witnesses to the Resurrection. Apostle means "one sent." These were the people sent to preach the Gospel to the whole world.

Apostles' Creed a statement of Christian belief that developed out of a creed used in Baptism in Rome. The Apostles' Creed lists simple statements of belief in God the Father, Jesus Christ the Son, and the Holy Spirit. The profession of faith used in Baptism today is based on the Apostles' Creed.

apostolic one of the four Marks of the Church. The Church is apostolic because it continues to hand on the teaching of the apostles through their successors, the bishops, in union with the successor of Saint Peter, the pope.

Ark of the Covenant a portable box that held the tablets of the Ten Commandments. The Ark was the most important item in the shrine that was carried through the desert and then placed in the holiest part of the Temple in Jerusalem. Two angels are depicted on the cover of the Ark of the Covenant. The wings of the angels curve upward, representing the place where God came close to Israel and revealed his will.

Ascension the entry of Jesus into God's presence in heaven. In the Acts of the Apostles, it is written that Jesus, after his Resurrection, spent 40 days on earth, instructing his followers. He then returned to his Father in heaven.

Assumption Mary's being taken, body and soul, into heaven. Mary had a special relationship with her Son, Jesus, from the very beginning, when she conceived him. Because of this relationship, she enjoys a special participation in Jesus' Resurrection and has been taken into heaven where she now lives with him. We celebrate this event in the feast of the Assumption on August 15.

B

Baptism the first of the seven sacraments. Baptism frees us from Original Sin and is necessary for salvation. Baptism gives us new life in Jesus Christ through the Holy Spirit. The celebration of Baptism consists of immersing in water or pouring water upon a person while declaring that he or she is baptized in the name of the Father, the Son, and the Holy Spirit.

Beatitudes the teachings of Jesus in the Sermon on the Mount in Matthew's Gospel. The Beatitudes are eight ways of living the Christian life. They are the fulfillment of the commandments given to Moses. These teachings present the way to true happiness.

benediction a prayer service in which we honor Jesus in the Blessed Sacrament and receive his blessing

Bible the collection of books containing the truths of God's Revelation to us. These writings were inspired by the Holy Spirit and written by human beings. The Bible is made up of the 46 books in the Old Testament and 27 books in the New Testament.

bishop a man who has received the fullness of Holy Orders. As a successor to the original apostles, he takes care of the Church and is a principal teacher in it.

blasphemy speaking or thinking words of hatred or defiance against God. It extends to language that disrespects the Church, the saints, or holy things. It is also blasphemy to use God's name as an excuse to enslave people, to torture them, or to put them to death. Using God's name to do these things can cause others to reject religion.

Blessed Sacrament the hosts, which are the Body of Christ, that have been consecrated at Mass. They are kept in the tabernacle to adore and to be taken to those who are sick.

blessing a prayer that calls for God's power and care upon some person, place, thing, or special activity

Body and Blood of Christ consecrated by the priest at Mass. In the Sacrament of the Eucharist, all of the risen Lord Jesus Christ—body, blood, soul, and divinity—is present under the appearances of bread and wine.

Buddhism a philosophy based on the teaching of Siddhartha Gautama, who was known as the Buddha, which means "Enlightened One." The Buddha was born to a royal family in northern India about five and a half centuries before Jesus. At age 29 he became disillusioned with life and left his comfortable home to find an answer to the question of why humans suffer.

C

calumny (slander) a false statement about the reputation of someone that makes other people think badly of that person. Calumny, also called *slander,* is a sin against the Eighth Commandment.

canon law the official laws that guide all aspects of Church life. Canon law assists the Church in its task of revealing and communicating God's saving power to the world.

capital sins those sins that can lead us to more serious sin. They are pride, avarice (greed), envy, wrath (anger), gluttony, lust, and sloth.

cardinal virtues the four main virtues that direct right living: prudence, justice, temperance, and fortitude. Cardinal comes from the Latin word *cardo,* which means "hinge."

catechumen a person being formed in the Christian life through instruction and by the example of the parish community. Through conversion and maturity of faith, a catechumen is preparing to be welcomed into the Church at Easter through the Sacraments of Baptism, Confirmation, and the Eucharist.

catechumenate the process of becoming a Christian through the Rite of Christian Initiation for Adults (RCIA). In the early Church, the process took several years.

catholic one of the four Marks of the Church. The Church is catholic because Jesus is fully present in it, because it proclaims the fullness of faith, and because Jesus has given the Church to the whole world. The Church is universal.

Catholic Social Teaching the body of teaching on social justice issues, action on behalf of justice, and work to create a more just world. The Church makes judgments about economic and social matters that relate to the basic rights of individuals and communities. The Church's social teaching is a rich treasure of wisdom about how to build a just society.

charity a virtue given to us by God that helps us love God above all things and love our neighbor as ourselves

chastity the integration of our physical sexuality with our spiritual nature. Chastity helps us be completely human, able to give to others our whole life and love. All people, married or single, are called to practice chastity.

chrism a perfumed oil, consecrated by a bishop, that is used in the Sacraments of Baptism, Confirmation, and Holy Orders. Anointing with chrism signifies the call of the baptized to the threefold ministry of priest, prophet, and king.

Christ a title that means "anointed one." It is from a Greek word that means the same thing as the Hebrew word *Messiah,* or "anointed." It is the name given to Jesus as priest, prophet, and king.

Christian the name given to all those who have been anointed through the Gift of the Holy Spirit in Baptism and have become followers of Jesus Christ

Christmas the feast of the birth of Jesus (December 25)

Church the People of God throughout the whole world, or diocese (the local Church), or the assembly of those called together to worship God. The Church is one, holy, catholic, and apostolic.

clergy those men who are set apart as sacred ministers to serve the Church through Holy Orders

collegiality shared decision making between the pope and the bishops

commandment a standard, or rule, for living as God wants us to live. Jesus summarized all of the commandments into two: love God and love your neighbor.

Communion of Saints the unity of all, dead or living, who have been saved in Jesus Christ. The Communion of Saints is based on our one faith, and it is nourished by our participation in the Eucharist.

confession the act of telling our sins to a priest in the Sacrament of Penance and Reconciliation. The sacrament itself is sometimes referred to as "confession."

Confirmation the sacrament that completes the grace we receive in Baptism. It seals, or confirms, this grace through the seven Gifts of the Holy Spirit that we receive as part of Confirmation. This sacrament also makes us better able to participate in the worship and apostolic life of the Church.

conscience the inner voice that helps each of us judge the morality of our own actions. It guides us to follow God's law by doing good and avoiding evil.

consecration the making of a thing or a person to be special to God through a prayer or blessing. At Mass, the words of the priest are a consecration that transforms the bread and wine into the Body and Blood of Jesus Christ. People or objects set apart for God in a special way are also consecrated. For example, churches and altars are consecrated for use in liturgy, and bishops are consecrated as they receive the fullness of the Sacrament of Holy Orders.

contrition the sorrow we feel when we know that we have sinned, followed by the decision not to sin again. Perfect contrition arises from a love that loves God above all else. Imperfect contrition arises from other motives. Contrition is the most important act of the penitent preparing to celebrate the Sacrament of Penance and Reconciliation.

Corporal Works of Mercy kind acts by which we help our neighbors with their everyday material needs. Corporal Works of Mercy include feeding the hungry, giving drink to the thirsty, clothing the naked, sheltering the homeless, visiting the sick and the imprisoned, and burying the dead.

Council of Jerusalem the name of the meeting that happened about A.D. 50 that is described in chapter 15 of the Acts of the Apostles. The meeting was the result of a disagreement between Paul and his followers and the Jewish Christian followers of James, the leader of the Jerusalem Church. James felt that those who became Christians should also observe the rules of traditional Judaism and that the men should be circumcised. Paul said that there should be no such necessity. It was finally agreed that circumcision was not necessary for Gentiles who became Christians.

counsel one of the seven Gifts of the Holy Spirit. Counsel helps us make correct choices in life through reflection, discernment, consulting, and the advising of others.

covenant a solemn agreement between people or between people and God. God made covenants with humanity through agreements with Noah, Abraham, and Moses. These covenants offered salvation. God's new and final covenant was established through Jesus' life, Death, and Resurrection. *Testament* is another word for covenant.

covet to want to take what belongs to someone else. The Ninth and Tenth Commandments tell us it is sinful to covet.

creation God's act of making everything that exists outside himself. Creation is everything that exists. God said that all creation is good.

Creator God, who made everything that is and whom we can come to know through everything he created

creed a brief summary of what people believe. The word *creed* comes from the Latin *credo,* which means "I believe." The Nicene Creed is the most important summary of Christian beliefs.

culture the activity of a group of people that includes their music, art, language, and celebrations. Culture is one of the ways people experience God in their lives.

D

deacon a man ordained through the Sacrament of Holy Orders to the ministry of service in the Church. Deacons help the bishop and priests by serving in the various charitable ministries of the Church. They also help by proclaiming the Gospel, preaching, and assisting at the Liturgy of the Eucharist. Deacons can also celebrate Baptisms, witness marriages, and preside at funerals.

detraction the act of talking about the faults and sins of another person to someone who has no reason to hear this and cannot help the person. Detraction damages the reputation of another person without any intent to help that person.

devil a spirit created good by God who became evil through disobedience. The devil tempted Adam and Eve to sin and still tempts us today. But God's grace is stronger than the works of the devil.

dignity of the human person a basic principle at the center of Catholic Social Teaching. It is the starting point of a moral vision for society because human life is sacred and should be treated with great respect. The human person is the clearest reflection of God among us.

dignity of work a basic principle at the center of Catholic Social Teaching. Since work is done by people created in the image of God, it is not only a way to make a living but an important way we participate in God's creation. In work, people fulfill part of their potential given to them by God. All workers have a right to productive work, to decent and fair wages, and to safe working conditions.

diocese the members of the Church in a particular area, united in faith and the sacraments, and gathered under the leadership of a bishop

disciple a person who has accepted Jesus' message and tries to live as he did, sharing his mission, his suffering, and his joys

discrimination the act of mistreating other people because of how they look or act, or just because they are different

Divine Providence the guidance of God over all he has created. Divine Providence exercises care for all creation and guides it toward its final perfection.

Doctor of the Church a man or a woman recognized as a model teacher of the Christian faith

doctrine the revealed teaching of Christ, which the Magisterium of the Church has declared Catholics are obliged to believe. Growth in the understanding of doctrine continues in the Church through the prayer and study of the faithful and theologians and through the teaching of the Magisterium.

E

Easter the celebration of the bodily raising of Jesus Christ from the dead. Easter is the festival of our redemption and the central Christian feast, the one from which other feasts arise.

Eastern Catholic Church a group of churches that developed in the East (in countries such as Lebanon) that are in union with the Roman Catholic Church, but have their own liturgical, theological, and administrative traditions. They show the truly catholic nature of the Church, which takes root in many cultures.

ecumenical council a gathering of Catholic bishops from the entire world, meeting under the leadership of the pope or his delegates. Ecumenical councils discuss pastoral, legal, and doctrinal issues. There have been 21 ecumenical councils recognized by the Catholic Church. The first was the First Council of Nicaea in 325. The most recent was the Second Vatican Council, which took place between 1962 and 1965.

ecumenism the movement for unity among Christians. Christ gave the Church the gift of unity from the beginning, but over the centuries that unity has been broken. All Christians are called by their common Baptism to pray and work to maintain, reinforce, and perfect the unity Christ wants for the Church.

Emmanuel a Hebrew name from the Old Testament that means "God with us." In Matthew's Gospel, Jesus is called Emmanuel.

encyclical a letter written by the pope and sent to the whole Church and sometimes to the whole world. It expresses Church teaching on specific and important issues.

epistle a letter written by Saint Paul or another leader to a group of Christians in the early Church. Of the 27 books of the New Testament, 21 are epistles. The second reading at Mass on Sundays and holy days is always from one of these books.

eternal life the never-ending life after death with God, granted to those who die as God's friends, with the grace of God alive in them

Eucharist the sacrament in which we give thanks to God for giving us Jesus Christ. The Body and Blood of Christ, which we receive at Mass, brings us into union with Jesus' saving Death and Resurrection.

Eucharistic Liturgy the public worship, held by the Church, in which the bread and wine are transformed into the Body and Blood of Jesus Christ which we receive in Holy Communion. The Sunday celebration of the Eucharistic Liturgy is at the heart of Church life.

euthanasia an act with the intent to cause the death of a handicapped, sick, or dying person. Euthanasia is considered murder and is gravely contrary to the dignity of the human person and to the respect due to the living God, our Creator.

evangelist anyone engaged in spreading the gospel. Letters in the New Testament, along with the Acts of the Apostles, list evangelists along with apostles and prophets as ministers in the Church. The term is principally used to describe the writers of the four Gospels: Matthew, Mark, Luke, and John.

evangelization the sharing of the good news, by word or example, of the salvation we have received in Jesus Christ. Jesus commissioned his disciples to go forth into the world and tell the good news. Evangelization is the responsibility of every Christian. The New Evangelization calls believers to a deeper faith and invites those who have heard the Gospel but not been transformed by it to have a true encounter with Christ.

examination of conscience the act of prayerfully thinking about what we have said or done in light of what the Gospel asks of us. We also think about how our actions may have hurt our relationship with God or with others. An examination of conscience is an important part of our preparing to celebrate the Sacrament of Penance and Reconciliation.

excommunication a severe penalty that is imposed by Church authorities for serious crimes against the Catholic religion. A person who is excommunicated is excluded from participating in the Eucharist and the other sacraments and from ministry in the Church.

Exile the period in the history of Israel between the destruction of Jerusalem in 587 B.C. and the return to Jerusalem in 537 B.C. During this time, many of the Jewish people were forced to live in Babylon, far from home.

Exodus God's liberation of the Hebrew people from slavery in Egypt and his leading them to the Promised Land

F

faith a gift of God that helps us believe in him. We profess our faith in the Creed, celebrate it in the sacraments, live by it through our good conduct of loving God and our neighbor, and express it in prayer. It is a personal adherence of the whole person to God, who has revealed himself to us through words and actions throughout history.

fasting limiting the amount we eat for a period of time to express sorrow for sin and to make ourselves more aware of God's action in our lives. Adults 18 years old and older fast on Ash Wednesday and Good Friday. The practice is also encouraged as a private devotion at other times of penitence.

fear of the Lord one of the seven Gifts of the Holy Spirit. This gift leads us to a sense of wonder and awe in the presence of God because we recognize his greatness.

fortitude the strength to choose to do the right thing, even when it is difficult. Fortitude is one of the four central human virtues, called the cardinal virtues, by which we guide our conduct through faith and the use of reason. It is also one of the Gifts of the Holy Spirit.

free will the ability to choose to do good because God has made us like him. Our free will is what makes us truly human. Our exercise of free will to do good increases our freedom. Using free will to choose sin makes us slaves to sin.

G

Gentiles the name given to foreign people by the Jews after the Exile. They were nonbelievers who worshiped false gods. They stand in contrast to the Jewish people, who received God's law.

Gifts of the Holy Spirit the permanent willingness, given to us by the Holy Spirit, that makes it possible for us to do what God asks of us. The Gifts of the Holy Spirit are wisdom, understanding, counsel, fortitude, knowledge, piety, and fear of the Lord.

Gospel the good news of God's mercy and love that we experience by hearing the story of Jesus' life, Death, and Resurrection. The story is passed on in the teaching ministry of the Church as the source of all truth and right living. It is presented to us in four books in the New Testament—the Gospels of Matthew, Mark, Luke, and John.

grace the gift of God, given to us without our meriting it. Sanctifying grace fills us with God's life and makes it possible for us always to be his friends. Grace is the Holy Spirit alive in us, helping us live out our Christian vocation. Grace helps us live as God wants us to.

Great Commandment Jesus' commandment that we are to love God and to love our neighbor as we love ourselves. Jesus tells us that this commandment sums up everything taught in the Old Testament.

greed too great a desire for wealth, material possessions, or power. It is also called *avarice* and is one of the seven deadly, or capital, sins.

H

heaven union with God the Father, Son, and Holy Spirit in life and love that never ends. Heaven is a state of complete happiness and the goal of the deepest wishes of the human heart.

Hebrews the descendants of Abraham, Isaac, and Jacob, who were enslaved in Egypt. God helped Moses lead these people out of slavery.

hell a life of total separation from God forever. In his infinite love for us, God can only desire our salvation. Hell is the result of the free choice of a person to reject God's love and forgiveness once and for all.

heresy a religious belief that opposes or denies any divinely revealed truth of the Catholic faith

holiness the fullness of Christian life and love. All people are called to holiness, which is made possible by cooperating with God's grace to do his will. As we do God's will, we are transformed more and more into the image of the Son, Jesus Christ.

holy one of the four Marks of the Church. It is the kind of life we live when we share in the life of God, who is all holiness. The Church is holy because it is united with Jesus Christ.

Holy Communion the reception of the Body and Blood of Christ during holy Mass. It brings us into union with Jesus Christ and his saving Death and Resurrection.

holy days of obligation the principal feast days, other than Sundays, of the Church. On holy days of obligation, we celebrate the great things that God has done for us through Jesus and the saints. Catholics are obliged to participate in the Eucharist on these days, just as we are on Sundays.

Holy Family the family of Jesus as he grew up in Nazareth. It included Jesus; his mother, Mary; and his foster father, Joseph.

Holy of Holies the holiest part of the Temple in Jerusalem. The high priest entered this part of the Temple once a year to address God and to ask God's forgiveness for the sins of the people.

Holy Orders the sacrament through which the mission given by Jesus to his apostles continues in the Church. The sacrament has three degrees: deacon, priest, and bishop. Through the laying on of hands in the Sacrament of Holy Orders, men receive a permanent, sacramental mark that calls them to minister to the Church.

Holy Spirit the third Person of the Trinity, who is sent to us as our helper and, through Baptism and Confirmation, fills us with God's life. Together with the Father and the Son, the Holy Spirit brings the divine plan of salvation to completion.

homily the explanation by a bishop, a priest, or a deacon of the Word of God in the liturgy. The homily relates the Word of God to our life as Christians today.

hope the confidence that God will always be with us, make us happy now and forever, and help us live so that we will be with him forever

I

idolatry The worship of false gods, either a person or a thing, in place of worshiping God. Idolatry is worshiping a creature, which could be power, pleasure, or money, in place of the Creator. Idolatry is a sin against the First Commandment.

Immaculate Conception the Church teaching that Mary was free from Original Sin from the first moment of her life. She was preserved through the merits of her Son, Jesus, the Savior of the human race. It was declared a belief of the Catholic Church by Pope Pius IX in 1854 and is celebrated on December 8.

Incarnation the Son of God, Jesus, being born as a full human being in order to save us. The Son of God, the second Person of the Trinity, is both true God and true man.

indulgence a lessening of the punishment due for sins that have been forgiven. Indulgences move us toward our final purification, when we will live with God forever.

inerrancy the teaching of the Church that the Bible teaches the truths of the faith necessary for our salvation without error. Because God inspired the human authors, he is the author of the Sacred Scriptures. This gives us the assurance that they teach his saving truth without error, even though certain historical and scientific information may not be accurate. With the help of the Holy Spirit and the Church, we interpret what God wants to reveal to us about our salvation through the sacred authors.

infallibility the gift the Holy Spirit has given to the Church that assures that the pope and the bishops in union with the pope can proclaim as true the doctrines that involve faith or morals. It is an extension of the fact that the whole body of believers cannot be in error when it comes to questions of faith and morals.

Infancy Narrative accounts of the infancy and childhood of Jesus that appear in the first two chapters of Matthew's and Luke's Gospels. Each Gospel contains a different series of events. They have in common that Jesus was born in Bethlehem through the virginal conception of Mary. The intention of these stories is to proclaim Jesus as Messiah and Savior.

inspired influenced by the Holy Spirit. The human authors of Scripture were inspired by the Holy Spirit. The creative inspiration of the Holy Spirit makes sure that the Scripture is taught according to the truth God wants us to know for our salvation.

intercession prayer or petition on behalf of another or others. Intercession for others in prayer knows no boundaries and includes even those who might wish to do us harm.

interpretation explanation of the words of Scripture, combining human knowledge and the teaching office of the Church, under the guidance of the Holy Spirit

interreligious dialogue the work to build a relationship of openness with the followers of non-Christian religions. The Church's bond with non-Christian religions comes from our common bond as children of God. The purpose of this dialogue is to increase understanding of one another, to work for the common good of humanity, and to establish peace.

Islam the third great religion, along with Judaism and Christianity, professing belief in one God. *Islam* means "submission" to that one God.

Israelites the descendants of Abraham, Isaac, and Jacob. God changed Jacob's name to "Israel," and Jacob's 12 sons and their children became the leaders of the 12 tribes of Israel. (*See* Hebrews.)

J

Jesus the Son of God, who was born of the Virgin Mary and who died and was raised from the dead for our salvation. He returned to God and will come again to judge the living and the dead. His name means "God saves."

Jews the name given to the Hebrew people, from the time of the Exile to the present. The name means "the people who live in the territory of Judah," the area of Palestine surrounding Jerusalem.

Joseph the foster father of Jesus, who was engaged to Mary when the angel announced that Mary would have a child through the power of the Holy Spirit. In the Old Testament, Joseph was the son of Jacob who was sold into slavery in Egypt by his brothers and then saved them from starvation when famine came.

Judaism the name of the religion of Jesus and all the people of Israel after they returned from exile in Babylon and built the second Temple

justice the virtue that guides us to give to God and others what is due them. Justice is one of the four central human virtues, called the cardinal virtues, by which we guide our Christian life.

justification being in a right relationship with God through moral conduct and observance of the Law. We have merit in God's sight and are able to do this because of the work of God's grace in us. Paul speaks of justification in a new way that is no longer dependent on observance of the Law. It comes through faith in Jesus and in his saving Death and Resurrection. To be justified or made righteous in Jesus is to be saved, vindicated, and put right with God through his grace.

K

Kingdom of God God's rule over us, announced in the Gospel and present in the Eucharist. The beginning of the kingdom here on earth is mysteriously present in the Church, and it will come in completeness at the end of time.

knowledge one of the seven Gifts of the Holy Spirit. This gift helps us know what God asks of us and how we should respond.

L

laity those who have been made members of Christ in Baptism and who participate in the priestly, prophetic, and kingly functions of Christ in his mission to the whole world. The laity is distinct from the clergy, whose members are set apart as ministers to serve the Church.

Last Judgment the final judgment of all human beings that will occur when Christ returns in glory and all appear in their own bodies before him to give an account of all their deeds in life. In the presence of Christ, the truth of each person's relationship with God will be laid bare, as will the good each person has done or failed to do during his or her earthly life. At that time God's kingdom will come in its fullness.

Last Supper the last meal Jesus ate with his disciples on the night before he died. At the Last Supper, Jesus took bread and wine, blessed them, and they became his Body and Blood, Soul and Divinity. Jesus' Death and Resurrection, his sacrifice that we celebrate in the Eucharist, were anticipated in this meal.

Law the first five books of the Old Testament. The Hebrew word for *law* is *Torah*. The ancient law is summarized in the Ten Commandments.

Lectionary the official book that contains all the Scripture readings used in the Liturgy of the Word

Lent the 40 days before Easter (not counting Sundays) during which we prepare, through prayer, fasting, and giving aid to the poor, to change our lives and to live the Gospel more completely

liturgical year the celebrations throughout the year of all the mysteries of Jesus' birth, life, Death, and Resurrection. The celebration of Easter is at the heart of the liturgical year. The other feasts celebrated throughout the year make up the basic rhythm of the Christian's life of prayer.

liturgy the public prayer of the Church that celebrates the wonderful things God has done for us in Jesus Christ, our high priest, and the way in which he continues the work of our salvation. The original meaning of *liturgy* was "a public work or service done for the people."

Liturgy of the Eucharist the second half of the Mass, in which the bread and wine are transformed into the Body and Blood of Jesus Christ, which we then receive in Holy Communion

Liturgy of the Hours the public prayer of the Church to praise God and to sanctify the day. It includes an office of readings before sunrise, morning prayer at dawn, evening prayer at sunset, and prayer before going to bed. The chanting of psalms makes up the major portion of each of these services.

Liturgy of the Word the first half of the Mass, in which we listen to God's Word from the Bible and consider what it means for us today. The Liturgy of the Word can also be a public prayer and proclamation of God's Word that is not followed by the Liturgy of the Eucharist.

Lord the name used for God to replace *Yahweh,* the name he revealed to Moses, which was considered too sacred to pronounce. It indicates the divinity of Israel's God. The New Testament uses the title *Lord* for both the Father and for Jesus, recognizing him as God himself. (*See* Yahweh.)

Lord's Day Sunday is the day Christians set aside for special worship of God. Each Sunday Mass commemorates the Resurrection of Jesus on Easter Sunday. Besides requiring us to offer God the worship owed him, the Third Commandment tells us Sunday is a day to relax the mind and body and to perform works of mercy.

M

Magisterium the living, teaching office of the Church. This office, through the bishops and with the pope, provides an authentic interpretation of the Word of God. It ensures faithfulness to the teaching of the apostles in matters of faith and morals.

Magnificat Mary's song of praise to God for the great things he has done for her and planned for us through Jesus

Marks of the Church the four most important aspects of the Church found in the Nicene Creed. According to the Nicene Creed, the Church is one, holy, catholic, and apostolic.

martyrs those who have given their lives for the faith. *Martyr* comes from the Greek word for "witness." A martyr is the supreme witness to the truth of the faith and to Christ to whom he or she is united. The seventh chapter of the Acts of the Apostles recounts the death of the first martyr, the deacon Stephen.

Mary the mother of Jesus. She is called blessed and "full of grace" because God chose her to be the mother of the Son of God, the second Person of the Trinity.

Mass the most important sacramental celebration of the Church, established by Jesus at the Last Supper as a remembrance of his Death and Resurrection. At Mass, we listen to God's Word from the Bible and receive the Body and Blood of Jesus Christ in Holy Communion.

Matrimony a solemn agreement between a woman and a man to be partners for life, both for their own good and for bringing up children. Marriage is a sacrament when the agreement is properly made between baptized Christians.

meditation a form of prayer using silence and listening that seeks through imagination, emotion, and desire to understand how to adhere and respond to what God is asking. By concentrating on a word or an image, we move beyond thoughts, empty the mind of contents that get in the way of our experience of God, and rest in simple awareness of God. It is one of the three major expressions of the life of prayer.

Mendicant Order a unique variety of religious order that developed in the 13th century. Unlike monks who remain inside a monastery, members of Mendicant Orders have ministries of preaching, teaching, and witnessing within cities. They are called *mendicant* from the Latin word for "begging," which is their main means of supporting themselves. The two main Mendicant Orders are the Dominicans, founded by Saint Dominic de Guzman, and the Franciscans, founded by Saint Francis of Assisi.

Messiah a title that means "anointed one." It is from a Hebrew word that means the same thing as the Greek word *Christ*. Messiah is the title that was given to Jesus as priest, prophet, and king.

miracles signs or acts of wonder that cannot be explained by natural causes but are works of God. In the Gospels, Jesus works miracles as a sign that the Kingdom of God is present in his ministry.

mission the work of Jesus Christ that is continued in the Church through the Holy Spirit. The mission of the Church is to proclaim salvation in Jesus' life, Death, and Resurrection.

missionary one who proclaims the Gospel to others and leads them to know Christ. Missionaries are lay, ordained, and religious people engaged in mission.

monasticism a form of religious life in which men and women live out their vows of poverty, chastity, and obedience in a stable community life in a monastery. The goal of monasticism is to pursue, under the guidance of a rule, a life of public prayer, work, and meditation for the glory of God. Saint Benedict of Nursia, who died around A.D. 550, is considered the father of Western monasticism.

moral choice a choice to do what is right or not do what is wrong. We make moral choices because they are what we believe God wants and because we have the freedom to choose what is right and avoid what is wrong.

moral law a rule for living that has been established by God and people in authority who are concerned about the good of all. Moral laws are based on God's direction to us to do what is right and avoid what is wrong. Some moral laws are "written" in the human heart and can be known through our own reasoning. Other moral laws have been revealed to us by God in the Old Testament and in the new law given by Jesus.

mortal sin a serious decision to turn away from God by doing something that we know is wrong. For a sin to be mortal it must be a very serious offense, and the person must know how serious the sin is and freely choose to do it anyway.

Mother of God the title for Mary proclaimed at the Council of Ephesus in 431. The council declared that Mary was not just the mother of Jesus, the man. She became the Mother of God by the conception of the Son of God in her womb. Because Jesus' humanity is one with his divinity, Mary is the mother of the eternal Son of God made man, who is God himself.

Muslim a follower of the religion of Islam. *Muslim* means "one who submits to God."

mystagogy the last stage of the Rite of Christian Initiation of Adults, in which the newly initiated reflect on the deep meaning of the sacraments they have celebrated and on living the Christian life fully

mystery a religious truth that we can know only through God's Revelation and that we cannot fully understand. Our faith is a mystery that we profess in the Creed and celebrate in the liturgy and sacraments.

Mystical Body of Christ the members of the Church formed into a spiritual body and bound together by the life communicated by Jesus Christ through the sacraments. Christ is the center and source of the life of this body. In it, we are all united. Each member of the body receives from Christ gifts fitting for him or her.

N

natural law the moral law that is "written" in the human heart. We can know natural law through our own reason because the Creator has placed the knowledge of it in our hearts. It can provide the solid foundation on which we can make rules to guide our choices in life. Natural law forms the basis of our fundamental rights and duties and is the foundation for the work of the Holy Spirit in guiding our moral choices.

New Testament the 27 books of the second part of the Bible, which tell of the teaching, ministry, and saving events of the life of Jesus. The four Gospels present Jesus' life, Death, and Resurrection. The Acts of the Apostles tells the story of the message of salvation as it spread through the growth of the Church. Various letters instruct us in how to live as followers of Jesus Christ. The Book of Revelation offers encouragement to Christians living through persecution.

Nicene Creed the summary of Christian beliefs developed by the bishops at the first two councils of the Church, held in A.D. 325 and 381. It is the Creed shared by most Christians in the East and in the West.

O

obedience the act of willingly following what God asks us to do for our salvation. The Fourth Commandment requires children to obey their parents, and all people are required to obey civil authority when it acts for the good of all. To imitate the obedience of Jesus, members of religious communities make a special vow of obedience.

Old Testament the first 46 books of the Bible, which tell of God's Covenant with the people of Israel and his plan for the salvation of all people. The first five books are known as the Torah. The Old Testament is fulfilled in the New Testament, but God's Covenant presented in the Old Testament has permanent value and has never been revoked.

one one of the four Marks of the Church. The Church is one because of its source in the one God and because of its founder, Jesus Christ. Jesus, through his Death on the Cross, united all to God in one body. Within the unity of the Church, there is great diversity because of the variety of the gifts given to its members.

Ordinary Time the part of the liturgical year outside of the seasons and feasts and the preparation for them. *Ordinary* means not common, but counted time, as in ordinal numbers. It is devoted to growth in understanding the mystery of Christ in its fullness. The color of Ordinary Time is green to symbolize growth.

ordination the rite of the Sacrament of Holy Orders, by which a bishop gives to men, through the laying on of hands, the ability to minister to the Church as bishops, priests, and deacons

Original Sin the consequence of the disobedience of the first human beings. They disobeyed God and chose to follow their own will rather than God's will. As a result, human beings lost the original blessing God had intended and became subject to sin and death. In Baptism, we are restored to life with God through Jesus Christ, although we still experience the effects of Original Sin.

P

parable one of the simple stories that Jesus told to show us what the Kingdom of God is like. Parables present images drawn from everyday life. These images show us the radical choice we make when we respond to the invitation to enter the Kingdom of God.

parish a stable community of believers in Jesus Christ, who meet regularly in a specific area to worship God under the leadership of a pastor

particular judgment a judgment made by Christ received by every person at the moment of death that offers either entrance into heaven (after a period of purification, if needed) or immediate and eternal separation from God in hell. At the moment of death, each person is rewarded by Christ in accordance with his or her works and faith.

Paschal Mystery the work of salvation accomplished by Jesus Christ through his passion, Death, Resurrection, and Ascension. The Paschal Mystery is celebrated in the liturgy of the Church, and we experience its saving effects in the sacraments. In every liturgy of the Church, God the Father is blessed and adored as the source of all blessings we have received through his Son in order to make us his children through the Holy Spirit.

Passover the Jewish festival that commemorates the delivery of the Hebrew people from slavery in Egypt. In the Eucharist, we celebrate our passover from death to life through Jesus' Death and Resurrection.

penance the turning away from sin with a desire to change our life and more closely live the way God wants us to live. We express our penance externally by praying, fasting, and helping the poor. This is also the name of the action that the priest asks us to take or the prayers that he asks us to pray after he absolves us in the Sacrament of Penance and Reconciliation. (*See* Sacrament of Penance and Reconciliation.)

Penitential Act that part of the Mass before the Liturgy of the Word in which we ask God's forgiveness for our sins. The Penitential Act prepares us to celebrate the Eucharist.

Pentateuch Greek for "five books." It refers to the first five books of the Bible: Genesis, Exodus, Leviticus, Numbers, and Deuteronomy. The Pentateuch tells of Creation, the beginning of God's special people, and the Covenant. In Hebrew it is called *Torah*, which means "law."

Pentecost the 50th day after Jesus was raised from the dead. On this day, the Holy Spirit was sent from heaven, and the Church was born. It is also the Jewish feast that celebrated the giving of the Ten Commandments on Mount Sinai 50 days after the Exodus.

perjury lying while under oath or making a promise under oath without planning to keep it. Perjury is both a sin and a crime. Perjury is a violation of the Second and Eighth Commandments.

personal sin a sin we choose to commit, whether serious (mortal) or less serious (venial). Although the consequences of Original Sin leave us with a tendency to sin, God's grace, especially through the sacraments, helps us choose good over sin.

Pharisees a party or sect in Judaism that began more than 100 years before Jesus. They saw Judaism as a religion centered on the observance of the Law. The Gospels present a picture of mutual hostility between Jesus and the Pharisees. Pharisees were later found in the Christian community in Jerusalem. (Acts of the Apostles 15:5) Paul was proud to call himself a Pharisee.

piety one of the seven Gifts of the Holy Spirit. It calls us to be faithful in our relationships, both with God and with others. Piety helps us love God and behave responsibly and with generosity and affection toward others.

pope the Bishop of Rome, successor of Saint Peter, and leader of the Roman Catholic Church. Because he has the authority to act in the name of Christ, the pope is called the Vicar of Christ. The pope and all the bishops together make up the living, teaching office of the Church, the Magisterium.

poverty a vow taken by religious men and women to live a simple lifestyle and to give up control of material possessions

prayer the raising of our hearts and minds to God. We are able to speak to and listen to God in prayer because he teaches us how to pray.

prayer of petition a request to God asking him to fulfill a need. When we share in God's saving love, we understand that every need is one that we can ask God to help us with through petition.

precepts of the Church those positive requirements that the pastoral authority of the Church has determined are necessary to provide a minimum effort in prayer and the moral life. The precepts of the Church ensure that all Catholics move beyond the minimum by growing in love of God and love of neighbor.

pride a false image of ourselves that goes beyond what we deserve as God's creation. Pride puts us in competition with God. It is one of the seven capital sins.

priest a man who has accepted God's special call to serve the Church by guiding it and building it up through the ministry of the Word and the celebration of the sacraments

priesthood all the people of God who have been given a share of the one mission of Christ through the Sacraments of Baptism and Confirmation. The ministerial priesthood, which is made up of those men who have been ordained bishops and priests in Holy Orders, is essentially different from the priesthood of the faithful because its work is to build up and to guide the Church in the name of Christ.

prophet one called to speak for God and to call the people to be faithful to the Covenant. A major section of the Old Testament presents the messages and actions of the prophets.

Protestant Reformation a religious, political, and economic movement that swept Europe in the 16th and 17th centuries and separated Protestants from the Catholic Church. The Catholic Reformation, or Counter-Reformation, was an attempt to respond to the major concerns of the Reformers by a sincere reform within the Catholic Church.

prudence the virtue that directs us toward the good and helps us choose the correct means to achieve that good. When we act with prudence, we carefully and thoughtfully consider our actions. Prudence is one of the cardinal moral virtues that guide our conscience and influence us to live according to the law of Christ.

psalm a prayer in the form of a poem, written to be sung in public worship. Each psalm expresses an aspect of the depth of human prayer. Over several centuries, 150 psalms were assembled into the Book of Psalms in the Old Testament. Psalms were used in worship in the Temple in Jerusalem, and they have been used in the public worship of the Church since its beginning.

purgatory a state of final cleansing after death of all our human imperfections to prepare us to enter into the joy of God's presence in heaven

R

racism the opinion that race determines human traits and capacities and that a particular race has an inherent, or inborn, superiority. Discrimination based on a person's race is a violation of human dignity and a sin against justice.

rationalism an approach to philosophy developed by René Descartes. It dominated European thought in the 17th and 18th centuries. The main belief of rationalism was that human reason is the principal source of all knowledge. It stresses confidence in the orderly character of the world and in the mind's ability to make sense of this order. Rationalism recognizes as true only those religious beliefs that can be rationally explained.

real presence the way in which the risen Jesus Christ is present in the Eucharist under the appearances of bread and wine. Jesus Christ's presence is called real because in the Eucharist, his Body and Blood, soul and divinity, are wholly and entirely present.

reconciliation the renewal of friendship after that friendship has been broken by some action or lack of action. In the Sacrament of Penance and Reconciliation, through God's mercy and forgiveness, we are reconciled with God, the Church, and others.

Redeemer Jesus Christ, whose life, sacrificial Death on the Cross, and Resurrection from the dead set us free from the slavery of sin and bring us redemption

redemption our being set free from the slavery of sin through the life, sacrificial Death on the Cross, and Resurrection from the dead of Jesus Christ

religious life a state of life recognized by the Church. In the religious life, men and women freely respond to a call to follow Jesus by living the vows of poverty, chastity, and obedience in community with others.

Resurrection the bodily raising of Jesus Christ from the dead on the third day after his Death on the Cross. The Resurrection is the crowning truth of our faith.

Revelation God's communication of himself to us through the words and deeds he has used throughout history to show us the mystery of his plan for our salvation. This Revelation reaches its completion in his sending of his Son, Jesus Christ.

rite one of the many forms followed in celebrating liturgy in the Church. A rite may differ according to the culture or country where it is celebrated. A rite is also the special form for celebrating each sacrament.

Rite of Christian Initiation of Adults (RCIA) a series of rituals, accompanied by religious instruction, through which a person is formed in the Christian life through instruction and by the example of the parish community. Through conversion and maturity of faith, a catechumen is preparing to be welcomed into the Church at Easter through the Sacraments of Baptism, Confirmation, and Eucharist. Baptized Christians who are preparing to be received into full communion with the Roman Catholic Church may also take part in the Rite of Christian Initiation of Adults.

Roman Missal the book containing the prayers used for the celebration of the Eucharist. It is placed on the altar for the celebrant to use during Mass.

Rosary a prayer in honor of the Blessed Virgin Mary. When we pray the Rosary, we meditate on the mysteries of Jesus Christ's life while praying the Hail Mary on 5 sets of 10 beads and the Lord's Prayer on the beads in between. In the Latin Church, praying the Rosary became a way for ordinary people to reflect on the mysteries of Christ's life.

S

Sabbath the seventh day, when God rested after finishing the work of creation. The Third Commandment requires us to keep the Sabbath holy. For Christians, Sunday became the Sabbath because it was the day Jesus rose from the dead and the new creation in Jesus Christ began.

sacrament one of seven official rites through which God's life enters our lives in the liturgy through the work of the Holy Spirit. Christ's work in the liturgy is sacramental because his mystery is made present there by the power of the Holy Spirit. Jesus gave us three sacraments that bring us into the Church: Baptism, Confirmation, and the Eucharist. He gave us two sacraments that bring us healing: Penance and Reconciliation and Anointing of the Sick. He also gave us two sacraments that help members serve the community: Matrimony and Holy Orders. (*See also* sacramental.)

Sacrament of Penance and Reconciliation the sacrament in which we celebrate God's forgiveness of sin and our reconciliation with God and the Church. Penance and Reconciliation includes sorrow for the sins we have committed, confession of sins, absolution by the priest, and doing the penance that shows our willingness to amend our ways.

sacramental an object, a prayer, or a blessing given by the Church to help us grow in our spiritual life

Sacraments at the Service of Communion the Sacraments of Holy Orders and Matrimony. These two sacraments contribute to the personal salvation of individuals by giving them a way to serve others.

Sacraments of Healing the Sacraments of Penance and Reconciliation and Anointing of the Sick, by which the Church continues the healing ministry of Jesus for soul and body

Sacraments of Initiation the sacraments that are the foundation of our Christian life. We are born anew in Baptism, strengthened by Confirmation, and receive in the Eucharist the food of eternal life. By means of these sacraments, we receive an increasing measure of divine life and advance toward the perfection of charity.

sacrifice a ritual offering of animals or produce made to God by the priest in the Temple in Jerusalem. Sacrifice was a sign of the people's adoration of God, giving thanks to God, or asking for his forgiveness. Sacrifice also showed union with God. The great high priest, Christ, accomplished our redemption through the perfect sacrifice of his Death on the Cross.

Sacrifice of the Mass the sacrifice of Jesus on the Cross, which is remembered and mysteriously made present in the Eucharist. It is offered in reparation for the sins of the living and of the dead and to obtain spiritual or temporal blessings from God.

sacrilege deliberate damage or harm to a sacred person, place, or thing. A sacrilege can be a mortal or venial sin, depending on the seriousness of the evil done.

saint a holy person who has died united with God. The Church has said that this person is now with God forever in heaven.

salvation the gift, which God alone can give, of forgiveness of sin and the restoration of friendship with him

salvation history the story of God's loving relationship with his people, which tells how God carries out his plan to save all people

sanctify to make holy, to separate from sin, to set aside for sacred use, to consecrate

sanctifying grace the gift of God, given to us without our earning it, that introduces us to the intimacy of the Trinity, unites us with its life, and heals our human nature that has been wounded by sin. Sanctifying grace helps us respond to our vocation as God's adopted children, and it continues the work of making us holy that began at our Baptism.

Satan the enemy of anyone attempting to follow God's will. Satan tempts Jesus in the Gospels and opposes his ministry. In Jewish, Christian, and Muslim thought, Satan is associated with those angels who refused to bow down before human beings and serve them as God commanded. They were thrown out of heaven as a punishment. Satan and the other demons tempt human beings to join them in their revolt against God.

Savior Jesus, the Son of God, who became human to forgive our sins and to restore our friendship with God. *Jesus* means "the Lord saves."

scandal leading another person to sin by bad example

schism a willful split or separation in the Church, stemming from a refusal to obey lawful authority

Scripture the holy writings of Jews and Christians collected in the Old and New Testaments of the Bible

Second Vatican Council the 21st and most recent ecumenical council of the Catholic Church. It met from October 11, 1962 to December 8, 1965. Its purpose, according to Pope John XXIII, was to renew the Church and to help it promote peace and unity among Christians and all humanity.

Sermon on the Mount the words of Jesus, written in chapters 5 through 7 of the Gospel of Matthew, in which Jesus reveals how he has fulfilled God's law given to Moses. The Sermon on the Mount begins with the eight Beatitudes and includes the Lord's Prayer.

sexism a prejudice or discrimination based on sex, especially discrimination against women. Sexism leads to behaviors and attitudes that foster a view of social roles based only on sex.

sin a deliberate thought, word, deed, or failure to act that offends God and hurts our relationships with other people. Some sin is mortal and needs to be confessed in the Sacrament of Penance and Reconciliation. Other sin is venial, or less serious.

social justice the fair and equal treatment of every member of society. It is required by the dignity and freedom of every person. The Catholic Church has developed a body of social principles and moral teachings described in papal and other official documents issued since the late 19th century. This teaching deals with the economic, political, and social order of the world. It is rooted in the Bible as well as in the traditional theological teachings of the Church.

social sin social situations and institutions that are against the will of God. Because of the personal sins of individuals, entire societies can develop structures that are sinful in and of themselves. Social sins include racism, sexism, structures that deny people access to adequate health care, and the destruction of the environment for the benefit of a few.

Son of God the title revealed by Jesus that indicates his unique relationship to God the Father. The revelation of Jesus' divine sonship is the main dramatic development of the story of Jesus of Nazareth as it unfolds in the Gospels.

soul the part of us that makes us human and an image of God. Body and soul together form one unique human nature. The soul is responsible for our consciousness and for our freedom. The soul does not die and is reunited with the body in the final resurrection.

spirituality our growing, loving relationship with God. Spirituality is our way of expressing our experience of God in both the way we pray and the way we love our neighbor. There are many different schools of spirituality. Some examples of these schools are the monastic, Franciscan, Jesuit, and lay. These are guides for the spiritual life and have enriched the traditions of prayer, worship, and living in Christianity.

Spiritual Works of Mercy the kind acts through which we help our neighbors meet the needs that are more than material. The Spiritual Works of Mercy include counseling the doubtful, instructing the ignorant, admonishing sinners, comforting the afflicted, forgiving offenses, bearing wrongs patiently, and praying for the living and the dead.

suicide the act of deliberately and intentionally taking one's own life. Because we are stewards, not owners, of the life God has given us, suicide is a sin against the Fifth Commandment. But serious psychological disturbances, fears, and suffering can lessen the responsibility of the person committing suicide. By ways known to him alone, God can offer salvation to people who have taken their own life. The Church encourages us to pray for such people.

Summa Theologiae the major work of Saint Thomas Aquinas that organized and clarified thinking on many religious topics in the 13th century. In it Thomas addressed topics such as proof for the existence of God, the nature of the human soul, making moral decisions, the Incarnation, and transubstantiation.

synagogue the Jewish place of assembly for prayer, instruction, and study of the Law. After the destruction of the Temple in 587 B.C., synagogues were organized as places to maintain Jewish faith and worship. Jesus attended the synagogue regularly to pray and to teach. Paul went to the synagogue first in every city he visited. The synagogue played an important role in the development of Christian worship and in the structure of Christian communities.

Synoptic from the Greek word meaning to "see together," it describes the Gospels of Matthew, Mark, and Luke. These are called the Synoptic Gospels because although they are different from one another, there are similarities that can be seen by looking at them together. Most Scripture scholars agree that Mark was the first Gospel written and that Matthew and Luke used Mark as the pattern for their Gospels.

T

tabernacle the container in which the Blessed Sacrament is kept so that Holy Communion can be taken to the sick and the dying. *Tabernacle* is also the name of the tent sanctuary in which the Israelites kept the Ark of the Covenant from the time of the Exodus to the construction of Solomon's Temple.

temperance the cardinal virtue that helps us control our attraction to pleasure so that our natural desires are kept within proper limits. This moral virtue helps us choose to use created goods in moderation.

Temple the house of worship of God, first built by Solomon. The Temple provided a place for the priests to offer sacrifice, to adore and give thanks to God, and to ask for forgiveness. It was destroyed and rebuilt. The second Temple was also destroyed, this time by the Romans in A.D. 70, and was never rebuilt. Part of the outer wall of the Temple mount remains to this day in Jerusalem.

temptation an attraction, from outside us or inside us, that can lead us to disobey God's commands. Everyone is tempted, but the Holy Spirit helps us resist temptation and choose to do good.

Ten Commandments the 10 rules given by God to Moses on Mount Sinai that sum up God's law and show us what is required to love God and our neighbor. By following the Ten Commandments, the Hebrews accepted their Covenant with God.

Theological Virtues those virtues given us by God and not by human effort. They are faith, hope, and charity.

Torah the Hebrew word for "instruction" or "law." It is also the name of the first five books of the Old Testament: Genesis, Exodus, Leviticus, Numbers, and Deuteronomy.

Tradition the beliefs and practices of the Church that are passed down from one generation to the next under the guidance of the Holy Spirit. What Christ entrusted to the apostles was handed on to others both orally and in writing. Tradition and Scripture together make up the single deposit of the Word of God, which remains present and active in the Church.

transubstantiation the unique transformation of bread and wine in the Eucharist into the Body and Blood of the risen Jesus Christ, while retaining its physical appearance of bread and wine

Trinity the mystery of the existence of God in three Persons—the Father, the Son, and the Holy Spirit. Each Person is God, whole and entire. Each is distinct only in the relationship of each to the others.

U

understanding one of the seven Gifts of the Holy Spirit. This gift helps us make the right choices in life and in our relationships with God and others.

V

venial sin a choice we make that weakens our relationship with God or with other people. Venial sin wounds and lessens the divine life in us. If we make no effort to do better, venial sin can lead to more serious sin. Through our participation in the Eucharist, venial sin is forgiven when we are repentant, strengthening our relationship with God and with others.

viaticum the Eucharist that a dying person receives. It is spiritual food for the last journey we make as Christians, the journey through death to eternal life.

virtue an attitude or way of acting that enables us do good

vocation the call each of us has in life to be the person God wants each to be and the way we each serve the Church and the Kingdom of God. Each of us can live out his or her vocation as a layperson, as a member of a religious community, or as a member of the clergy.

vow a deliberate and free promise made to God by people who want especially to dedicate their lives to God. The vows give witness now to the kingdom that is to come.

W

wisdom one of the seven Gifts of the Holy Spirit. Wisdom helps us understand the purpose and plan of God and live in a way that helps bring about this plan. It begins in wonder and awe at God's greatness.

witness the passing on to others, by our words and by our actions, the faith that we have been given. Every Christian has the duty to give witness to the good news about Jesus Christ that he or she has come to know.

worship the adoration and honor given to God in public prayer

Y

Yahweh the name of God in Hebrew, which God told Moses from the burning bush. *Yahweh* means "I am who am" or "I cause to be all that is."

Index

dignity, human, 223, 225, 247
diligence, 193
diocese, 80, 307
disciple, 24, 307. *See also* apostle
discrimination, 307
Divine Providence, 307
Doctor of the Church, 64, 307
doctrine, 308
domestic church, 24, 27, 223
Dominic, Saint, 129, 130
Dominicans, 130
Dulles, Cardinal Avery, 22

E

Easter, 213, 261, 308
    Jesus' words at, 262
    symbols of, 262
    Triduum, 260
Eastern Catholic Churches, 73, 74, 308
ecumenical council, 103, 308. *See also specific councils*
ecumenism, 56, 308. *See also* Christian Unity, Week of
    Prayer for
Edict of Milan, 111
Elizabeth Ann Seton, Saint, 31, 176
Emmanuel, 308. *See also* Jesus
encyclical, 165, 308
Epiphany, 255
epistles, 94, 308
eternal life, 308
Eucharist, Sacrament of the, 205, 276, 277, 294, 308
    completeness of, 208
    importance of, 208
    Jesus' real presence in, 209
    liturgy (*see* Eucharistic Liturgy; Mass)
    nourishes us, 213
    unites the Church, 55, 59
Eucharistic Liturgy, 308
euthanasia, 171, 308
evangelist, 308
evangelization, 74, 75, 77, 308
Evangelization, New. *See* New Evangelization
examination of conscience, 107, 267, 268, 269, 272, 298, 309.
    See also conscience
excommunication, 128, 309
Exile, the, 309
Exodus, the, 309

F

faith, 121, 125, 293, 309
family, as domestic church, 24
Family Tree of Faith, 14
fasting, 205, 309

fear of the Lord, 293, 309
First Vatican Council, 160
forgiveness, 273. *See also* Penance and Reconciliation,
    Sacrament of
fortitude, 99, 121, 125, 293, 309
Franciscans, 130
Francis de Sales, Saint, 167, 224
Francis of Assisi, Saint, 31, 129, 130
Francis Xavier, Saint, 78, 151
free will, 309
French Revolution, 159

G

Galileo, 157
genealogy, 13
generosity, 192
Gentiles, 309
Germanic tribes, 119, 120
Gibbons, James Cardinal, 177
Gifts of the Holy Spirit, 49, 309
Gloria Patri, 285. *See also* Glory Be to the Father
Glorious Mysteries, 288
Glory Be to the Father, 285, 286, 287
God
    love for all, 71, 189
    loves us, 205
    name, power of his, 202
    with us always, 281
Good News, 77
Good Shepherd, 5. *See also* Jesus
Gospels, 16, 299, 309
grace, 309
Great Commandment, 291, 310
greed, 310
Greek Christians, 73
Gregory the Great, Pope Saint, 120, 138
Gregory XI, Pope, 64
Gregory VII, Pope Saint, 127
Guadalupe, Our Lady of, 185

H

Hail, Holy Queen, 286
Hail Mary, 285
    Rosary, as part of, 286, 287
heaven, 310
Hebrews, 310
Hedwig, Saint, 12
hell, 310
Henry VIII, King, 63, 144, 145, 151, 234
Henry IV, King, 127
heresy, 112, 113, 129, 137, 310
    Arian, 112, 113, 206
    Nestorian, 113

Ave Maria, 285
Gloria Patri, 285
Hail, Holy Queen, 286
Hail Mary, 285
Liturgy of the Hours, 31, 32–33, 313
Lord's Prayer (*see* Our Father)
Morning Prayer, 31–32
Nicene Creed, 51, 54, 113, 284, 244, 315
Night Prayer, 31
Our Father, 30, 285
Pater Noster, 285
Rosary, 286–287
precepts of the Church, 292, 317
pride, 317
priests, definition of, 317
priesthood, 317
prophets, 317
Protestant Reformation, 143, 317
prudence, 121, 125, 293, 317
psalm, 317
purgatory, 16, 317

R

racism, 317
rationalism, 160, 317
Ratzinger, Joseph Cardinal, 168. *See also* Benedict XVI, Pope Emeritus
real presence, 317
reconciliation, 317
Redeemer, 318
redemption, 318
religious life, 318
Rerum Novarum, 165, 177
Resurrection, 21, 318
Revelation, 15, 17, 19, 318
reverence, 66
rite, 318
Rite of Christian Initiation of Adults (RCIA), 318
Robert Bellarmine, Saint, 28
Roman Empire, fall of, 119, 123
Roman Missal, 318
Rosary, 286, 287, 288, 318
Rose of Lima, Saint, 186

S

Sabbath, 207, 318. *See also* Lord's Day
sacramentals, 318
sacraments, 318. *See also specific sacraments*
    mysteries, celebrate, 62
    seven, 62, 69
Sacraments at the Service of Communion, 319
Sacraments of Healing, 319
Sacraments of Initiation, 319

Sacred Tradition, 15, 155, 321
sacrifice, 202, 319
Sacrifice of the Mass, 319
sacrilege, 200, 319
St. Peter's Basilica, 160
saints, 319. *See also specific saints*
    as spiritual family, 19
    prayer life of, 31
    strengthen us, 251
salvation, 319
salvation history, 13, 17, 319
sanctifying grace, 319
Satan, 200, 319
Satanism, 200
Saul of Tarsus, 101
Savior, 319
scandal, 319
science, 163
schisms, 128, 319
    Great (East-West), 128, 131
    Great Western, 141
Scripture, 15, 319. *See also* Bible; New Testament; Old Testament
Second Vatican Council, 7, 103, 107, 140, 167, 168, 169, 171, 319
September 11th tragedy, 119
Sermon on the Mount, 291, 319
sexism, 320
Sext, 31
sexuality, 226, 228, 233
Sign of the Cross, 285
    Rosary, as part of praying, 286, 287
Signum Crucis, 285. *See also* Sign of the Cross
sin, 320
    capital sins, 191, 305
    conversion from, 271
    mortal, 314
    Original, 315
    personal, 316
    social, 320
    venial, 321
Sisters of Notre Dame, 159
slander, 239
Smith, Alfred E., 178
social justice, 320
social sin, 320
Society of Jesus. *See* Jesuits
Solanus Casey, Venerable, 64
Son of God, 320. *See also* Jesus
Sorrowful Mysteries, 288
soul, 320
spiritual family, 16
spiritualism, 200
spirituality, 320
    Mendicant Orders as guidance
Spiritual Works of Mercy, 11, 293, 320

Stations of the Cross, 289–90
Stephen, Saint, 95, 96, 99
suicide, 219, 320
Summa Theologiae, 130, 320
Syllabus of Errors, 160, 161
symbols, Christian. *See specific symbols*
synagogue, 320
Synoptic, 321
Syrian Church, 73

T

tabernacle, 321
Taizé prayer, 147
Teaching of the Twelve Apostles, 191
temperance, 121, 125, 192, 293, 321
Temple, 321
temptation, 321
Ten Commandments, 292, 321
Terce, 31
Teresa of Ávila, Saint, 20, 150, 156
Teresa of Calcutta, Blessed, 72
Theological Virtues, 121, 125, 192, 293, 321
Thérèse of Lisieux, Saint, 31, 167
Thomas More, Saint, 63, 151, 234
Torah, 321. *See also* Pentateuch
Tradition, 15, 321
transubstantiation, 321
Trent, Council of, 150, 153
Triduum, 260
Trinity, 117, 321

U

understanding, 293, 321
Urban II, Pope, 128

V

Vatican City, 80
venial sin, 321. *See also* sin
Vespers, 31
viaticum, 322
Vincent de Paul, Saint, 158–59, 161
    Society, 163
Vincentian Fathers, 158
violence, 219
virtues, 197, 293, 322. *See also specific virtues*
    cardinal (*see* cardinal virtues)
    definition, 121, 192, 195

help us, 195
    Jesus, brings us closer to, 121
    power of, 121
    Theological (*see* Theological Virtues)
vocations, 41, 322. *See specific vocations*
vow, 202, 322

W

Way of the Cross, 137. *See also* Stations of the Cross
Wenceslaus, Saint, 126
wisdom, 293, 322
Wise Men. *See* Magi.
witchcraft, 200
witnessing, 41, 322
Wojtyla, Karol (Saint, Pope), 168.
        See also John Paul II (Saint, Pope)
worship, 322

Y

Yahweh, 322

Z

Zacchaeus, 218

Scripture Index

Lesson Pullouts

- **Map of Palestine**

- **Reconciliation Booklet**

- **Scripture Prayer Booklet**

- **My Parish Booklet**

- **History Timelines**

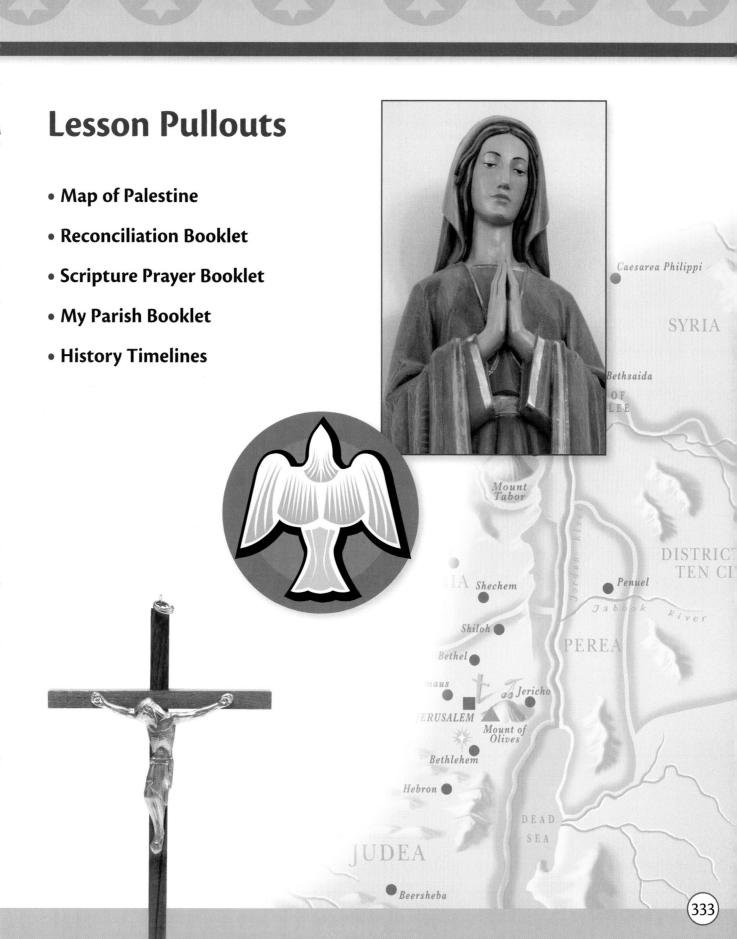

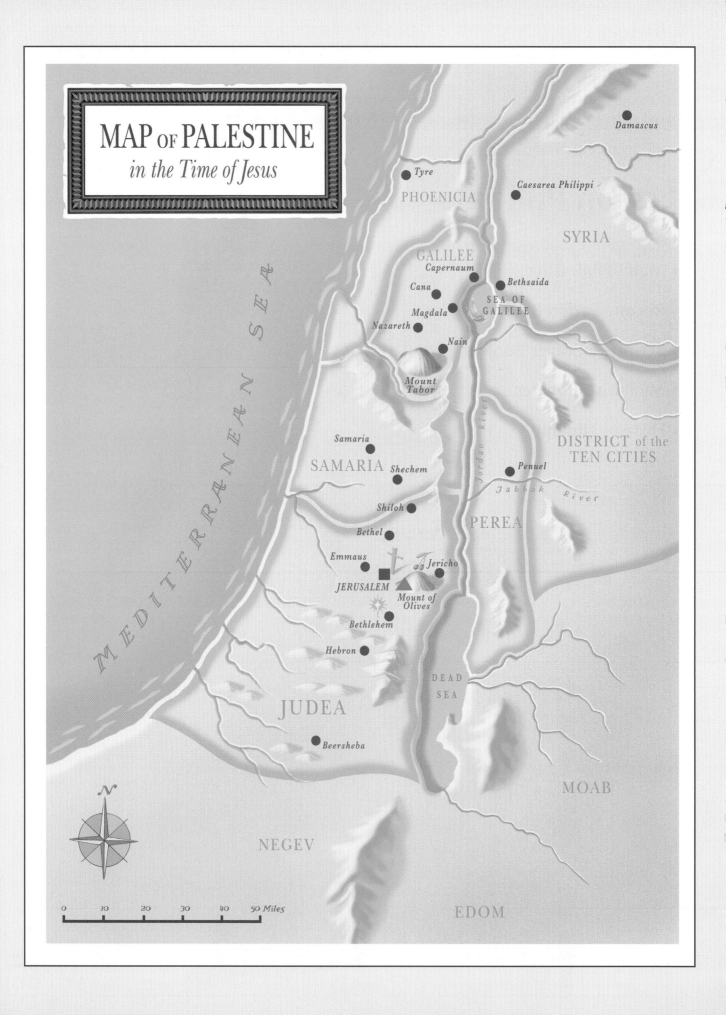

Deepening Your Spiritual Life

Now you may wish to take further steps toward deepening your spiritual life, toward learning to know Jesus better. The Sacrament of Penance can help you recognize your weaknesses. This awareness should lead you to overcome your faults. The Sacrament of Penance can help you become a stronger follower of Christ and create a plan for responding to Christ's mercy. Select one area you want to work on, such as truthfulness, cheerfulness, patience, or setting a good example. Then try some of the following suggestions:

☐ Celebrate the Sacrament of Penance regularly.

☐ Pray every day to become more like Christ in the area you selected.

☐ Describe daily in your reflection notebook your efforts to follow Christ more closely.

☐ Read about the life of a saint who needed strength in the same area you are working on. Learn from the saint how to be more like Christ.

☐ During the Penitential Act of the Mass, think of your progress in the area you selected.

☐ Before going to bed at night, ask yourself if during the day you omitted an action that could have helped you to grow like Christ.

☐ Read short passages from Scripture daily.

☐ Listen, participate, and ask questions in religion class.

☐ Offer to help someone who is in need physically (Corporal Works of Mercy) or spiritually (Spiritual Works of Mercy).

☐ Ask the priest in confession if you need to give up something to get your spiritual life in shape.

☐ Read a Scripture passage slowly—Matthew 14:22–33, for example. Then reflect. In this passage, am I most like Jesus? Peter? The disciples? Why?

The next time you receive the Sacrament of Penance, take some time to reread the suggestions above. Check the ones you have done.

Reconciliation Booklet

On this cover of your Reconciliation Booklet, copy Hebrews 4:16, or write your favorite psalm or prayer.

Name: _____

Acts of Contrition

My God,
I am sorry for my sins with all my heart.
In choosing to do wrong
and failing to do good,
I have sinned against you
whom I should love above all things.
I firmly intend, with your help,
to do penance,
to sin no more,
and to avoid whatever leads me to sin.
Our Savior Jesus Christ
suffered and died for us.
In his name, my God, have mercy.
Rite of Penance

Lord Jesus, Son of God,
have mercy on me, a sinner.

My own prayer of sorrow and of desire to become more like Christ, so that
I can continue to bring reconciliation to others:

_____
_____
_____
_____
_____
_____
_____

Prayer for Light and Courage

Before celebrating the Sacrament of Penance and Reconciliation, it is
important to call upon the Holy Spirit for help in seeing ourselves as we
really are. The Spirit will also help us to confess our sins without fear and
to be open to God's mercy.

Write your own prayer for light and courage with these parts:

1. Call on the Spirit to open your heart to God.
2. Ask the Spirit to give you courage to confess your sins honestly.
3. Petition the Spirit to give you strong determination to become more
   like Christ in the days ahead.

My Prayer for Light and Courage

_____
_____
_____
_____
_____
_____
_____
_____

Rite of Reconciliation

- Greet the priest.
- Pray the Sign of the Cross.
- Listen as the priest prays.
- Read or listen to the Word of God from Scripture (optional).
- If the priest does not know you, tell how long it has been since your last confession. You can begin with words such as, "Bless me, Father, for I have sinned. It has been _____ (days/weeks/months/years) since my last confession." Or you can use words of your own.
- Confess your sins. (For mortal sin, tell how often it occurred.)
- If you wish, speak about anything that is troubling you. Ask the priest to help you begin a plan to improve in a certain area. Ask forgiveness for all your sins. You can use words such as, "For these and for all my sins, I am sorry."
- Listen to the priest's advice.
- Accept your penance.
- Pray an Act of Contrition. (In a communal penance service, sometimes an Act of Contrition is prayed as a community before or after individual confessions.) You may use your own words or a memorized Act of Contrition.
- Receive absolution, silently making the Sign of the Cross. Respond "Amen."
- Proclamation of praise and dismissal:
  Priest's prayer: "Give thanks to the Lord for he is good."
  Response: "His mercy endures forever."
- Say, "Thank you, Father."

Afterward, spend some time in prayer and thanksgiving.
Do your penance.

Reading God's Word

God's Word is alive and powerful. It is full of challenge and full of love. God's Word can change our lives.

Prayerfully reflect on the following Scripture readings. Let the questions guide your reflections.

Read 1 John 3:16–24. Summarize the reading.

_____

_____

Read again verses 17–18. How does your family see that God's love is real and active in you and not "mere talk"?

_____

_____

Read again verses 21–22. What can you do now to better live the kind of life Jesus wants?

_____

_____

Read Luke 17:4. Summarize the reading.

_____

_____

How do these words challenge you?

_____

_____

_____

Examination of Conscience

When you examine your conscience, try to look not only at what you did wrong, but why you did it. Think of positive ways to grow closer to Christ.

How Is My Relationship with God?

Have I

- refused to pray or listen to God? ignored opportunities to pray?
- laughed or talked during the celebration of the Eucharist or in religion class?
- been lazy about singing or giving responses at the celebration of Mass?
- missed Mass? come late? caused others to do so?
- talked to friends during Mass, then walked up to Holy Communion without preparing?
- failed to use the name of God reverently?
- purposely stayed away from the Sacrament of Penance and Reconciliation?
- rejected God by thinking I can do everything on my own?

Why? Because

- I was lazy.
- I feared what others might think.
- I wanted my own way.
- I did not trust God.

How Do I Deal with My Responsibilities to Myself?

Have I

- failed to take care of my health by not eating a balanced diet and getting the proper amount of sleep?
- harmed my body by taking drugs or using alcohol?
- used my body for my own pleasure? or let others use my body for sexual pleasure?
- harmed my character by reading or viewing pornographic books, magazines, films, or Web sites?
- used vulgar language?

Why? Because

- I feared what others might think of me.
- I was lazy or selfish.
- I wanted attention.

How Is My Relationship with Others?

Have I

- been angry with others? hated them?
- told lies about my actions? friends? clothes? family? events?
- teased or ridiculed others? played unkind jokes? dared others to carry out forbidden or dangerous actions?
- had uncharitable thoughts? felt bitterness? refused to speak to others?
- been unfair to others? dishonest?
- cheated at games? tests? copied others' assignments?
- damaged another's property? failed to make restitution?
- failed to reverence the bodies of others? used another's body for my own pleasure? encouraged impure talk?
- damaged the reputation of another?
- refused to help those poorer than myself?
- encouraged others to view forbidden movies and Web sites?

Why? Because

- I didn't get my own way. I was jealous or envious.
- I wanted to be "in" to be popular, or to show off.
- I wanted to avoid punishment.
- I wanted to win, to be on top, or to appear smart or talented.

How Is My Relationship with My Parents and Family.

Have I

- failed to show love and respect for my parents or guardians?
- ignored them? turned them off? given them the "silent treatment"? talked back to them?
- acted ashamed of them? "used" them to get me out of trouble?
- demanded they buy me things I did not deserve?
- been angry or pouted when corrected?
- quarreled with my brothers and sisters?
- used their belongings without permission?
- refused to do the things assigned to me at home?
- blamed others when it was not their fault?

Why? Because

- I feared what my friends might think of me.
- I resented authority and wanted my own way.
- I was jealous.

Guidelines to Goodness

Saint Paul, in his letters, gave the early Christians and us many helpful hints to become the best people we can be.

Read Romans 12:9–21. Think and pray about Paul's advice. Then see if you can form 10 guidelines for life today. Give them a title, such as "A Teenager's Guide to Following Jesus." List your guidelines below.

Title: _____

1. _____
2. _____
3. _____
4. _____
5. _____
6. _____
7. _____
8. _____
9. _____
10. _____

Add to your list. Use the following references to form more guidelines, or search for your own.

Romans 13:1 _____

Romans 13:7 _____

Romans 13:10 _____

Romans 14:13 _____

1 Corinthians 9:22 _____

Scripture Prayer Booklet

Name: _____

Leadership: Christ's Way

Much is written about leadership and the qualities of a leader. The Acts of the Apostles offers suggestions for Christian leadership. Look up the references below and list the qualities or practices suggested. The first one is done for you. Reflect on how you can live each one.

Reference	Leadership Quality or Practice
Acts of the Apostles 5:42	Praise God and spread the Good News daily.
1. Acts of the Apostles 8:60	
2. Acts of the Apostles 10:1–2	
3. Acts of the Apostles 13:42	
4. Acts of the Apostles 14:22	
5. Acts of the Apostles 15:37–38	
6. Acts of the Apostles 18:9–10	
7. Acts of the Apostles 20:19	
8. Acts of the Apostles 20:20	
9. Acts of the Apostles 20:24	
10. Acts of the Apostles 20:35	

The last chapters in Acts of the Apostles contain more suggestions. How many are you able to find?

Reference   **Leadership Quality or Practice**

Jesus and Prayer

Jesus often prayed, spending time in communion with his Father. Scripture tells us that Jesus prayed before important events of his life. Locate and read the Scripture references below and tell what event or occasion followed Jesus' prayer.

Reference   **Occasion**

Luke 3:21–22 _____

Mark 1:35–38 _____

Luke 9:18–21 _____

Luke 6:12–16 _____

Luke 11:1–4 _____

Luke 22:39–41 _____

Luke 23:33–34 _____

How can we imitate Jesus' prayer life in our own lives?

_____

_____

_____

Jesus Teaches Us to Pray

The apostles, aware of the prayerfulness of Jesus, asked him to teach them to pray. Imagine you are with the apostles as they ask Jesus and hear his answer. (Read Luke 11:1–4 and Matthew 6:9–13.)

In daily newspapers, there is typically a summary of major news events entitled something like "News in Brief." We might say that the Our Father, or the Lord's Prayer, is the "Good News in Brief." It is actually a short summary of the mission and teaching of Jesus.

Mary's Seven Words

Complete Mary's "words" from the references on page 9. Fill in the remaining words to the verses listed in parentheses.

1. How can this be (Luke 1:34) _____

2. I am the (Luke 1:38) _____

3. May it be (Luke 1:38) _____

4. My soul proclaims (Luke 1:46) _____

5. Son, why have you (Luke 2:48) _____

6. They have no (John 2:3) _____

7. Do whatever (John 2:5) _____

All young people can look to Mary and find a totally unselfish people who could bravely accept an uncertain future. Both Mary and Joseph in their youthful generosity responded in dedicated love to the great things that were asked of them.

In today's world, young people are eager to promote justice and peace in the face of many obstacles. Like Mary, they will effectively influence their society and the world only when their lives are completely given to God in faith, hope, and love.

adapted from *Behold Your Mother*, par. 143–144

So we look to Mary as the model of all that we are striving to be as people. We want to imitate her obedience to God's will, her faith, her purity, her humility, and all her other virtues. No matter what vocation God calls us to, Mary is the example of how to live out that vocation perfectly. Now spend some time in silent prayer. Ask Mary for help and protection, especially during these important years of your life, as you seek to listen to God and to obey God's will.

The Lord's Prayer

The Greeting—"Our Father"

This is not just an opening to the prayer, but a very important truth: God is Jesus' Father, but he is also our Father! What does it mean to you to have God as your Father?

_____

Petitions

Six petitions follow. Three refer to God and three to us. For each, look up the Scripture reference and prayerfully reflect on what Jesus is telling us. The first three petitions ask for the help we need to live God's kingdom on earth.

Hallowed be thy name (John 17:26)

Thy kingdom come (John 17:21)

Thy will be done (Luke 22:42)

The next three petitions ask God to help us with our needs as we await the kingdom.

Give us this day our daily bread (John 6:50,57)

Forgive us our trespasses (Luke 23:34)

Lead us not into temptation (John 17:11,15)

Thinking it over:

- How do I honor (or fail to honor) God's name?
- Do I see God's kingdom in the people around me? In events?
- What is God's will for me at this time in my life? How can I best carry it out?
- How do I show appreciation for my "daily bread"? Forgiveness? Protection from evil?

Praying about it:

- Pray the Our Father slowly and thoughtfully.
- Ask our Lord to help you not only to pray this prayer but to live it as well.

Acting on it:

- Decide what you will do today to show Jesus what you have learned from his teaching.

Mary: Mother of the Church and Model of the Ideal Person

During the Second Vatican Council, the pope honored Mary by giving her the title "Mother of the Church." She is the spiritual mother of the Mystical Body, the Church, of which Christ is the head.

Since Mary is the Mother of God by her free response to God's call, she is also the Mother of the members of the Church. She cooperated with her Son's saving work and he, in turn, gave her to us as mother. In Mary, the whole Church sees the perfect example of the virtues that Christ preached.

Led by the Holy Spirit, Mary devoted her whole life to Christ. Through the same Holy Spirit, Jesus is brought forth in the lives and hearts of all who do his will.

adapted from *Behold Your Mother*, par. 118

As you read, think, and pray about the following incidents in the life of Mary, you will also find the "seven words" of Mary that Scripture records. These seven words or phrases of Mary, like the "seven words" of Jesus on the Cross, give us a glimpse into the spirituality and personality of the speaker.

Take one incident at a time. Follow the steps of meditation given on page 4 (Recall, Read, Enter in, Think, Pray, Act, Remember). Ask yourself: How does Mary show great faith in this incident? What virtues or qualities does she practice? How can I imitate her, the model of holiness?

Incident	Scripture
Annunciation	Luke 1:26–38
Visitation	Luke 1:39–56
Jesus	Luke 2:41–52
Cana at Wedding	John 2:1–12
Calvary	John 19:25–27

Kinds of Prayer

Praying the Our Father or any other prayer that has a definite pattern of words is called vocal prayer. Another kind of prayer or way of praying is meditation, or mental prayer. Meditation is thinking about God, trying to become aware of God's action in our lives, and applying what we have learned to our way of living. It combines thinking about God and talking to God. Here are some helpful steps to follow for meditation, especially when you first begin to meditate:

* Recall—Place yourself in God's presence, and ask God to help you in your prayer.
* Read Scripture, the lives of the saints, or other inspirational literature.
* Enter in—Mentally put yourself in the place or situation. See, hear, feel, smell, and taste! These are ways of making the event real to you.
* Think about the situation, the persons, the words, the actions, and so on.
* Pray about it. (Often, thinking and praying will go together naturally.)
* Act on it—Do something specific as a result of your thinking and praying.
* Remember—Use a quotation, word, phrase, or symbol to help remember your meditation.

You have followed some of these steps in the section Jesus Teaches Us to Pray. In the next section, you will follow all the steps in a meditation on two of Jesus' miracles.

Moments of Meditation

Father Mark Link, S.J., said, "Meditation is reflecting upon God, or seeking to become aware of God's action or presence in human life . . . it is needed to bring God's presence in focus." (*The Seventh Trumpet*)

Now that you have learned a method for meditation, you might want to follow it in meditations of your own. Any incident in Scripture lends itself to meditation, but some are more vivid than others. Several suggestions are given here. Choose what appeals to you or fits your present mood.

Luke 1:26–38	The Annunciation
John 2:1–11	The Wedding Feast at Cana
Matthew 13:44–46	The Treasure in the Field, The Pearl
Luke 17:11–19	The 10 Lepers
Matthew 22:1–14	The Parable of the Wedding Banquet
Mark 9:17–29	Healing of the Epileptic Boy
Luke 5:1–11	The Miraculous Catch of Fish
Luke 9:28–36	The Transfiguration of Jesus
John 6:1–15	The Multiplication of Loaves
John 2:13–22	The Cleansing of the Temple
Luke 22:39–46	The Agony in the Garden
John 20:19–25	Jesus Appears to His Apostles (after the Resurrection)
John 20:24–29	Thomas
Luke 24:13–32	The Appearance on the Road to Emmaus
Acts of the Apostles 16–11	Ascension

Confidence in Christ, Lord of the Wind and the Waves

Jesus must have loved the water, for he worked several miracles on or near the Sea of Galilee, also called Lake Gennesaret or the Sea of Tiberias.

This lake, 13 miles long and about 6 miles wide, is 695 feet below sea level. It is surrounded by hills with steep cliffs and deep ravines that the weather had cut into them. Because of its saucerlike position and the meeting of warm lake air and cold ravine air, the lake is a place of rapid weather changes, especially after sundown. Within minutes, it can change from a calm, mirrorlike lake to a raging white-capped sea of six-foot waves.

In this prayer activity you will experience God's power in Jesus as he works two miracles on the Sea of Galilee.

Recalling Recall that God is everywhere. Right now, you are in God's presence. Ask him to help you learn what he is trying to teach you in these miracles.

Jesus Calms the Storm at Sea

Reading Mark 4:35–41 (Also Matthew 8:23–27; Luke 8:22–25)

Entering In Get into the boat with Jesus and the apostles. Smell the freshness of the lake breeze, feel the gentle splash of water on your face, see the stars reflected in the calm surface of the lake, hear the dipping of oars into the water.

Thinking, Praying How happy the apostles are! They have Jesus all to themselves. Here in the boat he can rest. After a long day of preaching and teaching, he is very tired. In fact, he is already asleep on a cushion. The apostles will take him safely across the lake, even though it is near nightfall and the lake can be dangerous then. After all, aren't they experienced boatmen? They probably feel that nothing can happen to Jesus when they are around. Lord, how great we sometimes think we are! Help us remember that all our talents and abilities come from you!

Without warning, gales of wind sweep across the lake. The rudder is hard to control and the sails are unmanageable. Wave after wave pours over the boat, and the hull begins to fill. The boat will surely sink or capsize! The once bold apostles suddenly lose their courage. Lord, save us or we'll be lost! Do we look to Christ when we've lost our nerve and in times of difficulty?

A familiar voice sounds through the darkness, *Where is your courage? How little faith you have! Trust me!*

Jesus stands in the boat, raises his hands, and commands the winds and the waves to be still. Everything becomes perfectly calm. Jesus has worked another miracle! Do we realize how many times Christ comes to our rescue when we ask for help through prayer? Sometimes he helps us even before we ask.

Mark ends his account by asking, "Who then is this whom even wind and sea obey?" (Mark 4:41)

Who do you say he is?

Acting When difficulties come my way today, I will trust Jesus.

Remembering Where is your courage? Trust me!

Jesus Walks on the Water

Recalling Remember that God is with you.

Reading Matthew 14:22–33 (Also Mark 6:45–52; John 6:16–21)

Entering In Imagine that you are in the boat during the storm. Hear the roar of the wind and feel it against you. See the lightning and hear the thunder. Sense the rocking of the boat and your wet clothes. Feel the panic at the storm and then at the ghostlike vision walking across the water.

Thinking, Praying The apostles obey Jesus' wishes and set out to sea while he stays behind to pray. Again the apostles are at the mercy of the sea. The waves lash at their boat, tossing it about while the winds whip the sails. In the middle of the storm, Jesus appears to them, walking on the water! He pretends to walk right by them. He is longing to help them, but he wants them to ask for help first. Do we realize that God is always ready to help us but waits for us to ask?

At first the apostles don't recognize Jesus. They think he is a ghost. After all, no human being walks on water. In their fear they cry out. Then the figure speaks, "Take courage, it is I; do not be afraid." (Matthew 14:27) How often does Jesus speak to me, telling me to have courage, that he's there for me, to trust him? Do I hear him? Do I trust him?

Finally the apostles grasp the situation. Jesus is with them; no harm can come to them now. What trust! But Peter is either fascinated by Jesus' miracle, or he wants more proof. He says, "Lord, if it is you, command me to come to you on the water." (Matthew 14:28) Peter shows faith and courage to make such a request. After all, if this is really Christ, Peter isn't asking too much. Would we have asked? Is our faith and courage as strong as Peter's?

Jesus replies with one word: "Come." (Matthew 14:29) That's enough for Peter. Full of confidence, he looks at Jesus, steps out of the boat, and starts walking across the water toward Jesus. As long as he keeps his eyes on Jesus, all goes well. Suddenly a large wave rolls toward him. Peter looks at the wave, momentarily frightened. He loses sight of Jesus and immediately begins to sink. Do we keep our eyes on Jesus in times of trouble?

Peter cries out, "Lord, save me!" (Matthew 14:30) Jesus reaches out his hand and pulls Peter from the water. How many times do we lose confidence in Jesus and come to him with "wet feet"? Jesus chides Peter for his lack of trust. "[W]hy did you doubt?" (Matthew 14:31) Then, hand in hand, Jesus and Peter walk back to the boat, and the storm suddenly dies down. Do we walk hand in hand with Jesus through the storms of life?

Now spend some time silently talking to Jesus about your confidence and trust in him.

Acting How can I show my confidence and trust in Jesus? What specific thing can I do today?

Remembering [He] hushed the storm to a murmur; the waves of the sea were stilled. (Psalm 107:29)

My Parish Booklet

Write the name of your parish on the line. In the space, paste a photo of your church or draw a picture of it.

Patron saint of your church: _____

Summary of the saint's life: _____
_____
_____
_____

Name: _____

Ministries: _____
_____
_____

Your favorite parish celebration: _____
_____

Parish customs: _____
_____

Ways that you are (or can be) involved in your parish: _____
_____
_____
_____
_____
_____
_____

Special rooms in the building: _____

_____

Kind of music (choirs, instruments): _____

Draw a diagram of the interior of the church:

[blank framed box]

Year the church was founded: _____

Founding pastor: _____

Interesting fact of its history: _____

_____

Outstanding parishioner past or present: _____

How this person was outstanding: _____

_____

Unique feature of architecture or furnishings: _____

_____

Description of statues: _____

_____

Description of windows: _____

_____

Description of baptismal font: _____

_____

History Timelines

Throughout *The Church Then and Now* book, we explore how the mission of Jesus Christ has been carried out by the Church over history. On the following pages, you will find timelines of the Journey of the Church Through Time, indicating many significant events in Church history over the past 2,000 years. Below are listed some significant events in world history that provide a context for the Church history events on the pages that follow.

Events in World History (A.D.)

98–116	Roman Empire reaches its greatest geographical extent.
305	Empire is split into East and West.
313	Edict of Milan legalizes Christianity in Roman Empire.
360	Huns invade Europe. ❯
476	Fall of the Western Roman Empire
570	Muhammed, founder of Islam, is born.
c. 600	Arab (Islamic) expansion
800	Charlemagne crowned first Holy Roman Emperor.
c. 900	❮ Rise of feudalism, building of castles
c. 950	Europe in the "Dark Ages"
c. 1000	The rise of city-states
1000	Norse explorer Leif Ericson travels to America.
1215	Magna Carta written
1271	Marco Polo travels to China.

1347	Black Death devastates Europe. *(shown above)*
1453	Fall of Constantinople, the end of the Middle Ages
c. 1450	Invention of the printing press
1492	Colonization of the Americas
c. 1500	Renaissance in Europe
c. 1700	The Age of Enlightenment
1775	American Revolution
1789	French Revolution
c. 1800	Industrial Revolution
1804–1815	Napoleonic Wars
c. 1850	Rise of Socialism and Communism
1914–1918	World War I
1929–1933	The Great Depression ❯
c. 1920	Rise of fascism
1939–1945	World War II
c. 1945	Beginning of the Cold War
1989	Fall of Berlin Wall
1991	Collapse of Soviet Union

❮ Berlin Wall

Birth of Christ · Paschal Mystery Pentecost—the Church begins. · Council of Jerusalem · Persecutions begin. · Gospels finished. · Monasticism begins. · Age of Church Fathers · Edict of Milan ends persecution. · Council of Nicaea · Council of Constantinople · Invasions by Germanic tribes · Council of Ephesus · Irish Church organized · Council of Chalcedon · Benedictines founded. · Gregory the Great elected pope. · Germanic conversions begin. · Charlemagne crowned Holy Roman Emperor. · Slavic conversions begin. · The Great Schism · Reform of Pope Gregory VII

c. 6 B.C. · c. A.D. 30 · c. 50 · 64 · 95 · c. 251 · c. 300 · 313 · 325 · 381 · c. 400 · 431 · 432 · 451 · 529 · 590 · 722 · 800 · 863 · 1054 · 1073

Journey of the Church

B.C.

c. 6 Christ is born in Bethlehem.

A.D.

c. 30 Christ dies and rises. The Holy Spirit comes at Pentecost.

c. 50 The Council of Jerusalem decides that Gentile converts need not follow Jewish practices.

64 Persecution of Christians begins under the Roman emperor Nero.

67 Peter and Paul are martyred in Rome.

95 Evangelists finish writing the Gospels.

c. 100 Apostolic Age ends.

c. 251 Monasticism begins due to the influence of Saint Anthony of Egypt.

c. 300 The great Fathers influence Church history.

311 The emperor Constantine ends persecution of Christians.

325 The Council of Nicaea refutes the Arian heresy and composes the Nicene Creed.

324–343 Saint Augustine influences Church thought.

381 The Council of Constantinople affirms and expands the Nicene Creed. The Council also defines the divine nature of the Holy Spirit.

c. 400 Tribes from the East gradually invade Europe.

431 The Council of Ephesus refutes the Nestorian heresy and states that Mary is truly the Mother of God.

432 Saint Patrick begins missionary work in Ireland.

451 The Council of Chalcedon defends the divine nature of Christ.

529 Saint Benedict founds an order of monks, which helps preserve Christianity in Europe.

590 Saint Gregory the Great is elected pope. Saint Augustine is sent to convert England.

722 Saint Boniface begins the conversion of the Germanic tribes.

800 Charlemagne is crowned Holy Roman Emperor.

863 Saints Cyril and Methodius begin the conversion of the Slavic tribes.

1054 The Great Schism splits the Eastern and Western Churches.

1073 Gregory VII is elected pope and begins to reform the Church.

1095 Pope Urban II calls for crusades to free the Holy Land from Muslim control.

1209 Saint Francis founds the Franciscan Order.

1215 Saint Dominic founds the Dominican Order.

1266 Saint Thomas Aquinas writes the *Summa Theologiae*.

1291 The Crusades end without success.

1378–1415 The Western Schism splits the Roman Church, with two or three men claiming to be pope at one time.

1521 Martin Luther breaks with the Catholic Church. The Protestant Reformation begins.

1534 King Henry VIII differs with the pope and begins the Anglican Church.

Crusades begin. **1095**
Mendicant Orders founded. **c. 1200**
Summa Theologiae of Thomas Aquinas **1266**
Crusades end. **1291**
The Western Schism **1378 – 1415**
The Protestant Reformation **c. 1521**
Anglican Church **1534**
Jesuits founded. **1540**
Council of Trent **1545 – 1563**
Evangelization of the Americas begins. **c. 1600**
The French Revolution John Carroll made first bishop of the U.S. **1789**
Religious freedom protected in U.S. **1791**
First Vatican Council **1870**
Social encyclical Rerum Novarum **1891**
Second Vatican Council **1962**
John Paul II becomes pope **1978**
Catechism of the Catholic Church is published. **1992**
Pope John Paul II dies. Benedict XVI becomes pope. **2005**
Pope Benedict XVI resigns, Francis becomes pope. **2013**

Through Time

1540 Saint Ignatius founds the Society of Jesus.

1545–1563 The Council of Trent promotes Church reformation.

c. 1600 Missionaries begin to evangelize the Americas.

1789 The French Revolution clashes with the Catholic Church. John Carroll is appointed first bishop of the United States.

1791 Freedom of religion is protected by the U.S. Constitution.

1870 The First Vatican Council convenes.

1891 Pope Leo XIII writes the first major social encyclical, *Rerum Novarum*.

1914–1918 The Church endures World War I.

1917 The Communist Revolution occurs. An atheistic government limits religious freedom.

1933 Nazi government persecutes Christians and Jews in Europe.

1939–1945 The Church endures World War II.

1959 Pope John XXIII calls the Second Vatican Council (1962–1965) to renew the Church's vitality and relevance. The ecumenical movement begins.

1978 John Paul II becomes pope.

1992 *Catechism of the Catholic Church* is published.

2005 Pope John Paul II dies. Benedict XVI becomes pope.

2013 Pope Benedict XVI resigns, and Francis becomes pope.

2014 Pope John XXIII and Pope John Paul II are canonized.

The Church in North America

1642–1672 North American martyrs are killed.

1769–1823 Twenty-one Spanish missions are founded, most of them by Junipero Serra.

1774 The British government grants religious freedom to French Catholics in Canada.

1789 John Carroll is appointed first U.S. bishop.

1791 The first Catholic seminary, Saint Mary's in Baltimore, opens.

1809 Elizabeth Ann Seton founds the first American religious community, the Daughters of Charity.

1820–1920 Nine million Catholic immigrants come to the United States.

1884 At the Council of Baltimore, the U.S. bishops create a Catholic school system and commission the *Baltimore Catechism*.

1911 Maryknoll, the first American mission association, is started.

1919 The National Catholic Welfare Conference, now the United States Catholic Conference, begins.

1960 John Fitzgerald Kennedy, a Catholic, is elected president.

1975 Elizabeth Ann Seton is canonized as first native-born American saint.

1993 Pope John Paul II visits World Youth Day in Denver.

2013 Kateri Tekakwitha is canonized as the first Native American saint.

Art Credits

Page positions are abbreviated as follows: (t) top, (c) center, (b) bottom, (l) left, (r) right.

FRONT MATTER:

i Lori Lohstoeter. **iv**(t) Stockbyte/PunchStock; (b) The Crosiers/Gene Plaisted, OSC. **v**(t) Getty Images/Staff/Getty Images Sport/Getty Images; (bl) David Madison/The Image Bank/Getty Images. **vi**(t) © iStockphoto.com/double_p; (b) The Crosiers/Gene Plaisted, OSC.

UNIT 1:

1 AgnusImages.com. **2** Friedrich-stark.de. **3**(t) Carsten Koall/Stringer/Getty Images News/Getty Images; (cl) Charles Smith/Corbis; (ccl) Bill Wittman; (ccr) Bill Wittman; (cr) Phil Martin Photography; (bl) PD-1923 Wikimedia Commons; (br) Bill Wittman. **4** Tracy Montana/Photodisc Green/Getty Images. **5** Hemera Technologies/Photos.com. **6**(b) Photos.com. **7** Lars Justinen/Licensed from GoodSalt.com. **8** AgnusImages.com. **9** The Crosiers/Gene Plaisted, OSC. **10** The Crosiers/Gene Plaisted, OSC. **11** © iStockphoto.com/yelo34. **12** The Crosiers/Gene Plaisted, OSC. **13**(t) Jack Hollingsworth/Photodisc/Getty Images. **14** Robert Voights. **15** Tobin Rogers/Licensed from GoodSalt.com. **16** The Crosiers/Gene Plaisted, OSC. **17** © iStockphoto.com/4x6. **19** Warling Studios. **20** The Crosiers/Gene Plaisted, OSC. **21** © iStockphoto.com/Kiyyah. **22** The Crosiers/Gene Plaisted, OSC. **23** Bill Wittman. **24**(b) Burke/Triolo Productions/Jupiter Images. **27** fStop Photography/Veer. **28** The Crosiers/Gene Plaisted, OSC. **29** Myrleen Pearson/PhotoEdit. **30** PhotoDisc, Inc. **31**(t) The Crosiers/Gene Plaisted, OSC; (b) Rob Melnychuk/Digital Vision/Getty Images. **32** Hemera Technologies/Photos.com. **33** Sally Weimer/Llcensed from GoodSalt.com. **34** PhotoDisc, Inc. **35** Lars Justinenl/Licensed from GoodSalt.com. **37** Jaren Jai Wicklund/Shutterstock. **38** The Crosiers/Gene Plaisted, OSC. **39** Ocean/Corbis. **40** Susan Van Etten/PhotoEdit. **41** Alistair Berg/Taxi/Getty Images. **42** Anita Patterson Peppers/Dreamstime.com. **43** SW Productions. **44** Spencer Grant/PhotoEdit. **46**(t) Dreamstime. **46–47**(b) The Crosiers/Gene Plaisted, OSC. **49** © iStockphoto.com/aldomurillo. **50** The Crosiers/Gene Plaisted, OSC.

UNIT 2:

51 Brand X Pictures/Punchstock. **52** Paula Bronstein/Getty Images News/Getty Images. **53** Lars Justinen/Licensed from GoodSalt.com. **54** © iStockphoto.com/omgimages. **55** By Edgar Jiménez from Porto, Portugal (Papa rock star) [CC-BY-SA-2.0 (http://creativecommons.org/licenses/by-sa/2.0)], via Wikimedia Commons. **56** Sudhi/Dreamstime.com. **58** The Crosiers/Gene Plaisted, OSC. **60** The Crosiers/Gene Plaisted, OSC. **61**(t) Laurence Mouton/PhotoAlto Agency RF Collections/Getty Images; (b) Adri Berger/Photographer's Choice/Getty Images. **62** Vasic/Dreamstime.com. **63** The Crosiers/Gene Plaisted, OSC. **64** © The Father Solanus Guild. **65** Valueline/Punchstock. **66** The Crosiers/Gene Plaisted, OSC. **67** Zedcor Wholly Owned/Photos.com. **68** The Crosiers/Gene Plaisted, OSC. **69** Warling Studios. **70** jorisvo/Shutterstock. **72** Bill Wittman. **73** The Crosiers/Gene Plaisted, OSC. **74** Jeffrey L. Rotman/Corbis. **76** The Crosiers/Gene Plaisted, OSC. **77** Warling Studios. **78** The Crosiers/Gene Plaisted, OSC. **79**(t) The Crosiers/Gene Plaisted, OSC; (b) Design Pics Inc./Alamy. **80** Tony Gentile/epa/Corbis. **81** The Crosiers/Gene Plaisted, OSC; **82** AgnusImages.com. **83** Stockbyte/PunchStock. **84** The Crosiers/Gene Plaisted, OSC. **85** Alessandro Bianchi/Reuters/Corbis. **88** Stockbyte/Getty Images. **89** Jupiterimages. **90** The Crosiers/Gene Plaisted, OSC.

UNIT 3:

91 © San Lorenzo Maggiore-Capella Di Sant' Aquilino, Milano, Italy/Mauro Magliani/SuperStock, Inc. **93**(t) Alfredo Dagli Orti/The Art Archive/Corbis; (b) The Crosiers/Gene Plaisted, OSC. **94** © iStockphoto.com/Lenorlux. **95** Alinari Archives/Corbis. **97** Photos.com. **98** The Crosiers/Gene Plaisted, OSC. **100** © Basilica of the National Shrine of the Immaculate Conception Washington DC 2009/Geraldine M. Rohling. **101** Myrleen Pearson/PhotoEdit. **102** The Crosiers/Gene Plaisted, OSC. **103** THINK Design Group. **104** Brand X Pictures/PunchStock. **105** © iStockphoto.com/kulicki. **106** The Crosiers/Gene Plaisted, OSC. **107** Juanmonino/iStock/Thinkstock. **108** By Anonymous (Florence) (www.rijksmuseum.nl : Home : Info : Pic) [Public domain], via Wikimedia Commons. **109** Don Mammoser/Licensed from GoodSalt.com. **110** © Ursuline Sisters of Cleveland. **111**(t) The Crosiers/Gene Plaisted, OSC. **112** The Crosiers/Gene Plaisted, OSC. **113** Valueline/PunchStock. **114**(t) The Crosiers/Gene Plaisted, OSC. **115** Giraudon/The Bridgeman Art Library. **117** Jupiterimages/Stockbyte/Thinkstock. **119**(t) Maigi/Dreamstime.com. **120** © Iconotec. **122** Gianni Dagli Orti/Corbis. **123** © iStockphoto.com/iofoto. **124** The Crosiers/Gene Plaisted, OSC. **125** Darrin Henry/iStock/Thinkstock. **126** The Crosiers/Gene Plaisted, OSC. **127**(t) AgnusImages.com; (b) The Crosiers/Gene Plaisted, OSC. **128**(t) Gianni Giansanti /Sygma/Corbis; (b) De Agostini Picture Library/The Bridgeman Art Library. **129** The Crosiers/Gene Plaisted, OSC. **130**(t) The Crosiers/Gene Plaisted, OSC; (b) © iStockphoto.com/DNY59. **131** The Crosiers/Gene Plaisted, OSC. **132**(t) The Crosiers/Gene Plaisted, OSC; (b) The Crosiers/Gene Plaisted, OSC. **133** THINK Design Group. **135** SW Productions. **137** Warling Studios. **138** The Crosiers/Gene Plaisted, OSC.

UNIT 4:

139 David Lees/Corbis. **140** Valueline/PunchStock. **141** Photos.com. **142** Sylvester Adams/Photodisc/Getty Images. **143** Pacific Press/licensed from GoodSalt.com. **144**(r) Gianni Dagli Orti/Corbis. **145–146** The Crosiers/Gene Plaisted, OSC. **147** © iStockphoto.com/Juanmonino. **148** Sterling Hundley. **149**(t) David Lees/Corbis. **150**(b) The Crosiers/Gene Plaisted, OSC. **151** Fine Art Images/SuperStock. **152–154** The Crosiers/Gene Plaisted, OSC. **155** Warling Studios. **156** The Crosiers/Gene Plaisted, OSC. **157**(t) Index/The Bridgeman Art Library. **158** The Crosiers/Gene Plaisted, OSC. **159** Gianni Dagli Orti/Corbis. **160** David Lees/Corbis. **162** Bettmann/Corbis. **163** bikeriderlondon/Shutterstock. **164** Service Central des Archives SNJM (Longueuil, Quebec) Blessed Marie Rose Durocher by Annette Chouinard. **165** Alfredo Dagli Orti/The Art Archive/Corbis. **166** SW Productions. **167**(t) PD wikimedia commons; (b) The Crosiers/Gene Plaisted, OSC. **168** Thierry Orban/Corbis Sygma. **169** Alessandro Bianchi/Reuters/Corbis. **170**(t) The Crosiers/Gene Plaisted, OSC; (b) Lars Justinen/licensed from GoodSalt.com. **171** iStock/Thinkstock. **173** Richard Cummins/Corbis. **174**(t) Brooklyn Museum/Corbis; (b) The Crosiers/Gene Plaisted, OSC. **175**(t) Bob Krist/Corbis; (b) PD wikimedia commons. **176**(t, c, b) The Crosiers/Gene Plaisted, OSC. **177**(t) Catholic News Service; (b) Glenna Carroll, OP. **178** Ralf-Finn Hestoft/Corbis. **179** SW Productions. **180** Bettmann/Corbis. **181** THINK design group. **182** The Crosiers/Gene Plaisted, OSC. **182–183** Con Tanasiuk/Design Pics/Corbis. **184** The Crosiers/Gene Plaisted, OSC. **185** Darrin Henry/Shutterstock. **186** The Crosiers/Gene Plaisted, OSC.

UNIT 5:

187 Brand X Pictures/PunchStock. **188** Bill Wittman. **189** Alloy Photography/Veer. **190**(t) Bill Wittman; (b) PD Wikimedia Commons. **191**(t) The Crosiers/Gene Plaisted, OSC; (b) Robert W. Ginn/PhotoEdit. **192** SW Productions. **193**(t) UpperCut Images/PunchStock; (b) Stockbyte/Getty Images. **194**(t) The Crosiers/Gene Plaisted, OSC; (b) SW Productions. **196** AgnusImages.com. **197** Jacek Chabraszewski/Shutterstock. **198** Photos.com/Thinkstock. **200** The Stapleton Collection/The Bridgeman Art Library International, Ltd. **202** Michael Newman/PhotoEdit. **207** Bill Wittman. **208** Amy Etra/PhotoEdit. **209** Bill Wittman. **211–212** The Crosiers/Gene Plaisted, OSC. **214** The Crosiers/Gene Plaisted, OSC. **217** Asia Images Group/Getty Images. **220** Jim West/age fotostock/SuperStock. **221** Tim Brown/Stone/Getty Images. **223** SOMOS/SuperStock. **224** The Crosiers/Gene Plaisted, OSC. **225** SW Productions. **228** The Crosiers/Gene Plaisted, OSC. **229** © iStockphoto.com/CEFutcher. **230** Brand X Pictures/PunchStock. **231** Bob Daemmrich/PhotoEdit. **232** The Crosiers/Gene Plaisted, OSC. **234** The Crosiers/Gene Plaisted, OSC. **235** Myrleen Pearson/PhotoEdit. **236** Design Pics/PunchStock. **237**(t) Ocean Photography/Veer. **238** © iStockphoto.com/xavierarnau. **239** Photodisc/PunchStock. **241** Brand X Pictures/PunchStock. **243** THINK Design Group. **244–245** Photos.com. **245** Design Pics/PunchStock. **246** Valueline/PunchStock. **248** The Crosiers/Gene Plaisted, OSC.

SPECIAL SEASONS AND LESSONS:

249(t, c) AgnusImages.com; (bl) Christian Kober/Robert Harding World Imagery/Media Bakery. (br) Stockbyte/Punchstock. **250** Julie Lonneman/www.thespiritsource.com. **251**(t) Phil Martin Photography; (b) Robert Voigts. **252**(t) The Crosiers/Gene Plaisted, OSC; (cl) Leif Skoogfors/Corbis; (cr) The Crosiers/Gene Plaisted, OSC; (b) Christian Kober/Robert Harding World Imagery/Media Bakery. **253**(t) Thomas Northcut/Photodisc/Getty Images; (b) Photos.com. **254**(t) Lars Justinen/Licensed from GoodSalt.com; (b) Stockbyte/Punchstock. **255**(t) Jeff Preston/Licensed from GoodSalt.com; (b) The Crosiers/Gene Plaisted, OSC. **256**(t) The Crosiers/Gene Plaisted, OSC; (b) Giraudon/The Bridgeman Art Library. **257**(t, b) AgnusImages.com. **258**(t) SW Productions; (b) AgnusImages.com. **259**(t) AgnusImages.com; (b) Jeff Preston/Licensed from GoodSalt.com. **260**(t, b) AgnusImages.com. **261**(t) Commissioned by All Saints Church Cotgrave, Nottinghamshire/The Bridgeman Art Library. **262**(t) Zedcor Wholly Owned/Photos.com; (b) Photos.com. **263** Lars Justinen/Licensed from GoodSalt.com. **264**(t) The Crosiers/Gene Plaisted, OSC; (b) Giraudon/The Bridgeman Art Library. **267** Bill Wittman. **268** © iStockphoto.com/asiseeit. **269** Bill Wittman. **272** Bettman/Corbis. **273** Design Pics/Fotosearch. **274** Design Pics/Fotosearch. **275** The Crosiers/Gene Plaisted, OSC. **276**(t) © Cleo Freelance Photography; (b) The Crosiers/Gene Plaisted, OSC. **277** Bill Wittman. **278** The Crosiers/Gene Plaisted, OSC.

WHAT CATHOLICS SHOULD KNOW:

279 © iStockphoto.com/abalcazar. **280**(t) © iStockphoto.com/colevineyard; (b) Rob Melnychuk/Digital Vision/Getty Images. **281** Jack Hollingsworth/Photodisc/Getty Images. **285**(b) The Crosiers/Gene Plaisted, OSC. **286** AgnusImages.com. **287** Greg Kuepfer. **288** Design Pics/Fotosearch. **290** From Fourteen Mosaic Stations of the Cross © Our Lady of the Angels Monastery Inc., Hanceville, Alabama. All Rights Reserved. **291**(b) Digital Vision/Getty Images. **292** Stock Montage, Inc./Alamy. **293** © iStockphoto.com/Lightguard. **294** © iStockphoto.com/TerryHealy. **295** Bob Daemmrich/PhotoEdit. **297**(t) © iStockphoto.com/hidesy. **298** Myrleen Pearson/PhotoEdit. **300**(t) SuperStock/SuperStock. **301**(t) The Crosiers/Gene Plaisted, OSC; (b) Jeff Greenberg/Alamy. **302** © iStockphoto.com/Nnehring.

LESSON PULLOUTS:

333(t) Mark Karrass/Corbis. Digital Stock Corp; (c) Robert Voigts; (br) Bill Wood. **334** Bill Wood.
Reconciliation Booklet, p. 1, 6, 7, 8: Robert Voigts.
Scripture Prayer Booklet Cover: © PhotoDisc, Inc.
Scripture Prayer Booklet, p. 9: (t) The Crosiers/Gene Plaisted, OSC.
Scripture Prayer Booklet, p. 5, 6, 7: Robert Voigts.
My Parish Booklet, p. 4: © iStockkphoto.com/tpuerzer.
History Timelines: (t) North Wind Picture Archives/Alamy; (c) Universal Images Group/Getty Images; (bl) Hemera Technologies/Photos.com; (bc) Jupiterimages/Getty Images. (br) Bettmann/Corbis. (band) Robert Voigts.

Loyola Press has made every effort to locate the copyright holders for the cited works used in this publication and to make full acknowledgment for their use. In the case of any omissions, the Publisher will be pleased to make suitable acknowledgments in future editions.